NutriSearch
COMPARATIVE GUIDE
TO
NUTRITIONAL
SUPPLEMENTS™

NutriSearch
COMPARATIVE GUIDE
TO
NUTRITIONAL
SUPPLEMENTS™

A Compendium of Products Available
in the United States and Canada

Fourth Edition

BY LYLE MACWILLIAM, MSc FP

for

NUTRISEARCH
CORPORATION

**Northern
Dimensions**
PUBLISHING

NutriSearch Comparative Guide to Nutritional Supplements™

A Compendium of Products Available in the United States and Canada

Printed and bound in the United States of America.

This guide is produced for educational and comparative purposes only. No person should use the information herein for self-diagnosis, treatment, or justification in accepting or declining any medical treatment for any health-related problems. Some medical therapies, including the use of medicines, may be affected by the use of certain nutritional supplements. Therefore, any individual with a specific health problem should seek advice by a qualified medical practitioner before starting a supplementation program. The decision whether to consume any nutritional supplement rests with the individual, in consultation with his or her medical advisor. Furthermore, nothing in this manual should be misinterpreted as medical advice.

This guide is intended to assist in sorting through the maze of nutritional supplements available in the marketplace today. It is not a product endorsement and does not make any health claim, other than to document recent findings in the scientific literature.

This guide was not commissioned by any public sector or private sector interest, or by any company whose products may be represented herein. The research, development, and findings are the sole creative effort of the author and NutriSearch Corporation, neither of whom is associated with any manufacturer or product represented in this guide. Those manufacturers highlighted in the Top-rated Product Section of the guide were invited by NutriSeach Corporation to submit a brief profile of their respective companies and product lines for the benefit of the readership of this guide. No financial compensation was given or received by NutriSearch Corporation or the author for the inclusion of this material.

Library and Archives Canada Cataloguing in Publication

MacWilliam, Lyle Dean
  NutriSearch comparative guide to nutritional supplements : a compendium of products available in the United States and Canada / by Lyle MacWilliam. -- 4th ed.

Previous ed. had title: Comparative guide to nutritional supplements.
Includes bibliographical references and index.
ISBN 978-0-9732538-6-3

1. Dietary supplements. I. Title.

RM258.5.M33 2007   615'.1   C2007-900969-7

To my children,
Laurie, Matthew, Tana, and Karalyn,
who make me feel blessed to be their father.

And to my wife, Arlene,
who gently leads me to knowing
that love is all there is.

WITH THANKS

This book is the culmination of several years of effort in developing the scientific rationale and in refining and enhancing the analytical models used to conduct our comparative analysis. With each edition, we have built on our previous work in order to provide consumers with a comprehensive, up-to-date, and reliable source of information on the science of nutritional supplementation and the products available. To do so, we have admittedly stood on the shoulders of others; the guidance from the scientific authorities we have referenced in developing our analytical models has been invaluable. In borrowing from their scientific insights to construct our analytical standard, we recognize the immense contribution each has made, individually and collectively, to the advancement of scientific knowledge and the pursuit of optimal health.

I am deeply indebted to my editor and wife, Arlene, who has patiently endured my emotional highs and lows, as I have struggled to pull together a seemingly endless volume of scientific and product research. Without her sharp editorial eye, her unwavering demand for neutrality and rigour, and her innate ability to bring me back to centre, the quality of this final work would not be what it is.

I am also indebted to Mr. Gregg Gies, Vice President of Research and Technical Services at NutriSearch. Gregg is a true master in the science of information technology and a tireless researcher, whose ability to ferret out information knows no bounds. As the project's technical director, Gregg's hand is written large throughout this publication. Thanks, also, to Anne Firby, whose tireless efforts in data input and verification helped keep the project on track.

To Ian Black of Ian Black Concepts, I owe a heartfelt thank you. Ian's creative talents in graphic design have provided immeasurable value throughout the finished product.

Last, but certainly not least, all of us extend thanks to you, the purchaser of this guide, for your continued support. In particular, I am grateful to those of my readership who have provided feedback on previous editions of this guide; the encouragement, support, and constructive criticism received from so many of you continues to inspire me to reach beyond myself, in what has truly become a labour of love.

May health be your constant companion,

Lyle MacWilliam

February, 2007

Table of Contents

Section I: Supplementation and Degenerative Disease

Chapter One: The Case for Supplementation 2
    Eat Your Fruits and Veggies 2
    Nutrient-deficient Foods 5
    It Pays to Take Your Vitamins 5

Chapter Two: Degenerative Disease 6
    Living Longer, but Not Healthier 6
    Preventing Degenerative Disease 7
    The Mechanisms of Onset 8

Chapter Three: Oxidative Stress 9
    Oxygen—Friend and Enemy 9
    Nature's Fire Wardens 10
    Synergy—the Power of Teamwork 11
    Antioxidant Enzyme Systems 11
    Implications 12

Chapter Four: Inflammation 13
    Cardiovascular Disease 13
    Other Degenerative Processes 13
    What is Inflammation? 14
    The Inflammatory Cascade 15
    Preventing Chronic Inflammation 15
    The Link to Oxidative Stress 17
    Implications 18

Section II: The Safety of Supplements

Chapter Five: The Safety of Nutritional Supplements 20
    Relative Risks 21
    The Real Issue of Safety 22
    New Research Discloses Problems 25
    Summary 26

Chapter Six: Optimal Nutrition 27
    Misreading the RDAs 27
    RDAs Fail to Address Deficiencies 28
    New DRIs Also Fall Short 29
    Fueling the Biological Spark Plugs 29
    Genes, Enzymes, and Mutations 31
    Genetic Polymorphisms Common 31
    Implications 32

Chapter Seven: Nutritional Supplements Under Attack 33
    Teasing Fact from Fiction 33
    Scientific Sensationalism 37
    The Wrong Yardstick 39
    Tools for a New Paradigm 40

Section III: Rating the Products

Chapter Eight: How the Comparisons Are Made 42
    Creation of the Blended Standard 44
    Limitations of the Study 45
    Interpreting the Graphs 47
    Qualifying the Products 48
    The Nutrient Profile Score 48

Chapter Nine: Product Rating Criteria 49
    Changes to the Criteria 49
    Show Me the Science 49
    1. Completeness 49
    2. Potency 50
    3. Mineral Forms 50
    4. Bioactivity of Vitamin E 51
    5. Gamma Tocopherol 51
    6. Antioxidant Support 52
    7. Bone Health 53
    8. Heart Health 53
    9. Liver Health (detoxification) 54
    10. Metabolic Health 55
    11. Ocular Health 55
    12. Methylation Support 57
    13. Lipotropic Factors 57

14. Inflammation Control 58
15. Glycation Control 59
16. Bioflavonoid Profile 61
17. Phenolic Compounds Profile 62
18. Potential Toxicities 62
Summary 64
Chapter Ten: Medals of Achievement 65
How the Program Works 65
Beyond the Stars: Proof of Quality 66
Certification Programs Overview 66
Summary 69

Section IV Top-rated Products

Chapter Eleven: Top-rated Products 72
Top-rated Stand-alone Products 72
Top-rated Combination Products 72
Going for the Gold 72
Gold Medal Recipients 74

Section V: Graphical Comparisons

Stand-alone Product Comparisons 82
Combination Product Comparisons 116

Section VI: Product Ratings

Appendix A: Stand-alone Products Alphabetically 131
Appendix B: Stand-alone Products Alphabetically by Star Rating 149
Appendix C: Combination Products Alphabetically 167
Appendix D: Combination Products Alphabetically by Star Rating 171
Appendix E: Products Exceeding Upper Limits 175
Bibliography: References by Chapter 177
Index of Terms 187

Illustrations

Figure 1-1: Depleted Soil: Fertilizer Use Skyrockets Post-World War II 5
Figure 2-1: Number of US Residents Surviving to Selected Ages 6
Figure 2-2: Change in Cause of Death between 1987 and 2004 7
Figure 3-1: Free Radical Molecule 9
Figure 3-2: Important Cellular Antioxidants 11
Figure 4-1: Activated Phagocytes (White Blood Cells) 14
Figure 4-2: Prostaglandin Metabolism 16
Figure 5.1: The Risk Management Continuum 21
Figure 6-1: Brin's Schema of Vitamin B1 Deficiency (1964) 28
Figure 6-2: Methylation Reactions 30
Figure 9-1: *d*-Alpha Tocopherol Form of Vitamin E 51
Figure 9-2: Human Heart with Associated Blood Vessels 53
Figure 9-3: Methylation 56
Figure 9-4: Flavone Ring Skeleton 60
Figure 9-5: Quercetin 61
Figure 9-6: *p*-Hydroxycinnamic Acid 61
Figure 9-7: *p*-Hydroxybenzoic Acid 62
Figure 9-8: Oleuropein 62
Figure 11-1: Eighteen Important Health Support Criteria 80

Tables

Table 5-1: Deaths from Unintended Causes and Adverse Reactions to Dietary Supplements 20
Table 5-2: Lead Content in Calcium Supplements 22
Table 5-3: Products Failing Both Disintegration Tests 26
Table 5-4: Products Failing Stage I Disintegration Tests 26
Table 5-5: Products Passing Both Disintegration Tests 26
Table 6-1: Common Vitamins, Coenzymes, and their Functions 29
Table 11-1: Top Products Stand-alone 73
Table 11-2: Top Products Combination 73
Table 11-3: Table of Recommended Daily Intakes (Blended Standard) 78

Section I

Supplementation and Degenerative Disease

This section provides the reader
with an in-depth look at:

■ The Case for Supplementation
■ Degenerative Disease
■ Oxidative Stress
■ Inflammation

*The value of nutritional supplements in overcoming
common dietary deficiencies leads into a discussion
regarding the aetiology of degenerative disease. The processes
of oxidative stress and inflammation as mechanisms
for the genesis of degenerative disease are discussed in depth.*

From nature comes the disease,
and from nature will come the cure.
— *Paracelsus (1493-1541)*

CHAPTER ONE

THE CASE FOR SUPPLEMENTATION

The word is out—it pays to take your vitamins.

After 20 years, the American Medical Association (AMA) has completely reversed its previous anti-vitamin stance and now encourages all adults to supplement daily with a multiple vitamin. A landmark review of 38 years of scientific evidence by Harvard researchers, Dr Robert Fletcher and Dr Kathleen Fairfield, has convinced the conservative *Journal of the American Medical Association (JAMA)* to rewrite its policy guidelines regarding the use of vitamin supplements. In two reports, published in the June 19, 2002 edition of *JAMA*, the authors conclude that the current North American diet, while sufficient to prevent vitamin-deficiency diseases, such as scurvy and pellagra, is inadequate to support the need for optimal health.[1,2]

Insufficient vitamin intake is apparently a cause of chronic diseases. Recent evidence has shown that suboptimal levels of vitamins (below standard), even well above those causing deficiency syndromes, are risk factors for chronic diseases such as cardiovascular disease, cancer, and osteoporosis. A large portion of the general population is apparently at increased risk for this reason.
— Dr Robert Fletcher and Dr Kathleen Fairfield

In the study, the authors examine several nutrients, including vitamins A, B_6, B_{12}, C, D, E, K, folic acid, and several of the carotenoids (including alpha- and beta-carotene, cryptoxanthin, zeaxanthin, lycopene, and lutein). In their conclusions, they note:

✔ folic acid, vitamin B_6, and vitamin B_{12} are required for proper homocysteine metabolism, and low levels of these vitamins are associated with increased risk of heart disease;

✔ inadequate folic acid status increases the risk of neural tube defects and some cancers;

✔ vitamin E and lycopene appear to decrease the risk of prostate cancer;

✔ vitamin D is associated with a decreased risk of osteoporosis and fracture when taken with calcium;

✔ inadequate vitamin B_{12} is associated with anaemia and neurological disorders;

✔ low dietary levels of carotenoids, the brightly coloured pigments in peppers and fruits, appear to increase the risk of breast, prostate, and lung cancers;

✔ inadequate vitamin C is associated with increased cancer risk; and,

✔ low levels of vitamin A are associated with vision disorders and impaired immune function.

In a striking departure from *JAMA's* anti-vitamin rhetoric of the last 20 years, the authors conclude that, given our modern diet, supplementation each day with a multiple vitamin is a prudent preventive measure against chronic disease. The researchers base their guidance on the fact that more than 80% of the American population does not consume anywhere near the five servings of fruits and vegetables required each day for optimal health.

JAMA's last comprehensive review of vitamins, conducted in the 1980s, concluded that people of normal health do not need to take a multivitamin and can meet all their nutritional needs through diet alone. This sudden about-face, along with *JAMA's* public declaration that supplementation is now deemed important to your health, underscores the strength of the scientific evidence that now prevails.

The *JAMA* declaration also highlights a growing concern among nutrition experts that the current recommended intakes for vitamins and minerals are too low. The Recommended Dietary Allowances, also known as the RDAs, were originally established to prevent vitamin-deficiency disorders; however, there has been a growing volume of evidence supporting the need for higher levels of intake for many vitamins and minerals in order to maintain optimal health. Consequently, the United States and Canada have undertaken a comprehensive revision of these recommendations. The reader is referred to Chapter 6 for more detailed information on these evolving reference standards.

Eat Your Fruits and Veggies

The Fletcher-Fairfield reviews published in *JAMA* also highlight the common knowledge that today's diet is not providing sufficient nutritional value to ward off chronic diseases. While nutrient intakes in North America are generally sufficient to avoid overt vitamin deficiencies, sub-clinical deficiencies are common. Fruits and vegetables are the main dietary sources of most vitamins and minerals and health experts have long recommended at least five daily servings of each.

An analysis of data from four US Department of Agriculture surveys of adolescent food intakes from 1965 to 1996 found significant shifts in the adolescent diet during that period.[3] Total energy intake, as well as the proportion of energy from fat, decreased considerably during this time; however, this beneficial trend was offset by a 36% drop in milk consumption and a concomitant rise in the consumption of soft drinks and sugary juices. Moreover, an initially encouraging trend in vegetable intakes was found to be the result of a large increase in the consumption of french fries. Overall, the number of servings for fresh fruits and vegetables remained well below the recommended five servings per day. Disturbingly, the intake of dietary iron, folic acid, and calcium in adolescent girls also remained significantly below recommended levels.

A more recent survey of African-American children showed that consumption of foods from the tip of the food pyramid, including discretionary fat and added sugar, contributed to almost 50% of the diet.[4] Another survey found that nearly one quarter of all vegetables consumed by children and adolescents were french fries. Moreover, only one in five children consumed five or more servings of fruits and vegetables per day.[5]

Similar patterns within the adult population are evident. A 1995 US food frequency survey, conducted by telephone among almost 24,000 adults in 16 states, found that only 20% of the population consumed the recommended five or more daily servings of fruits and vegetables (likely an optimistic figure, as such telephone-based studies tend to over-report actual values). A 1998 study of fruit and vegetable consumption among rural African Americans paralleled the findings of other national studies. In all cases, the intakes of fruits and vegetables fell agonizingly short of meeting the recommended intakes for good health.[6]

Recent US Department of Agriculture data show an encouraging trend in national fruit and vegetable consumption over a three-decade period from 1965 to 1987. During this time, fruit consumption increased 19% and vegetable consumption rose 24%, along with a 22% reduction in fat.[7, 8] However, another recent survey found a disturbing counter-trend reflective of the level of fitness and activity of the individual. Between 1990 and 1996, consumption of fruits and vegetables, while improving among active individuals with normal weights, showed a significant decline among sedentary and obese people.[9] Such a finding has disturbing implications, considering that the incidence of overweight and obesity has climbed to almost two thirds of the US adult population. While the level of overweight and obesity is not as high in Canada, similar trends are apparent.

Let us look at three of the major killers in our modern world—heart disease, cancer, and stroke, which, collectively, account for two thirds of all reported deaths—and investigate the important role that nutrition plays in their prevention.

Heart Disease

It is hard to believe that cardiovascular disease, Public Enemy #1, is a problem cultivated by modern society. In 1912, the *Journal of the American Medical Association* published the first clinical report on cardiovascular disease in America. At the time, the disease was so rare it took years to find.[10] Yet, in less than 100 years, the changes wrought to our lifestyle, environment, and to the food we eat have made cardiovascular disease the number one killer in North America.

Not long ago, common wisdom held that heart disease was a malady of the elderly. Today, this is just not so. Heart disease starts in childhood: the patterns of diet and exercise that develop during our early years cast the mould for lifelong habits. In fact, atherosclerosis (hardening of the arteries) has now been documented in infants and children two-to-fifteen years of age. A 1998 study, reported in the *New England Journal of Medicine,*

found that the prevalence of atherosclerosis begins in childhood and increases with age.[11] Post-mortem examinations of young persons who had died from various accidental causes showed strong correlations between coronary atherosclerosis and cardiovascular risk factors, including body-mass index, blood pressure, serum cholesterol and triglycerides, and smoking. The findings reveal a startling progression of fibrous lesions (plaque) that begins early in life and affects about 30% of adolescents 16 through 20 years of age, 50% of young adults 21 through 25, and 75% of adults 26 through 39. Read those numbers again: by the time we reach the ripe young age of 39, three quarters of us have definitive signs of cardiovascular disease, and most of us have absolutely no knowledge of the fact. For many, our first warning barely precedes our last breath.

The 18-year Baltimore Longitudinal Study of Aging, which concluded in 2004, investigated the contributions of saturated fats, fruits, and vegetables to both coronary heart disease (CHD) and all-cause mortality. The authors found that each serving of fruits and vegetables was associated with a 6% decrease in all-cause mortality and a remarkable 21% decrease in CHD mortality. Total mortality was 31% lower and CHD mortality was a stunning 76% lower among those subjects with both low-fat intakes and high-fruit/vegetable intakes, relative to those with high-fat and low-fruit/vegetable intakes.[8] The findings concur with a previous epidemiological study, which observed a strong inverse relationship between fruit and vegetable intakes and the risk of subsequent cardiovascular disease.[12] Both studies support the general consensus that increased intakes of fresh fruits and vegetables are beneficial for heart health.[13, 14]

The largest and longest investigation to date on the effect of diet on heart disease (part of the Harvard-based Nurses' Health Study and the Health Professionals' Follow-up Study) recently found that the risk of developing cardiovascular disease was inversely proportional to the dietary intake of fruits and vegetables. Simply put, the more fresh fruits and vegetables you eat, the lower is your risk of heart disease. The study included almost 110,000 men and women whose health and dietary habits were followed for 14 years. Compared with those in the lowest category of fruit and vegetable intakes (less than 1.5 servings per day), those who averaged eight or more servings per day were 30% less likely to have a heart attack or stroke.[15] Even a *single* daily serving of leafy green vegetables was sufficient to reduce the risk of heart disease by 11%.

Surprisingly, the data from the two contributing cohort studies also revealed that only 2% to 3% of the study participants—medical professionals who would presumably be knowledgeable about the value of nutrition—actually consumed more than four to five servings of vegetables per day.[16]

Cancers

On July 13, 2000, a groundbreaking report, published in the *New England Journal of Medicine,*[17] tied the development of most cancers to lifestyle plus exposure to environmental and occupational risk factors. While not negating genetic influence, which appears to account for approximately 30% of total cancer risk, the findings place the burden of guilt on poor dietary habits, smoking, alcohol consumption, lack of exercise, and exposure to environmental toxins. A 1997 report, released by the American Institute for Cancer Research and the World Cancer Fund, also highlights the importance of diet in cancer prevention. The report claims that dietary change alone could prevent three to four million cases of cancer worldwide every year.[18] Its key recommendation is to choose a diet that is predominantly plant-based and includes a wide variety of vegetables, fruits, and grains. According to the report, an estimated 30% to 35% of all cancers are related to diet. A comprehensive review of some 200 epidemiological studies from around the world drew similar findings. Researchers from the University of California at Berkeley found overwhelming evidence that fruits and vegetables in the diet provide a huge protective effect against almost every type of cancer.[19] According to the authors, persons with low fruit and vegetable intakes experience about twice the risk of cancer compared to those with high intakes.

Yet, despite what we know about the importance of lifestyle and nutrition, cancer continues to be the second-leading cause of death in North America. The lifetime risk for developing some form of cancer is now one in three for women and one in two for men. According to figures released in a 1994 report that reviewed epidemiological data from 1973 through 1987, adult males entering their 40s and 50s had more than twice the cancer rates of their grandfathers. Women who smoked had five to six times the cancer rates of their grandmothers.[20]

Epidemiologists have long regarded vegetables and fruits as key features of a diet associated with a reduced risk of colorectal cancer. In 1997, a panel of leading epidemiologists, convened by the American Institute for Cancer Research, concurred that fresh vegetables were the dietary components possessing the highest scientific certainty of reducing the risk of colorectal cancer.[16] While the findings have not always been consistent, several recent investigations concur that high intakes of fruits and vegetables confer protective effects over a wide variety of cancers.[15, 21-30]

In a comprehensive review of the scientific literature on the relationship between vegetable and fruit consumption and cancer risk, results from 206 human epidemiological studies and 22 animal studies found evidence of a protective effect from increased vegetable and fruit consumption that is consistent for cancers of the stomach, oesophagus, lung, oral cavity and pharynx, endometrium, pancreas, and colon.[31] The types of food that most often appear to be protective are raw vegetables, followed by allium (onion-like) vegetables, carrots, green vegetables, cruciferous vegetables, and tomatoes. Unquestionably, some constituents of fruits and vegetables are chemo-protective; low intake carries a greater than twofold risk of cancer. In fact, the risk of cancer associated with low fruit or vegetable consumption may only be exceeded by that of smoking.[32]

Stroke

Stroke has been the third-leading cause of death in the most developed countries for decades. A stroke occurs when blood flow to the brain is cut off, generally due to a thrombotic (clot-forming) event in one of the major arteries feeding the brain. It is a major cause of disability among adults and a principal factor in late-life dementia. It is likely that many small strokes go unnoticed, leading to an underreporting of the true incidence of the disease. During the 1950s and early 1960s, countries such as the United States and Canada were characterized by increasing trends in stroke mortality; however, stroke mortality (but not necessarily incidence) declined steeply for the following two decades, before levelling off in the 1980s.[33-36]

Interestingly, since 1998, in both the United States and Canada, folic acid fortification of grain products has been fully implemented. Since then, average blood folate concentrations have increased and blood homocysteine concentrations have decreased (homocysteine is a primary risk factor for cardiovascular disease and stroke). Subsequent to this, from 1998 to 2002, there occurred a discernible decline in stroke mortality in both the US and Canada. The decline is consistent with the hypothesis that folic acid supplementation helps reduce the risk of stroke.[37]

Disturbingly, the number of stroke deaths in Canada and America has one again begun to climb—a possible reflection of the advancing demographic bulge of baby boomers—and the incidence is expected to rise sharply in coming years. Researchers predict that by the middle of the next century, the numbers of Americans to suffer a first stroke will more than double current rates. According to Dr Frank Silver of the Canadian Heart and Stroke Foundation, as baby boomers move into the golden years of their 60s and 70s, Canada will witness a correspondingly large increase in the incidence of strokes. Moreover, a new study by the University of Cincinnati Medical Center suggests that the number of strokes in the United States may be dramatically higher than previously estimated. According to the findings, approximately 700,000 strokes occur in the United States every year—40% higher than previous estimates.[38]

In most epidemiological studies, increased fruit and vegetable intakes in the ranges commonly consumed are associated with a reduced risk of stroke. A recent systematic review of studies investigating the association between fruit and vegetable intakes and chronic disease found that low consumption of fruits and vegetables was a major contributor to the global burden of disease. According to the review, reported in the 2002 World Health Report, 19% of the global burden of ischemic stroke can be attributed to a low consumption of fruits and vegetables.[39] Two recent meta-analyses,* published in 2005 and 2006, found a strong association between fruit and vegetable consumption and a reduction in the risk of stroke. One analysis demonstrated a linear dose-response relationship, with a risk reduction of 11% for each additional portion of fruit consumed and 3% for each vegetable consumed.[40] Moreover, the second study suggested that individuals who have three-to-five servings of fruits and vegetables per day have a 26% lower risk for stroke compared to individuals who consume less than three servings.[41] Since hypertension is the major cause of stroke, the blood pressure-lowering attribute of potassium, plentiful in fresh fruits and vegetables, is thought to be a principal factor contributing to reduced risk. Many other nutrients, including folic acid, bioflavonoids, polyphenols, and assorted antioxidants, are also believed to play

---

* A meta-analysis is a statistically based study that pulls together findings from several other studies to tease out a common thread. A well-designed meta-analysis can be a useful tool; however, a poorly designed meta-analysis can furnish results that are very misleading. For that reason great care must be taken in the study design.

an important role. Consumption of citrus fruit juices, which contain high levels of vitamin C, and cruciferous vegetables (such as broccoli, cabbage, Brussels sprouts, bok choy, and cauliflower), which are rich sources of sulphur-containing glucosinolates, appear to confer the greatest protection against stroke.[42]

Nutrient-deficient Foods

Not only are we not eating enough of the proper food groups, the foods we *do* eat can sometimes be woefully short in vital nutrients and alarmingly high in calories. Nothing can replace the value of a carefully balanced diet. Unfortunately, in today's high-stress world, we face a dearth of beneficial physical activity and a steady diet of meals on the run, fast-food restaurants, and processed foods devoid of nutritional value. Today, it is the exception, rather than the rule, that children or adults will sit down to home-cooked meals with fresh-from-the-garden fruits and vegetables. Even for those fortunate enough to do so, there is no guarantee that they are receiving all the nutrients they need. In our time, relatively few families in America or Canada can boast garden-fresh produce. Most shoppers must rely on commercial agriculture to meet their daily nutritional needs. Yet, for the last 60 years, commercial farms have been relying largely on chemical fertilizers to grow their crops. During the late forties, growers found that three minerals, nitrogen (N), phosphorus (P), and potassium (K), left over from the post-war armaments industry, produced fine-looking crops. The subsequent use of these nutrients quickly replaced traditional mulching and manuring, and, over time, the use of NPK fertilizers contributed to the depletion of many essential micronutrients from our soils. The long-term consequence of this folly has been a steady erosion in the nutritional health of our nations and an inexorable rise in the incidence of degenerative disease. Unquestionably, NPK fertilizers, a destructive legacy of World War II, have played a major role in contributing to sub-clinical nutritional deficiencies and chronic degenerative diseases that afflict our world.[10]

To make matters worse, commercial processing of nutrient-deficient foods further depletes their nutritional value. The mass-production processes of storing, drying, cooking, freeze-drying, extracting, and hydrogenating wreak havoc on an already marginal nutrient content. Processing of cereal grains depletes the magnesium content by 80%. Up to 50% of the folic acid content in foods is lost through preparation, processing and storage. Commercial milling of cereals depletes the vitamin B_6 content by 50% to 90%.[32] Store asparagus for a week and 90% of its vitamin C is gone. Blanch vegetables or fish and up to one half of their B-complex vitamins and vitamin C is lost.[10, 43]

Our bodies need more than just nitrogen, phosphorus, and potassium. They also need iron, copper, selenium, chromium, calcium, magnesium, iodine, molybdenum, zinc, cobalt, boron, vanadium, and other trace elements.[44] Even with the best of intentions and the most careful planning, daily consumption of commercially processed foods grown in nutrient-deficient soils will not provide us with the quality of nutrition we require for a lifetime of optimal health. Simply put, if the nutrients are not in our soils, they are not in our foods; and if they are not in our foods, they are not in our bodies. The long-term consequence of chronic sub-clinical mineral deficiencies is a spiralling epidemic of chronic degenerative disease. For this reason, daily supplementation with a quality vitamin-mineral supplement is a vital component in our quest for optimal health.

It Pays to Take Your Vitamins

We should *never* neglect the importance of a well-balanced diet, high in fruits and vegetables, and we should take every opportunity to eat as close to the earth as possible. However, in today's fast-food world, it is difficult to escape the high-calorie, low-nutrition, over-processed, corporate food culture; prudence dictates that we take extra steps to optimize our nutritional needs. To do so, we need to fortify our diets with a high-quality nutritional supplement that replenishes the body with same vitamins, minerals, antioxidants, and important plant-based nutrients that *ought* to be provided in the food we eat.

As Dr Robert Fletcher, co-author of the groundbreaking JAMA study, states:

> *All of us grew up believing that if we ate a reasonable diet, that [sic] would take care of our vitamin needs. But, the new evidence, much of it in the last couple of years, is that vitamins also prevent the usual diseases we deal with every day—heart disease, cancer, osteoporosis, and birth defects.*

If you value your health, it only makes sense to take that extra step—begin supplementing your diet with a high-quality broad-spectrum nutritional supplement, then stay on it every day for the rest of your life. Supplementation is your *personal* health insurance plan that will help you to age gracefully. It is not just there to assist you when you fall ill; it is there to keep you healthy in the first place.

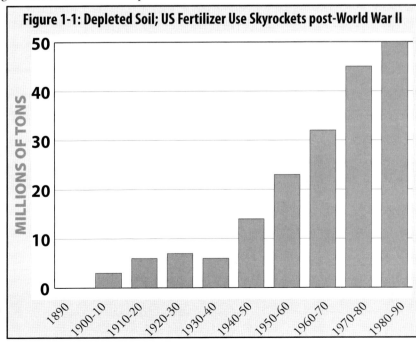

Figure 1-1: Depleted Soil; US Fertilizer Use Skyrockets post-World War II

I don't want to achieve immortality through my work.
I want to achieve immortality through not dying.
—Woody Allen (1935-)

CHAPTER TWO

DEGENERATIVE DISEASE

In our modern and hectic world, health is a rapidly declining commodity. We complain about being "run off our feet"; however, the phrase rarely involves the type of physical exertion for which our bodies were designed. "Too busy" really means that too many things are getting in the way of exercising and eating well. "Too busy" really means that our long-term health is, once again, hurriedly dismissed for the more immediate and seemingly urgent matters of the day.

Bob Seger's song captures our dilemma: "Deadlines and commitments; what to leave in, what to leave out." We have come to take our health for granted. We are, indeed, "running against the wind," conveniently placing considerations of health on the back burner. Unfortunately, for many, that day suddenly presses upon us with the diagnosis of a serious degenerative disease.

Degenerative diseases are characterized by their slow progression and long duration. They include the diseases we discussed in the previous chapter, heart disease, cancer, and stroke— today's three major killers. Arthritis, diabetes, osteoporosis, inflammatory bowel disorder, Alzheimer's, and Parkinson's diseases are but a few of the many other forms of chronic disorders that share a common aetiology (cause). In most cases, chronic degenerative disease steals years from its victims or debilitates them in such a way that their final days are filled with needless pain and suffering. These are protracted diseases; ones for which there is no immediate recovery and rarely a complete cure. Generally speaking, a chronic degenerative disease is a life sentence.

Chances are very good that each of us knows someone whose life has been burdened with a chronic degenerative disease: a family with a parent claimed by cancer; a relative with Alzheimer's disease; a grandmother or aunt with osteoporosis; or a cousin who requires daily insulin injections for diabetes. Before our lives are through, chronic degenerative disease will touch each one of us in a personal way.

Living Longer, but Not Healthier

While technology has increased our lifespan dramatically over the past few centuries, it has, ironically, not secured for us the holy grail of long-term health. In the 17th century, an adult in his late 30s was considered old. Even less than 100 years ago, we were not expected to live past the age of 50. By 2002, the average lifespan hovered around 77 years of age for men and 79 for women. Rapid mortality declines in the first half of the 20th century, largely due to enhanced hygiene and advances in medical science (particularly, the development of antibiotics), increased the average life expectancy in the US by almost 50%. By the end of the 20th century, the average life expectancy stood at 76.9 years, driven largely by reductions in mortality of the elderly.[1] Over the course of the 20th century, the number of individuals reaching the 75-year milestone nearly tripled and the percentage living to 85 exploded six-fold.

At the dawn of the last century, individuals who reached 65 years of age could expect to live another 12 years; by end of the century, the remaining life expectancy for individuals 65 years of age had increased by 50%. Throughout the 21st century, mortality rates are expected to decline further, allowing life expectancy to reach even higher levels, perhaps well past the 100-year mark.[2,3] If you are part of the baby boom generation or younger, and are in generally good

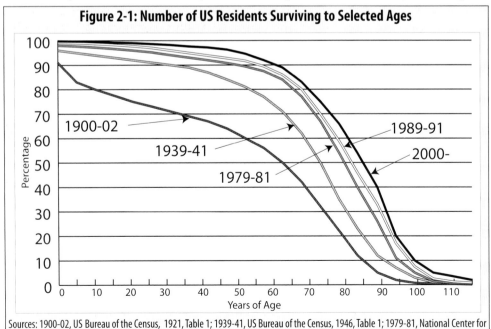

Figure 2-1: Number of US Residents Surviving to Selected Ages

1900-02
1939-41
1979-81
1989-91
2000-

Percentage
Years of Age

Sources: 1900-02, US Bureau of the Census, 1921, Table 1; 1939-41, US Bureau of the Census, 1946, Table 1; 1979-81, National Center for Health Statistics (NCHS), 1985, Table 1; 1989-91, NCHS, 1995, Table 1; 2000, NCHS, 2001b, Table 1.

health today, chances are very good that you will make it to that centennial milestone.

Many experts predict that, within a decade, every passing year will witness the addition of more than a year to the scale of human life expectancy. Renowned longevity expert and gerontologist, Aubrey de Grey, believes that within the next 20 to 25 years human therapies will have been invented that will actually halt and reverse the biological aging process.[4]

While extending one's lifespan certainly has appeal, the tragic reality is that, for many, our golden years are too often spent in debilitating pain. Today, more than 14 million Americans over the age of 65 are disabled from some form of chronic disease, such as heart disease, arthritis, diabetes, and neurodegenerative disorders.[1] Today, 80% of American seniors suffer from at least one chronic health condition and 50% suffer from at least two degenerative conditions that seriously impede their ability to function. Similarly, more than four out of five Canadian seniors living at home suffer from one or more of the same chronic health conditions as their American cousins.

Chronic diseases develop over a lifetime. Their rise to today's list of top killers is, curiously, a product of our increased lifespan. We have slain the dragons of infectious disease, such as polio and tuberculosis, only to find that our own lifestyle has now become our next mortal adversary. The fact is, living longer allows our dietary and lifestyle choices to *create* the circumstances of today's most common causes of death.

Preventing Degenerative Disease

The good news is that there is something we can do right now, regardless of our age or our health, to retard the progression of degenerative diseases and reduce the risks of their premature expression. According to former US Surgeon General, Dr Everett Koop:

> *The preponderance of the evidence . . . substantiates an association between dietary factors and rates of chronic diseases. In particular, the evidence suggests strongly that a dietary pattern that contains excessive intake of foods high in calories, fat (especially saturated fat), cholesterol, and sodium, but that is low in complex carbohydrates and fiber, is one that contributes significantly to the high rates of major chronic diseases among Americans. It also suggests that reversing such dietary patterns should lead to a reduced incidence of these chronic diseases.[6]*

As we learned in the previous chapter, there is an undeniable link between our level of nutrition and the prognosis for our long-term health; those of us who consume a healthy diet and keep fit are likely to live longer, healthier lives than those whose diets and lifestyles are below par. The dietary recommendations for chronic disease prevention are consistent from one specific condition to the next. In the same report mentioned above, the Surgeon General advocates a diet rich in fruits and vegetables, complex carbohydrates, and fibre. The report recommends a varied and balanced plant-based diet and warns against high-fat, calorie-dense foods that are devoid of any real nutritional value, such as those made with refined sugars and flour.

Figure 2-2: Change in Cause of Death between 1987 and 2004

Cause of death	1987	2004	%Change
Heart Disease	35.7%	35.0%	-0.8%
Cancers	22.4%	29.7%	7.3%
Stroke	7.0%	8.0%	1.0%
Repiratory	3.7%	6.5%	2.9%
Diabetes	1.8%	3.9%	2.1%
Alzheimer's	0.0%	3.5%	3.5%
Liver and Kidney	1.2%	2.3%	1.1%
Subtotal	71.8%	89.0%	17.2%
All other causes	28.2%	11.0%	-17.2%

Sources: Extracts of The Surgeon General's Report on Nutrition and Health. Washington, DC: U.S. Department of Health and Human Services; 1988; WISQARS Internet program. WISQARS Leading Causes of Death Reports, 1999 - 2004. Atlanta, GA: Office of Statistics and Programming, National Center for Injury Prevention and Control, Centers for Disease Control and Prevention; 2004.

In fact, we knew the importance of good nutrition well before it became the focus of the US Surgeon General's report. Scientists who helped eradicate infectious diseases warned some time ago that we would be facing new health challenges based on our lifestyle choices. Most people simply accept the onset of arthritis, heart disease, and diabetes as inevitable results of the aging process. The truth is that these conditions are largely preventable.

For instance, up to 30% of heart disease can be attributed directly to obesity and high cholesterol, two conditions that are lifestyle and diet related. Up to 35% of all cancer deaths, especially breast, prostate, and colon cancers, are related to diet. In 1997, the American Institute for Cancer Research and the World Cancer Fund released a report claiming that a change in diet could prevent 3 to 4 million cancer cases throughout the world each year.[7] As well, osteoporosis has been traced to diets low in calcium and vitamin D; macular degeneration and cataracts arise, in part, from low intakes of antioxidants such as vitamins C and E—and the list goes on.[8]

In 1987, almost 72 out of every 100 American citizens died from a chronic degenerative disease; By 2004, 89% of deaths were caused by chronic disease—an increase of over 17% in less than two decades.[6, 9] These diseases develop silently over a long time, perhaps decades. There is no warning—progression of a chronic condition is a process of stealth. Our bodies generally give no noticeable indication that we are heading down a path that will lead to cancer or heart disease. For one third of those who will experience their first heart attack, it will be their *only* and their last warning sign—that's not much of a chance for lifestyle change.

Yet, 60 to 70% of heart disease cases can be prevented; of stroke, 80% are avoidable. Some experts believe that up to 80% of all cancer deaths are also preventable. As well, 90% of the incidents of type 2 diabetes, a major health risk for tens of thousands of Americans and Canadians alike, can be avoided through simple modifications in diet and exercise.

Mark Twain strikes a jocular cord when he says, "The only way to keep your health is to eat what you don't want, drink what you don't like, and do what you'd rather not." We chuckle, but, unfortunately, many of us feel the same way. Health is a matter of choice—choosing to eat a healthy meal instead of a burger and fries or choosing to take a brisk walk instead of watching TV. The fact is, far too many of us are making poor nutrition and lifestyle choices on a consistent, often daily, basis. If, instead, we would choose to make good nutrition and an active lifestyle a daily habit, we could add 5 to 15 *healthy* years to our lives. Apart from the future benefit, eating well and exercising regularly will also enable us to enjoy life so much more right now!

The Mechanisms of Onset

Over the past several decades, scientists have attempted to ferret out the causative factors of degenerative disease. Unlike infectious diseases, which present a clear and present danger to the body—and are met with an intense inflammatory defence by the body's immune system—chronic disease processes are exceedingly subtle. Like stealth fighters, they pass beneath our radar screens until well advanced.

A good example is cancer: if you don't protect yourself, your chance of avoiding cancer is about as good as the flip of a coin. Unfortunately, once you have contracted the disease, your overall chance of survival is considerably lower. Cancer does not happen overnight. Developing silently for perhaps 10 to 20 years, most cancers are already well advanced by the time they are discovered. Upon diagnosis, doctors immediately roll out their heavy artillery—surgery, chemotherapy, radiation—but in reality, there is not a lot that they can do at this point. "Cut, burn, and poison" have become the indispensable tools of the trade.

Over the last 35 years, survival rates for cancer have not significantly improved. Since former US President Richard Nixon's 1971 declaration of "War on Cancer," hundreds of billions of dollars have been poured into a campaign some critics have labelled a "medical Vietnam." According to Nobel Laureate, Linus Pauling, "Everyone should know that the war on cancer is largely a fraud." We have been desperately searching for a magic bullet, while ignoring the underlying cause.

Cancer is not a single disease, but a group of over 100 diseases with a generally similar aetiology. There is growing medical evidence that, like many other chronic diseases, cancer may initially develop through oxidative damage to the cell's biological machinery, including its molecular blueprint, or DNA, and through inflammatory events caused by oxidation. The fact that oxidative stress and inflammation are so closely linked to diet and lifestyle suggests that the onset of cancer and other chronic disease processes are based on long-standing inadequacies in the body's nutritional and physiological status that have left it vulnerable to attack.

Oxidative Stress

Back in 1954, biochemist and professor emeritus of medicine, Dr Denham Harman, proposed that disease and aging occur when cells, unprotected by proper levels of endogenous and dietary antioxidants, sustain repeated injury from an unrelenting attack of molecular fragments known as free radicals. According to Harman's *Free Radical Theory*, the carnage inflicted by repeated oxidative assaults damages the integrity of important cellular molecules—the proteins, fats, carbohydrates, and nucleic acids of the cell. Like many bold scientific advances that dare to broach conventional wisdom, Harman's theory was largely ignored, even derided, until several studies in the late 1960s overwhelmingly validated his brilliant insight.

According to Harman, the cumulative damage from unchecked oxidative stress eventually destroys the molecular fidelity of the cell and impairs its function. These initial molecular lesions inflict collateral damage to neighbouring biomolecules, to eventually impact tissues and organs—propagating a catabolic* cascade that ultimately manifests in some form of degenerative disease.

Since Harman first posited his theory, investigators have linked over 80 degenerative diseases to the consequences of oxidative stress. Today, most researchers believe that such diseases are not separate entities at all, but are simply different forms of expression of a catabolic process influenced by genetic endowment, environment, and lifestyle. Which disease strikes *you* depends as much on your individual lifestyle and lifelong dietary choices as it does on your genetic predisposition.

Systemic Inflammation

Research shows that, beyond the immediate damage that oxidative stress invokes on the cell's molecular structures, it also kick-starts a process of systemic inflammation by activating key inflammation-promoting molecules within the cell. Nuclear factor kappa beta (NFkB) is a nuclear transcription factor, one of several such signalling proteins activated in response to oxidative stress. Once mobilized, NFkB switches on genes that control the manufacture of numerous proinflammatory cytokines.† These signalling proteins, in turn, unleash a cascade of inflammatory reactions that damage neighbouring cellular structures and lead to the onset of disease and accelerated aging. The process is silent—and deadly.

Hence, the ability to control oxidative stress and to inhibit inflammation is vital to the long-term health of the cell.[10] The link between oxidative stress and silent inflammation, and the roles that both processes play in the manifestation of degenerative disease will be discussed more fully in the next two chapters.

---

* Catabolism is a metabolic process that involves degradative chemical reactions within the cell. These reactions are responsible for the breakdown of large biomolecules into smaller units. Catabolism is associated with cellular aging and leads to the destruction of cells and tissues.

† Cytokines are proteinaceous signalling compounds, similar to hormones and neurotransmitters. They are used extensively for localized inter-cellular communication.

**Science is wonderfully equipped to answer the question "How?"
but it gets terribly confused when you ask the question "Why?"**
—Albert Einstein (1879-1955)

CHAPTER THREE

OXIDATIVE STRESS

In chemistry, radicals (often referred to as free radicals) are atomic or molecular species with unpaired electrons. Highly unstable and extremely short lived, free radical intermediates have a lifespan measured in trillionths of a second or less. Their presence in biological systems was first reported in the 1960s when scientists observed exceedingly short-lived events in enzyme-controlled oxidation-reduction (redox) reactions similar to those that take place inside our cells.[1,2] Unlike ions, free radicals generally do not carry a net charge on the molecule, so their reactivity is different from the reactivity of similar ions. However, the unpaired electrons of a free radical create an activated energy state, making the molecule highly reactive chemically. Consequently, free radicals are aggressive participants in chemical reactions within the cell, reacting with other biomolecules at the instant of their creation.

During their fleeting existence, highly unstable free radicals can inflict considerable damage to the cell. Like sparks from a spitting fire that burn holes in your living room carpet, these supercharged particles leave a virtual killing field of destruction in their wake. For example, when a free radical interacts with a lipid (fat) molecule in the cell membrane, it sets in motion an autocatalytic reaction that is self-perpetuating. Once oxidized, a lipid molecule interacts with and damages its neighbouring molecule. This newly formed lipid peroxide (oxidized lipid) then attacks *its* neighbour and the process repeats unless quenched by a membrane-active antioxidant. Lipid peroxidation is *extremely* damaging to the cell because it seriously impairs the selective permeability of the cell membrane and, with this, the ability of the cell to control its internal environment—nasty stuff, with nasty consequences for the cell.

Oxygen—Friend and Enemy

Life's quintessential paradox is that oxygen—the giver of life—is also our mortal enemy. While absolutely essential for life, oxygen's involvement in the cell's respiratory processes lies at the very heart of growing old. A constant flow of energy moves through every living cell with an intricate transfer of electrons from one molecule to the next. When a molecule gives up electrons it is *oxidized;* when it accepts electrons it is *reduced.* The redox process is a chemical "yin-yang," that powers the machinery of the cell and lets the life-force flow. Scientists call this process *respiration.*

It begins with a molecule of glucose, the principal energy source of the cell. Through a complex series of redox reactions, glucose is broken into its component parts and energy is cap-

tured. At each step, electrons (carried by special energy-transfer agents, NADH and $FADH_2$) shuttle between molecules to the terminal reaction sequence, located deep within the cell's mitochondria (respiratory centres). Here, the electrons combine with molecular oxygen and hydrogen ions to form water.

In simple terms, respiration is nothing more than controlled oxidation or combustion, much like the burning of wood or the rusting of iron. In our cells, however, biological catalysts—specialized proteins called enzymes—control each step. Enzymes allow the oxidative fires of the cell to burn at a much lower temperature, releasing energy in small packets that the cell can capture and store in the form of adenosine triphosphate (ATP), a specialized molecule that acts as the energy currency of the cell. The result of this biologically controlled oxidation is essentially the same as simple combustion: complex molecules are broken down to water and carbon dioxide, releasing energy. In cellular

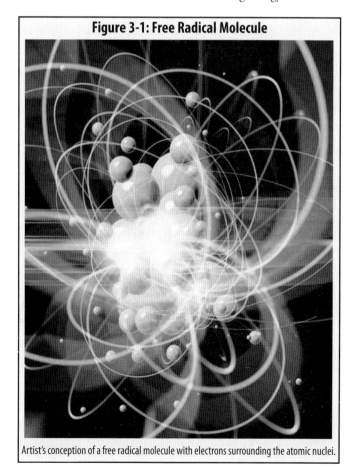

Figure 3-1: Free Radical Molecule

Artist's conception of a free radical molecule with electrons surrounding the atomic nuclei.

respiration, the energy captured by ATP is later used to power the machinery of the cell as it performs its daily tasks.

During cellular respiration some of the exchanged electrons invariably escape, leaking out of the cell's respiratory centres to react with ambient oxygen and generate toxic oxygen radicals, known as reactive oxygen species (ROS). ROS include the super-oxide anion ($\cdot O_2^-$), the hydroxyl radical (OH$\cdot$), singlet oxygen (an activated form of molecular O_2), and hydrogen peroxide (H_2O_2). These molecular predators, because of their unstable electron configurations, are extremely aggressive, reacting with and damaging other molecules in the cell. It is estimated that 2% to 5% of the electrons that pass through the cell's respiratory processes are converted to damaging superoxide molecules and other ROS.[3]

Oxygen is not the only molecular species that forms free radi-cals. There are also a number of endogenous* reactive nitrogen species (RNS), derived from nitric oxide (NO). Of these, perox-ynitrite (ONOO$^-$) appears to have the most biological activity.[4] As well, several atmospheric and water-borne pollutants, absorbed into our bodies through the foods we consume, contain persistent free radical-generating toxins. These xenobiotics (mate-rials foreign to the body) include chlorinated hydrocarbons, pesticides, smog residues, chemical carcinogens from cigarette smoke, metals (such as mercury, lead, and arsenic) and other sources. They are all prodigious generators of RNS, ROS, and other free radical species.

Normally, a cell will snuff out free radicals by neutralizing them with endogenous and dietary antioxidants, which donate electrons to convert the free radicals to a more stable form. In the process, the antioxidant, itself, becomes oxidized and needs to be replenished; however, if the cell's antioxidant status has been depleted through excessive physiological demands or chronic nutritional insufficiency, the continuous flux of free radicals will exhaust the cell's capacity to extinguish this destructive power.

Not everything about free radicals is bad for the cell. Outside of the central role that they play in respiration, free radicals are important in a number of other biological processes. Their pro-duction is central to the body's immune response; for example, the killing of bacteria and other invading pathogens by neu-trophil granulocytes (specialized white blood cells) is accomplished by a burst of ROS that is lethal to the invading organism. Free radicals have also been implicated in certain cell signalling processes, including the initiation of the inflammatory response.

While we can't live with free radicals, we also can't live without them—much like many human relationships! The secret lies in *balance,* for it is when the redox balance in the body goes awry that cellular damage takes root. Therefore, it is essential that the cells of your body be maintained in their *optimal* nutritional state. Even moderate exercise can tilt the body's cellular redox balance, causing the release of a damaging flood of free radicals. For this reason, elite athletes, who press themselves to the limits of physi-cal endurance, need high levels of antioxidant protection. Unchecked, free radical damage threatens the integrity of essen-tial biomolecules and structural components within the cell. These include the lipids that compose the delicate membranes of the cell, the enzymatic and structural proteins, and the nucleic acids (DNA) that encode the cell's genetic blueprint. Once the damage begins, so, too, does the process of degenerative disease and accelerated aging.

Unfettered generation of free radicals, due to inadequate antioxidant stores or chronic inflammation in the cells and tissues of the body, is what must be avoided at all cost—and that is what this book is all about.

Nature's Fire Wardens

According to Dr Edward West,[5] "It is essential that in biolog-ical oxidation-reduction the transfer [of energy] takes place in a manner that controls the potentially destructive effects of free radical formation and conserves biological function [within the cell]." The fundamental control mechanisms, referred to by West, lie in the enzyme systems needed for the reactions to proceed, as well as in the cell's natural defence mechanisms—antioxidants.

Antioxidants are nature's fire wardens—complex biomolecules that police the chemical processes of the cell and snuff out the firestorm of free radicals that erupts from the metabolic activities of the cell or is inflicted through persistent environmental toxins. As long as we have sufficient antioxidant stores in our cells, the damage is minimized. However, if we lack sufficient antioxidant reinforcement, the cumulative damage of these molecular "sparks" will severely injure the cell. Such oxidative damage is now believed to be the dark force behind the onset of degenera-tive disease. In fact, a multitude of degenerative disease processes have now been linked to oxidative stress.[6] Dr Ray Strand, in his book, *Bionutrition,* adroitly calls the battle against oxidative stress, "the war within."[7]

Until the proffering of Harman's Free Radical Theory in 1954,

---

Telomeres tick off time

Scientists have proposed that our internal biological clock may be located on the ends of the chromosomes, the tiny threads of genetic material that lie coiled within the nucleus of each of our cells. Each of our 23 pairs of chromosomes contain molecular caps, called telomeres, which act much like the protective plastic caps on shoelaces. Telomeres play an important role in cell division. Each time a cell replicates, the telomeres get a bit shorter until, after about 50 cell divisions, the caps are but a fraction of their original length. Scientists now believe that the length of the telomeres may be the timing mechanism that limits further cell division and signals the end of the cell's productive lifespan.

In the early '70s, Russian scientist Alexaie Olovnikov and Nobel Laureate James Watson (co-discoverer of the molecular structure of DNA) individually proposed that the shortening of the telomeres might lead to cellular aging. As the cell repeatedly divides, the telomeres get shorter and, as they do so, they are increasingly able to influence the way the cell expresses its genetic code. The consequence, each concluded, is cellular aging. Recent studies concur that the shortening of telomeres increases their control over gene expression and may determine the ultimate age of the cell and the risk for degenerative disease.

---

* An endogenous substance is one manufactured by the ongoing biochemical processes of the cell. While several endogenous antioxidants, like coenzyme Q_{10}, are manufactured within the body, they can also be supplied through the diet.

free radicals were thought to exist only outside the body. In 1968, further work by Harman showed that a small amount of vitamin E added to the diet increased life spans in mice by about 5%.[8] Until then, not much was known about the relevance of vitamin E or other biological antioxidants; science simply did not understand the importance of such molecules in the protection of the cell against oxidative assault. My own research on free radicals and dietary supplementation with vitamin E, conducted in the 1970s, showed that ionizing radiation (gamma rays) caused severe damage to cell membranes, punching tiny holes in their surfaces and causing them to become "leaky."[9] The work also shed some light on the ability of vitamin E to quench the peroxidation of membrane lipids as a consequence of radiation-induced membrane damage.[9, 10]

In 1971, Dr Richard Passwater became the first scientist to publicly describe the nutritional role of antioxidants. Since that time, research on these important nutrients has grown prodigiously. Today, vitamin A, vitamin C, vitamin E, beta-carotene, coenzyme Q_{10}, selenium, zinc, l-glutathione, alpha-lipoic acid, n-acetyl-cysteine, proanthocyanidins, bioflavonoids, and many other tongue-twisting names, have stepped into the limelight—an army of free radical fighters poised to battle the tens of thousands of oxidative attacks that each cell of your body sustains every day.[11]

Antioxidants quench highly reactive free radicals, stopping them dead in their tracks *before* they can cause structural damage to the cell. They do this by scavenging the unpaired electron from the free radical, rendering the molecule harmless. In the process, the antioxidant, itself, is altered chemically. Some antioxidants are regenerated by the presence of other antioxidants—a principal reason why you should always supplement with a wide spectrum of antioxidants, rather than just one. Other antioxidants are converted to entirely different compounds or are excreted from the body. Your body produces some antioxidants, while others must be obtained through the diet.

The endogenous antioxidants include many of the body's natural enzymes, coenzymes, and sulphur-containing molecules, such as glutathione and n-acetyl-cysteine. The dietary antioxidants include vitamin A (and the related carotenoids, including beta-carotene), vitamins E and C, and the myriad of bioflavonoids and sulphur-containing compounds derived from fruits and vegetables. While not themselves antioxidants, many minerals also form vital parts of the different antioxidant systems in the body. These include selenium, manganese, copper, and zinc.[11]

The evidence is now irrefutable that the right use of antioxidants can prevent and reverse many forms of cancer, heart disease, atherosclerosis, adult-onset diabetes and a host of other diseases whose primary cause is excess (free radical) oxidation.

—Dr Michael Colgan

Synergy—the Power of Teamwork

To debate which antioxidant is the *magic bullet* misses the point. Like firefighters on the front line, who reinforce one another, antioxidants work best when they work together. This is known as *synergy*, an idiom coined by Passwater, who stresses that antioxidants require the presence of other antioxidants to effect proper electron transfer to the oxidizing agent—a kind of molecular relay team, if you will. Synergy implies that the effect of the whole is greater than the sum of its parts.

Antioxidants also work in different areas of the cell. Vitamin E is the premier antioxidant of the cellular membrane, quenching free radical-induced lipid peroxidation within the membrane itself. Vitamin C is king in the extracellular fluids and works alongside glutathione in the cytosol (fluid portion) of the cell. Both vitamin C and vitamin E, along with selenium, enhance the effect of beta-carotene, itself a potent antioxidant and a metabolic precursor of vitamin A. Coenzyme Q_{10} (CoQ_{10}) works deep within the mitochondrion, assisting in the energy-transfer reactions and rejuvenating vitamin E. Together with vitamin E, CoQ_{10} protects the mitochondrial membranes from the oxidative fires of respiration. Alpha-lipoic acid, along with a family of powerful antioxidants, the proanthocyanidins (found in grape seed and pine bark extracts), regenerates vitamin C, which in turn rejuvenates vitamin E. Working together, these free radical fighters choreograph their daily battle, protecting the cell in a symphony of synergy—it is a masterpiece written by Mother Nature.

Antioxidant Enzyme Systems

The first line of defence employed by the cells of our bodies against free radicals consists of the protective enzyme systems, superoxide dismutase (SOD), catalase, and glutathione peroxi-

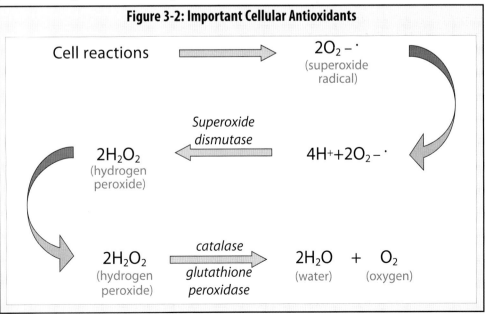

Figure 3-2: Important Cellular Antioxidants

Cell reactions → $2O_2 -\cdot$ (superoxide radical)

Superoxide dismutase

$2H_2O_2$ (hydrogen peroxide) ← $4H^+ + 2O_2 -\cdot$

$2H_2O_2$ (hydrogen peroxide) — catalase / glutathione peroxidase → $2H_2O$ (water) + O_2 (oxygen)

dase. These three antioxidant complexes work together to rid our cells of toxic ROS generated through respiration. Figure 3-2 provides a good example of the interconnectedness and synergy developed through these coordinated systems:

Step 1: Under the prodding of the superoxide dismutase (an antioxidant enzyme), toxic superoxide radicals, produced by the cell's metabolic activities, combine with hydrogen ions to form hydrogen peroxide.

Step 2: To rid itself of hydrogen peroxide, itself a potent oxidizing agent, the cell next enlists the talents of two more antioxidant enzyme systems: catalase and glutathione peroxidase.

Step 3: Working together, catalase and glutathione peroxidase cleave the hydrogen peroxide molecules to produce harmless water and molecular oxygen.

There are several other detoxification processes at work within our cells, but this simplified reaction model is a good example of how the cell's principal detoxification mechanisms team up to rid the body of damaging superoxide radicals, generated by the cell's own metabolic processes.

As we age, we gradually lose our ability to produce these important antioxidant enzymes. This may be related to the shortening of the end caps of chromosomes (see "Telomeres tick off time"), which appears to increase their control over genetic expression. It may also be due to the accumulation of errors in the genes regulating the manufacture of a particular antioxidant enzyme. Whatever the cause, once cells can no longer manufacture sufficient working enzymes to quench oxidative stress, free radicals begin to accumulate and oxidative damage—the genesis of the aging process—ensues. Simply put, our bodies slowly begin to "rust away" from within.

Implications

The scientific evidence points increasingly to oxidative distress as a principal causative factor in biological aging and the development of chronic diseases. It appears that damage caused by relentless oxidative assault to the cell causes its metabolic machinery to malfunction and eventually fail. We have much to learn about the precise mechanisms through which antioxidants counteract these free radical assaults. The challenge now is to clarify the means by which the initial oxidative damage caused by free radicals propagates outward to affect the organs and the body itself.

Recently, the body's inflammatory response has become the focus of intensive investigations that are now revealing insights as to how this damaging oxidative cascade unfolds. We will investigate some of these key relationships in the next chapter.

Don't dig your grave with your own knife and fork.

— English Proverb

CHAPTER FOUR

INFLAMMATION

In April, 2005, a paper published in the *Archives of Internal Medicine* revealed startling new findings about the nature of heart disease. The paper, a systematic review on the effect of various lipidemic (fat lowering) agents on heart disease, combined the data from 97 individual clinical trials and compared the reductions in cardiac death rates from various interventions to treat hypercholesterolemia (high cholesterol). Mortality data involving 137,000 patients from six types of intervention—including the use of cholesterol-busting drugs, cholesterol-binding resins, high-dose niacin, fish oil supplementation, and dietary change—were compared to data from 139,000 control subjects.

The researchers found that, by large measure, the greatest benefit was obtained from *fish oil*, which provided a remarkable 23% reduction in the overall risk of death.[1] Conversely, mainstream medicine's weapon of choice—statin drugs—conferred only a 13% reduction in risk. When the risk of death from heart disease alone was examined, fish oil lowered mortality by 32% compared to only 22% from statin drugs. Even more remarkable, fish oil provided this extraordinary protection while exhibiting the *least* ability amongst all forms of intervention to actually lower cholesterol levels.

The findings strongly refute the classic view of heart disease based on the contemporary model of cholesterol blockage—a model that utterly fails to explain why 70% of heart attacks occur in people with little or no previous arterial blockage. The authors of the study suggest that the protective effect of fish oil must be expressed through some *alternate* mechanism unrelated to cholesterol levels.

That mechanism rests upon a hypothesis proffered over 150 years ago by the renowned 19th century pathologist, Rudolph Virchow, who proposed that *inflammation* may be the trigger that precipitates a fatal cardiac event. From research conducted since the 1980s, we are now closing the circle to embrace Virchow's original paradigm: cardiovascular disease, the leading cause of preventable death in our modern world, is a bona-fide inflammatory condition.[2]

Cardiovascular Disease

Harvard cardiologist, Paul Ridker, has come to view heart disease as an inflammatory process that is similar to rheumatoid arthritis. Based on several studies that suggest up to 25 million Americans with normal cholesterol have markedly higher risks for heart attack due to systemic inflammation,[3-5] Ridker believes that chronic inflammation is implicated in no less than 50% of diagnosed heart disease cases.

Ridker's research has identified C-reactive protein (CRP) as a principal clinical marker for systemic inflammation. Produced by the liver and in the endothelial cells that line the arterial walls, levels of this signalling molecule can shoot up 1,000-fold or more during an acute illness. Focusing on low levels of CRP (less than 10 mg/L), Ridker demonstrated that healthy middle-aged men with extremely low levels—less than 0.5 mg/L—rarely have heart attacks,[6] while those with levels greater than 3 mg/L have triple the risk of heart attack or stroke.[7-9] Furthermore, studies have found that the specificity of CRP in predicting a cardiovascular event is extraordinarily high. Associated clinical markers for inflammation, including fibrinogen and homocysteine, and the signalling molecules, interleukin-6 and tumor necrosis factor-alpha, are also strong predictive markers for a heart attack—far more predictive than the measure of cholesterol alone.[10-12] Several recent studies suggest that cholesterol, in fact, may not pose any real danger unless it is first weakened by the processes of inflammation and oxidative damage.[13, 14]

Other Degenerative Processes

While heart disease is the current poster boy for systemic inflammation, it is certainly not alone. The more researchers probe systemic inflammation, the more they expose its links to other disease processes. Many researchers now believe that low-grade, systemic inflammation is the basis for accelerated aging and the development of degenerative disease. Chronic inflammation is also an underlying cause of excess body fat and the inability to lose weight, and may be the important missing link in the current obesity epidemic.[15] It is associated with the onset of diabetes, Alzheimer's, Huntington's, and Parkinson's diseases, amyotrophic lateral sclerosis, and multiple sclerosis, to name but a few. As well, several autoimmune diseases, such as rheumatoid arthritis, multiple sclerosis, lupus, and Crohn's disease, can occur when there is too much *friendly fire* from the immune system.

The presence of activated microglial cells (which scavenge damaged tissues and pump out harmful neurotoxins and free radicals), found in the brains of patients with neurodegenerative disorders, are clinical indicators of chronic inflammation of the central nervous system (CNS).[16] In a 25-year study evaluating the risks of dementia, men with high levels of CRP were up to three times more likely to contract Alzheimer's disease (AD) or vascular dementia than were men with low levels. Of note was the finding that silent, but deadly, inflammatory processes were evident long before clinical symptoms of dementia appeared.[17]

A recent study on inflammation and type 2 diabetes provides support for a common inflammatory basis for both AD and diabetes.[18] Diabetics have elevated levels of deep inflammation, and many such individuals commonly suffer from both diseases. In patients with AD, inflammation of brain tissues increases the production of soluble beta-amyloid protein* and its conversion to insoluble amyloid fibrils. Accumulation of these harmful protein fibrils is closely associated with the deterioration of brain function. Moreover, because of a molecular structure that is similar to immunoglobulins (antibodies), beta-amyloid fibrils can, in turn, over-stimulate the immune system, leading to further inflammation.[19, 20] In type 2 diabetics, amyloid protein deposits similar to those found in the AD brain can form in the pancreas, knocking out of action the cells responsible for the production of insulin. Chronically elevated levels of insulin and blood sugar, common to those suffering from metabolic syndrome (a pre-diabetic state), trigger inflammatory events, similar to those seen in the AD brain, that lead to the formation of these harmful protein plaques.

Inflammation of the gastrointestinal tract can have far-reaching consequences, including the inability to absorb essential nutrients and the development of osteoporosis. Patients with inflammatory bowel disorder (IBD), a chronic inflammatory condition of the gut, demonstrate an inordinately high risk of osteoporosis.[21, 22] Chronic inflammation of the endothelial cells lining the digestive tract appears to contribute to an imbalance in bone remodelling, triggering the release of bone-destroying inflammatory cytokines into the blood. This, in turn, leads to bone mineral loss and even greater systemic inflammation.[23]

Inflammation also promotes several types of cancer. People with the highest blood levels of CRP and interleukin-6, another important inflammatory marker, are much more likely to contract colorectal, oesophageal, and other cancers than those with the lowest levels.[24-26] It is well known that non-steroidal anti-inflammatory drugs (NSAIDs), such as aspirin and ibuprofen, reduce inflammation and with it the risk of contracting several types of cancer.[27, 28]

Studies now show that systemic inflammation is involved in:

✔ Allergy
✔ Alzheimer's disease
✔ Anemia
✔ Ankylosing spondylitis
✔ Aortic valve stenosis
✔ Arthritis
✔ Cancer
✔ Congestive heart failure
✔ Diabetes
✔ Fibromyalgia
✔ Fibrosis
✔ Hypertension
✔ Heart attack
✔ Huntington's disease
✔ Irritable bowel disorder
✔ Kidney disease
✔ Lupus
✔ Metabolic syndrome
✔ Osteoporosis
✔ Parkinson's disease
✔ Psoriasis
✔ Stroke

With so many notches in its belt and more undoubtedly to come, inflammation—a survival mechanism from our evolutionary past—is both saviour and executioner in our modern world. Consequently, understanding the process of chronic inflammation is critical to our longevity.

What is Inflammation?

Viewed through its textbook definition, inflammation is a normal part of the body's defence against pathogens. The increase in body temperature, flood of toxic free radicals and inflammation-signalling proteins, and release of killer macrophage cells are the hallmarks of an inflammatory event that is the body's long-established means of defending against a clear and present danger. In modern man, however, this vigorous adaptive response, honed from millions of years of evolution, can become a harbinger of debilitating disease. University of Vermont pathologist, Russell Tracy, believes that the aging process may, in fact, be linked to the very defence mechanism that keeps us healthy when we are young.[29]

As we age, our ability to regulate inflammation begins to wane. Then, rather than protecting us, inflammation becomes silent and systemic, morphing into a process of stealth through which degenerative disease takes root. The symptoms of silent inflammation are entirely different from the cardinal signs of acute inflammation—*rubor* (redness), *calor* (heat), *tumor* (swelling), and *dolor* (pain)—and can lie undetected until catastrophe strikes.[19]

When inflammation turns silent, things turn ugly. Silent inflammation causes the body to turn on itself, its immune defences attacking its own organs.[30] Over time, dangerous proinflammatory cytokines (specialized signalling proteins), such as C-reactive protein and interleukin-6, and inflammation-producing eicosanoids (oxygenated essential fatty acids), such as prostaglandin E-2 and leukotriene B-4, begin to destroy tissues throughout the body. In response to this systemic attack from within, the body produces even more inflammatory cytokines and damaging free radicals, creating a self-perpetuating cycle.[31] Like a smouldering fire that slowly consumes itself, silent inflammation damages arteries, destroys nerve cells and organs, compromises the immune system, and promotes cancerous growths. If you have silent inflammation, despite how well you may feel today, you are on a fast track toward degenerative disease tomorrow.

On the bright side, instead of requiring different radical treatments for the degenerative diseases you may face in your

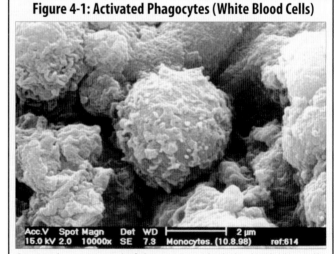

Figure 4-1: Activated Phagocytes (White Blood Cells)

| Acc.V | Spot | Magn | Det | WD | | | 2 μm |
| 15.0 kV | 2.0 | 10000x | SE | 7.3 | Monocytes. (10.8.98) | | ref:614 |

Scanning electron micrograph of phagocytes, specialized white blood cells, engulfing and digesting foreign bacteria and cellular debris. Magnification 10,000x

---

* Amyloids are insoluble fibrous protein aggregations deposited in the brain tissues of Alzheimer's patients. The name *amyloid* comes from the early mistaken identification of the substance as starch (amylum in Latin). It is not yet certain whether these fibrous plaques are a cause or a result of the disease.

lifetime—including heart disease, cancer, diabetes, and Alzheimer's—preventive measures to reduce inflammation, taken today, could prevent all of these ailments tomorrow.

The Inflammatory Cascade

Eicosanoids are a large class of fat-like molecules that are derived from the essential fatty acids, linoleic and alpha-linolenic acid, supplied through our diet. Eicosanoids are actually primitive hormones from our evolutionary past; however, unlike the endocrine hormones that travel throughout the body, these specialized signalling molecules act only at the cellular and inter-cellular levels and only in the immediate vicinity where they are formed. The family of eicosanoids is large and includes different classes: prostaglandins, thromboxanes, leukotrienes, lipoxins, isoprostanoids, and endocannabinoids, among others.

These oxygenated essential fatty acids are the central players in regulating the levels of inflammation in the body; some eicosanoids are inflammatory, others are anti-inflammatory. Together, they form the command centre for the immune response, creating a dynamic balance between their opposing forces. It is when these forces get out of balance that inflammation ensues. Working in a coordinated fashion, eicosanoids can quickly shift the prevailing equilibrium to either incite or attenuate the body's inflammatory response. Eicosanoids are also important in the regulation of blood pressure, heart and kidney function, allergic response, nerve transmission, hormone synthesis, and steroid production.

The proinflammatory or *bad* eicosanoids are the storm troopers of the inflammatory cascade and include the prostaglandins, which cause pain, and the leukotrienes, which cause swelling. While certainly necessary in the body's defence against acute trauma and infection, their continued over-expression is a factor in the onset of degenerative disease. Both classes of these inflammatory eicosanoids are manufactured from arachidonic acid (AA), present in red meats, shellfish, egg yolks, and other animal-based products. Arachidonic acid is also manufactured in the body from linoleic acid, an omega-6 essential fatty acid found in the oils extracted from plants. Evening primrose oil, black current seed oil, and borage oil are rich sources of linoleic acid.

The Arachidonic Acid Pathway

The arachidonic acid pathway is a key metabolic pathway for the manufacture of inflammation-promoting eicosanoids. Details of this pathway are provided in Figure 4-2.

A principal proinflammatory eicosanoid manufactured from AA is prostaglandin E2 (PG-E2). Release of this signalling molecule will activate specialized white blood cells to search out and destroy invading pathogens. When released, PG-E2 promotes platelet stickiness, hardening of the arteries, heart attacks, and strokes, and will also activate the release of proinflammatory cytokines, signalling proteins that help coordinate the body's immune response.

Leukotriene B4 (LT-B4) is also a product of AA metabolism (see Figure 4-2) and is associated with several inflammatory conditions, including arthritis, asthma, atherosclerosis, and inflammatory bowel disease.[32-34] Thromboxane A2 (Tx-A2) is another inflammatory eicosanoid produced by the conversion of AA, and it is a powerful constrictor of vascular and respiratory smooth muscles. Excessive production of Tx-A2 leads to cardiovascular hypertension.

The conversion of AA to inflammatory PG-E2, which occurs at the terminal step of the omega-6 metabolic pathway (see Figure 4-2), is controlled by the cyclooxygenase-2 (COX-2) enzyme. Research shows that COX-2 is inhibited by gamma tocopherol. By inhibiting COX-2, gamma tocopherol can effectively block the production of inflammatory PG-E2. This ability is not seen in alpha tocopherol,[35,36] suggesting that the gamma-form has unique anti-inflammatory powers not shared by its vitamin E analogue. Curcumin, a phenolic compound that is the principal agent in the Indian spice, turmeric, also blocks the activity of both COX-2, and lipoxygenase (LOX). Inhibition of these key inflammation-promoting enzymes allows curcumin to choke off the production of both PG-E2 and LT-B4, to depress the inflammatory cascade.[37]

Eicosapentaenoic Acid Pathway

The *good* eicosanoids are manufactured from eicosapentaenoic acid (EPA), which is derived from alpha-linolenic acid (ALA), an essential omega-3 fatty acid found in flax, canola, and pumpkin seeds. Another rich source of EPA is the oil of fatty cold-water fish, such as salmon and sardines. Prostaglandin-E3 (PG-E3) and certain leukotrienes are derivatives of EPA; they are strongly anti-inflammatory. Production of these chemical messengers serves to dampen the immune response and return the body to a normal physiological state.

DHA, another essential omega-3 fatty acid found in fish oil, is a major constituent of the phospholipid matrix in sperm, brain, and retinal tissues. DHA contributes to eicosanoid synthesis through its conversion to EPA via the removal of two carbon units. As noted in Figure 4-2, not only do EPA and DHA manufacture *good* eicosanoids, these important omega-3 fats also inhibit the delta-5-desaturase enzyme and, consequently, block the formation of AA. This has the beneficial effect of reducing the downstream production of inflammatory eicosanoids.

The provision of fish oil in the diet, consequently, serves as a double knockout punch to the propagation of the inflammatory response. First, fish oil ramps up the production of *good* eicosanoids, PG-E3 and the anti-inflammatory leukotrienes, by providing the needed substrates (EPA and DHA) to the omega-3 metabolic pathway. Second, fish oil blocks the production of the *bad* eicosanoids, PG-E2 and the inflammatory leukotrienes, by inhibiting delta-5-desaturase and the formation of AA—not a bad day's work for a simple marine oil. Many nutritional experts believe that daily consumption of high-quality fish oil is the single most important thing one can do to reduce systemic inflammation.

Preventing Chronic Inflammation

When opposing *good* and *bad* eicosanoids are in balance, a state of wellness prevails; however, when they become chronically unbalanced, problems arise. Interestingly, this balance is highly dependent on the level of insulin in the body—in turn, a reflection of one's girth.[38] High insulin levels—whether induced by chronic sugar overload, the onset of insulin resistance, or the hormonal effects of excess fat—set the stage for systemic inflammation. When insulin levels climb, oxidative stress increases dramatically and the conversion of dihomo-gamma-linolenic acid (DGLA) to proinflammatory AA is favoured (see Figure 4-2). This results in the formation of proinflammatory PG-E2 and leukotriene B-4. Insulin also increases the production of inter-leukin-6 (IL-6), another proinflammatory cytokine that raises blood levels of CRP.

Apart from being too high in refined sugar, the average North American diet is stuffed with inflammation-promoting omega-6 fats but scarce in inflammation-reducing omega-3 fats. The consequence of this chronic fatty acid imbalance is an increase in systemic inflammation. As inflammation rises, so does the production of cortisol, an anti-stress hormone that attempts to stem this rising tide. Produced within the adrenal glands, cortisol is intricately involved in the body's response to stress.

Problematically, in attempting to dampen inflammation, cortisol increases blood pressure, elevates blood-sugar levels, and suppresses the immune system. Systemic inflammation produces chronically elevated levels of cortisol, which, in turn, place a heavy physiological burden on all organs and dramatically increase the risk of degenerative disease.

Many researchers now believe that the stimulatory effect of high insulin levels, combined with the consumption of high-glycemic foods deficient in omega-3 fatty acids, is the *smoking gun* that directly implicates diet and obesity to the collateral damage caused by chronic inflammation.

Fortunately, changing the balance within the body to favour the production of anti-inflammatory eicosanoids can be attained through conscious dietary change. A recent Canadian study suggests that simply eating a healthy diet that includes almonds (which are also a rich source of gamma tocopherol) reduces

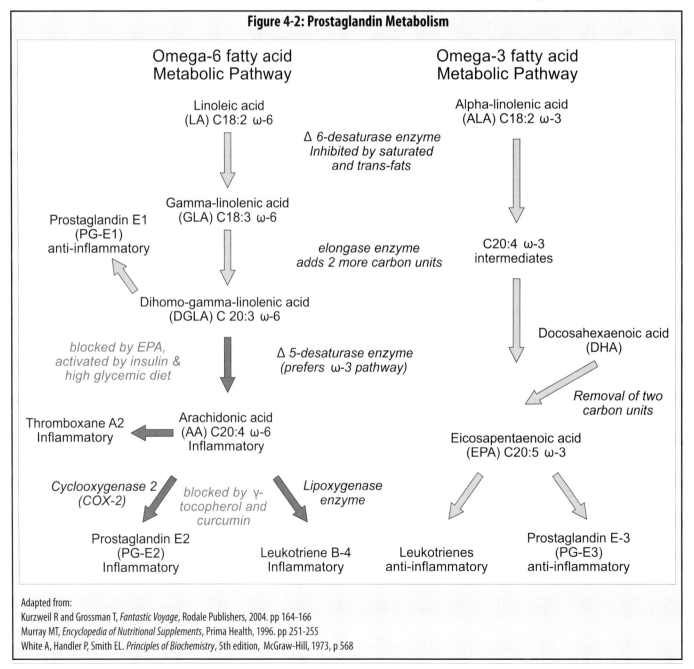

Figure 4-2: Prostaglandin Metabolism

Omega-6 fatty acid Metabolic Pathway

Linoleic acid
(LA) C18:2 ω-6

Δ 6-desaturase enzyme
Inhibited by saturated
and trans-fats

Gamma-linolenic acid
(GLA) C18:3 ω-6

Prostaglandin E1
(PG-E1)
anti-inflammatory

elongase enzyme
adds 2 more carbon units

Dihomo-gamma-linolenic acid
(DGLA) C 20:3 ω-6

blocked by EPA,
activated by insulin &
high glycemic diet

Δ 5-desaturase enzyme
(prefers ω-3 pathway)

Thromboxane A2
Inflammatory

Arachidonic acid
(AA) C20:4 ω-6
Inflammatory

Cyclooxygenase 2
(COX-2)

blocked by γ-
tocopherol and
curcumin

Lipoxygenase
enzyme

Prostaglandin E2
(PG-E2)
Inflammatory

Leukotriene B-4
Inflammatory

Omega-3 fatty acid Metabolic Pathway

Alpha-linolenic acid
(ALA) C18:2 ω-3

C20:4 ω-3
intermediates

Docosahexaenoic acid
(DHA)

Removal of two
carbon units

Eicosapentaenoic acid
(EPA) C20:5 ω-3

Leukotrienes
anti-inflammatory

Prostaglandin E-3
(PG-E3)
anti-inflammatory

Adapted from:
Kurzweil R and Grossman T, *Fantastic Voyage*, Rodale Publishers, 2004. pp 164-166
Murray MT, *Encyclopedia of Nutritional Supplements*, Prima Health, 1996. pp 251-255
White A, Handler P, Smith EL. *Principles of Biochemistry*, 5th edition, McGraw-Hill, 1973, p 568

chronic inflammation to about the same level as taking a first generation statin drug.[39]

When insulin levels are reduced through weight loss and dietary modification, production of anti-inflammatory prostaglandins is favoured and inflammation is kept in check.[40] The basic goal is to reduce the production and dietary intake of AA and increase the levels of healthy fats to promote the production of *good* prostaglandins.[41, 42] Because the modern North American diet contains 10 to 20 times the amount of omega-6 oils that we need, the most sensible dietary approach is to reduce sources of omega-6 oils and supplement with high-dose omega-3 oils, to bring us back to an optimal 4:1 ratio of omega-6 and omega-3 fatty acids.[43]

This can be achieved by increasing your dietary intake of fatty fish (salmon, in particular), eating raw nuts and grains rich in healthy fats, and supplementing with a high-quality cold-pressed fish oil or flaxseed oil. Concurrently, decreasing your dietary intake of red meats, eggs, high-glycemic foods, and foods high in saturated fats will reduce the levels of proinflammatory AA and further shift the balance in favour of the beneficial omega-3 fats.

> *Because the modern North American diet contains 10 to 20 times the amount of omega-6 oils that we need, the most sensible dietary approach is to reduce sources of omega-6 oils and supplement with high-dose omega-3 oils*

The Link to Oxidative Stress

As we have learned, reducing the level of insulin in the body and the level of sugar in the diet and optimizing the ratio of essential fatty acids can do much to dampen systemic inflammation. However, these are not the only mechanisms by which inflammation can be managed. It is well established that oxidative stress will also result in an inflammatory response;[44-47] however, the answer to the question of *how* the processes of inflammation and oxidation are linked is only now being revealed.

Recent evidence suggests that oxidative damage to the cell membrane and to other membranous structures within the cytoplasm of the cell leads to the production of AA within the lipid environment of the membrane.[48] The AA produced by autocatalytic lipid peroxidation is further modified by enzyme systems to yield proinflammatory products. In addition, other fats oxidized within these membranes are believed to mimic proinflammatory chemical messengers that, in turn, trigger an inflammatory response at the cellular level. This leads to increased free radical production inside the cell and activates an important transcription molecule, nuclear factor kappa beta (NFkB), which is capable of choreographing the entire inflammatory cascade.

Nuclear Factor kappa Beta

NFkB is believed to be the *master switch* that regulates the level of inflammation in the body. Present in the cytoplasm of the cell, NFkB is normally bound to a protein that keeps it in an inactive state. When a cell is exposed to an invading pathogen or undergoes attack from free radicals or environmental toxins, NFkB swings into action. Much like a smoke detector that senses imminent danger, NFkB responds by switching on the genes that produce an inflammatory response. Once activated, this transcription factor migrates to the cell's nucleus, attaching to the DNA, and orders the transcription (copying) of over 400 genes that control the manufacture of numerous proinflammatory cytokines and enzymes.[49] Messenger RNAs* (mRNA) then migrate out of the nucleus, travel to the endoplasmic reticulum (internal membranous structures) and attach to tiny protein structures, called ribosomes. Here, the genetic message is decoded and the appropriate amino acids (building blocks of proteins) are assembled into the specified cytokine or enzyme protein. Once manufactured, these foot soldiers immediately launch into action, ramping up the inflammatory response against the invader—and you thought cells were simple!

So, here lies the critical link between oxidative stress and inflammation: NFkB is revealed as a key signalling molecule that is capable of monitoring and responding to oxidative insults by commanding the cell's genetic machinery to marshal a vast biological armada against an impending threat. The result is an inflammatory cascade that, in turn, ramps up the level of oxidative stress. In short, as oxidative stress promotes inflammation, so, too, does inflammation promote oxidative stress.

As the master switch, NFkB controls the genes encoding the proinflammatory cytokines, interleukin-1 (IL-1), IL-2, IL-6, tumor necrosis factor alpha (TNF-alpha), various chemokines and adhesion molecules, as well as the cyclooxygenase enzymes and inducible nitric oxide synthase (iNOS) enzyme. All of these agents are central to the inflammatory cascade and all augment the level of oxidative stress. These proteins, along with the inflammatory eicosanoids manufactured from AA, control the entire inflammatory sequence and can initiate widespread cellular destruction that is typical of chronic inflammation.

For several years, Life Extension Foundation (LEF), a non-profit, research-based organization dedicated to exploring the causes for aging and disease, has been warning about the dangers of over-expression of NFkB. Much of the work in elucidating the critical role played by NFkB has, in fact, been uncovered through research conducted by LEF scientists. Through their work, we now know that expression of NFkB in the body increases as we age, provoking systemic inflammation and setting the stage for the progression of degenerative disease.[49] Inflammation is now thought to be the initiating factor in most degenerative diseases and is estimated to underlie up to 98% of all diseases afflicting humans.[50] Over-expression of NFkB can spark the smouldering embers of arthritis and asthma, it can stir inflammatory fires in the nervous system to set the stage for neurodegenerative disease, and it can switch on genes that initiate the development of several cancers. In fact, NFkB has recently emerged as a critical link between chronic inflammation and cancer.

Nature to the Rescue

Fortunately, Mother Nature, in her wisdom, has provided generously for our protection with plant-based nutrients that can

---

* mRNA molecules are copies of the coded sequence of nucleotides on the DNA blueprint, specific for a given gene. Once the genetic code is transcribed, mRNA carriers migrate outside the nucleus and attach to ribosomes. Ribosomal proteins then decipher the molecular codes to assemble the required amino acids and construct the specified protein.

regulate this powerful protagonist. The polyphenols, with well over 8,000 known structural variants, are the most prolific family of NFkB inhibitors known to science. Polyphenols are secondary metabolites of plants—effective free radical antagonists and metal chelators that comprise a vast range of complex molecular structures. Polyphenols commonly found in higher quality nutritional supplements include the citrus bioflavonoids, from fruits and berries; resveratrol, found in red wine and grapes; curcumin, isolated from turmeric (*Curcuma longa*) rhizome; and the catechins (including catechin, epicatechin, and their gallic acid esters), isolated from green tea, grape seeds, assorted nuts and berries, and pine bark. Oligomers* of the catechins, called procyanidolic oligomers (PCOs), comprise approximately 60% to 70% of the polyphenol content of grapes.

Early research on polyphenols viewed these substances as antioxidants; however, their pharmacology could not be adequately explained, based solely on their antioxidant prowess. New research has revealed that polyphenols not only serve as potent free radical scavengers, they effectively modulate cellular signalling processes that control inflammatory events and may, themselves, serve as signalling agents to attenuate inflammation.[51] Importantly, the polyphenols found in resveratrol, the green tea catechins, and turmeric *all* suppress the activation of NFkB. The ability of polyphenols to inhibit NFkB is absolutely critical to the ability of the cell to reduce inflammation, which is why a diet high in fresh fruits and vegetables is important to long-term health.[52] For a more detailed discussion on the scientific evidence supporting the use of polyphenols in controlling inflammation, please see Chapter 9.

Many other natural compounds exert some of their beneficial effects through interaction with NFkB. Early investigations showed that supplementation with alpha-lipoic acid can stimulate the production of anti-inflammatory prostaglandins.[53] Lipoic acid has also been found to bind to and inhibit NFkB within the cell's nucleus.[54] Very recently, researchers investigating the use of lipoic acid as a therapeutic agent against bone loss associated with systemic inflammation found that inhibition of cyclooxygenase-2 by the antioxidant can reduce the production of inflammatory PG-E2.[55] Alpha-lipoic acid has also been found to interfere with the release of inflammatory toxic metabolites and reactive oxygen species (ROS) from activated macrophages (specialized white blood cells), and may also protect against the inflammatory effects of oxidative stress associated with bronchial asthma in lung tissues.[56, 57] This important antioxidant, which is present in both the lipid and aqueous phases of the cell and can penetrate the blood-brain barrier with ease to protect the central nervous system (CNS), is a front-line weapon in the body's arsenal against silent inflammation.

While most antioxidants demonstrate some level of anti-inflammatory activity, vitamin C, in particular, has been shown to reduce several inflammatory markers, including the release of tumor necrosis factor alpha, C-reactive protein, and inflammatory cytokines associated with NFkB activation.[58-60] As well, n-acetyl-cysteine and s-adenosyl methionine are strong inhibitors of NFkB.[61] Finally, EPA and DHA, aside from their ability to block the inflammatory AA pathway, have been found to reduce NFkB activity.

Implications

Systemic, low-grade inflammation is an underlying cause of the vast majority of chronic degenerative diseases. The fact that this type of inflammation increases with age and with poor dietary and lifestyle choices means that most North Americans unknowingly suffer from this silent, but deadly, affliction. Unfortunately, as aging baby boomers reach their senior years, the problem promises to worsen.

Yet, it does not have to be like this. We have the solution at hand to resolve this dilemma: all that is necessary is to understand that what we put *into* our bodies and do *with* our bodies will largely determine our longevity and quality of life. Simply put, we have to stop digging our graves with our own knife and fork—it all comes down to the choices we make along the way.

Cutting down, today, on those elements in our diet that fan the fires of inflammation will reduce our risk of dying tomorrow from cancer or cardiovascular disease: choose the braised salmon rather than the barbequed burger; snack on fresh fruits and vegetables rather than gorging on deep-fried onion rings and french fries; get out for a brisk daily walk rather than "wasting away again in Margaritaville"; use olive oil and healthy fats rather than saturated and unhealthy fats; reach for nuts and natural juices rather than candy bars and cokes; and supplement with a quality nutritional rather than a cold six-pack.

Each passing year, the impact of silent inflammation looms large in the cold statistical enumeration of deaths by cancer, heart disease, stroke, diabetes, and Alzheimer's disease—and each passing year we see waistlines continuing to grow larger and people continuing to grow softer. Each passing year, we see a medical system stretched beyond breaking, trying to stem a rising tide of degenerative disease that appears to be without end—and each passing year we see millions more squandered by that same medical system, intent on treating the *symptoms* rather than dealing with the *causes*. Each passing year, we witness friends and loved ones succumb to an undisclosed cancer or heart condition that struck swiftly, silently, and without remorse—and each passing year we cross our fingers and offer a silent prayer that we are not next.

---

* Oligomers are repeating units of the parent molecule. Like a beaded chain, they consist of several units chemically united.

Section II

The Safety of Supplements

This section provides the reader with an in-depth look at:

- The Safety of Nutritional Supplements
- Optimal Nutrition
- Nutritional Supplements Under Attack

The relative risks of nutritional supplements, in comparison to pharmaceutical drugs, are discussed and the real issue of safety is explored. The regulatory environments in the United States and Canada are reviewed. Several recent studies and their media headlines disputing the efficacy of nutritional supplements are critiqued.

**Vitamins, if properly understood and applied,
will help us to reduce human suffering to an extent
which the most fantastic human mind would fail to imagine.**

— Albert Szent-Györgyi (1893-1986)
Nobel Laureate in Physiology and Medicine

CHAPTER FIVE

THE SAFETY OF NUTRITIONAL SUPPLEMENTS

The most fundamental of forensic arguments is, "Where are the bodies?" For years, the US Food and Drug Administration (FDA) has advanced the argument that vitamin/mineral and herbal supplements are unsafe and, consequently, must be closely regulated. Yet, the *2004 Annual Report of the American Association of Poison Control Centers Toxic Exposure Surveillance System*[2] (TESS) confirms that there were fewer deaths caused by dietary supplements that year than were caused by air fresheners. According to the study, not a single death was reported from an adverse reaction or unintended cause from the consumption of dietary supplements (vitamins, minerals, antioxidants, and herbal supplements). Considering that almost half of the American population consume nutritional supplements every day, for an annual consumption of some 53 billion doses, this is a safety record without equal.

Table 5-1 shows the number of deaths reported by TESS over the decade from 1994 to 2004 resulting from the use of dietary

supplements. Eight deaths were ascribed to accidental infant poisonings with iron-containing supplements (principally, ferrous sulphate), three were attributed to the use of Ma huang *(Ephedra sinica)*, two were caused by adverse reactions to yohimbe *(Pausinystalia yohimbe)* and ginseng *(Panax ginseng)*, and one death was caused by an unknown herbal supplement. In total, 14 unintentional deaths in 10 years were caused by the use of dietary supplements, the majority of which were accidental infant poisonings.

Conversely, pharmaceutical drugs—simply taken as prescribed—kill with vengeance. A 1998 study, reported in the *Journal of the American Medical Association*,[3] showed that in one year (1994) there were over *2.2 million* serious adverse drug reactions in the United States, accounting for an annualized death rate of 106,000.[4] To put this into perspective, in any given year, more Americans die after taking prescription medications than gave their lives in the entire Viet Nam war. What's more, some

Table 5-1: Deaths from Unintended Causes and Adverse Reactions to Dietary Supplements (US) 1994 to 2004					
Year	Minerals	Vitamins	Multiple Supplement	Herbal/ homeopathic	
2004	0	0	0	0	
2003	0	0	0	2	adverse reactions: yohimbe; ginseng
2002	0	0	0	1	adverse reaction: unknown herbal supplement
2001	0	0	0	3	adverse reactions: Ma huang; multiple herbal composite
2000	0	0	0	0	
1999	1	0	0	0	unintended infant (14 mo) ingestion: iron supplement
1998	0	0	0	0	
1997	1	0	0	0	unintended infant (16 mo) ingestion: iron sulphate
1996	2	0	0	0	unintended infant (16, 17 mo) ingestion: prenatal iron supplement
1995	1	0	1	0	unintended infant (12, 22 mo) ingestion: prenatal multiple/iron sulphate
1994	2	0	0	0	unintended infant (12, 18 mo) ingestion: iron sulphate
Total	7	0	1	6	

Data summarized from Annual Reports of the American Association of Poison Control Centers Toxic Exposure Surveillance System
Available at: http://www.aapcc.org

Data include only those cases where death occurred due to adverse reaction or unintended causes
and do not include death due to therapeutic error, intentional abuse, or suicide

physicians estimate that the actual number of drug-induced deaths may be far higher than reported.[5]

Moreover, a further 44,000 to 98,000 citizens die each year as a result of grievous medical errors.[6, 7] Estimates of the combined effects of medical errors and adverse effects that occur because of iatrogenic damage (injury brought on by a healer in the course of therapy) include:[3, 8, 9]

✔ 12,000 deaths/year from unnecessary surgery;

✔ 7,000 deaths/year from medication errors in hospitals;

✔ 20,000 deaths/year from other errors in hospitals;

✔ 80,000 deaths/year from nosocomial infections (infections resulting from treatment for a condition unrelated to the infection); and

✔ 106,000 deaths/year from adverse effects of prescription medications.

In all, some 225,000 deaths per year from iatrogenic causes make it very clear that a visit to your local clinic, or a trip to the emergency ward, can be a risky proposition. According to Dr Barbara Starfield, Johns Hopkins School of Hygiene and Public Health, iatrogenic death constitutes the *third* leading cause of death in the United States, after death from heart disease and cancer.[4]

Within this context, the relative safety of dietary supplements as a preventive measure to maintain optimal health is unassailable. Simply put, it seems a lot less risky to *prevent* yourself from falling ill, through adopting a good diet, healthy lifestyle, and a daily regime of supplementation, than it does to be treated *after* the fact for a serious illness requiring medical intervention. Consequently, it seems prudent—if only from a risk management perspective—to consider the value of preventive health through supplementation. Well-known sports nutritionist, Dr Michael Colgan, sums it up nicely: "Used in any sensible amounts, vitamins and minerals are about as toxic as apple pie."

Relative Risks

Compared to the very narrow margins of safety separating beneficial from toxic doses for many common prescription drugs, the safety margins between effective daily intakes and harmful effects of most vitamins, minerals, and herbal supplements are wide. When viewed on a risk management continuum from one to ten (Figure 5-1), where one means *risk-free* and ten means *high-risk*, vitamins, minerals, and herbal supplements would generally fall between one and three. Over-the-counter non-steroidal anti-inflammatories (OTC NSAIDs), such as aspirin, ibuprofen, and naproxen, would comprise the middle ground. Prescription drugs, on the other hand, would span the upper limits of risk.

The facts speak for themselves: while over 100,000 Americans die each year from prescription drugs taken as directed, a decade of supplement use, from 1994 to 2004, recorded only 14 deaths, most of which were accidental infant poisonings from dietary supplements containing iron (see Table 5-1).

The Food and Nutrition Board of the Institute of Medicine (United States) recently published a list of tolerable upper intake levels (UL) for a number of nutrients common to dietary supple-

ments. These include vitamins A, D, B_3, B_6, C, E, folic acid, and choline. ULs have also been established for several minerals, which tend to display more potential for toxicity at high dosages than do vitamins. Minerals with defined ULs include boron, calcium, copper, iron, iodine, magnesium, manganese, molybdenum, phosphorus, selenium, vanadium, and zinc. The UL is the upper level of intake of a nutrient that is deemed safe for use by adults.

The *Table of Recommended Daily Intakes* (Table 11-3, page 78) shows that for several nutrients the UL is significantly higher than the advanced levels of daily supplementation cited in most published recommendations. In fact, for several nutrients, including thiamin, riboflavin, biotin, vitamin B_5 (pantothenic acid), vitamins B_6 and B_{12}, and vitamin K, there are *no* levels of intake for which adverse effects from food or supplements have been reported. Limits set for these nutrients are merely precautionary.

Several nutrients, particularly the antioxidants, have safe levels of intake that are magnitudes higher than suggested in the new *Dietary Reference Intake* (DRI) standards jointly established by the

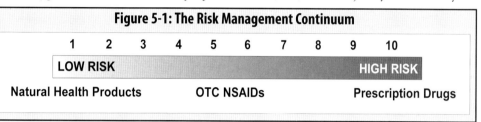

Figure 5-1: The Risk Management Continuum

| 1 | 2 | 3 | 4 | 5 | 6 | 7 | 8 | 9 | 10 |

LOW RISK — HIGH RISK

Natural Health Products — OTC NSAIDs — Prescription Drugs

US and Canada. For example, the UL for vitamin E (1,000 mg) is almost 70 times that of its DRI (15 mg). For vitamin C, the UL (2,000 mg) is 22 times that of its DRI (90 mg). Many individuals, including the late Nobel Laureate, Dr Linus Pauling, have regularly taken up to 20,000 mg/day of vitamin C with no harmful consequences (Dr Pauling lived a healthy, productive life until his death at 93 years of age).

Two nutrients commonly found in multivitamin formulations, however, *do* warrant a note of caution due to their potential for cumulative toxicity. Long-term intakes of high levels of vitamin A and iron have been associated with harmful and even fatal toxicity problems.

✔ Ingestion of too much vitamin A can be toxic, particularly if there are defects in liver function.[10, 11] At doses greater than 10,000 IU, vitamin A has been shown to cause birth defects, particularly during the first seven weeks after conception. Women who may become pregnant should limit their supplemental vitamin A intake to below 5,000 IU or, preferably, supplement with beta-carotene.[12]

✔ Iron at high doses becomes a potent oxidant and free radical generator that can accelerate oxidative damage of cholesterol, with the consequent onset of atherosclerosis. Iron overload causes increased risks of infection, cancer, and myocardial infarction (heart attack).[13, 14] Most fatalities concerning dietary supplements have involved accidental overdosing in children. Hence, caution is warranted, particularly with tasty and chewable children's tablets, if using nutritional supplements containing iron.

In short, with the exception of those few nutrients that demonstrate potential for cumulative toxicity—and providing you add a dose of common sense—nutritional supplements containing vitamins and minerals are a safe and effective way to optimize your daily health. So, to paraphrase Dr Michael Colgan, go ahead and enjoy your "apple pie."

Similarly, most herbal products used in nutritional supplements are completely safe. While there are legitimate toxicity concerns for a small percentage of herbals, including Ma huang (ephedra), kava, berberine, lobelia, foxglove (digitalis), and mistletoe, the majority of herbal products are generally considered to have low or no recognized toxicity.

The *Real* Issue of Safety

The *real* issue of safety resides not in the toxicity of any particular nutrient within a formulation, but rather in the *manner* in which the final product has been manufactured. Here, the concerns expressed by the FDA, and quietly voiced by responsible members of the dietary supplement industry, have resonance. The fact is, sloppy and unhygienic manufacturing practices and disregard for the need to validate content and purity have frequently led to adulterated and contaminated products. Such practices are inexcusable and pose a far greater threat to public safety than the individual toxicities of active ingredients in a formulation.

Products not manufactured according to Good Manufacturing Practice (GMP) may contain more (or less) in the bottle than what is on the label—and this is *not* a good thing. Adulteration and contamination of raw materials during the manufacturing process, and finished products whose potency, purity, and content do not meet minimal standards, are common amongst products not manufactured in accordance with established GMP standards. This is particularly true for products containing herbal ingredients, which may be contaminated with pesticides and herbicides from the growing cycle, or contain animal residues, moulds, and insect parts from inappropriate harvesting and storage.

Purity, potency, and safety are foremost in any nutritional supplement when you are likely to be taking it on a daily basis. For these reasons, consumers should ensure that the products they use are of the highest quality. This means adherence to quality manufacturing through compliance with GMP standards that reflect the pharmaceutical model.

Calcium Supplements: the Need for Purity

A good example of the importance of purity in a nutritional product is calcium. Many consumers supplement their daily calcium intake with bone meal, a dried, processed powder made from finely ground bones (usually bovine). Bone meal is one of the 25 top-selling nutritional products in the United States, with

sales increasing over 400% in 2003 alone.[15] Two other popular calcium supplements are dolomite, a mineral consisting of calcium magnesium carbonate $(CaMg(CO_3)_2)$, and unrefined calcium from powdered oyster shells. While calcium, itself, has virtually no toxicity, studies indicate that natural source calcium supplements may contain substantial amounts of lead, a potent neurotoxin linked to several neurological and behavioural disorders.

A 1993 Canadian study of calcium products, conducted at Trent University, Ontario, measured the lead content in 70 brands of US and Canadian calcium supplements. The products were grouped into the following five categories: laboratory-refined calcium carbonate, calcium bound to organic chelates, dolomite, unrefined calcium carbonate derived from limestone, and bone meal. The results shown in Table 5-2 give the average lead content in micrograms (µg) per 800 mg of calcium.[16]

Less than 20% of the supplements tested had lead levels comparable to or lower than that reported for cow's milk. Moreover, the average levels of lead found in the bone meal, dolomite, and unrefined calcium products were magnitudes higher than the levels found in the refined calcium products. None of the products tested in the dolomite and bone meal groups and only two out of 25 in the unrefined calcium carbonate group had lead levels below the recommended limit of 1 µg per 800 mg of calcium. The group that displayed the greatest variance in its lead content was the unrefined calcium carbonate group (oyster shells), with one product containing a startling 25 µg of lead per 800 mg of calcium.[16]

Fully 25% of the calcium products evaluated in the study exceeded the FDA total tolerable daily intake of 6 µg of lead for children 6-years old and under. According to the findings, natural calcium products, including bone meal, dolomite, and natural source calcium supplements, can harbour significant lead contamination. In fact, more than half of the products in these categories had levels of lead that exceeded the FDA's tolerable daily intake for young children.[17] According to these findings, individuals who consume high doses of natural source calcium may be inadvertently placing themselves at high risk for cumulative lead toxicity—*not* something a health-conscious consumer would willingly pay for.

Good Manufacturing Practices Essential

As previously discussed, from a risk-management perspective, vitamin/mineral and herbal products are inherently safe. The *real* safety issue lies in quality control. Without stringent quality control measures at all stages of the manufacturing process, you cannot be certain that what is on the label is actually *in* the bottle. Understandably, it is simply not feasible for consumers, themselves, to test supplements for lead contamination or any other contamination for that matter—*that* should be the responsibility of the manufacturer and should be backed up with tough regulatory oversight. Products tainted with lead or any other contaminants should not be allowed on the retail shelf—period. Sadly, disregard for the standardization of manufacturing practices and quality control measures have allowed many inferior, mislabelled, unsanitary, and unsafe products to find their way into the markets of both the United States and Canada.

Table 5-2: Lead Content in Calcium Supplements (µg/800 mg Ca)	
Refined calcium carbonate	0.92 µg
Calcium chelates	1.64 µg
Dolomite	4.17 µg
Unrefined calcium carbonate	6.05 µg
Bone meal	11.3 µg

A good example is *Echinacea*, a popular herbal remedy for colds and flu, and a general immune system booster. Between 1908 and 1991, due to errors in species identification, more than half of the *Echinacea* sold in the US was *Parthenium integrifolium,* a medicinally inferior form of Missouri snakeroot.[18] Unbelievably, for almost 90 years, many US consumers had been taking the *wrong* herbal remedy! No wonder *Echinacea* was getting such a bad rap.

Another example is ginseng, a popular herbal ingredient now found in several broad-spectrum dietary supplements and cold remedies. The herb is well known for its immunostimulatory action, as evidenced by its ability to enhance antibody responses, increase cell-mediated immunity, and augment natural killer T-cell activity. *Panax ginseng* (also known as Korean or Chinese ginseng) contains at least thirteen different steroid-like compounds, called ginsenosides. Ginsenoside R_g1, which contributes to the herb's stimulatory effect, is present in appreciable quantities in the Asian variety of ginseng. In contrast, American ginseng *(Panax quinquefolius)* contains primarily parthenolide R_b1, which has a sedative effect, and very little (if any) of the stimulatory R_g1. Consequently, Amercian ginseng possesses a pharmacologic action far different from its Asian cousin.[19] Many consumers, believing they are taking Asian ginseng for immunological enhancement are, in fact, taking the less effective and sedating American variety.

Case law dating back to the 1930s shows that the FDA, the US regulatory watchdog for food and drug safety, has long been battling unscrupulous manufacturers of dietary supplements who posed concerns for public safety because what was on their product label was not necessarily in the bottle.

The Canadian Example

The importance of the need to develop quality manufacturing practices may be best exemplified by recent events in Canada. In the mid-1990s, the Canadian nutritional marketplace was growing rapidly, along with the arrival of innovative and exotic varieties of natural remedies from offshore markets. Canadian consumers, dissatisfied with the failures of the pharmaceutical approach to healthcare, were becoming pro-active with their personal health. Turning to nutritional supplements and natural remedies found in the indigenous cultures as well as those of traditional Chinese and Ayurvedic medicines, health-conscious consumers began driving a new market niche that was, at the time, largely unrecognized and uncontrolled. Under the *Canada Food and Drug Act,* vitamins and minerals were regulated, at the time, as drugs; herbs, on the other hand, were considered foods and regulated, at the time, under relatively lax food-model GMP. Canada's outdated food and drug statute failed to recognize the growing therapeutic role of herbal medicines in dosage form. Within this laissez-faire regulatory environment, entrepreneurs began throwing herbal products onto retail shelves that, in some cases, were literally concocted in the bathtub. In addition, importers, eager to satisfy the burgeoning demand, were bringing into Canada herbal ingredients from the Far East with little or no

authentication of purity, potency, or safety. This led to a flood of questionable products into the market, with the inevitable discovery of serious contamination (including animal feces and insect parts) and rising concern for public safety.

Alerted to the threat to public safety, the Government of Canada acted quickly. Health Canada sent out inspectors from its federal Health Protection Branch to seize suspected contaminated products from retail shelves. Their actions, at times overly aggressive, caused an immediate uproar within the natural health community. Failing to appreciate the magnitude of the safety issue, consumers retaliated. During the 1997 federal election, frustrated consumers pressed the power of their democratic franchise to extract from the Minister of Health a concession to investigate Health Canada's actions and to develop new regulations that would assure access to safe, quality natural health products. From this would come the creation of a new regulatory agency charged with the oversight of the manufacture and sale of vitamins, minerals, and herbal products. This new body would recognize all products containing vitamins, minerals, and botanicals in dosage form as Natural Health Products (NHPs) and—with safety and quality being paramount—would develop an innovative regulatory structure with specified manufacturing criteria. To ensure quality and safety, the regulations would demand both product and site licensing for any manufacturer selling a natural health product (dietary supplement) in or into Canada.

Now a reality, Canada's innovative Natural Health Products Directorate (NHPD) is mandated "to ensure Canadians access to natural health products that are safe, effective and of high quality, while respecting freedom of choice and philosophical and cultural diversity."[20] Regulations were brought into force on January 1, 2004.

Its critics contend that Canada's natural health product regulations are a dilution of the stringent pharmaceutical criteria that formerly governed the manufacture and sale of vitamin/mineral products. Practitioners within the natural health community, on the other hand, applaud the new regulations that acknowledge and reflect the greater safety of vitamin and herbal products, when compared to drug products, within the context of risk-management. Moreover, the new regulations serve to bring together two formerly separate product categories, vitamins/minerals and herbal products, under a single regulatory window, and

> *Between 1908 and 1991, due to errors in species identification, more than half of the Echinacea sold in the US was Parthenium integrifolium, a medicinally inferior form of Missouri snakeroot*

Get the Lead Out

Lead toxicity is a significant problem in all industrialized countries, including the United States and Canada. The level of lead in the body has been shown to be directly linked to IQ and criminal behaviour. High blood levels in children are also linked to the development of learning dysfunctions, such as attention deficit disorder (ADD), attention deficit hyperactivity disorder (ADHD), and autism.[1]

According to a 1998 report by the US Agency for Toxic Substances and Disease Registry, 17% of all US children younger than 12 years of age had unacceptably high blood levels of lead.

they ensure industry compliance with an established GMP for natural health products as a guarantee of product quality and safety.

The American Scene

The US *Dietary Supplementation and Health Education Act* (DSHEA) was enacted in 1994 to promote health by providing easier access to dietary supplements. Under provisions of the *Act*, the language regarding GMP compliance is modelled after food-processing practices. Compliance with pharmaceutical-model GMP standards, pre-market approval, and site/product licensing are *not* required in the manufacture of dietary supplements. Except in the case of a new dietary ingredient, where law requires pre-market review of safety data and other information, a manufacturer does not have to provide the FDA with evidence to substantiate safety or effectiveness before or after it markets its products.

The *manufacturer* is responsible for determining that the supplements it makes are safe and that any claims made about the products are substantiated. The burden of proof for unsafe or adulterated products and false or misleading labelling, however, lies wholly with the FDA, rather than the manufacturer. Consequently, the US market for dietary supplements is one where, according to some authorities, the majority of US dietary supplements fail to meet label claims.

While the enactment of the DSHEA relaxed the regulatory hurdles for the manufacturing and marketing of nutritional products in the United States, it retained the FDA's authority to enforce industry compliance with established GMP standards as a means of ensuring product quality and safety. To date, however, the agency has chosen *not* to invoke this authority. Consequently, there are no current US regulations that enforce minimum standards of practice, no requirements for pre-market approval, no post-market surveillance, and no site licensing or product licensing required for the manufacturing of dietary supplements in the United States. Current reference standards are *voluntary*. This lack of regulatory oversight has created a market open to abuse, misrepresentation, and sub-optimal and unsafe products. In short, it is a case of "buyer beware."

Subsequent to the passage of the DSHEA in 1994, several issues have come to light that have given rise to a growing concern about quality and safety. It is important to reiterate that this is not so much about the inherent safety of the active ingredients as it is about the potential for inferior, mislabelled, adulterated, and contaminated products.

In one case, a dietary supplement that claimed to "gently assist in the systematic cleansing of the body, and in the removal of impurities from the intestinal tract" was found to contain high levels of digitalis, a powerful cardiotonic botanical.[21] This was discovered when two women who had used the product reported classical symptoms of digitalis toxicity. These symptoms include nausea, vomiting, heart palpitations, visual distortions, arrhythmia, and possible heart failure. Investigation revealed that a raw

material labelled "plantain," used in the manufacture of the supplement, mistakenly contained the herbal ingredient *Digitalis lanata*. Nationwide, it was estimated that 183 companies may have inadvertently used the contaminated product, indicating the extent of the safety issue.[22]

In a more recent investigation, researchers found that some Ayurvedic herbal supplements were seriously contaminated with heavy metals and metalloids, including lead, mercury, and arsenic. The 2004 study by Harvard researchers found that one-fifth of the Ayurvedic herbal medicine products produced in South Asia and available in grocery stores in the Boston area contained potentially harmful levels of lead, mercury, and/or arsenic.[23] In one case, ingesting the recommended dose would have exposed a child to 20,000 µg/day of mercury; the US Environmental Protection Agency reference dose for mercury exposure is 1µg/day.[22, 23] The authors concluded that users of Ayurvedic medicines sold in the US market are at risk for heavy metal toxicity, and that testing of these products for toxic heavy metals should be mandatory. As well, a 1998 survey conducted by the American Herbal Product Association revealed that 43 botanical ingredients used in the manufacture of various dietary supplements were seriously contaminated, some with carcinogenic aflatoxins and other harmful mycotoxins produced by fungi.[22]

The FDA has recently identified several products in the US market that were not accurately labelled or that contained potentially harmful contaminants. The cited violations include:[24]

✔ the use of non-food-grade chemicals in the manufacture of dietary supplements;

✔ product contamination with excessive amounts of lead;

✔ sub-optimal levels of nutritional components as claimed on the label (One product had only 35% of the amount of folic acid claimed on the label); and

✔ products exceeding safe upper levels of some nutrients. (One manufacturer recalled a niacin product after it received reports of nausea, vomiting, liver damage, and heart attack associated with the use of its product. A supply firm had mislabelled a bulk-ingredient container subsequently used by another firm, which resulted in the inadvertent manufacturing of a product that contained ten times more niacin than the allowable safe upper limit.)

High batch-to-batch variability is another reason cited for the need to consider the imposition of a national GMP standard for dietary supplements. In spot-surveys of products on retail shelves, investigators have found that the active ingredient was not even present in 25% of *Ginkgo biloba* products; 20% of saw palmetto products; 33% of glucosamine, chondroitin, and combination products; and in 50% of s-adenosyl methionine (SAMe) products.[23] According to well-known naturopath, Dr Michael Murray, chemical analyses of over 35 commercial preparations of feverfew *(Tanacetum parthenium)* for active ingredients found a wide variation in the amounts of parthenolide, with the majority of

> *There are no current US regulations that enforce minimum standards of practice, no requirements for pre-market approval, no post-market surveillance, and no site licensing or product licensing required for the manufacturing of dietary supplements in the United States.*

products containing no parthenolide or only trace amounts of the active constituent.[18]

Additionally, unsanitary conditions of manufacture, packaging and storage, including pest infestations, moulds, and leaking pipes that drip onto stored supplements, have been cited as further cause for concern regarding product safety and as justification for the imposition of mandatory compliance with federally mandated GMP standards. The FDA has also been involved in recalls of dietary supplements contaminated with salmonella, *Klebsiella pneumonia,* botulism, and glass, as well as super-potent and sub-potent ingredients (including vitamin A, vitamin D, and selenium), and undeclared colour additives and sulphites.[25]

In its 2001 *Overview of Dietary Supplements* the FDA concedes, "It is often difficult to know what information is reliable and what is questionable, [therefore] consumers may want first to contact the manufacturer about the product they intend to purchase."[26] Dr John Cardellina, of the US-based Council for Responsible Nutrition, believes that 20% to 40% of US dietary supplement products fail to meet analyses for label claim. Other experts feel that Cardellina's estimate may to be too conservative. According to Dr Srini Srinivassa, of the United States Pharmacopeia Dietary Supplementation Verification Program, the majority of nutritional products in the US market today would fail to substantiate the claims made on their labels. With quality control like that, people *should* be asking if what is on the label is *really* in the bottle.

New Developments in the US Market

Responding to the growing plethora of unsafe nutritional products on retail shelves, the US federal watchdog published in the Federal Register in March 2003 a proposed rule for current GMP (cGMP) for the manufacture, packaging, and storage of dietary supplements. As required by law, comments from all stakeholders were then solicited.

The rule is generally science-based and requires manufactures to establish and meet detailed specifications for identity, purity, quality, potency, and composition of dietary supplements. While modelled under the cGMP for foods, the rule gives a nod to the fact that dietary supplements fall somewhere between foods and drugs along the risk-management continuum. Encouragingly, the proposed rule recognizes the need for the cGMP to address the unique hazards and requirements that stem from the "hybrid" nature of such natural health products.

The rule states that the authority has been vested by Congress for the FDA "to develop dietary supplement cGMP that are not identical to US food GMP and that are appropriately tailored to the manufacturing, packaging, and holding of dietary ingredients and dietary supplements."[25] This suggests that the final rule for cGMP standards for US dietary supplements may be similar in nature to those recently adopted by Canada, falling somewhere between GMP standards modelled after foods, on the one hand, and GMP standards modelled after pharmaceuticals, on the other. Accordingly, the new standard will acknowledge and reflect the modicum of risk posed by dietary supplements. While the final rule was expected in 2005, it had not been published as of February, 2007.

Nevertheless, when/if the ruling *does* come into force—and provided it is not substantially modified—it will serve as a major step forward in assuring access to safe and effective dietary supplements within the US marketplace. Of benefit will be the knowledge that natural health products will contain the specified types and amounts of ingredients listed on the bottle and will not contain toxic or unidentified contaminants. The final challenge will then be to secure full industry compliance through appropriate regulatory oversight.

New Research Discloses Problems

Disintegration is one of the most basic quality-control parameters in the natural health products industry. If a tablet or capsule cannot disintegrate, the individual nutrients within it are unable to dissolve into the intestinal fluids and, hence, are incapable of being absorbed into the bloodstream. Nurses have a description for dietary supplements that fail to dissolve: they call them "bedpan bullets." Often, you can still read the label imprinted on the pill when it is excreted in the stool!

Simply put, if a supplement does not disintegrate fully, it will do you little good. Most of your investment is literally flushed down the toilet. Unfortunately, a great number of popular nutritional supplements in the United States and Canada cannot pass a simple disintegration test.

ConsumerLab.com's Startling Findings

In January 2007, ConsumerLab.com, a provider of independent test results to help consumers evaluate nutritional products, published the findings of an investigation of several popular dietary supplements. Out of the 39 brands tested by ConsumerLab.com for content and purity, 12 brands failed the test.[27] The supplements were purchased in the marketplace and each was assayed for calcium, vitamin A (retinol and beta-carotene), and folic acid. For products not containing some of these nutrients, vitamin C, iron, and zinc levels were also assessed. In addition, the products were tested for disintegration and heavy metal contamination (lead). Finally, each product was assayed to see whether it contained nutrients in excess of the upper tolerable limits (UL) established by the US Food and Nutrition Board.

Among 21 products for adults and children that were tested, *less than half* met labelling and quality standards. Several products failed to pass more than one of the test criteria. It must be emphasized that the tests conducted by ConsumerLab.com were by no means onerous, sampling only a few of the more common nutrients found in everyday supplements. To put these findings into perspective, product verification procedures modeled after pharmaceuticals (in the US) or natural health products (in Canada) would have required these products to pass criteria that are considerably more stringent, including a validation of the identity, potency, and purity of all active ingredients and a screening for several potential chemical and biological contaminants. Looking at the ConsumerLab.com results, exceedingly few of these products would likely have survived these more rigorous product-content evaluations.

The fact that over 50% of the adults' and children's products tested failed to pass ConsumerLab.com's nominal benchmarks raises serious questions regarding the manufacturing practices and the levels of quality assurance in the United States dietary supplement industry today.

Earlier tests by this same company have uncovered several nutritional products that failed to meet label claims, failed to dissolve properly, or were contaminated with heavy metals. Further information about the particular products that have passed or failed their testing protocols is available at www.ConsumerLab.com.

Alberta Study Finds Disintegration Problems

A recent study, conducted by researchers at the University of Alberta, also investigated disintegration patterns of a number of Canadian and US nutritional products.[28] The study, conducted in 2006 and reported in the *Journal of Pharmacy and Pharmaceutical Sciences*, investigated 39 tableted formulations and 10 encapsulated formulations. Disintegration tests were conducted on tableted and encapsulated products, using simulated intestinal fluid (SIF USP 28) buffered to a pH* of 6.8. Twenty-one of the 39 tablets and four of the 10 capsules failed to disintegrate within the 20-minute time limit. In other words, 25 out of 46 products (54%) that *should* have disintegrated *did not do so* and, consequently, failed the test.

Products that did not disintegrate in the Stage-I tests were again tested using US Pharmacopoeia (USP Chapter 2040) disintegration conditions for dietary supplements. Nine of the tableted products tested did not fully disintegrate; however, all capsules passed the test. None of the three "timed release" products disintegrated under the applied conditions. Four products did not pass the test.[28] The results of the tests are shown in Tables 5-3 to 5-5 below.

The authors of the study observed that many products contained inaccurate, vague and misleading label claims, such as: "contains all the finest ingredients," "most advanced complete daily nutrient from A to Z," "guarantee of absolute purity and full potency," "scientifically balanced formula," and "highest bioavailability…all ingredients are the highest quality and purity

available." They argue that there are products sold in or into the Canadian market using label claims that are difficult to define, and that add pseudoscientific and unjustified apparent value to the product.

The authors urge Health Canada to clarify its guidance criteria for acceptable labelling standards and allow only recognized test methods on product labels. "Health professionals need to know how to identify a product with unknown quality. Meaningful disintegration standards accompanied with dissolution criteria are needed. Only this will ensure therapeutically efficacious dosage forms." [28]

Summary

Annual mortality data and records of adverse events reported annually by the American Association of Poison Control Centers confirm that the consumption of dietary supplements and natural health products is exceedingly safe. Witness the handful of fatalities from a decade of supplement use by tens of millions of Americans (most of these due to acute iron poisoning of infants) and compare this to the annual carnage of over 100,000 deaths from the use of prescription drugs—indeed, it is a study in contrasts.

As we have learned, when it comes to nutritional supplements, the *real* issue of safety lies in how the finished product is made. The formulation of a nutritional product can be a complex and exacting procedure, one that requires stringent quality control and attention to detail through every step of the manufacturing process. As the evidence shows, simply ensuring that the finished product disintegrates is a challenge that obviously confounds many well-known manufacturers. Guarantees of identity, purity, and potency are easy to claim, but are a fragile commodity in the competitive world of supplement manufacturing.

Table 5-3:[†] Products Failing Both Disintegration Tests

Costco Kirkland Signature Formula Forte	Swiss Herbal Swiss One "80"
GNC Mega Men Timed Release	Swiss Herbal Super Swiss One "50"
NuLife Ultimate One for Men Active	Trophic Multiple Vitamins & Minerals
Sisu Only One	

Table 5-4:[†] Products Failing Stage I Disintegration Tests

Atkins Nutritionals Basic 3	NaturPharm Nutri-plex
Body Wise Right Choice PM Formula	NuLife Ultimate One for Women Active
Douglas Laboratories Ultra Balance III	Pharmavite Essential Balance
Ehn Multi+	Quest Extra Once a Day
Jamieson Mega Vita	Seroyal International Super Orti Vite
Melaleuca Cell Wise	Thorne Research Multi-encap
Metagenics Multigenics Optimum	Tyler Holdings Multi Ils
Metagenics Multigenics Optimum without Iron	Wampole Multivitamins and Minerals
	Wampole Complete Multi-Adult Tabs

Table 5-5:[†] Products Passing Both Disintegration Tests

Body Wise Right Choice AM Multi Formula	Omnivite Nutrition Omnivite
Centrum Multi Vitamin Mineral Formula	One-A-Day Advance Adults
Centrum Forte	Pharmetics Multiple Vitamins plus Iron
Douglas Laboratories Ultra-Preventive III	Professional Health Products Multidyn
GNC Mega Multi Pro Performance	Safeway Adults One Tablet Daily
Holista Health Advanz	Safeway Select Central-Vite Forte
Jamieson Basic Vita-Vim	Selekta Multis without copper
Loblaws Exact Multivitamins	Seroyal International Multi Vite 109
Loblaws Exact Essentra Forte	Solaray Spectro Multi-Vita-Min
London Drugs One Tablet Daily	Ultragenesis Comprehensive Multi without Iron & Copper
London Naturals Multivitamin Iron-free	
Melaleuca Mel-Vita	USANA Health Sciences Essentials
Natural Factors Super Multi plus Iron	Vital Life Multivitamin complex

---

* pH is a measure of acidity. On a scale of 1 to 14 , a pH of 7.0 is neutral. Increasing the acidity of a solution will cause the pH to drop; increasing the alkalinity of a solution will increase the pH above 7.

† as reported in Lobenberg R, Steinke W. Investigation of vitamin and mineral tablets and capsules on the Canadian market. *J Pharm Pharm Sci* 2006;9(1):40-9

Optimal nutrition is the Medicine of the Future.

— *Dr Linus Pauling*
Nobel Laureate in Chemistry and Peace

CHAPTER SIX

OPTIMAL NUTRITION

The Food and Nutrition Board of the Institute of Medicine, US National Academy of Sciences, has been setting national standards for nutrient intake for over 60 years. These recommendations are collectively known as the Recommended Dietary Allowances (RDAs). Similar standards, based on the US RDAs, have been adopted by over 40 countries. In Canada, the allowances are known as the Recommended Nutrient Intakes (RNIs).

The RDAs were originally developed during World War II, under the auspices of the US National Research Council. At the time, it was determined that a comprehensive set of standards was required in order to establish scientifically valid baselines for nutrient intake. The standards were to provide guidance for the development of wartime rationing measures amongst the armed forces and civilian populations. As such, the recommendations were minimal in nature, establishing the lowest levels of nutrient intake required to avoid common maladies associated with acute nutritional deficiencies—diseases such as rickets, scurvy, pellagra, and beriberi. The RDAs were not designed—nor were they ever intended—to address the levels of intake required for optimal health.

The RDA for a particular nutrient is based on the amount of nutrient required to prevent the failure of a specific function or the development of an observable clinical deficiency. Because they were developed for demographic groups within a population, there are separate recommendations for different ages, genders, and physiological states (e.g. pregnancy). The recommendations pertain to healthy individuals only and do not consider the particular nutritional needs of different disease states.

Since their inception in 1943, The RDAs have been revised each decade, ostensibly taking into account the emergence of new scientific evidence. In some cases, these revisions have resulted in the lowering of the recommended intake for certain nutrients— decisions that have been soundly criticized by experts knowledgeable in the field. For example, in 1989, the RDA for folic acid was halved from 400 to 200 µg/day. Similarly, the 1989 RDA for vitamin E was reduced from 30 to 15 IU/day. This general lowering of RDAs for some nutrients was based on the questionable assumption that the American population is generally healthy, and since US citizens consume diets that routinely fail to meet the earlier (higher) RDA, a nutrient intake half that of the previous RDA was deemed sufficient to maintain general health.[1]

The logic that the American population is "healthy" simply because its citizens fail to exhibit classical symptoms of clinical nutritional deficiencies is seriously flawed. While it is rare, today, for people in America or Canada to suffer from scurvy or rickets, when considered within the context of a nutritional basis for the onset of chronic diseases, the decision of the US Food and Nutrition Board to reduce further the RDAs of several important nutrients appears nonsensical, indeed.

America and Canada are nations awash in illness, where two thirds of adults are overweight and obesity is epidemic; where the incidence of heart disease—today's major killer—reflects the appalling dietary and lifestyle choices of generations of couch potatoes; and where the rising prevalence of several cancers, type 2 diabetes, osteoporosis, and neurodegenerative disorders threatens to swamp our respective healthcare systems.

Misreading the RDAs

The explosive increase in the consumption of nutritional supplements to achieve long-term health has not gone unnoticed by the pharmaceutical industry or the regulatory authorities in Europe and North America. Consequently, some governments have developed recommendations on tolerable upper levels of intake for several nutrients. Likely for reasons of pure expediency—or due to pressure from the pharmaceutical lobby—some governments have viewed the RDAs as convenient *upper limits* for intake. Such an irrational approach has no scientific validity and is, in fact, the antithesis of the principle that the RDAs are a *baseline* of intake needed to avoid disease.

The 1989 summary report on the RDAs states, "The Recommended Dietary Allowances (RDAs) are the levels of intake of essential nutrients that, on the basis of scientific knowledge, are judged by the Food and Nutrition Board to be *adequate* to meet the known nutrient needs of practically all healthy persons." It adds, "For certain nutrients, the requirement may be the amount that will prevent failure of a specific function or the development of specific deficiency signs—*an amount that may differ greatly from that required to maintain body stores*"[2] (emphasis added).

In other words, the RDA recommendations define the lower limits of daily nutrient intake that are necessary to avoid acute nutritional deficiencies; they do *not* address the requirements for optimal nutrition—they were not designed to do so.

Consequently, the fact that some governments are considering using the US RDAs as a means of limiting the levels of nutrients in commercial dietary supplements poses a serious threat to the public interest and to the future of the natural healthcare industry. If implemented, such a misguided policy would dismiss the validated benefits of high-dose supplementation for the maintenance of optimal health and the treatment of specific disease processes. This serves no possible public health benefit other than to protect the commercial interests of Big Pharma—an industry whose bottom line is dependent upon people becoming ill.

Nutrients Exceeding the RDAs

There has also been discussion amongst several countries regarding the imposition of drug regulations for products containing levels of nutrients greater than the RDAs. This argument has been promulgated by the pharmaceutical industry, which has long wanted to see nutritional supplements brought under stringent regulatory control. According to Dr John Hathcock, of the US Council for Responsible Nutrition, treating high-potency natural health products as drugs would preclude the validated benefits of high-dose supplementation for several disease states, except under the care of a registered physician.[3] In other words, the consumer would not be able to obtain high-dose vitamin formulations without a doctor's prescription. Considering the

relative safety of natural health products, such a senseless constraint would serve only the interests of Big Pharma.

Consider also that many nutrients with well-established pharmacological benefits, such as lutein, lycopene, boron, coenzyme Q_{10}, alpha-lipoic acid, and others, have no established RDA. Should RDA-based limits be implemented, the concern arises that those nutrients *without* established RDAs may be banned from inclusion in nutritional supplements. Absurd, you say? The hard reality is that the government minions who make these decisions are not known for their infallible insight and unassailable logic—particularly when their political bosses are faced with relentless lobbying from a drug cartel bent on eliminating the preventive healthcare industry.

Simply put, the use of baseline RDAs to establish maximum allowable levels of nutrient content in nutritional products has no scientific basis and provides no conceivable benefit to public health. Governments that choose this route will inflict a profound blow to the rights and freedoms of their citizens to take control of their own health.

RDAs Fail to Address Deficiencies

An insightful analysis of the progression of vitamin deficiency, published by Dr Myron Brin in 1964, outlines a five-stage developmental process[4] (Figure 6-1). Using vitamin B_1 (thiamine) in red blood cells as a model, Brin showed that the first stage of B_1 deficiency leads to reduced urinary excretion of the vitamin. In the second (biochemical) stage, the activity of a key cellular enzyme, transketolase, is significantly reduced. In the third (physiologic) stage, vague symptoms, such as reduced appetite, insomnia, irritability, and general malaise, begin to develop. It is only at the fourth (clinical) stage that the classic symptoms of vitamin B_1 deficiency disease, beriberi, are expressed. These clinical symptoms include intermittent claudication (leg pain upon exertion), polyneuritis (inflammation of nerves), bradycardia (unusually slow heartbeat), peripheral oedema (swelling of the limbs), and opthalmoplegia (paralysis of the eye muscles). In the fifth and final (anatomical) stage, damage to cellular structures, such as cardiac hypertrophy (swelling of the heart muscle), arrhythmia (irregular heartbeat), and degeneration of structures within the central nervous system are seen. While the five-stage schema was modelled after vitamin B_1, Brin notes that its principle is applicable to any nutrient deficiency.[1]

What is particularly illuminating about Brin's schema, as it pertains to the RDAs, is that the "failure of specific functions or the development of specific deficiency signs" (as outlined in the RDA criteria) are only seen at the fourth (clinical) and fifth (anatomical) stages in the developmental continuum. Thus, the first three phases of deficiency—because they do not involve specific deficiency symptoms or the failure of specific functions—pass below the radar screen of the RDA standards. While these sub-clinical stages, indeed, exhibit physiologic responses to increasingly inadequate levels of nutrient intake, the dietary intakes established by the RDAs do not consider these levels as inadequate. *Consequently, the RDAs utterly fail to protect the public from the first three stages of nutrient deficiency—and it is precisely at this sub-clinical level that many experts now believe the seeds of degenerative disease are sown.*

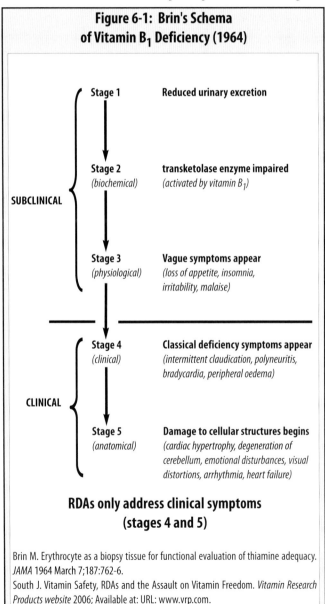

Figure 6-1: Brin's Schema of Vitamin B₁ Deficiency (1964)

SUBCLINICAL

Stage 1 — **Reduced urinary excretion**

Stage 2 *(biochemical)* — **transketolase enzyme impaired** *(activated by vitamin B₁)*

Stage 3 *(physiological)* — **Vague symptoms appear** *(loss of appetite, insomnia, irritability, malaise)*

CLINICAL

Stage 4 *(clinical)* — **Classical deficiency symptoms appear** *(intermittent claudication, polyneuritis, bradycardia, peripheral oedema)*

Stage 5 *(anatomical)* — **Damage to cellular structures begins** *(cardiac hypertrophy, degeneration of cerebellum, emotional disturbances, visual distortions, arrhythmia, heart failure)*

RDAs only address clinical symptoms (stages 4 and 5)

Brin M. Erythrocyte as a biopsy tissue for functional evaluation of thiamine adequacy. *JAMA* 1964 March 7;187:762-6.
South J. Vitamin Safety, RDAs and the Assault on Vitamin Freedom. *Vitamin Research Products* website 2006; Available at: URL: www.vrp.com.

New DRIs Also Fall Short

Advances in nutritional science have led to a growing awareness of the need to determine *optimal* levels of nutrient intake as a means of preventing degenerative disease. In response, the United States and Canada embarked on a joint review of the scientific data with the purpose of developing a new, harmonized nutritional standard that embraces the concept of optimal nutrition. Through Health Canada and the National Academy of Sciences in the United States, Canadian and US nutritional experts have, over recent years, worked together to create new standards, called the *Dietary Reference Intakes* (DRIs). These harmonized reference standards represent a shift away from the simple avoidance of nutritional deficiencies and toward the recognition of nutritional intakes necessary to optimize health.

Today, DRI standards have been determined for a number of vitamins and minerals. Ultimately, they will replace the RDA standards in the United States and RNI standards in Canada. While a step in the right direction, it is the concern of many nutritional experts that the new DRI standards still fall short when considering the nutritional needs for long-term prevention and optimal health.

The scientific evidence shows that effective prevention of chronic disease requires levels of some nutrients that far exceed the recommendations contained in these new standards. For example, the newly revised DRI for vitamin E is 22-23 IU per day. Yet, several clinical and epidemiological studies show that much higher doses (100-800 IU/day) are needed to reduce the risk of heart disease. The 1995 Cambridge Heart Antioxidant Study (CHAOS) showed that patients with angina who consumed 400-800 IU per day of vitamin E suffered 47% fewer non-fatal heart attacks than did patients who did not receive supplementation.[5] Other studies involving vitamin E also show that advanced intakes of this nutrient can reduce the risk of major cardiovascular events by 33% to 50% or more.[6-9] To do so, however, requires daily supplementation at levels significantly higher than the new Canada/US guidelines.

Advanced levels of other vitamins, minerals, and antioxidants have also demonstrated protective effects against several degenerative disease processes:

✔ Selenium, at 200 µg/day, rather than the 55 µg/day recommended in the DRI, was found to reduce the incidence of total cancer mortality, including prostate, colon, and lung cancer.[10]

✔ Administration of 2,000 µg/day of folic acid (DRI: 400 µg/day), 25mg/day of vitamin B_6 (DRI: 1.3-1.5 µg/day) and 400 µg per day of vitamin B_{12} (DRI: 2.4 µg/day) was found to lower plasma homocysteine levels in older men by substantial amounts. A high plasma concentration of homocysteine is associated with a greater risk of cardiovascular events.[11]

✔ Supplementation with high levels of vitamin C, well above the DRI standard of 75-90 mg per day, was shown to reduce the risk of cataracts by 83%. The findings also suggest that long-term (more than 10 years) consumption of vitamin C supplements may

substantially reduce the development of age-related lens opacities.[12]

✔ Advanced intakes of calcium and vitamin D have been shown to reduce the risk and slow the progress of osteoporosis.[13, 14] Concerns about osteoporosis and indications of a positive association between calcium intake and bone mass led an international scientific panel in 1994 to recommend daily supplementation of calcium at levels that greatly exceed the recommended intakes.[15]

✔ In a 2003 study, 130 adults who took a multiple vitamin/mineral supplement (containing levels of nutrients similar to what can be found in commercial dietary supplements) fell ill to infections far less frequently (43% vs. 73%) and experienced significantly less infection-related work loss than did a placebo-controlled comparison group. The differences were even more pronounced in those subjects who were type 2 diabetic: only 17% of the diabetic segment of the intervention group reported contracting at least one infection over the study interval compared to a whopping 97% in the diabetic segment of the control group.[16]

✔ In a 2002 meta-analysis of several previous studies involving mega-vitamin therapy (where the dosage given exceeds the US RDA for a given nutrient by at least a factor of ten), researchers at the University of California at Berkeley identified more than 50 genetically-related diseases caused by defective enzymes that could be successfully treated. When patients were administered a high dose of the vitamin component for the corresponding coenzyme (an assistant to the principal enzyme), a partial restoration in the activity of the defective enzyme was observed. The authors concluded that defects in the gene that controls the manufacturing of the associated enzyme reduces binding of the coenzyme and consequently lowers the activity of the enzyme; such defects can be remedied by raising cellular concentrations of the coenzyme through high-dose vitamin therapy.[17]

Interestingly, some of the above studies also highlight the requirement for long-term supplementation before reductions in risk become evident. Short-term use of nutritional supplements does not appear to exhibit such profound protective effects.

Fueling the Biological Spark Plugs

The bulk of food we eat—including proteins, fats, and carbohydrates—fuels the machinery of the cell; however, our bodies utilize micronutrients somewhat differently. Vitamins, minerals, and certain trace elements have specialized functions; each plays a distinct role in helping to drive the myriad of biochemical reac-

Table 6-1: Common Vitamins, Coenzymes, and their Functions

Vitamin	Coenzyme	Function
Niacin (B_3)	nicotinamide adenine dinucleotide (NAD+)	Oxidation/hydrogen transfer
Riboflavin (B_2)	flavin adenine dinucleotide (FAD)	Oxidation/hydrogen transfer
Pantothenic acid (B_5)	coenzyme A (CoA)	Acetyl group carrier
Cobalamin (B_{12})	coenzyme B_{12}	Methyl group transfer
Thiamin (B_1)	thiaminpyrophosphate (TPP)	Aldehyde group transfer

tions through which life's energy flows. Much like the spark plugs in an automobile engine ignite the fuel, vitamins and minerals—along with thousands of enzymes—act as the cell's *biological spark plugs*. Together, they furnish the means by which the cell converts foodstuffs into energy. This means that vitamins and minerals are not foodstuffs in the ordinary sense, but, rather, function catalytically.

Presently, there are 3,870 known enzymes and, of those, 22% require cofactors to catalyze their respective reaction processes. A cofactor is the non-protein component of an enzyme, such as a metal ion, which is required to activate the enzyme. A coenzyme is an organic cofactor and forms a functional component of an enzyme molecule, making up part of its active site. Without its attendant coenzyme, an enzyme will not function. Vitamins serve as precursors* to coenzymes (e.g. vitamins B_1, B_2, B_6, B_{12}, niacin, folic acid) or as cofactors themselves (e.g. vitamin C). Table 6-1 shows several of the common vitamins, their coenzymes, and the functions they perform.

As coenzymes, vitamins not only activate the principal enzymes and provide the electrochemical punch that drives cellular reaction processes, they link together disparate chemical reactions into an integrated whole. *It is precisely because vitamin-derived coenzymes can couple different enzyme systems that they are so central to proper cellular metabolism and so important to our diet.* They are the cell's biochemical gateways, through which the continuous exchange of materials and energy is made possible.

Homocysteine Metabolism

A good example of enzymatic coupling necessary to optimize physiologic function and health is the metabolism of homocysteine—an important intermediate in the metabolism of sulphur-containing amino acids. Unfortunately, homocysteine is also a potent oxidant. High blood levels of homocysteine can damage arterial linings, induce atherosclerotic lesions, and destroy the protective sheath of nerve fibres; consequently, the proper metabolism of homocysteine is fundamental to optimal health.

Healthy individuals utilize two different pathways to convert homocysteine to less harmful metabolites. One pathway results in the methylation of homocysteine to methionine; the other pathway converts homocysteine to cysteine and taurine, eventually to be incorporated into proteins.[18]

Figure 6-2 outlines the reaction sequences for the conversion of homocysteine to methionine and cysteine. This conversion requires vitamin B_{12} as a cofactor to the enzyme *methionine synthase*. This enzyme strips a methyl group (-CH_3) from the substrate, 5-methyl tetrahydrofolate. In turn, the reaction product, tetrahydrofolate, is converted back to 5-methyl tetrahydrofolate in a two-step process moderated by the action of the enzyme, *methylene tetrahydrofolate reductase* (MTHFR).

To perform this conversion, the enzyme requires the presence of the coenzymes FAD, derived from vitamin B_2 (riboflavin), and

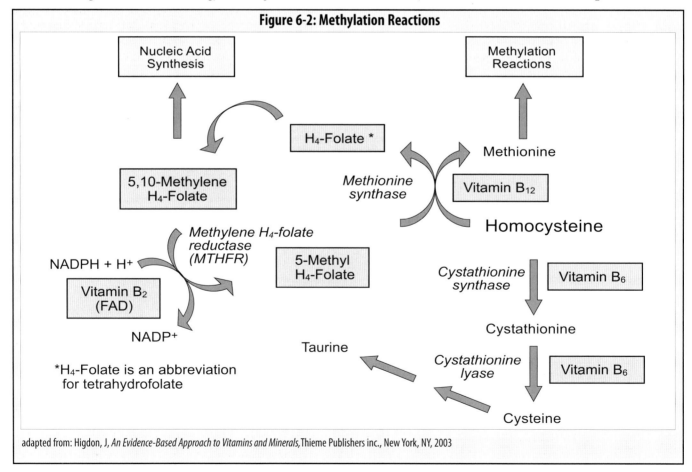

Figure 6-2: Methylation Reactions

Nucleic Acid Synthesis

Methylation Reactions

H_4-Folate *

5,10-Methylene H_4-Folate

Methionine synthase

Methionine

Vitamin B_{12}

Homocysteine

Methylene H_4-folate reductase (MTHFR)

NADPH + H+

Vitamin B_2 (FAD)

5-Methyl H_4-Folate

NADP+

Cystathionine synthase

Vitamin B_6

Cystathionine

Taurine

Cystathionine lyase

Vitamin B_6

*H_4-Folate is an abbreviation for tetrahydrofolate

Cysteine

adapted from: Higdon, J, *An Evidence-Based Approach to Vitamins and Minerals,* Thieme Publishers inc., New York, NY, 2003

---

* A metabolic precursor is a substance required by the cell to manufacture an active biomolecule. In the case of vitamin B_3 (niacin), the vitamin must first be converted into its active form, nicotinamide adenine dinucleotide (NAD), before it can be used by the cell for a wide variety of hydrogen-transfer reactions.

NADPH, derived from vitamin B_3 (niacin). Conversely, the conversion of homocysteine into cysteine occurs via transformation with two vitamin B_6-dependent enzymes, *cystathionine synthase* and *cystathionine lyase*. In the reaction sequence, the sole function of folate (folic acid) is to transfer single-carbon methyl groups (-CH_3), a process known as methylation.[19] Figure 6-2 shows that the conversion of homocysteine is, in fact, a multi-faceted process requiring several enzymes and at least five vitamin-derived cofactors (folate, vitamin B_2, vitamin B_3, vitamin B_6, and vitamin B_{12}) all working in unison, an elegant example of the "interconnectedness" of cellular processes—and of the critical role that vitamins play in driving these complex biochemical sequences.

The coupling of enzymatic reactions shown in Figure 6-2 also demonstrates how the failure of a single component through a genetic malfunction in one of the controlling enzymes can compromise the entire process and lead to harmful biochemical and physiological impediments. For example, an alteration in the gene for the MTHFR enzyme, known as the MTHFR polymorphism, leads to dangerously high levels of homocysteine in the blood. Implications of this common anomaly, hyperhomocysteinemia, will be discussed later in this chapter.

Genes, Enzymes, and Mutations

As mentioned previously, enzymes are chemically active proteins that control and sustain the myriad of chemical reactions that take place in a living cell. Each enzyme is manufactured by the cell from the genetic blueprint for that protein, stored within the cell's nucleus. The gene(s) controlling the manufacture of a specific enzyme are not infallible. Sometimes changes can occur to the coding within a gene that may alter the amino acid sequence of the corresponding enzyme manufactured by that gene. Mutations, perhaps caused by radiation, environmental toxins, or simply through errors introduced in the replication process, are some of the mechanisms that nature uses to drive evolutionary change.

According to renowned biochemist, Dr Bruce Ames, of the University of California at Berkeley, as many as one third of mutations occurring in a given gene result in the corresponding enzyme having a decreased affinity for its coenzyme. This weakened binding capacity results in a reduced rate of reaction governed by that enzyme. Simply put, enzymes modified through alterations (mutations) in their genetic code do not work very well. Their compromised activity often results in an observable physiological weakness and a greater susceptibility to disease.

In a groundbreaking discovery, Dr Ames and his research team at Berkeley recently surveyed the literature to connect the dots between genetic variations in the structure of critical enzymes and the manifestation of associated disease states. The Ames team uncovered no less than 50 human diseases caused by genetically defective enzymes. Moreover, the literature showed that each of these diseases could be remedied or ameliorated by the administration of high concentrations of the associated coenzyme. Study after study revealed that high-dose therapy with the vitamin precursor of the coenzyme enhanced the activity of the defective enzyme and brought about dramatic therapeutic results.

Of the 50 diseases the Ames team reviewed, eleven responded to vitamin B_6 (pyridoxine). In all cases, the researchers were able to isolate the problem to an impediment in how the defective enzyme binds to the cofactor derived from the vitamin. Twenty-two other diseases caused by defective cofactor binding involved other B-complex vitamins, including thiamin (B_1), riboflavin (B_2), niacin (B_3), biotin (B_7), and cobalamin (B_{12}).[20]

"These 50 diseases are just the tip of the iceberg," Ames said in a 2002 media release published to report his findings. "Individual doctors have noticed this, but nobody put it all together. Now doctors are going to try high-dose vitamin therapy the minute they know a coenzyme is involved in a disease or there is a problem with the substrate."[21]

The Ames theory of mega-vitamin therapy, where vitamins are given at dosages substantially greater than their respective RDA, has far greater implications than simply the treatment of overt disease. The human genome is rife with genetic variations that likely affect several enzyme-coenzyme interactions. Consequently, high-dose vitamin therapies tailored to an individual's unique genetic profile may soon offer the future of genetically individualized programs for optimal health and prevention. Such programs could also provide an effective means of slowing the aging process that is, in part, a consequence of cumulative oxidative damage to such cellular mechanisms.

Genetic Polymorphisms Common

An alternate form of a gene present in greater than 1% of the population is called a polymorphism. These single nucleotide* variations in the genetic sequence of the gene alter the amino acid sequence in the corresponding enzyme protein manufactured by that gene. This can occur at the binding site for the coenzyme, thereby reducing the affinity of the enzyme for its coenzyme. It can also occur at locations elsewhere along the protein chain, modifying the three-dimensional structure of the enzyme protein sufficiently to affect its activity. Such genetic variations are far more common than previously believed, affecting a significant portion of the population. A good example of a malady brought on by a common genetic polymorphism—and one that may be ameliorated effectively with high-dose vitamin therapy—is hyperhomocysteinemia.

Hyperhomocysteinemia

Hyperhomocysteinemia, the *Darth Vader* of cardiovascular disease, is characterized by abnormally high levels of homocysteine in the blood. An aggressive oxidant and neurotoxin, homocysteine can inflict widespread damage to cells and organs; high levels of the amino acid are implicated in the aetiology of several disease processes. The 1992 Physician's Health Study, conducted by Meir Stampfer[22] of the Harvard School of Public Health, looked at blood homocysteine levels in 15,000 physicians. The authors concluded that even mildly elevated levels of homocysteine are directly related to heart disease. Subsequent studies confirm that high levels of homocysteine place people at increased cardiovascular risk.[23] It is estimated that for every 10% increase in blood homocysteine levels there is a similar increase in

---

* A nucleotide is a chemical compound that consists of a nitrogenous base, a sugar, and one or more phosphate groups. Nucleotides are the structural units of RNA, DNA, and several cofactors. In the cell, they play important roles in information storage and replication, energy production, metabolism and cellular signalling.

the risk of heart disease.[24, 25] Other studies indicate that people with elevated blood homocysteine face four times the risk of peripheral vascular disease (damage to the blood vessels of the body, outside the heart) than do people with normal levels.[26]

The massive Framingham Heart Study,[27] which followed twins over a 26-year period, showed a significant increase in carotid artery stenosis (narrowing of the main arteries of the neck) consistent with elevated homocysteine levels. Other studies confirm a positive link between blood homocysteine levels and the risks of arteriosclerosis (hardening of the arteries without plaque formation) and myocardial infarction (sudden heart attack).[28] High homocysteine levels are implicated, as well, in the development of peripheral vascular disease, diabetes, arthritis, kidney disease, cancer, and neural tube birth defects.[29-31]

As a neurotoxin, homocysteine can destroy the myelin sheath protecting nerve cells and cause them to "short-circuit," much like a frayed electrical wire. Many neurological diseases, such as depression, schizophrenia, multiple sclerosis, Parkinson's disease, Alzheimer's dementia, and age-related cognitive decline, are associated with high levels of homocysteine and low levels of the B-complex vitamins. In fact, recent studies confirm that deficiencies in vitamin B_{12} and folate are common in older people, who often suffer from many of the above-mentioned degenerative diseases.[32]

Hyperhomocysteinemia can be caused by disruption of any of the interrelated pathways of its metabolism, such as a deficiency in the *cystathionine synthase* enzyme, defective vitamin B_{12} synthesis, or a genetic defect in the enzyme, *methylene tetrahydrofolate reductase* (MTHFR) (see Figure 6-2).

MTHFR Polymorphism

A common defect in the gene coding the MTHFR enzyme, known as the C677T MTHFR polymorphism,* is expressed in up to 20% of the population worldwide. It is characterized by the enzyme's decreased affinity for the coenzyme *flavin adenine dinuceotide* (NAD), derived from vitamin B_2.[33] As seen in Figure 6-2, the MTHFR enzyme plays a central role in the methylation of homocysteine to methionine. Individuals who express this common genetic abnormality have depressed serum folate and noticeably elevated plasma homocysteine levels. Consequently, their risks for cardiovascular and coronary artery disease,[34] diabetic nephropathy,[35] schizophrenia,[36] and dementia[37] are noticeably increased.

Most individuals with high levels of homocysteine respond well to supplementation with vitamins B_6, B_{12}, and folic acid; however, individuals who express the MTHFR polymorphism tend to be resistant to this nutritional intervention. This occurs because the defective MTHFR enzyme creates a biochemical bottleneck in the conversion of methylene tetrahydrofolate to methyl tetrahydrofolate (see Figure 6-2). Supplementing with vitamins B_6, B_{12}, and folic acid cannot effectively alleviate this bottleneck. However, studies show that the MTHFR enzyme *is* sensitive to riboflavin (vitamin B_2) deficiency.[38] Consequently, it has been suggested by the Ames group of Berkeley that mega-dose therapy

with vitamin B_2, the vitamin precursor to the FAD coenzyme required by MTHFR, would prove beneficial.[39] Studies are now underway to evaluate this hypothesis.

Recently, the Linus Pauling Institute of Corvallis, Oregon, has called to question whether the present RDA for folate is sufficient to normalize impaired MTHFR enzymes in individuals who are affected by this common genetic defect.[18] As well, Ames has called for clinical trials to explore further the efficacy of mega-dose B-vitamin therapy, including supplementation with both folate and riboflavin, in reducing homocysteine levels in hyperhomocysteinemic individuals.

The MTHFR polymorphism, and its attendant hyperhomocysteinemia, is but *one* of some 50 recognized genetic defects that can be ameliorated by high-dose vitamin therapy, which, according to Ames, is only "the tip of the iceberg." If so, high-dose vitamin therapy appears to be a very promising intervention. Ames' view is that prophylactic high-dose vitamin therapy might tweak enzyme functioning enough to improve the general health of many segments of society. Furthermore, with the advent of individualized genomic testing, it will soon become possible to customize such vitamin therapies to suit an individual's unique genetic profile.

Implications

Recent scientific findings demonstrate convincingly that several nutrients, in dosages considerably higher than their recommended intakes, can help optimize one's health and provide significant protective effects against the onset of degenerative disease. While a degree of prudence must always be exercised with those nutrients (some minerals, in particular) which exhibit known toxicities at high levels, it is evident that *optimal* nutrition goes well beyond the overly conservative requirements contained in the US and Canadian government guidelines. Establishing a DRI for a particular nutrient will soon become more complicated, once it is recognized that a sizeable portion of the population has a higher requirement for that nutrient because of a prevalent genetic polymorphism.

Moreover, the recent evidence showing the efficacy of treatment of polymorphisms through high-dose vitamin therapies suggests that mega-dose interventions with selected nutritional components may provide an effective means for targeted nutritional therapies. In the near future, such preventive and interceptive therapies will be possible through the advent of genetic profiling, thus providing individuals with a greater certainty of their biochemical "weak links" and a means of bolstering their metabolic defences against the onset of degenerative disease.

These developments argue strongly against the crass lobbying efforts of the drug cartel (proffered under the guise of safety) to limit the potencies of nutritional supplements and, consequently, constrain the future of the natural health products industry. The fact is, compared to drugs, natural health products are exceedingly safe. Their use in therapeutic doses in both preventive and therapeutic protocols should certainly continue to be explored and encouraged through future research.

---

* The strange name indicates that there is a substitution of the nitrogenous base, cytosine, with the nitrogenous base, thymine, at the 677th nucleotide on the gene coding for the MTHFR enzyme. Such a substitution alters the amino acid sequence of the protein structure and, with it, the functionality of the enzyme. The C677T MTHFR polymorphism is quite common, with 30% to 40% of the population being heterozygous (having at least one copy) for this defective gene.

A lie can travel halfway around the world
while the truth is putting on its shoes.
— *Mark Twain (1835-1910)*

CHAPTER SEVEN

NUTRITIONAL SUPPLEMENTS UNDER ATTACK

In recent years, the value of nutritional supplements in protecting and promoting human health has been intensely debated within the scientific/medical community and in the national press. Many researchers argue that supplements provide a convenient and effective means for supplying the optimal intakes of essential nutrients required to support long-term health; others counter that there is no conclusive proof that supplements provide any real health benefits at all.

Unfortunately, much of the debate has been framed by a media more interested in selling newspapers than in ferreting out the truth. Sloppy reporting, distorted editorial sensationalism, and conflicts of interest by researchers and publishers have unnecessarily alarmed the public and threatened to destroy our trust in complementary health care. These injustices must be addressed before irreversible harm is done to an industry committed to natural approaches to wellness and to a public increasingly confused about where to turn for sound advice on preventing disease and achieving optimal health.

Health-conscious consumers and medical practitioners, alike, have become frustrated at the mixed messages being promulgated through the headlines: one day we're told something is good for us and the next day we're told it's not. Why do so many recently published studies appear to refute the prevailing scientific evidence about the benefits of natural approaches to wellness? How can vitamin E be good for us one day and bad for us the next? For once, why can't the experts just get it straight?

Teasing Fact from Fiction

If there is any consolation, it may be helpful to understand that science *never* progresses smoothly—there will always be new findings that appear to refute long-held beliefs. Controversy is the crucible for change and paves the road that science *must* travel to arrive at a final truth. Unfortunately, media bias and conflicts of interest place unnecessary detours along the way.

Looking at the recent spate of negative studies, several explanations arise for findings that are seemingly incongruous with the prevailing scientific evidence. For one thing, several long-term dietary intervention trials have recently come to fruition. These studies were developed back in the early 1990s and fail to differentiate between the heart-healthy *good fats* (such as the omega-3 fats found in fish and grains, and the monosaturated oils found in nuts and olive oil), and *bad fats* (such as the saturated fats

> Much of the information contained in this chapter has been adapted from an article written by the author for Life Extension Magazine. A full text of the article is available online in the LEF magazine archives at:
>
> http://www.lef.org/magazine/mag2006/jun2006_cover_media_01.htm

found in red meats and the trans-fats found in deep-fried and processed foods). By design, these studies simplistically assumed that fat was fat and reducing fat meant cutting down on *all* fat. If anything, the mixed findings of these investigations demonstrate the folly of such an indiscriminate approach to fat reduction.

Second, out of 100 clinical studies that investigate a particular effect, probability dictates that five of these studies—no matter how well designed—will show results that are not real. There will always be a statistical fluke in the bunch.

Third, it is to be expected that about one fifth of clinical trials investigating a particular effect will not have the needed number of subjects to show a statistically significant result. This occurs because in most clinical trials the probability of finding a real result, known as the *power* of a test, is set at a minimum of 80%. Consequently, there is up to a 20% chance of missing your mark and failing to find a difference when one actually exists. This is merely the gremlin of statistical probability at work.

On a final point, some investigations are just *bad* science, improperly conducted, poorly reported, and inadequately reviewed. Unfortunately, as has recently been the case, these studies attract an inordinate amount of attention from a media hungry for headlines.

Let us look at some of the more egregious headlines and events that, in recent years, have captured public attention and compare them with the scientific truth behind the stories. Then, we will turn to the *central* issue in the debate on the value of nutritional

Statistical Power

Statistical power is the probability that one can detect an effect if there really is one. It is highly influenced by the size of a study (the number of subjects), such as when you toss a coin. Sometimes studies are discounted that show elevated, but not statistically significant, risks.

Often, negative studies have very low power. Therefore, one should be careful of dismissing a possible association on the basis of negative studies, unless those studies are designed to have high statistical power.[1]

supplementation—the unsuitability of the scientific paradigm by which nutritional supplementation, as a preventive measure, is currently assessed.

Omega-3 Study: Something's Fishy

In March of 2006, the world's largest international news agency, *Reuters*, published the headline, "Doubts over heart claims of omega-3 fats." Reporting on the findings of a study on omega-3 fats and heart health, published that same month in the *British Medical Journal,*[5] the *Reuters* article claimed that the systematic review of 89 studies showed no substantive evidence that omega-3 fats protected against cardiovascular disease or cancer. Halfway around the world, the *New Zealand Herald* picked up the spin and announced that the heart-healthy advice to eat more oily fish was wrong. The *Herald* article advised its readers to "place fish oils at the top of the list of medical shibboleths that turned out to be myths."

The omega-3 investigation, conducted by Lee Hooper and coworkers at the University of East Anglia School of Medicine, was a meta-analysis—a statistical technique where researchers combine data from several available clinical trials. Such analyses are highly speculative because differences in the scientific protocols between the included studies can make it extremely difficult to expose a common factor. A good meta-analysis is a useful tool that can put apparently contradictory evidence into perspective; a poorly designed analysis, however, can lead to bad science and faulty conclusions.

The Hooper analysis was reportedly a review of 48 randomized controlled trials* and 41 cohort studies;† however, the investigation used as few as 15 controlled trials and 3 cohort studies in compiling the data. Several of the included studies had very small sample sizes and provided little data on the effects under investigation. Inordinately low death rates in several of the included studies exacerbated this situation, resulting in very large confidence intervals (indicating insufficient information to detect differences) and a lower analytical power than was expected.

Moreover, there was a large degree of heterogeneity amongst

the included studies. Some had death rates in their control groups as low as 0.5%; others had inordinately high control-group death rates that, in two cases, exceeded 15% and 22% respectively. This indicates that the subjects had *large* disparities in their health. Such heterogeneity requires a high analytical power to expose meaningful results—something the Hooper study lacked.

Addressing these issues, the authors pointed out that, "There were too few events [deaths, associated cardiovascular events, and incidences of cancer] to rule out the possibility of important effects from various interventions." In layman's terms, the numbers did not show much of anything. In such a case, one must be very prudent in dismissing a possible association based on negative results. Dr Mike Knapton, Director of Prevention and Care for the *British Heart Foundation*, wisely cautioned, "People should not stop consuming omega-3 fats or eating oily fish as a result of this study." Dr Knapton's sage advice, however, did not stop the media from savaging the value of omega-3 fats.

Glucosamine/Chondroitin Findings Ignored

In February 2006, the world's largest daily newspaper, the venerable New York *Times,* declared, "2 Top-Selling Arthritis Drugs are Found to be Ineffective." The fact that the "drugs" mentioned in the article are not drugs at all, but two popular, natural nutritional supplements used successfully by millions of people worldwide, underscores the quality of investigative journalism that went into the article. The US newswire, Associated Press (AP), and its counterpart, Canadian Press (CP), also picked up the story and parroted the line that glucosamine and chondroitin sulphate were "… no better than dummy pills" in relieving knee pain associated with osteoarthritis. The findings of the $12.5 million study, published in the *New England Journal of Medicine,*[6] provide a very different view.

The Glucosamine/chondroitin Arthritis Intervention Trial (GAIT), the largest-ever clinical study of these supplements, was a randomized, double-blind, placebo-controlled intervention trial of 1583 patients with symptomatic osteoarthritis of the knee. The primary outcome was a 20% reduction in knee pain over 24 weeks. From a clinical perspective, the study was well powered, with a projected 85% probability of detecting change and a high adherence to the treatment protocol. It was expected to be *the* definitive word on the effectiveness of glucosamine and chondroitin in reducing the pain of osteoarthritis; however, a combination of poor experimental design and misrepresentation by the media succeeded only in clouding the findings and heightening the controversy.

The investigation suffered from an extraordinarily high placebo effect of over 60% that virtually destroyed the ability of the trial to detect valid change. The fact that six in ten patients in the placebo group found significant pain relief in a dummy pill is an enormous source of error! A possible reason for this was the free use of pain relievers allowed during the trial. Despite the fact that acetaminophen (Tylenol®) enhances the efficacy of osteoarthritis treatment, researchers allowed patients to take up to 4,000 mg of acetamino-

* A randomized controlled trial (RCT) is a form of clinical trial or scientific procedure used in the testing of the efficacy of medicines or medical procedures. It is widely considered the most reliable form of scientific evidence because it is the best-known design for eliminating the variety of biases that regularly compromise the validity of medical research.

† A cohort study is a study in which subjects who presently have a certain condition and/or receive a particular treatment are followed over time and compared with another group not affected by the condition under investigation.

phen daily. This further reduced the chance of finding significant differences between the intervention and comparison groups.

Another shortcoming was the *form* of glucosamine used in the study. While glucosamine sulphate is the standard form used in supplements, the type used in the study was glucosamine hydrochloride. This form of glucosamine does not contain the sulphate moiety (a specific segment of a molecule) found in glucosamine sulphate, which is believed to amplify its analgesic properties.

Despite these limitations, the study did find that for those individuals with moderate-to-severe knee pain, the combination of glucosamine and chondroitin sulphate provided a 25% to 26% improvement in pain relief—a response that exceeded the projected 20% design measure to prove efficacy. According to the study authors, "Treatment with chondroitin sulphate was associated with a [statistically] significant decrease in the incidence of joint swelling, effusion, or both." In fact, for those participants with moderate-to-severe pain, the *only* treatment that bore significant benefit was the combination of glucosamine and chondroitin sulphate, which outpaced the antiarthritic drug, Celebrex,® by a large margin.

Disregarding these findings, newswire coverage of the study celebrated the positive effects of Celebrex,® incorrectly affirming that the drug effectively reduced pain and claiming, "Nutritional supplements showed no overall benefit in treating arthritis." What the study *actually* showed was that for those patients needing it the most—individuals with moderate to severe pain—Celebrex® was *not* effective, whereas the combination of glucosamine and chondroitin *did* reduce pain in this group.

Rather than decipher the findings of the study, it appears the media took its negative spin from an editorial appearing in the same edition of the *New England Journal of Medicine*[7] that was critical of the use of glucosamine and chondroitin. The author of the critique is an individual who has received financial compensation from Pfizer Pharmaceuticals, the makers of Celebrex.® Interestingly, a number of the authors of the GAIT study also received compensation from Pfizer and McNeil Pharmaceuticals, the makers of Tylenol.®

Calcium-Vitamin D Study Flawed

In February 2006, the *New England Journal of Medicine* published the findings of an $18 million double-blind, placebo-controlled study conducted by the Women's Health Initiative (WHI) on the protective effect of calcium and vitamin D.[8] Reporting on the study, the New York *Times* declared, "Big Study Finds No Clear Benefit of Calcium Pills." In its account of the findings, the *Times* article dismissed the fact that those women who stuck to their supplementation regime experienced a 29% reduction in hip fractures, a result rarely achieved with even the strongest pharmaceuticals.

The WHI study was designed to test whether postmenopausal women given calcium and vitamin D would have a lower risk of hip fracture. The intervention group received 1,000 mg per day of calcium carbonate and 400 IU of vitamin D. While these women showed a greater preservation of hipbone density, as a whole, the decrease in the risk of fracture (12%) was not significant. Given the fact that many of the women included in the

study were under 60, and therefore not typically at risk for fractures, these results, while disappointing, are not surprising.

The results were also skewed by the fact that, by the end of the study, compliance with the prescribed daily intake was only 59%. Fully 41% of the study participants had stopped taking the prescribed daily dosage of calcium and vitamin D and 24% had discontinued the supplements altogether. This unexpectedly low compliance rate, combined with a projected hip fracture rate that was over twice that observed, reduced the power of the study to a paltry 48%. Consequently, the trial, as designed, had less chance than the flip of a coin to detect anything but the largest of differences in fracture risk.

Despite these shortcomings, when researchers looked at subgroups, a different picture emerged. They found that those women who mostly stuck to their prescribed regime had a marked 29% reduction in fractures, and women over 60 experienced a significant 21% reduction in the risk of fracture—results that are frankly remarkable, considering the many problems that clouded the data. Unfortunately, in their slanted account of the study, the media failed to acknowledge the significance of these findings.

Exclusion of Magnesium a Fatal Flaw

In designing the WHI study, the authors disregarded the fact that reduction of fracture risk is dependent upon several factors other than calcium. Studies show that magnesium is equally important in the treatment and prevention of osteoporosis, and its deficiency plays a central role in the development of the disease.[9]

Postmenopausal women and those with osteoporosis generally have low bone-magnesium content and exhibit other indicators of magnesium deficiency not seen in non-osteoporotic women.[10, 11] Moreover, calcium competes for absorption with magnesium.[12] Consequently, postmenopausal women who increase their calcium intake *without* also increasing their intake of magnesium—as was the case in the WHI study—can impair their absorption of magnesium. Within this context, the failure of the researchers to include magnesium supplementation along with the calcium and vitamin D strongly biased the findings in *favour* of harm—a glaring and irresponsible oversight for an $18 million study.

Other Crippling Design Failures

Several other factors conspired to erode the impact of the

Media Spin

A *New York Times* article on the WHI calcium study disparaged the 29% reduction in fractures (for those women who mostly stuck to their prescribed regime) as being only a "hint" of benefit.

It argued that to protect against osteoporosis women should consider, instead, taking several prescription drugs proven in clinical trials to prevent fractures.

The article failed to mention that, for some of these drugs, the benefits are more modest than those obtained through simple vitamin D and calcium supplementation; for others, the drugs only work effectively when adequate calcium and vitamin D are present.[3]

WHI calcium trial. For one, the study's prescribed dosage of 400 IU per day of vitamin D had already been shown to have a negligible effect on the risk of hip fracture.[13, 14] Most of the studies supporting a benefit provided vitamin D at a dose of 600 IU per day or higher.[15-19]

In addition, more than half the women in both the intervention and comparison groups were already taking estrogen hormone therapy, known to increase bone-mineral density. This further confounded the interpretation of the findings. Furthermore, all study participants, including those in the comparison group, were allowed to continue their personal use of calcium and vitamin D. It is, therefore, quite conceivable that some of the women (those who normally take a calcium/vitamin D supplement) in the control group were actually taking *more* calcium and vitamin D than many of those women in the intervention group who did not take the prescribed daily amount. No wonder the results are confusing!

Yet another weakness was the *type* of calcium used in the WHI trial. Calcium carbonate is one of the least bioavailable forms of calcium on the market. Because of its low solubility, absorption of calcium carbonate is highly dependent on the acidity of the stomach. Studies show that people with normal levels of stomach acid absorb only 22% of the calcium in the form of calcium carbonate (When the form of calcium is changed to the more bioavailable calcium citrate, absorption increases up to 45%). As we age, our ability to produce stomach acid is reduced. Studies reveal that individuals with insufficient stomach acid, which includes 40% of postmenopausal women, absorb as little as 4% of the oral dose of calcium carbonate. [12, 20, 21] Assuming that 40% of the intervention group was absorbing as little as 4%, or only 40 mg, of their daily calcium intake, it is astounding that any positive results were apparent. This fact, alone, so handicapped the study, it may be sufficient cause to disregard the findings altogether.

Despite the investigation's serious shortcomings and contrary to the media spin that the study "dispels long-held beliefs about

the benefits of calcium and vitamin D," the authors concluded that the results *do* provide evidence of a positive effect of calcium and vitamin D on the bone health of older postmenopausal women.

WHI Trial Results Mixed

In February 2006, the *Journal of the American Medical Association* (*JAMA*) published three studies based on data from the eight-year, $415 million WHI Dietary Modification Trial, the largest long-term trial ever conducted, involving 48,835 postmenopausal women. Reporting on two of the studies, the New York *Times* claimed that low-fat diets do not cut health risks. According to the *Times* articles, low-fat diets have virtually no effect on invasive colon cancer, heart attacks, or strokes. Canada's *Globe and Mail* followed suit, declaring, "Everything you know about your health is wrong (again)." According to journalist Margaret Wente, low-fat diets are of no benefit at all and the only people who benefit from calcium and vitamin D are those who work in the supplements industry. "Salads and supplements are useless in warding off the deadly diseases we all dread." "Give up health advice," she counselled. "You'll feel 100% better in no time."

Wente's tirade is typical of the journalistic hyperbole that serves to confuse, rather than enlighten. Her commentary is a perfect example of author Norman Mailer's caution that, "Once a newspaper touches a story, the facts are lost forever."

So, let us look at the facts. The three-part WHI dietary modification trial was designed to test whether behavioural intervention intended to produce a dietary pattern low in total fat, along with increased intakes of vegetables, fruits, and grains, would decrease the risks of cardiovascular disease, breast cancer, and colorectal cancer in postmenopausal women. The primary outcomes were fatal and non-fatal cardiac events or stroke,[22] invasive breast cancer,[23] and invasive colorectal cancer.[24] Each of these three primary outcomes was reported in a separate study.

Women in the intervention group for each study were counselled to reduce dietary fat intake to 20% of total daily caloric intake. However, over the eight-year trial period, the intervention groups achieved only 70% of this goal. This resulted in a substantial loss in the power (ranging from 40% to 60%) to detect reductions in *any* of the three outcomes. In other words, despite the trial's gigantic sample size, failure to meet the design targets for fat reduction eroded the probability of detecting benefit to about the flip of a coin.

Such studies require high power, large sample sizes, and clear discrimination between the intervention and comparison groups in order to detect relatively rare events (It is not every day you die of a heart attack or cancer). Consequently, failure to detect a preventive effect does *not* necessarily mean there is none. Although these limitations were clearly reported in all three studies, they were either not understood or purposely disregarded by the media.

Low Fat and Risk of Cardiovascular Disease

Although the WHI study investigating the effect of total dietary fat reduction on the risk of cardiovascular disease[25] found that long-term reduction of total dietary fat did not influence the risk of coronary heart disease (CHD), stroke, or cardiovascular

---

Australian Study Finds Long-term Compliance Tough

A more recent Australian study, published in the April 2006 edition of the Archives of Internal Medicine,[4] reported results similar to the WHI study. Although the main finding of the Australian study showed no statistically significant benefit to using calcium, the authors similarly noted that compliance was a huge problem—only 57% of the subjects continued the prescribed dosage of calcium throughout the five-year duration of the study.

When researchers analyzed the data from those women who consistently took their calcium, the risk of fracture fell by 34%. The authors concluded that supplementation with calcium in preventing fractures is effective only in those individuals who are compliant (take the prescribed dosage) over the long term.

According to principal author, Richard Prince, associate professor at the School of Medicine and Pharmacology, University of Western Australia, patients must make their calcium regimen a life-long habit to get the full treatment effect.

---

disease (CVD), it did achieve a modest—yet significant—reduction in CVD risk factors, including LDL-cholesterol and diastolic blood pressure. Trends toward reduction in CVD risk were evident among those women who reached the lowest intake of fat and the highest intakes of fresh fruits and vegetables, and for those women without previous CVD. Moreover, those women in the intervention group with the lowest fat intake had a lower risk of CHD than the control group.

Hobbled with a scant 40% chance of detecting a benefit, it is not surprising that the study failed to achieve statistical validity. Nevertheless, it does show just how hard it is to achieve a dramatic reduction in total fat over the long haul through behavioural intervention. Far from being the "definitive answer" on the effect of reduction of dietary fat, as suggested by the media, the study only helps confirm what we already know—simply eliminating all fats is *not* the solution to reducing cardiovascular risk.

Low Fat and Risk of Breast Cancer

Similar to the cardiovascular study, the WHI investigation on the effect of fat reduction on invasive breast cancer[26] did not find a significant decrease in cancer rates. After eight years of follow-up, the dietary intervention group had a relative decrease of 9% in the incidence of invasive breast cancer compared to the control group—a level of risk reduction that nudged, but did not achieve, statistical significance. Cancer can take years, even decades, to be expressed; considering the relatively short timeframe for this study, it is very likely that, given more time for the trial to proceed, evidence of a preventive benefit would have been revealed.

While the inability of the intervention group to reach the targeted level of fat reduction crippled the power of the trial, the investigators took care to point out certain trends in their findings. For example, it was found that those women who had the highest levels of fat intake at the start of the trial showed a stronger trend toward breast cancer reduction than did the intervention group as a whole. Such variation would *not* be expected if the dietary intervention had no effect on breast cancer. Researchers also found that the low-fat diet was associated with a 15% reduction in circulating levels of estradiol, the form of estrogen that increases the risk of breast cancer. This finding is consistent with the results of other clinical trials demonstrating the protective effect of estradiol reduction in breast cancer treatment.[27] Similarly, this would not be expected if dietary intervention had no effect on cancer risk reduction.

Simply put, we have a study that lacked the diagnostic power to do the job it was designed to do, primary results that nudged the boundaries of statistical significance, and secondary findings that exhibited supportive trends for reduction in breast cancer risk. While it is disappointing that the results were not definitive, it is hardly cause to throw out the salad and give up health advice, as one Canadian journalist espoused.

Low Fat and Risk of Colorectal Cancer

Findings in the colorectal cancer study,[28] likewise, revealed that dietary intervention did not reduce the incidence of this type of cancer in postmenopausal women. Again, this is not surprising. The study had a low probability of detecting a reduction in col-

orectal cancer risk, due to the inability of the intervention group to meet the goal for reduction in dietary fat intake.

Interestingly, the intervention was accompanied by a statistically significant decrease in total vitamin E and gamma tocopherol intakes—an outcome that does not appear to have been anticipated or controlled for. The study was designed in 1991, a time when the authors would not have been aware of the negative influence that a concomitant reduction of vitamin E, particularly gamma tocopherol, would have on cancer risk.[29] An across-the-board reduction in all fats, mandated in the study, would have inadvertently reduced blood levels of the fat-soluble tocopherols—precisely what was observed. Because of the important role played by gamma tocopherol in reducing the risk of colorectal cancer,[30-34] its concomitant reduction within the intervention group may have had the unforeseen effect of actually *enhancing* colorectal cancer risk.

Summary of the WHI Fat-loss Trial

What can we conclude from this costly three-part fat-reduction trial? The investigation was fatally flawed: to reduce total fat intake *without* consideration for the differences in *types* of fat was a fundamental error that doomed the studies from the outset. Even in 1991, when the dietary modification trial was conceived, these differences were clearly understood; however, the indiscretion does reinforce—albeit at considerable taxpayer expense—our current understanding that an across-the-board, non-discretionary reduction of total fat is of limited value in reducing CVD and cancer risks.

Scientific Sensationalism

There are some within the scientific community, anxious for their fifteen minutes of fame—not to mention future research handouts from Big Pharma—who must share the blame for much of the public's confusion about conflicting study results. Researchers and peer-reviewed journals bear a heavy responsibility and a fiduciary duty to report the results of clinical trials in a fair an unbiased manner. To their credit, the vast majority of investigators take great pains to ensure proper study design and an unbiased reporting of their findings. There are, however, exceptions to the rule. Simply put, attention-grabbing headlines and researchers elbowing for the limelight are not conducive to the advancement of good science.

Norwegian Vitamin Intervention Trial

Consider a recent study showing that modest reductions in homocysteine did not reduce heart attack risk in those with sig-

Gamma Tocopherol and Cancer

Gamma tocopherol appears to play a central role in the prevention of colorectal cancer through its ability to act as a chemo protective agent in the colon. New evidence shows that both alpha and gamma tocopherol can shield the cells lining the colon from cancerous growth.

Gamma tocopherol and its water-soluble metabolite, gamma-CEHC, have been found to combine with and remove fecal mutagens and quench oxidative stress in the colon.

nificant pre-existing arterial disease. The announcement at the 2005 European Society of Cardiology Congress that, "The homocysteine hypothesis is dead"[35] certainly got everyone's attention. According to Dr Kaare Bonaa, principal author of the study, the results "tell doctors that prescribing high doses of B vitamins will not prevent heart disease or stroke."[35] At the time of the public pronouncement, the trial had neither been peer reviewed nor published. Full details of the study were later released in March 2006, in the *New England Journal of Medicine.*[36]

The Norwegian Vitamin Intervention Trial (NORVIT) study was a secondary prevention trial—a study designed to evaluate whether treatment with folic acid and vitamin B_{12} would lower the incidence of recurrent heart attack (MI) or stroke. The trial included 3749 men and women who had experienced an acute MI within seven days prior to commencement. With a follow-up period of 40 months, the primary end-point was a composite of recurrent MI, stroke, and sudden death attributable to coronary artery disease. While the findings suggest that there was no protective effect, the data reveal a significant 28% lowering of plasma homocysteine levels.

Because it was a *secondary* prevention trial, the NORVIT study was investigating the efficacy of vitamin supplementation from a therapeutic (treatment/cure) perspective and not from one of *primary* prevention. The study participants were *already* seriously ill with heart disease prior to the commencement of the trial. Consequently, in these individuals, atherosclerotic damage was well advanced. The homocysteine hypothesis, developed in 1969, proffers that by reducing homocysteine levels as a *primary* preventive measure one can interrupt the development of atherosclerotic plaque and the consequent prothrombotic events that can lead to cardiovascular disease. The hypothesis is mute about the effectiveness of vitamin B intervention once the damage is done.

Dr Kilmer McCully, father of the homocysteine hypothesis, contends that once heart disease strikes, vitamin therapy is likely of little benefit. According to McCully, "The evidence is clear that

---

Mixed Messages on Vitamin E

A recent headline in the OB/Gyn News declared, "Vitamin E Shown Not to Reduce Cardiovascular Disease." The OB/Gyn article discussed the findings of a recent study on vitamin E, reported in JAMA (July 2005). The objective of the study was to test whether vitamin E supplementation decreased the risks of cardiovascular disease and cancer among healthy women. According to the OB/Gyn article, the study concluded, "Vitamin E showed neither benefit nor harm in all clinical parameters examined."

However, reading the fine print, an entirely different picture emerges. The study also found that for cardiovascular death there was a significant 24% reduction in risk. This is a HUGE decrease in death!

So, why was this finding not heralded as a significant discovery and headlined in all major dailies? Because cardiovascular death was not, in itself, one of the specified clinical parameters set up by the study (although it was a component of a composite parameter). Instead, the authors concluded that vitamin E supplementation is not recommended for cardiovascular disease prevention.

After all, it only reduced cardiovascular death by 24%.

---

this type of vitamin therapy is really not effective in reversing or benefiting advanced vascular disease."

So, while the NORVIT data suggests that vitamin-B therapy is not much good *after* cardiovascular disease strikes, the findings do not discredit the fact, well supported in the literature, that homocysteine is an independent risk factor in cardiovascular disease[37, 38] and one that can be effectively modulated through vitamin therapy. The NORVIT findings, despite weaknesses, certainly deserve attention; however, rumours of the demise of the homocysteine hypothesis are greatly exaggerated.

Johns Hopkins Vitamin E Trial

The 2005 Johns Hopkins University announcement that high-dose vitamin E can increase the risk of death among elderly patients certainly set the scientific world astir.[39] Here was a finding at complete odds with a surfeit of studies supporting the vitamin's protective benefits.

The study by Dr Edgar Miller and coworkers was a meta-analysis, where researchers combine data from several available clinical trials. In selecting their studies for inclusion in the analysis, the authors disqualified several smaller investigations and those where there were fewer than 10 deaths reported in the trial. This served to introduce a sampling bias, which skewed the data to *support* the argument of harm. Moreover, many of the studies included in the analysis involved elderly subjects—many of whom were already seriously ill—rather than healthy adults. In one such trial, 31% (60) of the subjects died during the study period. Nutritional intervention with gravely ill individuals can be a legitimate objective for a clinical study within a therapeutic context; however, applying the findings of such studies to the general population, within the context of prevention, is not legitimate.

On a final point, the studies included in the analysis used the synthetic (*d/l*) form of vitamin E. While there is no evidence of adverse effects from the consumption of the natural (*d*) form of vitamin E, the US National Academies of Science reports evidence of adverse effects from high doses of synthetic vitamin E, including hemorrhagic toxicity—a serious and potentially fatal complication with elderly subjects likely to be on blood thinners.

While publicly suggesting that high-level intake of vitamin E may be dangerous, the authors, in their written report, comment that, "Overall, vitamin E supplementation did not affect all-cause mortality." The authors also reported that, at the highest dosages, the risk of death was actually *lower*—a finding that the media completely missed or chose to ignore.

So, what does the Johns Hopkins study actually reveal? First, the findings fail to make the case that high-dose vitamin E intake will increase the risk of death. Most importantly, the study was conducted on elderly people, many of whom were gravely ill; therefore, whatever the findings, they simply cannot be extended to the general, healthy population.

Unfortunately, when announcing their findings, it appears that the authors disregarded their own written guidance not to generalize the results to a healthy population, thus raising the spectre of harm to the public. The fallout was predictable: giving no consideration to the wealth of scientific evidence to the contrary, the media took the bit at a full run, declaring that high-dose vitamin E may be deadly. Reacting with fear, consumers dumped vitamin E down the toilet by the truckload.

The Wrong Yardstick

As the previous examples demonstrate, media bias, conflicts of interest, and faulty study design have collectively contributed to needless confusion about the value and efficacy of nutritional supplements. However, much of the controversy also stems from peering through the narrow lens of the pharmaceutical treatment/cure model by which we currently evaluate the effectiveness of therapies. While this may be appropriate for pharmaceutical products, it is entirely inappropriate for natural health products, such as vitamins, minerals, and botanicals. Such products are, by nature, more *preventive* than *curative*. In other words, when it comes to evaluating preventive therapies, we are measuring success with the *wrong* yardstick.

To date, the vast majority of studies on the health benefits of natural health products have tested individual supplements as though they were pharmaco-therapeutic agents, able to work in isolation and expected to provide dramatic health benefits over the short term in acutely ill people. In fact, contemporary medical research is almost entirely geared toward fast-acting pharmaceutical treatment/cure protocols that are fundamentally incompatible with the evaluation of long-term primary preventive measures, such as nutritional supplementation. Consequently, natural health products are often tested inappropriately and the results interpreted incorrectly, while equally valid non-clinical confirmation, such as epidemiological* evidence, is most often discounted or completely ignored.[40]

In Search of the "Magic Bullet"

Within the prevailing pharmacologic model, the objective of most clinical trials is to evaluate a single biochemical entity for its therapeutic effect on a particular symptom or disease. Once a measurable therapeutic effect has been established, the drug can be patented and sold at great profit by pharmaceutical companies more interested in the bottom line than in the patient. This is a system of high-tech, disease-centered medicine, based on a promise of powerful fast-acting drugs that produce therapeutic results overnight.[40]

Isolating and testing a single compound may make for good science in the test tube, but it is *not* appropriate from a holistic perspective when dealing with a complex biological system. The human body does not rely on a single nutrient to prevent or treat a particular ailment or disease; instead, it summons the powers of the intricate biochemical synergies that exist *between* nutrients. For this reason, evaluating individual nutrients in isolation from others will inevitably lead to scientific distortions and invalid conclusions.

A good example of the error of this approach is the alpha tocopherol and beta-carotene cancer prevention study conducted in Finland in 1994.[41] The initial results of this study, when the effects of beta-carotene (a type of antioxidant) were viewed in isolation, led to the erroneous conclusion that high levels of beta-carotene increased the risk of cancer in male smokers.

Despite objections that the study was flawed, the charge stuck and vitamin use dropped worldwide. Fast-forward to July 2004, when the same data, using total antioxidant status, was reviewed in the *American Journal of Epidemiology*.[42] When *total* antioxidant intake was evaluated, the findings of the original study were found to be in error. The new analysis—using the *same* data as the original study—came to a remarkably different observation: beta-carotene in combination with other dietary antioxidants significantly *reduced* cancer risk in the same male smokers. The authors concluded, "These findings support the hypothesis that a combination of dietary antioxidants reduces lung cancer risk in male smokers." So, there you have it: two different paradigms, two different conclusions—same data.

The fact is, humans require a full range of some 25 or more essential vitamins, minerals, and antioxidants in properly balanced amounts to support good health. Vitamins and minerals do not work well in isolation; they work best in *teams* to support the myriad of cellular metabolic functions. Similarly, antioxidants work most effectively when they work together. Each plays a supportive role in regenerating other antioxidants and in quenching the chain-like series of oxidative reactions that can precipitate from a single oxidative event.

According to nutritional researcher, Dr Tim Wood, high doses of a single nutrient represent an incomplete and inappropriate approach to nutritional therapy and should not be evaluated within that context. "This would be analogous to testing the hypothesis that broccoli has cancer-preventive properties by putting people on a broccoli-only diet. It's not likely to work, and it carries the risk of creating severe nutrient imbalances, unwanted side effects, and misleading experimental artefacts." [40]

A Disease-centered Model

The other defining characteristic of the pharmaceutical model is that it is *disease-centered*. Clinical trials focus on treating subjects who are already ill. This is known as *secondary* prevention, which is about preventing further progression of a disease that people already have. It is fundamentally different from *primary* prevention, which is about preventing the development of chronic disorders in the first place. Moreover, because chronic diseases like heart disease and osteoporosis develop over a lifetime, primary prevention needs to be viewed as a lifelong undertaking—not as a quick fix after the fact.

Within this context, many of the trials discussed earlier in this chapter were clearly secondary prevention trials:

✔ The omega-3 fish oil study evaluated the efficacy of high-dose fish oil on subjects already ill with heart disease and angina.

✔ The glucosamine trial investigated the antiarthritic effects of glucosamine and chondroitin on individuals already suffering from knee pain.

✔ The calcium trial involved postmenopausal women who, at that stage of their lives, were predisposed to osteoporosis.

✔ The vitamin E study was conducted on elderly individuals, most of whom were already seriously ill with cardiovascular disease.

To take the findings of such investigations and attribute them

---

* Epidemiology is the study of the factors affecting the health of communities and populations. A cornerstone of public health research, its use is highly regarded in evidence-based medicine for the identification of risk factors for various disease states.

to the general, healthy population amounts to a scientific slight-of-hand. As we have seen in several cases, once the findings of these studies are released to the media, this is exactly what occurs. No wonder the public is confused.

Prevention vs. Cure

Is it possible for something to be an effective primary preventive agent without being an effective secondary preventive agent? In his thesis, *The Case for Nutritional Supplements*,[40] Dr Wood presents the following analogy:

> *Dentists tell us to floss our teeth to prevent tooth decay and avoid the need for root canal surgery. If you were to select a group of people with advanced tooth decay, many who had chronic toothaches, and divide them into two groups, telling one to floss regularly and the other to refrain from flossing, what do you think would happen? Would the flossing group experience significantly fewer toothaches, fewer tooth extractions, and fewer root canal surgeries in the short term? Probably not—the flossing came too late in the day to change the course of the existing disease.*

Does this mean that flossing is useless? It depends upon your paradigm. Considered within the context of treatment/cure, flossing probably *is* useless; but, as a preventive measure, it is *very* effective. So, too, it is with natural health products.

The value of nutritional supplementation lies more in its *preventive* nature than in its curative powers. For example, epidemiological research supports the belief that vitamin E acting as an antioxidant over the long term helps prevent atherosclerosis. However, vitamin E may be completely ineffective in preventing the onset of a heart attack or stroke brought on by the rupture of an existing atherosclerotic plaque. The findings of several clinical studies support this view. As such, vitamin E supplementation may pass muster as an effective long-term measure for the *primary* prevention of heart disease, yet it may fail the test using standard clinical trial parameters designed to evaluate treatment/cure (*secondary* prevention). This does not mean that vitamin E is useless. It means we must come to recognize that its value as an agent in *prevention* is fundamentally different from its value as an agent of *intervention*.

Consequently, as instruments of *wellness*, natural health products lie outside the acute-care paradigm. For this reason, the efficacy of products and therapies intended for the maintenance of health (primary prevention) must not be viewed through the clinical lens of treatment/cure (secondary prevention). When they are evaluated within that paradigm for short-term treatment/curative benefits, they often fail. These failures are then publicly paraded by the media—cheered on by the pharmaceutical cartel—as evidence that vitamins, minerals, and other natural health products have no health benefit.

Clearly, it is time to develop a new paradigm.

Tools for a New Paradigm

As Albert Einstein once said, "The significant problems we face cannot be solved at the same level of thinking we were at when we created them." In other words, we have to change our ways of thinking, and we need to develop new tools for the job. One of those tools is the use of epidemiological studies as a recognized standard of evidence. While less controlled and precise than the standard clinical trial, such studies more easily embrace long timeframes and, as such, are invaluable in assessing preventive measures.[40] Another approach is to consider the use of long-term trials, modified to evaluate the preventive effect of multiple nutrients working *in concert* within healthy populations. Such studies would undoubtedly be time-consuming and costly. This is, however, the price of admission for a final resolution of the question of efficacy of complementary therapies.

Section III

Rating the Products

This section provides the reader
with an in-depth look at:

■ How the Comparisons are Made
■ Product Rating Criteria
■ NutriSearch Medals of Achievement

Construction of the Blended Standard *and its use in rating all
nutritional products evaluated in this guide is discussed. A
biographical profile of all published authorities, upon whose
recommendations the* Blended Standard *is based, is provided.
An overview of each of the 18 product-rating criteria is given
and an explanation of the* NutriSearch Medal of
Achievement Program™ *for all qualifying five-star products is
provided.*

Facts are the air of scientists. Without them you can never fly.
—*Linus Pauling (1901-1994)*
Nobel Laureate in Chemistry and Peace

CHAPTER EIGHT

HOW THE COMPARISONS ARE MADE

This chapter explains the *Blended Standard*, a compilation of recommended daily nutritional intakes deemed important for long-term health. These intakes are derived from the suggested daily intakes published by 12 independent nutritional authorities.

The *Blended Standard* is the foundation for our analytical model. This model provides a quantitative method for rating nutritional products relative to an established benchmark based on the *Blended Standard*. With this completely revised fourth edition of the *Comparative Guide*, we have added five published works to our seven original authorities (cited in the 3rd edition of our guide), providing us with an enhanced, comprehensive listing of recommended nutritional intakes.

The authors that we cite are acknowledged within their respective scientific, medical, and naturopathic fields. Each has published one or more works, and each has provided specific recommendations for daily nutritional intakes. A short biographical background on each authority is provided below:

Phyllis Balch, CNC

For more than 20 years before her death in 2004, Ms Balch was a leading nutritional consultant. Recognized for her expertise in nutrition-based therapies, she testified before the US Congress on the efficacy of natural healing. She has also authored several best-selling books, including: *Prescription for Dietary Wellness: Using Foods to Heal; Prescription for Herbal Healing: An Easy-to-Use A-Z Reference to Hundreds of Common Disorders and Their Herbal Remedies;* and *Prescription for Nutritional Healing: the A-to-Z Guide to Supplements,* co-authored by **Dr James Balch**. Dr Balch is a certified urologist, a graduate of Indiana University School of Medicine, a member of the American Medical Association, and a Fellow of the American College of Surgeons. Because of the co-authorship of *Prescription for Nutritional Healing (2002)*, on which we base their recommendations, we recognize the authors as a single reference source.

Michael Colgan, PhD, CCN

Dr Colgan is a best-selling author and internationally acclaimed speaker on anti-aging, sports nutrition, and hormonal health. As a senior member of the Science Faculty of the University of Auckland, Dr Colgan taught Human Sciences and conducted research on aging and physical performance. His first public book, *Your Personal Vitamin Profile*, written while a visiting scholar at the Rockefeller University in New York, was

considered a definitive guide for accurate, scientifically researched nutritional information. He has subsequently authored *Hormonal Health: Nutritional and Hormonal Strategies for Emotional Well-Being and Intellectual Longevity* and *The New Nutrition: Medicine for the Millennium*. Dr Colgan is a member of the American College of Sports Medicine, the New York Academy of Sciences, and the British Society for Nutritional Medicine. He also serves on the Council of the International and American Association of Clinical Nutritionists and the Editorial Board of the *Journal of Applied Nutrition*. In addition, he has consulted for the US National Institute on Aging and the New Zealand government. Now Chairman of the Colgan Institute, Salt Spring Island, British Columbia, Dr Colgan and the Colgan Institute are known internationally for their research in sports nutrition.

Earl Mindell, RPh, MH

Earl Mindell has written 48 books on nutrition and health, including the best-seller, *Dr Mindell's Vitamin Bible*, published in the mid 1980s. Subsequent publications include *Earl Mindell's Vitamin Bible for the 21st Century; Dr Mindell's What You Should Know About Creating Your Own Personal Health Plan; Earl Mindell's Herb Bible; Earl Mindell's Food as Medicine; Shaping up with Vitamins;* and *Earl Mindell's Anti-Aging Bible*. Mindell received a Bachelor of Science in Pharmacy from North Dakota State University in 1964, earning his Master's in Herbal Medicine from Dominion Herbal College in 1995. He is a registered pharmacist in the State of California and is a Fellow of the British Institute of Homeopathy. Mindell serves as a Director of the Corporate Board for the Illinois College of Physicians and Surgeons and is a professor of nutrition. While some of his theories on nutrition have been controversial, he is recognized for introducing the benefits of soy with his book, *Soy Miracle*. Due to his notability as a nutritionist and pharmacologist, Mindell is a frequent guest on national radio and television programs.

Michael Murray, ND

Dr Murray is one of the world's leading authorities on natural medicine. He is a graduate and faculty member of Bastyr University, Seattle, Washington, where he also serves on the Board of Trustees. A meticulously researched author and lecturer, Dr Murray has published more than 20 books on natural medicine, including the *Encyclopedia of Natural Medicine* and the *Encylopedia of Nutritional Supplements,* from which we base his recommendations. In addition to his private practice as a consultant to the health food industry, he has been instrumental in bringing many effective natural products to North America (including glucosamine sulphate, St. John's wort extract, *Ginkgo biloba* extract, silymarin, and enteric-coated peppermint oil). Dr Murray is currently Director of Product Development and Education for Natural Factors, manufacturers of quality natural health products.

Richard Passwater, PhD

Dr Passwater received his BS in Chemistry from the University of Delaware in 1959 and his PhD in Biochemistry from Bernadean University (Nevada) in 1975. He was certified by the American Chemical Society in 1959 and in 1984 was elected Fellow of the American Institute of Chemistry. Twice honoured by the Committee for World Health (1978 & 1980), his scientific contributions have garnered him worldwide recognition. Dr Passwater's discovery of biological antioxidant synergism in 1962 has been the focus of his research since that time. In 1973, Dr Passwater's article, *Cancer: New Directions,* was the first to report that a synergistic combination of antioxidant nutrients significantly reduces cancer incidence. He was the first to publish an epidemiological study showing that vitamin E reduces heart disease risk. His research with selenium led to innovations in reducing free radical pathology, slowing the aging process, and reducing cancer incidence; his investigations into the role of chromium shed light on the conundrum of obesity and diabetes. Dr Passwater's pioneering work with Drs Linus Pauling and James Enstrom highlighted the protective effect of vitamin E against heart disease. His best selling book, *Supernutrition: Megavitamin Revolution*, published in 1975, is credited with legitimizing megavitamin therapy; many leading nutritional researchers credit this book with igniting their interest in nutrition. Dr Passwater's most recent public books include *The Antioxidants; The New Supernutrition;* and *Cancer Prevention and Nutritional Therapies.* He is the nutrition editor for *The Experts Journal of Optimal Health* and the scientific editor for *Whole Foods*, and he serves on the editorial board of the *Journal of Applied Nutrition.* Dr Passwater is the Director of the Solgar Nutritional Research Center in Berlin, Maryland.

Ray Strand, MD

Dr Ray Strand is a graduate of the University of Colorado Medical School (1971) and completed his postgraduate education at Mercy Hospital in San Diego. He has practised family medicine for over 30 years, focussing over the past decade on nutritional medicine. An articulate advocate for the integration of optimal nutrition and advanced nutritional therapies in preventive healthcare, he is a member of the Medical Advisory Board of USANA Health Sciences. Dr Strand has lectured on nutritional medicine across the United States, Canada, Australia, New Zealand, and England. His publications include *Bionutrition: Winning the War Within; Death by Prescription; Healthy for Life; What Your Doctor Doesn't Know About Nutritional Medicine May Be Killing You; Preventing Diabetes;* and *Living by Design.*

Julian Whitaker, MD

Dr Julian Whitaker graduated from Dartmouth College in 1966 and earned his medical degree at Emory University Medical School in Atlanta in 1970, completing his internship at Grady Memorial Hospital, also in Atlanta. Early in his career, Dr Whitaker was struck by the preventive and healing powers of nutrition and natural therapies. In 1974, Dr Whitaker was instrumental in forming the California Orthomolecular Medical Society, its name borrowed from a term coined by Dr Linus Pauling and meaning "the preservation of good health and the treatment of disease by varying the concentrations in the human body of substances that are normally present in the body and are required for health." Practising at the Pritikin Longevity Center subsequent to 1976, Dr Whitaker remarked, "I saw patients get well—not as a result of dangerous drugs or risky surgical procedures, but through the powerful effects of a low-fat, high complex carbohydrate diet and exercise. And not only did these patients drop their medications, they *dropped their diseases*." In 1979, he launched the Whitaker Wellness Institute Medical Clinic in Newport Beach, California, where patients participate in an intensive program of diet, exercise, nutritional and herbal supplementation, and lifestyle change. Dr Whitaker publishes a monthly newsletter, *Health & Healing,* and is the author of several popular books, including *Reversing Diabetes; Reversing Heart Disease;* and *Dr Whitaker's Guide to Natural Healing.* Board certified in anti-aging medicine, Dr Whitaker belongs to the American College for Advancement in Medicine and is a founding member of the American Preventive Medicine Association.

New to this edition of the guide, we include the published recommendations of the following nutritional authorities who, with the exception of one, have published a recognized work subsequent to the release of the last edition of the Comparative Guide in 2003:

Robert Atkins, MD

The late Dr Atkins was the founder and medical director of the Atkins Center for Complementary Medicine, a world-renowned integrative medical center in New York City. An early proponent of the value of nutritional supplementation, Dr Atkins' bestselling book, *Dr Atkins' Vita-Nutrient Solution,* stresses the importance of daily supplementation in overcoming nutritional deficiencies found in our foods today. Until his accidental death in 2003, Dr Atkins was a practising physician, specializing in cardiology and internal medicine, and a professor of medicine at Capital University of Integrative Medicine. Dr Atkins first gained recognition in 1972 with the publication of his first book, *Dr Atkins' Diet Revolution.* Subsequent to this best-selling publication, he also wrote *Dr Atkins' Nutrition Breakthrough* and *Dr Atkins' Health Revolution,* and was host of a syndicated radio show, *Your Health Choices,* which reached over one million listeners each month.

Terry Grossman, MD and Ray Kurzweil

Dr Grossman and Ray Kurzweil are co-authors of *Fantastic Voyage*, an insightful book on the science behind radical life extension. Dr Grossman is the founder and medical director of Frontier Medical Institute in Denver, Colorado. A diplomat of the American Board of Chelation Therapy (ABCT) and a member of ACAM (The American Academy for Advancement of Medicine), IOMA (The International Oxidative Medicine Association), and A4M (The American Academy of Anti-aging Medicine), Dr Grossman's special field of interest is nutritional medicine. He is licensed as a homeopathic medical doctor and a naturopathic medical doctor. He is assistant professor of family practice at The University of Colorado School of Medicine and lectures frequently on topics related to alternative medicine. Dr Grossman is also a leading scientific expert in longevity. He is certified in anti-aging medicine and lectures internationally on longevity and anti-aging strategies. **Ray Kurzweil** is one of the world's leading inventors, thinkers, and futurists. Called the "restless genius" by the *Wall Street Journal* and the "ultimate thinking machine" by *Forbes* magazine, Kurzweil's ideas are touted by prominent individuals from Bill Gates to Bill Clinton. He is the author of three previous books, *The Age of Spiritual Machines; The 10% Solution for a Healthy Life;* and *The Age of Intelligent Machines.* He is a recipient of the $500,000 Lemelson-MIT Prize, the largest award for invention and innovation in the US, and was inducted in 2002 into the National Inventor Hall of Fame for his work in computer systems. He also received the 1999 National Medal of Technology, America's highest honour in technology, from President Clinton and is the recipient of the 1994 Dickson Prize, Carnegie Mellon University's top science prize. In 1988, Kursweil was named Inventor of the Year by MIT and the Boston Museum of Science. He was also named Honorary Chairman for Innovation of the White House Conference on Small Business by President Reagan in 1986 and has received honours from Presidents Clinton, Reagan, and Johnson.

Jane Higdon, PhD

Until her tragic death in a cycling accident in the summer of 2006, Dr Higdon was a Research Associate at the Linus Pauling Institute, Oregon State University, in Corvallis, Oregon. With over 13 years of experience as a certified family nurse practitioner, she held a Master of Science in nursing and a Master of Science in exercise physiology, as well as a Doctorate in nutrition. The Linus Pauling Institute was established in 1996 at Oregon State University. Its mission is to determine the function and role of micronutrients and phytochemicals in promoting optimum health and in preventing and treating disease. The Institute conducts research to determine the role of oxidative stress and antioxidants in human health and disease. More than 65 scientists in ten laboratories focus their research on aging, cancer, heart disease, and neurodegenerative disease.

Philip Lee Miller, MD and Life Extension Foundation

Dr Miller is co-author of *The Life Extension Revolution: The New Science of Growing Older Without Aging* (2005) and is the founder and medical director of the Los Gatos Longevity Institute. A practising physician for over 30 years, he is a diplomat of the American Board of Anti-Aging Medicine and serves on the Medical Advisory Board of Life Extension Foundation (LEF), the world's largest organization dedicated to the science of pre-

venting and treating degenerative disease and aging. In addition to developing unique disease treatment protocols, LEF funds pioneering scientific research aimed at achieving an extended, healthy lifespan. At the heart of Life Extension's mission are its research programs for identifying and developing new therapies to slow and reverse the deterioration associated with aging.

Nicholas Perricone, MD

Dr Perricone is a board-certified clinical and research dermatologist. Dr Periconne completed his internship in Pediatrics at Yale Medical School and his Dermatology Residency at Ford Medical Center. An internationally recognized anti-aging expert, award-winning inventor, and a respected scientific researcher, Dr Perricone is an Adjunct Professor of Medicine at the Michigan State University's College of Human Medicine. He is certified by the American Board of Dermatology, is a Fellow of the New York Academy of Sciences, and a Fellow of the American College of Nutrition. He is also a Fellow of the American Academy of Dermatology and the Society of Investigative Dermatology. Dr Perricone has served as Assistant Clinical Professor of Dermatology at Yale School of Medicine and as Chief of Dermatology at the state of Connecticut's Veterans Hospital. He is author of *The Perricone Weight-loss Diet* and *The Acne Prescription.* Dr Periconne has also written three New York *Times* bestsellers: *The Wrinkle Cure; The Perricone Prescription;* and *The Perricone Promise.* His work has been the focus of a number of award-winning PBS specials.

Each of the preceding authors has published comprehensive recommendations for daily nutritional intakes through supplementation. In borrowing from their scientific insights to construct our analytical standard, we recognize the immense contribution that each has made, individually and collectively, to the advancement of scientific knowledge and the pursuit of optimal health.

Creation of the *Blended Standard*

To construct our analytical model, we pool the individual recommendations for daily nutrient intakes from our 12 cited authorities. While each author's recommendations may have characteristics not recognized by the others, there is substantial commonality amongst the whole. To create our blended nutritional standard (*Blended Standard*) we exploit these areas of commonality.

For a nutrient to qualify for inclusion in the *Blended Standard,* 3 of the 12 authorities must cite a recommended daily intake for the specified nutrient. In all, 47 nutrient categories, consisting of 19 vitamins or vitamin-like factors, 13 minerals, 5 phytonutrient complexes, 3 omega fatty acids, and 7 other nutritional factors, are identified and incorporated into this revised standard. The recommended daily intake for each nutrient is determined, wherever possible, by calculating the median value from those authorities who provide a specific dosage recommendation. In some cases, where recent scientific evidence has eclipsed the recommendations, *NutriSearch* provides a recommended daily intake—or removes a previously recommended nutrient—based upon these new findings.

Modifications from Previous Editions

In addition to broadening our field of cited authorities for this edition of the *Comparative Guide*, there are four instances where recent scientific findings have given us reason to both add and delete particular nutrients from the standard used in previous editions of the guide. These nutrients include gamma tocopherol, polyphenol compounds, iron, and para-aminobenzoic acid (PABA).

Gamma Tocopherol

Gamma tocopherol, an isomeric form of vitamin E found in high levels in the diet, is added as a required nutrient to our *Blended Standard.* The ability of gamma tocopherol to reduce the risks of cardiovascular disease, colorectal cancer, and dementia, as well as its recently discovered anti-inflammatory properties, have brought this little-recognized nutrient to the forefront of nutritional research.[1]

Polyphenols

The biochemistry of polyphenols is an emerging area of nutritional research that shows great promise in reducing inflammation and oxidative stress; however, quantitative consensus among our cited nutritional authorities is not yet available. While it is recognized that supplementation with polyphenols is highly desired, no median recommended daily intake, specific to phenolic compounds, is provided. Based on human consumption studies, research by Visioli and coworkers[2] suggests a recommended daily intake of 50 mg of olive oil, corresponding to approximately 25 mg of phenolic compounds. According to the authors, this amount is in the order of intake associated with a lower incidence of cardiovascular disease.

Iron

Recent evidence has shown that continuous low-dose supplementation with iron at as little as 31.25 mg per week (4.5 mg/day) over one year significantly increases the risk of iron overload and is an independent risk factor for iron overload toxicity.[3] Based upon this recent finding and the cautionary statements issued by several of our cited authorities regarding the use of iron as a supplement, we have discontinued its inclusion in our *Blended Standard.* However, many nutritional supplements have significant levels of iron in their formulations; therefore, iron continues to be included in our Potential Toxicities criterion.

Para-Aminobenzoic Acid (PABA)

The use of PABA as a dietary supplement receives mixed support in the scientific community. Some authorities argue that PABA has little or no support as an essential nutrient;[4] others contend that the nutrient is useful in fighting fatigue, treating chemical sensitivities, and in reducing cellular damage from ozone and other atmospheric pollutants.[5] Much of the confusion over the inclusion of PABA as a nutritional supplement pertains to the fact that PABA is converted in the human gut to folic acid by the action of intestinal bacteria. While the conversion rate is low, it is believed that much of the benefit ascribed to PABA is, in fact, derived from its conversion to and subsequent absorption as folic acid.

A thorough examination of the literature provides scant evidence of the efficacy of PABA in clinical trials, particularly at the milligram dosage ranges required for daily supplementation in a multiple vitamin. As well, most quality nutritional supplements are now providing high levels of folic acid in their formulations, some up to 1,000 mg. Consequently, there does not appear to be a need for additional supplementation with PABA. Moreover, the noted therapeutic benefits of PABA require multi-gram doses that are simply beyond the ability of a multiple vitamin tablet to deliver.

Authors' Recommendations

In addition to these modifications, several nutrients have been added to the *Blended Standard* due to the weight of the recommendations made by our newly cited authorities. Such nutrients include alpha-linolenic acid, eicosapentaenoic and docosahexaenoic acids, carnosine, acetyl l-carnitine and l-carnitine, trimethylglycine, mixed carotenoids, and lutein and zeaxanthin. These new nutrients comprise an enhanced *Blended Standard* that contains a total of 47 nutrients and nutrient categories.

With the exception of Passwater's recommendations (which are divided into four fitness categories based on diet, level of health, and level of physical activity), the recommended daily intakes published by each authority are presented for the general adult population. Passwater's lower two categories (C and D) are selected to develop the *Blended Standard.* These categories represent individuals who have poor-to-average diets, poor-to-average health, have little or no exercise and live a sedentary lifestyle. We chose these categories because they best represent today's general physiologic profile of the North American adult population. Using the range of values within these two categories, the minimum and maximum recommended daily intakes for each nutrient are determined.

Murray,[6] Passwater,[7] Strand,[8,9] Mindell,[10] Whitaker,[11] Balch,[12,13] and Kurzweil and Grossman[14] provide a range of recommended intakes for each nutrient. Colgan,[15] Perricone,[16] Atkins,[17] Miller,[18] and Higdon[19] generally cite a specified value. Therefore, for each authority, the *averaged* value for each nutrient is determined. Pooling these averaged values, the *median* recommended intake for each nutrient is calculated. The median (middle) value is used in preference to the mean (average) value because it is a better estimate of central tendency for the data derived from the small population of cited authorities.

The *Table of Recommended Daily Intakes* (Table 11-3, page 78) shows the specific nutritional recommendations of each authority, along with the median value for each nutrient incorporated into the *Blended Standard* derived from these recommendations.

Limitations of the Study

The products reviewed in this comparison represent a vast range of nutritional options available in the marketplace today. By necessity, *NutriSearch* has limited the selection to include only those products that meet specified criteria.

A qualifying product:

✔ must comprise a broad-spectrum nutritional supplement formulated for general preventive maintenance rather than a specified therapeutic use;

✔ must contain a comprehensive assortment of both minerals and vitamins;

✔ may contain assorted antioxidants and phytonutrients;

✔ must be formulated in tablet, capsule, powder, or liquid form and have a specified daily dosage; and

✔ must provide a comprehensive list of ingredients, along with specified amounts (in µg, mg or IU) for each nutrient in the formulation.

Individual products may contain nutrients other than those listed in the *Blended Standard*. With the exception of iron,* nutrients are *not* included in the comparison if those nutrients are not identified in the *Blended Standard*. Additionally, while a manufacturer may list a nutrient identified in the *Blended Standard*, the nutrient is not included in the comparison if the exact amount (µg, mg or IU) of the nutrient is not provided or cannot be determined. For example, if vitamin A in a product is shown as "5,000 IU of vitamin A with beta-carotene" the entire amount is entered as vitamin A because the precise amount of beta-carotene cannot be determined.

In the initial determination of product ratings, the presence or absence of various fillers, additives, preservatives, or coatings is not assessed. The appraisal of excipients, non-active ingredients, and possible contaminants more appropriately belongs as part of a comprehensive evaluation of the manufacturing process for each product. This generally requires an inspection of the manufacturing plant and an evaluation of its operational procedures. So, too, verification of product identity, potency, and purity requires the services of an analytical laboratory, at considerable cost for each product assayed. Consequently, compliance with current Good Manufacturing Practices (cGMP) and laboratory-based product quality verification are not evaluated in our initial product rating. Instead, products achieving a five-star rating, based on labelling criteria, are invited by *NutriSearch* to voluntarily demonstrate their commitment to product quality.

Each five-star recipient identified in our initial product-content analysis receives a personalized letter from NutriSearch encouraging them to further demonstrate their commitment to product quality by providing proof of their level of GMP compliance and by furnishing a notarized certificate of analysis for their product(s). For manufacturers, this generally requires an audit of their manufacturing practices for the level of GMP compliance and an independent laboratory analysis of product content, including identity, potency, and purity.

Manufacturers who provide such standards of evidence qualify for the *NutriSearch Medal of Achievement Program,*™ an award-based recognition program created by NutriSearch to highlight those manufacturers who have gone that extra mile to ensure exceptional product quality and safety. For more information on the requirements for GMP compliance, product testing, and the *NutriSearch Medal of Achievement Program,*™ please see Chapter 10.

Products with Phytonutrients

In constructing the *Blended Standard,* the bioflavonoids, including citrus flavonoids, soy isoflavones, quercetin, quercitrin, hesperidin, rutin, bilberry, and assorted berry extracts are listed under the category of Mixed Bioflavonoids. Phenolic compounds, including the olive-based polyphenols, green tea extract, and turmeric extract (curcumin), are listed under the category of Phenolic Compounds. The procyanidolic oligomers (PCOs), including resveratrol, grape seed extract, and pine bark extract, form a third component of the bioflavonoid complex. These are combined within the category of Mixed Bioflavonoids for inclusion in the *Blended Standard*.

Products with Ingredients Not Listed

Some products contain one or more ingredients not included in the *Blended Standard*. These products often include macronutritional components, such as amino acids, proteins, and assorted carbohydrate and nucleic acid complexes, which are easily obtained from the diet. Other products contain herbal components that, while recognized for their merit, are not generally acknowledged by the cited nutritional authorities whose published recommendations form the basis of the rating criteria.

Where a product contains ingredients not generally acknowledged in the recommendations from our cited authorities, those ingredients are deemed non-essential for the purpose of this comparison.

Products with Unspecified Dosages

In a few cases, the recommended daily dose of a product is unavailable from the data collected or the information provided by the company. In such cases, the daily dose is derived by adjusting the daily intake to provide for up to 400 IU of vitamin D, as indicated in the product formulation. For the vast majority of nutritional supplements, this is a standard daily dosage for vitamin D. In order to control for potential toxicity from excessive levels of vitamin A, the daily dosage of products containing vitamin A is limited to a maximum of 10,000 IU of vitamin A. Products with a derived daily dosage are clearly identified with an appropriate notation in the Appendices.

Combination Products

Many manufacturers are now selling nutritional products as packaged combinations of individual classes of nutrients. For the purpose of this comparison, we define these products as *combination* products because they consist of several individual products manufactured separately by the same company. A good example is a daily pack containing a company's foundational multiple vitamin/mineral, with an added calcium/magnesium supplement, perhaps an added phytonutrient complex (such as grape seed extract), and added essential fatty acids (perhaps supplied as a gelcap). While each supplement may be sold individually, they have been grouped for convenience into a daily pack. Such a product would not qualify as a *stand-alone* product, which we describe as

---

* Due to recent findings on its potential toxicity, we have eliminated iron as a component of the *Blended Standard*; however, because of its continued use in many supplements, iron continues to be included in the criterion for potential toxicity.

a single broad-spectrum multiple vitamin/mineral product provided in up to two tablets or capsules at a single serving.

For the purpose of this comparison, a *combination product* is defined as a product that contains more than two different tablets or capsules in a single serving.

Another example of a combination product is one that contains a multiple vitamin/mineral tablet, a calcium tablet, and an essential fatty acid gel-cap (three tablets/capsules in a single dose). Comparing this combination product with a stand-alone product would not be equitable because a stand-alone multiple is limited in the amounts and types of ingredients that it can include in tableted or capsule form. Formulating a broad-spectrum, vitamin/mineral tablet that also includes substantial amounts of essential fatty acids proves to be problematic when it comes to issues of tableting, stability, and shelf life. Although minor amounts can be added when stabilized in powdered form, the levels of fatty acids required for efficacy are considerably higher than can be put into a powder. Recognition of the limits of such technical challenges is the reason we choose to separate such products into the new category, called *Combination Products*.

Combination products are rated using the same criteria as the stand-alone products; however, the criteria for Completeness, Potency, and Inflammation Control for combination products also include the three essential fatty acids, EPA, DHA, and alpha-linolenic acid, which are not included in the same criteria for stand-alone products (for the reasons described earlier). Consequently, for purposes of fair comparison, combination products are evaluated separately from stand-alone products.

The Nutrient Profiles and Health Support Profiles for products reviewed in this guide are provided in Section V.

Sources of Information

The formulations of the nutritional products included in this comparative guide are obtained from information provided through:
✔ retail product labels;
✔ product monographs;
✔ corporate web sites; and
✔ direct communication with the manufacturer.

Interpreting the Graphs

The top-rated products (rating three stars and above) are shown graphically in Section V; each product is represented by two graphs. The vertical-bar graphs on the left-hand side of each page are the *Nutrient Profiles* for each product. The horizontal-bar graphs on the right-hand side of each page are the *Health Support Profiles* for each product.

At least one product from each manufacturer is graphically represented. Where a manufacturer has more than one product, NutriSearch will choose the product with the highest rating relative to all products evaluated from that manufacturer. In some cases, where a manufacturer offers products based on gender (separate supplements for men and women), more than one product may be graphically represented.

Nutrient Profile Graphs

These graphs highlight the potencies of each nutrient relative to the recommendations of the *Blended Standard*. For each product evaluated, the nutrient content is compared to that of the *Blended Standard*, based on the manufacturer's labelling information, including the maximum recommended daily dose. Each comparison rests on the assumption that the labelling is correct with respect to actual composition and dosage. The amount (μg, mg, or IU) of each nutrient in the product is compared to the *Blended Standard* for that nutrient.

With the exception of iron, which is no longer in the *Blended Standard* (but continues to be included in the graphs because of its potential toxicity), the nutrients included in the graphs are *only* those that are contained in the *Blended Standard*. In other words, if a nutrient (other than iron) is *not* included in the *Blended Standard* it is *not* included in the graph. The graphs are based on relative percentage values because this provides the simplest means of comparing different units of measure (μg, mg, or IU). The amount of each nutrient in the *Blended Standard*, therefore, represents 100% for that nutrient.

Colour of Graphs

Note that each graph changes colour for those nutrients that exceed 100% of the recommended daily intake, based on the *Blended Standard*. This makes it easy to depict those nutrients in a product that meet or exceed the recommended daily intakes of the *Blended Standard*. Each bar shown in dark blue represents the amount, up to 100%, of the daily intake of a nutrient in a product, compared to the recommended daily intake for that nutrient in the *Blended Standard*. Each bar shown in light blue represents the amount that a nutrient in a product exceeds 100% of the recommended daily intake for that nutrient in the *Blended Standard*. For the purpose of visual standardization, any daily intakes exceeding 150% of the *Blended Standard* are truncated (capped).

For vitamin A, daily intake up to 100% of the *Blended Standard* is highlighted in yellow. This simply denotes the need for cautionary use of this particular nutrient. Intake exceeding 100% of the value listed in the *Blended Standard* is highlighted in red. A red bar indicates that the level of vitamin A in the product, if taken over an extended period, raises concern with regard to potential toxicity (for more information on the potential toxicity of vitamin A, please see Chapter 9).

While iron was expunged from the *Blended Standard*, it continues to be included in the Nutrient Profiles of those products containing iron, due to its potential for cumulative toxicity. For iron, daily intake up to 5 mg/day is highlighted in yellow. This simply denotes the need for cautionary use of this particular nutrient. Intake exceeding 5 mg/day is highlighted in red. A red bar indicates that the level of iron in the product, if taken over an extended period, raises concern with regard to potential toxicity (for more information on the potential toxicity of iron, please read Chapter 9).

The Legend

A numerical nutrient code related to the specific nutrients in the *Blended Standard* is provided in the legend, located in the upper left-hand corner of each left-hand page. The legend makes it easier for the reader to determine the identity and potency of individual nutrients in a product. To identify the nutrient and its relative potency, its numerical value on the graph is matched to the numerical code in the legend.

Health Support Profile Graphs

New to this edition of the guide is the *Health Support Profile* **graph.** The *Health Support Profile* provides the consumer with a clear picture of how a product rates in each of the 18 analytical criteria. These horizontal bar graphs, shown on the right-hand sides of the product pages in Section V, provide the reader with an in-depth look at the strengths of each product and allow for the identification of products according to criteria that may be of particular interest (e.g. Heart Health, Liver Health, Antioxidant Support, etc). The *Health Support Profile* for a product is located to the immediate right of the *Nutrient Profile* for that same product on the page.

The length of the horizontal bars in the *Health Support Profile* of a product shows whether a product's rating is *low, moderate,* or *high* for each of the 18 criteria. These criteria are used to determine the five-star rating as depicted by a five-star scale. *Products that do not contain any of the appropriate nutrients for a particular health support criterion will be evident by the absence of a bar for that criterion.*

There is one exception to this generalization: in the criterion for Potential Toxicity, the absence of a bar indicates that there are no toxicity concerns for a product with regard to the levels of vitamin A and iron. **A bar extending half the length (***moderate***) indicates caution regarding potential toxicity for either vitamin A or iron; a bar extending the full length (***high***), indicates caution regarding potential toxicity for** *both* **vitamin A and iron.**

We believe that the intuitive nature of these graphs and their visual simplicity provide the consumer with a strong sense of relative product quality.

The Legend

A numerical code related to each health support criterion is provided in the legend, located in the upper right-hand corner of each left-hand page. The legend makes it easier for the reader to identify a particular criterion, such as Heart Health, by simply matching the numerical code for the criterion in the graph with its numerical code in the legend.

Qualifying the Products

The Upper Limit of daily intake (UL), shown in the right-hand column of the *Table of Recommended Daily Intakes* (Table 11-3, page 78) is a component of the new Dietary Reference Intake (DRI) standards recently developed by the United States and Canada. The UL represents the upper level of intake for a specific nutrient deemed safe for use by adults.* The ULs for several vitamins, minerals, and other nutritional factors have now been determined and are shown in the table.

All nutritional products considered for inclusion in this comparative guide are initially screened for excessive potency, according to the ULs established by the US Food and Nutrition Board. **Any product containing three or more nutrients with**

potencies exceeding 150% of the Upper Limit is eliminated from further consideration. In the 1,612 products evaluated in compiling this comparative guide, only 18 were screened out for reasons of excessive potency, for a total disqualification rate of only 1%. These disqualified products are listed in Appendix E with an appropriate notation.

The Nutrient Profile Score

All qualifying products are assessed quantitatively to provide a rating relative to the *Blended Standard.* Eighteen health support criteria are used to determine relative product ratings. To receive a full point for any single criterion, the product must meet or exceed the benchmark established for that criterion. Partial points are awarded for the partial fulfillment of each criterion. The last criterion penalizes the product if the formulation exceeds defined limits for those nutrients with potential cumulative toxicities.

The development of each criterion is based on the scientific evidence available in the literature and presented in Chapter 9. Nutrient potencies are based on the median values of the pooled recommendations for intake established in the *Blended Standard.* The 18 criteria, detailed in Chapter 9, are a significant enhancement of those developed for previous editions of the *Comparative Guide,* and effectively raise the bar for nutritional excellence by which all products are evaluated.

From these 18 criteria, a five-star rating is determined. This scale is divided into half-star increments to provide a 10-point rating scale. A five-star rating highlights those products possessing health support characteristics that are clearly superior to the majority of products on the market, based on the *Blended Standard.* Conversely, a one-star rating or less represents products possessing few, if any, of the health support characteristics reflected in the *Blended Standard.* We believe that this five-star scale provides an intuitive means by which the consumer can compare products, based on product content. **Please note that, due to the immense number of nutritional products on the market, not all products evaluated can be graphically compared.**

Each manufacturer with a product scoring three stars or more is represented with a graph in Section V. For those manufacturers that have more than one nutritional product rating three stars or more, the top-rated product(s) is/are chosen. In some cases, where a manufacturer has both a Canadian and a US product, or produces gender-specific products, the manufacturer may have more than one product represented in the graphs. In all, 394 individual American and Canadian manufacturers were identified in our field research.

New to this edition of the *Comparative Guide* **is the inclusion of combination products,** described earlier in this chapter, as a separate category. These products are evaluated using the same criteria for nutrient content, with modifications made to three criteria (Completeness, Potency, and Inflammation Control) to include essential fatty acids. Because of these differences, and for convenience of the reader, **standalone products and combination products are rated and listed separately within Section V of the guide.**

---

* The Food and Nutrition Board, Institute of Medicine, Washington, DC has recently established the ULs for a number of vitamins and minerals. These values are shown in the *Table of Recommended Daily Intakes* (Table 11-3, page 78).

There are in fact two things, science and opinion;
the former begets knowledge, the latter ignorance.

—Hippocrates (460 BC-377 BC)

CHAPTER NINE

PRODUCT RATING CRITERIA

This chapter explains the *Health Support Profile*, a comprehensive set of mathematical algorithms that are based on 18 health support criteria described below. The *Health Support Profile* ranks each product that is included in this comparative guide in accordance with nutrient intake recommendations described in the *Blended Standard*. As previously mentioned, this standard forms the basis of our analytical model. For a detailed explanation of the *Blended Standard*, please refer to the previous chapter.

When a product is evaluated, the rating for each criterion is calculated and pooled to provide a raw product score. This score is then used to rank each product against its peers. With four new criteria added to our analysis and all criteria strengthened, the revised *Health Support Profile* represents a significant enhancement from previous editions of the *Comparative Guide*. These revised criteria effectively raise the bar for nutritional excellence by which all products are evaluated in this guide.

Changes to the Criteria

In previous editions of the *Comparative Guide*, we gave full credit for nutrient potencies that met or exceeded 50% of the potency for each nutrient relative to the *Blended Standard*. For this edition of the guide, the benchmark has been raised considerably. Full credit for the potency of a given nutrient is now based on 100% of the value for that nutrient as described in the *Blended Standard*. In addition, we have added four new criteria, based on evolving scientific evidence. These new criteria are:

✔ Gamma Tocopherol Profile
✔ Ocular Health
✔ Inflammation Control
✔ Glycation Control

Furthermore, several of the previous criteria have been enhanced to accommodate new scientific findings. For example, the number of nutrients included in the criteria for Antioxidant Support, Heart Health, Metabolic Health, Liver Health (formerly called Glutathione Support), and Methylation Support (formerly called Homocysteine Reduction Support) has been increased. As well, the penalty-imposition point for excessive iron, which is part of the Potential Toxicities criterion, has been lowered. This decision is based upon recent evidence of cumulative iron toxicity at a dosage as low as 5 mg/day.[1]

To receive a full point for any single criterion, the product must *meet or exceed* the benchmark established for that criterion. Each criterion is rated using an ordinal (sliding) scale, where partial points are awarded for the partial fulfillment of each criterion. The last criterion, Potential Toxicities, penalizes the product if the formulation exceeds defined limits for those nutrients (vitamin A and iron) that demonstrate a potential cumulative toxicity.

The following is an overview of each criterion used in our *Health Support Profile*. For each criterion, we also provide the analytical question that addresses the criterion. Each question posed constitutes the logical argument that is embedded in the mathematical algorithm, and each algorithm evaluates the product based on the specified criterion.

Show Me the Science

For each *Health Support Profile* criterion, we provide a brief overview of the scientific justification for those nutrients included in the criterion. Those readers wanting to delve more deeply into the scientific evidence are invited to log on to our website at www.NutriSearch.ca, where you will find a more detailed scientific rationale for each criterion used in our analytical model. On the homepage, simply click on *SHOW ME THE SCIENCE*, where you can access a description for each criterion, along with relevant scientific references. While this information is somewhat technical, there is much that will be of interest to the lay reader.

1. Completeness

Over the years, scientific research has documented numerous micronutrients that are required for optimal health. We now know that the body requires approximately 17 vitamins and vitamin-like substances, a diverse group of plant-based antioxidants, at least 14 trace elements and minerals, and several essential fats necessary for proper cellular function. The body cannot manufacture many of these substances; they *must* be obtained through the diet. In all, 47 nutrients and nutrient categories are referenced in this guide, based upon the recommendations of our 12 cited authorities, and enhanced by emergent research that, in some instances, has eclipsed their published recommendations. These 47 nutrient categories comprise the cornerstone of our *Blended Standard*—the definitive benchmark upon which our analysis is built.

The criterion for Completeness poses the following question:

Does the product contain the full spectrum of nutrients and nutrient categories listed in the Blended Standard *and considered essential for optimal health? To qualify, a nutrient or nutrient category must be present at a dosage that is at least 20% of the value in the* Blended Standard.

Due to the technical challenges, including tableting, stability, and shelf-life, involved in the addition of high levels of essential fatty acids (fish oils and plant seed oils) in tableted products, the levels of these nutrient categories are only included in the Completeness criterion for those products categorized as Combination Products.

2. Potency

Recent epidemiological studies reveal that there is considerable genetic variation in the functionality of several key coenzymes in human cells.* In many instances, these genetic variations will hinder the ability of a coenzyme to bind to the active site of other enzymes, thus impairing the reactions that these enzymes control. This, in turn, can increase susceptibility to disease. Individuals affected with these genetic defects (polymorphisms) require supplementation with those nutrients serving as precursors for the affected coenzymes at potencies that may be substantially greater than their recommended dietary intakes (DRIs).

The potencies for the 47 essential nutrients and nutrient categories referenced in this guide are based upon the recommendations of our 12 cited authorities and reflect the need for supplementation with some nutrients at levels considerably higher than their DRIs. In those few instances where a specific recommendation is not definitive, but where there is clear support for the inclusion of the nutrient or nutrient category (such as in the case of phenolic compounds), we turn to emergent research for guidance.

The criterion for Potency poses the following question:

> *For each nutrient in the product, what is the level of potency relative to the potency for that nutrient in the Blended Standard?*

Due to the technical challenges, including tableting, stability, and shelf-life, involved in the addition of high levels of essential fatty acids (fish oils and plant seed oils) in tableted products, the levels of these nutrient categories are only included in the Potency criterion for those products categorized as Combination Products.

3. Mineral Forms

Minerals are essential components of our cells and serve as cofactors in the thousands of enzyme-controlled reactions that power the machinery of the cell. Throughout the body, minerals form critical structural elements, regulate the action of nerves and muscles, maintain the cell's osmotic (water) balance, and modulate the pH (acidity) of the cell and extracellular fluids. While minerals comprise only 4% to 5% of our total body weight, life would not be possible without them.

During the digestive process, minerals separate from the food and dissociate into ions (electrically charged atoms in solution). Ionized minerals can then pass freely through the intestinal wall and into the blood. They also attach themselves to amino acids, or other organic acids, and "hitch a ride" with these carriers, which are preferentially absorbed by the cells lining the small intestine. From here, the carriers and their attached minerals enter the blood and then travel to the liver to be readied for use by the cells of the body.

When nutritional supplements are consumed, the minerals are naturally conjugated (joined) to amino acids available in the gut during the digestive process.[2] This is why it is best to consume your supplements with a meal. This suggests that there should be no differences in mineral bioavailability† between supplements that use chelated mineral complexes and those that use less expensive inorganic mineral salts. However, such is not the case. For one thing, as people age, they lose their ability to produce sufficient stomach acid, making it increasingly difficult to dissolve and ionize common mineral salts. For another, complex mineral interactions can inhibit absorption and influence mineral bioavailability.

Many components of our daily diet, including other minerals, can interfere with, and sometimes block, the absorption of certain minerals, making them unavailable to the body.[3] Natural fibre, such as that found in fruits and cereals, has a depressing effect on the absorption of minerals supplied as inorganic mineral salts. Surprisingly, recent evidence shows that a fibre-rich diet can even deplete the body's mineral status when minerals are provided as inexpensive mineral salts, resulting in a *negative* mineral balance.[4, 5] Considering the ready availability of dietary supplements that use inexpensive mineral salts, these mineral-mineral and mineral-substrate interferences take on considerable importance. Imagine taking a mineral supplement in good faith and going into a negative mineral balance—actually *losing* ground for the very minerals you consumed! The short of it is this: avoid the use of supplements that provide minerals in the form of inorganic mineral salts (such as oxides, carbonates, sulphates and phosphates). While less expensive to manufacture, supplements using mineral salts do not appear to provide optimal nutritional value.

To resolve mineral-mineral interferences and increase the bioavailability of minerals, many manufacturers chemically bond the mineral to an amino acid or organic acid carrier. These chelated minerals are believed to mimic the natural mineral chelates that form during the digestion process. Beyond their reported superior bioavailability, chelated minerals appear to have lower absorptive interference and better tolerance in the gut than the less expensive mineral salts.[6] Moreover, minerals delivered in chelated form avoid the competitive inhibitions to absorption and the mineral-mineral interactions experienced by less expensive mineral salts.

While not chelates in the true sense of the word, minerals joined to organic acids, such as citrate, malate, succinate, alpha-

> *Avoid the use of supplements that provide minerals in the form of inorganic mineral salts (such as oxides, carbonates, sulphates and phosphates). While less expensive to manufacture, mineral salts do not appear to provide optimal nutritional value.*

---

* Coenzymes are small organic non-protein molecules that carry chemical groups between enzymes. Many coenzymes are activated water-soluble vitamins that have a phosphate group attached to the vitamin. Non-vitamins, such as ATP—the energy currency of the cell—can also act as coenzymes. While coenzymes are consumed in the reactions in which they assist, they are constantly regenerated and their concentration maintained at a steady level in the cell.

† Bioavailability is the ability of a given nutrient to be absorbed by the gut and to be utilized by the cells of the body.

ketoglutarate and aspartate (known, collectively, as Krebs cycle intermediates), are also believed to be preferentially absorbed. These organic acids are essential to the central metabolic pathway of the cell. Consequently, they are selectively absorbed through the gut, along with the attached mineral (which piggybacks along for the ride). Minerals chelated to Krebs cycle intermediates are better utilized and tolerated than inorganic or relatively insoluble mineral salts. Both Krebs cycle intermediates and amino-acid chelates fulfill all the requirements for an optimal carrier molecule:[7] they are easily metabolized; non-toxic; helpful in increasing the absorption of the mineral carried; and efficiently degraded and employed in other areas of the cell's metabolism. Organic-acid complexes also provide needed acidity to promote absorption in the gut. Moreover, both the mineral/amino-acid chelates and the mineral/organic-acid complexes appear to be better tolerated by the human gut than simple mineral salts.[8]

The Bottom Line

The question of mineral form versus bioavailability has been an issue of contention within the scientific community for some time. This is largely because of the complexities of the human digestive process and the multitude of interactions between minerals and other digestive products. Some studies appear to refute the claims of superior bioavailability of mineral chelates;[6, 9, 10] other studies provide convincing evidence that chelated minerals are preferentially absorbed.[11-16] While recognizing the controversy that continues to surround this issue, this guide acknowledges the consensus of our selected nutritional authorities, which supports the use of mineral/amino-acid chelates and mineral/organic-acid (Krebs cycle) complexes as superior mineral forms with respect to bioavailability.[2, 17-20]

The criterion for Mineral Forms poses the following question:

> *For those minerals included in a formulation, how many are found in their most bioavailable forms as amino-acid chelates or organic-acid complexes?*

4. Bioactivity of Vitamin E

Vitamin E is a fat-soluble vitamin that exists in eight different structural forms (four tocopherols and four tocotrienols). Each form, or isomer,* has its own biological activity, which is the measure of potency or functional use in the body. Alpha tocopherol is the name of the most active form of vitamin E in humans. It is the only form of vitamin E actively maintained in the human body and is, therefore, the form of vitamin E found in the largest quantities in the blood and tissue. Consequently, the type of vitamin E used in nutritional supplements is generally the alpha tocopherol form.

Alpha tocopherol functions as a chain-breaking antioxidant that prevents the propagation of lipid oxidation within the cell membrane. Found in leafy green vegetables, vegetable oils, and nuts, intakes of small quantities of this fat-soluble vitamin—as little as 100 IU per day—have been associated with a significantly reduced risk of heart disease in both men and women.[21] Natural

Figure 9-1: *d*-Alpha Tocopherol Form of Vitamin E

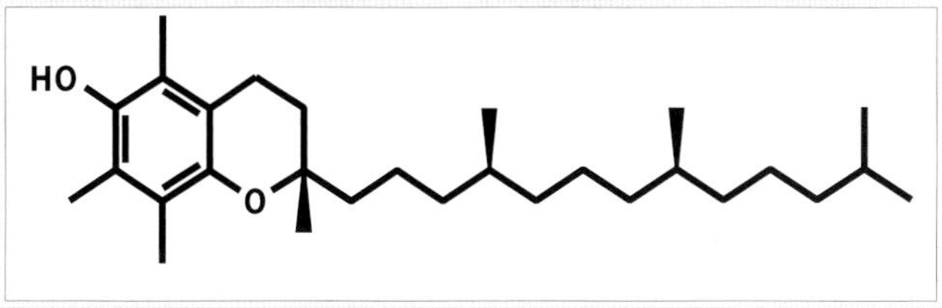

alpha tocopherol is called *d*-alpha tocopherol. Synthetic vitamin E, also known as *d/l*-alpha tocopherol, or *all-rac* tocopherol, is produced commercially in a process that yields both the *d*- and *l*-isomers. Like your right and left hands, these isomers are mirror images of each other.

Until recently, synthetic vitamin E was believed to possess a biological activity about two-thirds that of natural vitamin E. However, new evidence regarding the biological activity of synthetic vitamin E has prompted the National Academies of Science to recognize synthetic (*d/l*) alpha tocopherol as possessing only *one-half* the biological activity of natural (*d*) alpha tocopherol.[22]

As well as showing the highest level of biological activity, natural vitamin E appears to be quickly absorbed into human cells. In contrast, the synthetic forms are metabolized (broken down) and excreted in the urine. The assimilation of natural vitamin E appears to be a result of the action of specific binding proteins produced in the liver. These proteins preferentially bind and transport *d*-alpha tocopherol, to the exclusion of other forms of the vitamin. According to researchers at the Linus Pauling Institute, some of the forms of tocopherol present in synthetic vitamin E are simply not useable by the body. Consequently, *d/l*-alpha tocopherol is *less* bioavailable and only about half as potent as natural *d*-alpha tocopherol.

The Bottom Line

The evidence demonstrating the greater bioavailability, preferential absorption and assimilation, and lower rates of excretion of *d*-alpha tocopherol compared to the synthetic form of the vitamin is persuasive. Despite the use of the IU measure to account for differences in biological activity of natural versus synthetic vitamin E, the weight of evidence favours *d*-alpha tocopherol as the standard by which to judge nutritional quality. Accordingly, differentiation between these isomeric forms of vitamin E is incorporated, where applicable, throughout the product-rating criteria used in this guide.

The criterion for Bioactivity of Vitamin E poses the following question:

> *Does the product contain the natural (d) isomer of alpha tocopherol or does the product contain the synthetic (d/l) isomers of alpha tocopherol?*

5. Gamma Tocopherol

Regular consumption of natural vitamin E, with its complex mixture of tocopherols and tocotrienols, has long been known to

---

* Isomers are molecules with the same chemical formula and often with the same kinds of bonds between atoms, but in which the atoms are arranged differently to provide either a different structural formula (structural isomerism) or a different three-dimensional shape (stereoisomerism).

lower the risk of degenerative disease. A good deal of laboratory evidence and data from epidemiological and retrospective studies show that a high dietary intake of vitamin E can ward off heart disease[23-26] and keep several cancers at bay.[27-29] Findings from several prospective studies and clinical trials, however, have been ambiguous, failing to show consistent results.[30-34] One plausible explanation for this ambiguity may be that virtually all clinical trials have used alpha tocopherol, the primary form of vitamin E in dietary supplements, and many trials have used synthetic (*d/l*) vitamin E—known to cause adverse effects at high dosage—rather than the natural tocopherols found in the diet.[35] Researchers at Johns Hopkins University point out that the benefits of alpha tocopherol may, in fact, be compromised by a decrease in the levels of gamma tocopherol that is known to occur during high-dose supplementation with alpha tocopherol.[36]

Gamma tocopherol possesses distinctive chemical properties that differentiate it from its alpha analogue and may explain the observed differences in the physiologic effects of the two vitamin E forms. Gamma tocopherol has been shown to be more effective than alpha tocopherol in:

✔ reducing several prothrombotic events associated with oxidative stress;[37,38]

✔ reducing platelet aggregation and clot formation;[37]

✔ enhancing the activity of the antioxidant enzyme, superoxide dismutase (SOD), and inhibiting the proinflammatory COX-2 enzyme;[39,40]

✔ regulating the expression of genetic factors that can influence cancerous growth; and [41,42]

✔ subduing nitric oxide-induced oxidative stress by removing toxic nitrogen-based free radicals.[43]

Not surprisingly, gamma tocopherol is emerging as an important partner to alpha tocopherol in the science of preventive health. Both forms of vitamin E are recognized nutritional thoroughbreds, each possessing protective talents based upon their individual chemistries; however, it is their work as a team—both complementary and synergistic—that is the likely "power behind the punch" of vitamin E observed in epidemiologic, retrospective, and laboratory studies. The Bruce Ames research group at the University of California, Berkeley, contends that consumers taking vitamin E supplements containing an imbalance of the two principal forms of vitamin E are depriving themselves of the protection afforded by a mixture of tocopherols. Accordingly, the researchers argue that vitamin E supplements should contain a ratio of alpha/gamma tocopherol that is closer to what is found in nature.

> *Antioxidants do not work in isolation. When an antioxidant neutralizes a free radical, it is, itself, oxidized and must be replenished by another antioxidant before it can be used again.*

The Bottom Line

There are few studies that allude to an optimal alpha/gamma tocopherol ratio; however, some researchers have proposed a 2:1 to 1:1 blend.[44] We support the need for the inclusion of gamma tocopherol in any supplement containing high levels of the alpha-form. Consequently, we are adding the recommendation for the inclusion of gamma tocopherol at an alpha/gamma ratio of 2:1 as a new component in the *Blended Standard*.

The criterion for Gamma Tocopherol poses the following questions:

> *Does the product contain gamma tocopherol (or a mixture of gamma, beta, and delta-tocopherols) at a potency of up to one-half the potency of alpha tocopherol in the same product? What is the potency of gamma tocopherol or mixed tocopherols in the product, compared to the potency for gamma tocopherol in the* Blended Standard?

6. Antioxidant Support

The scientific evidence supporting the health benefits of supplementing with a balanced spectrum of antioxidants is impressive. Consequently, many health practitioners have begun to recommend higher dietary intakes of these important nutrients as a prudent preventive measure against oxidative stress. As was anticipated over two decades ago by leading researchers,[45] high-dose supplementation with antioxidants is gaining a significant role in the prevention and treatment of many of today's common ailments. However, antioxidants do not work in isolation. When an antioxidant neutralizes a free radical, it is, itself, oxidized and must be replenished by another antioxidant before it can be used again. For this reason, it is vital to supplement with a wide spectrum of antioxidants—an approach that is reflective of what occurs in nature.

As an aqueous-phase antioxidant, vitamin C (ascorbic acid) is the principal sentry against oxidative attack in the extra-cellular matrix and within the cytoplasm of the cell. Vitamin C is a cofactor or substrate for eight separate enzyme systems involved in various cellular functions, including collagen synthesis, ATP synthesis in the mitochondria, and hormone biosynthesis. Its primary antioxidant partners include vitamin E and beta-carotene, which help regenerate vitamin C.

Of all the antioxidants, vitamin E may offer the greatest protection against heart disease because of its ability to imbed itself into the LDL-cholesterol molecule and protect it from oxidative damage. Its solubility in lipids (fats) makes the vitamin an important component of the cell membrane, where it works to protect the cell against lipid peroxidation and attenuate oxidation-induced inflammatory events. More recently, the gamma tocopherol form of vitamin E has shown great promise in reducing the risks of several cancers. Researchers at the University of Uppsala, Sweden, found that gamma tocopherol proved even more effective than alpha tocopherol in reducing several prothrombotic events associated with oxidative stress.[46]

Beta-carotene, a member of a diverse group of auxiliary photosynthetic pigments, plays a dual role in human nutrition. As an antioxidant, its extensive conjugated double-bond structure reacts effectively with singlet oxygen radicals, absorbing and diffusing their destructive energy.[47] As a precursor for vitamin A (retinol), beta-carotene supplies a portion of the body's requirement for the vitamin, which plays a central role in the chemistry of vision. Both beta-carotene and vitamin A prevent the oxidation of cholesterol, reduce oxidative damage to DNA, and disable oxygen free radicals produced by exposure to sunlight and air pollution.[48] The yellow carotenoid is also involved in the activation of gene expression and the control of cell differentiation (cell specialization). Together, vitamin C, vitamin E, and beta-carotene form an important antioxidant triad that plays a central role in attenuating oxidative and inflammatory events.

Several other antioxidants play a synergistic role to the vitamin C, vitamin E, beta-carotene triad. These include vitamin A, alpha-lipoic acid, lycopene, coenzyme Q_{10}, and the antioxidant mineral, selenium. For further information on the scientific evidence supporting the use of these nutrients, please log on to www.NutriSearch.ca.

The Bottom Line

The criterion for Antioxidant Support poses the following question:

> *Does the product contain vitamin C, vitamin E (including alpha tocopherol and gamma tocopherol, or mixed tocopherols), vitamin A, beta-carotene, alpha-lipoic acid, lycopene, coenzyme Q_{10}, and selenium at potencies up to 100% of the potencies for these nutrients in the* Blended Standard?

7. Bone Health

As living tissue, healthy bones require at least 24 bone-building materials, including trace elements and protein. The most important minerals are calcium, magnesium, phosphorus, and potassium. Equally important is the balance between these minerals. Strong bones need lots of calcium, but calcium supplementation also requires the presence of magnesium, which increases calcium retention in the bone. Phosphorus, another important component in bone formation, must be in proper balance with calcium. Too much of it, from soft-drink consumption or high protein intake, will suck calcium out of the bone and weaken its integrity. Vitamins D and K are also vital for enhanced calcium deposition,[49] while silicon, boron, and zinc are required to strengthen the bone's mineral matrix.[50] Vitamin C stimulates formation of the collagen matrix, an important protein component that creates a framework for calcium crystallization.[49]

Silicon increases bone-mineral density and appears to have a role in the prevention and treatment of osteoporosis. Silicon deposition is found in areas of active bone growth, suggesting that it may be involved in the growth of bone crystals and the process of bone mineralization. Zinc is essential for the proper action of vitamin D; its status plays a central role in bone health. Increased zinc excretion, common in osteoporosis sufferers, is a likely consequence of accelerated depletion of bone-mineral content. Diets low in zinc have been shown to slow adolescent bone growth.[51] Last but not least, vitamins B_6, B_{12}, and folic acid reduce mineral loss by modulating blood homocysteine levels.[49] For further information on the scientific evidence supporting the use of these nutrients, please log on to www.NutriSearch.ca.

The Bottom Line

The scientific evidence supports the need for long-term supplementation with several key nutrients in the maintenance of bone health. This is particularly true for women in their peri- and post-menopause years. Accordingly, supplementation with vitamins D, K, C, B_6, B_{12}, folic acid, and the minerals boron, calcium, magnesium, silicon, and zinc, at levels deemed suitable for optimal nutritional health by our cited nutritional authorities, is included as an important component of our product-rating criteria.

The criterion for Bone Health poses the following question:

> *Does the product contain vitamin D, vitamin K, vitamin C, vitamin B_6, vitamin B_{12}, folic acid, boron, calcium, magnesium, silicon, and zinc at potencies up to 100% of the potencies for these nutrients in the* Blended Standard?

8. Heart Health

Epidemiological research has consistently revealed that individuals with a high dietary intake of antioxidant vitamins have a lower-than-average risk of cardiovascular disease.[52] This evidence is particularly consistent for vitamin E.[53] As well, many clinical studies show magnesium supplementation to be of significant benefit in the treatment of cardiac arrhythmias (irregular heart beat) and in reversing the depletion of potassium that accompanies a magnesium deficit. Many cardiovascular events, such as angina pectoris (chest pain), congestive heart failure (failure to pump blood efficiently), and cardiomyopathy (weakening or damaging of the heart muscle), are related to low magnesium status.[54] Coenzyme Q_{10} (CoQ_{10}), an essential component in cellular

Figure 9-2: Human Heart with Associated Blood Vessels

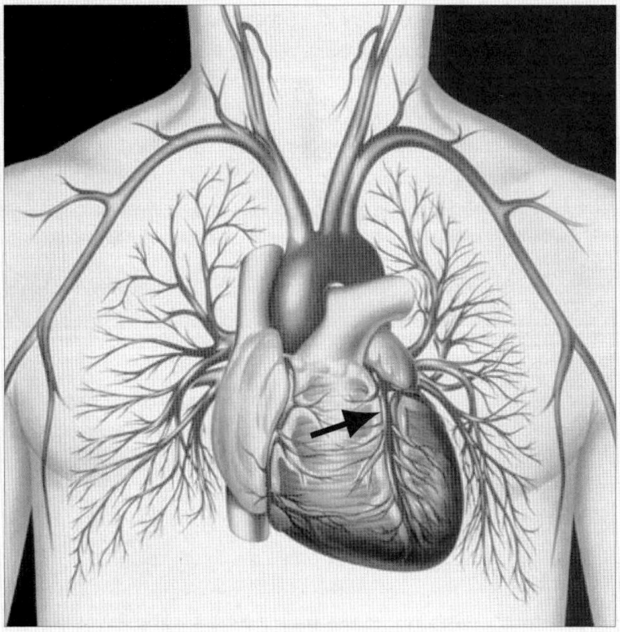

Note the left anterior coronary artery descending along the left ventricle to supply the heart muscle with oxygen. Narrowing of this artery by the buildup of atherosclerotic plaque is the basis for heart disease; blockage of this "widow-maker" (see arrow) by the formation of a thrombus or clot can precipitate a fatal heart attack (myocardial infarction).

energy production, is also prevalent in the heart muscle. Low tissue levels of CoQ_{10} have been associated with several cardiovascular complications, including angina, congestive heart failure, cardiomyopathy, hypertension (high blood pressure), and mitral valve prolapse (failure of the valve to close properly). Research suggests that this triad of nutrients—coenzyme Q_{10}, vitamin E, and magnesium—plays a central role in the maintenance of cardiac health and the prevention of disease states.

Vitamin E's cardio-protective effect appears to stem from its ability to bind to LDL cholesterol, protecting it from free-radical-induced oxidative damage and the consequent buildup of atherogenic plaque. Low levels of vitamin E in the blood are predictive of a heart attack almost 70% of the time. [55] A large study, conducted by the Harvard School of Public Health, showed that men who consumed at least 67 mg (100 IU) of vitamin E per day for at least two years had a 37% lower risk of heart disease than those who did not take supplements.[56]

Population studies suggest a link between calcium intake and blood pressure.[57] While results have not been consistent, several studies show that calcium supplementation can lower blood pressure in hypertensive individuals.[58] A recent review on the effects of mineral intakes in reducing hypertension concludes that a decrease of sodium and concurrent increase of calcium, along with increased potassium and magnesium intakes—modifications characteristic of the *Dietary Approaches to Stop Hypertension* (DASH) diet—have a dramatic impact in lowering blood pressure.[59] Regulation of intracellular calcium appears to play a key role in hypertension (as well as obesity).[60] Overall, sub-optimal calcium intakes contribute to hypertension. Dietary calcium appears to reduce blood pressure by normalizing intracellular calcium levels.

Supplementation with magnesium is of benefit in the treatment of cardiac arrhythmias and the prevention of potassium depletion; both minerals play an important role in the proper functioning of the heart.[61-64] Deficiency in magnesium has been observed in cardiomyopathy and mitral valve prolapse. In fact, over 85% of patients with mitral valve prolapse exhibit a chronic magnesium deficiency, which is relieved through supplementation.[65, 66] Several studies confirm improvement in heart function in patients with cardiomyopathies when supplemented with magnesium.[62-64, 67] Because the mineral acts in so many ways to enhance cardiac function and optimize cellular metabolism, magnesium is widely recognized as a critical nutrient for general cardiac support.

Several double-blind studies in patients with various cardiomyopathies show the benefits of CoQ_{10} supplementation. Langsjoen and co-workers reported an 89% improvement rate in 80 cardiomyopathy patients treated with CoQ_{10}.[68] The coenzyme also appears to moderate blood pressure through an unusual mechanism; by lowering cholesterol levels and stabilizing the vascular system through its antioxidant properties, it is able to reduce vascular resistance. Several studies confirm a lowering of both systolic (pumping) and diastolic (resting) pressures in the range of 10 percent through CoQ_{10} supplementation.[69-71]

Other nutrients play important roles in optimizing cardiovas-cular health and reducing hypertension. These include gamma tocopherol, calcium, magnesium, l-carnitine and acetyl-l-carnitine, procyanidolic oligomers (PCOs), phenolic compounds, and lycopene. For further details on the scientific evidence supporting the use of each of these nutrients, please log on to www.NutriSearch.ca.

The Bottom Line

The scientific evidence supports the need to supplement with a variety of heart-protective nutrients as a means of reducing cardiovascular risks. Accordingly, supplementation with these nutrients, at levels deemed suitable for optimal nutritional health by our cited nutritional authorities, is included as an important component of our product-rating criteria.

The criterion for Heart Health poses the following question:

> *Does the product contain vitamin E (including alpha tocopherol and gamma tocopherol, or mixed tocopherols), beta-carotene, coenzyme Q_{10}, calcium, magnesium, l-carnitine or acetyl-l-carnitine, procyanidolic oligomers (PCOs), phenolic compounds, and lycopene at potencies up to 100% of the potencies for those nutrients and nutrient categories in the* Blended Standard?

9. Liver Health (detoxification)

Glutathione (GSH) is a simple tripeptide, a small protein that consists of three amino acids: glutamic acid, cysteine, and glycine. Because of the chemical nature of sulphur-containing cysteine, glutathione effortlessly donates electrons, accounting for its powerful antioxidant properties.* Intracellular glutathione status is a sensitive indicator of cellular health and of the cell's ability to resist toxic challenges. An important water-phase antioxidant, glutathione is an essential component in the glutathione peroxidase system, one of three vital free-radical scavenging mechanisms in the cell. Glutathione peroxidase enzymes serve to detoxify peroxides, including hydrogen peroxide (H_2O_2), generated within cellular membranes and lipid-dense areas of the cell, particularly the mitochondrial membrane. Severe glutathione depletion quickly leads to cell death; experimental glutathione depletion has been found to induce cellular apoptosis (suicide).[72, 73]

Glutathione depletion at the cellular level invokes extensive damage to the mitochondria, the energy centres of the cell. Depletion of mitochondrial glutathione, in fact, may be the ultimate factor determining a cell's vulnerability to oxidative attack.[74] Nowhere is glutathione's presence more vital than in these cellular "furnaces," where a cascade of oxidation-reduction reactions complete the final steps in respiration—a process known as *oxidative phosphorylation*. Throughout this process, electrons invariably escape and react with ambient oxygen to generate toxic free radicals.[75] It is estimated that 2% to 5% of the electrons that enter the mitochondrial "furnaces" are converted to reactive oxygen species (oxygen-based free radicals),[75] generating considerable oxidative stress for the cell.[76, 77] These free radicals, like sparks from a fire, pose an immediate threat to other cellular components, such as the DNA, enzymes, structural proteins, and lipids.

---

* Oxidation-reduction reactions in biological systems involve a transfer of electrons from one chemical species to another. The ease by which an antioxidant donates an electron to reduce (neutralize) a free radical is, therefore, its defining prowess.

The cumulative damage wrought by oxygen and other free radical species is now recognized as a principal contributor to the degenerative disease process and the progressive loss of organ function, commonly recognized as aging.[77] Consequently, the cell is constantly challenged to destroy these free radical "sparks" before they can inflict lasting damage. Minimizing such oxidative assaults may prove to be the ultimate challenge of being alive. For this reason, the formidable reducing power of glutathione is of profound importance to the cell.

Glutathione helps regenerate other antioxidants that are, themselves, depleted from their task of fending off free radical challenges. Glutathione-induced regeneration, in fact, may be the mechanism used by the cell to conserve the lipid-phase antioxidants, vitamin A, vitamin E, and the carotenoids.[78] Recent investigations confirm that dietary vitamin C can protect against tissue damage resulting from glutathione depletion; likewise, supplementation with glutathione or its precursors can quickly replenish vitamin C deficiencies.[79, 80] Thus, glutathione and ascorbic acid—two of the pre-eminent cellular antioxidants—are tightly linked: glutathione can conserve vitamin C and vitamin C can conserve glutathione. Together, these two antioxidant powerhouses protect the entire spectrum of biomolecules within the cell and facilitate the cell's optimal performance.[74] According to Paris Kidd, PhD, "The glutathione status of a cell … will perhaps turn out to be the most accurate single indicator of the health of the cell. That is, as glutathione levels go, so will go the fortunes of the cell."

The Bottom Line

As the body's pre-eminent detoxicant, glutathione is essential for cellular health. While dietary glutathione is efficiently absorbed in the gut, the same may not be the case for nutritional supplementation. Oral dosing appears to raise glutathione levels, albeit with great variability between subjects. In one study, oral supplementation raised glutathione levels two- to five-fold.[81] In another study, absorption of a single dose of 3,000 mg was negligible.[82] Accordingly, supplementation with glutathione precursors and with those nutrients involved in the glutathione peroxidase pathway, including vitamin C, cysteine and n-acetyl-cysteine, selenium, vitamin B_2 (riboflavin), and vitamin B_3 (including niacin and niacinamide), at levels deemed suitable for optimal nutritional health by our cited nutritional authorities, is included as a component of our product rating criteria. For further information on the scientific evidence supporting the use of these nutrients, please log on to www.NutriSearch.ca.

The criterion for Liver Health poses the following question:

Does the product contain vitamin C, n-acetyl-cysteine (including cysteine), selenium, vitamin B_2, and vitamin B_3 (including niacin and niacinamide), at potencies up to 100% of the potencies for these nutrients in the Blended Standard?

10. Metabolic Health

Diabetes, now the seventh leading cause of death in the United States and Canada, is a chronic disorder of carbohydrate, fat, and protein metabolism. The disease first appears as a constel-lation of metabolic changes associated with hyperinsulinemenia (elevated insulin levels) and hyperglycemia (elevated blood-sugar levels). This condition, a precursor to full-blown diabetes, is called Insulin Resistance Syndrome. Untreated, insulin resistance will develop into full-blown diabetes; with it comes greatly magnified risks of heart disease, stroke, eye and kidney disease, and loss of nerve function. Frank diabetes is the principal cause of adult blindness and limb amputation.

Non-insulin-dependent (type 2) diabetes mellitus is a disease strongly associated with a sedentary lifestyle and the modern western diet. Inadequate physical activity, combined with a diet high in refined sugars, saturated fats, and proteins, and low in dietary fibre, has resulted in an epidemic of obesity throughout Canada and the United States. With it has risen the prevalence of type 2 diabetes. Obesity is, in fact, a hallmark of the disease: almost 90% of those diagnosed with type 2 diabetes are obese at the time of diagnosis.[83, 84] While there is disagreement as to whether obesity causes type 2 diabetes or whether diabetes begets obesity, one thing is clear: the disease involves a profound disturbance in the metabolic balance of the body, with dramatic consequences for the individual.

To reduce the risk of frank type 2 diabetes, one must prevent the onset of insulin resistance. However, millions of North Americans suffer unknowingly from this syndrome, placing them at an increased risk for cardiovascular and neurological dysfunctions. The development of insulin resistance is multi-factorial; however, research shows that complications associated with this pre-diabetic disorder may be mitigated effectively through conscientious dietary and lifestyle changes.

The Bottom Line

Vitamins B_3, B_6, B_{12}, C, E, biotin, coenzyme Q_{10}, and the trace elements chromium, magnesium, manganese, and zinc are all essential for proper metabolic support and the regulation of glucose metabolism. Accordingly, supplementation with these nutrients, at levels deemed suitable for optimal nutritional health by our cited nutritional authorities, is included as an important component of our product-rating criteria. For further information on the scientific evidence supporting the use of these nutrients, please log on to www.NutriSearch.ca.

The criterion for Metabolic Health poses the following question:

Does the product contain vitamin B_3 (including niacin and niacinamide), vitamin B_6, vitamin B_{12}, vitamin C, vitamin E (including alpha tocopherol and gamma tocopherol, or mixed tocopherols), biotin, coenzyme Q_{10}, chromium, magnesium, manganese, and zinc at potencies up to 100% of the potencies for these nutrients in the Blended Standard?

11. Ocular Health

Vitamin A is best known for its effects on the visual system. There are four types of photopigments produced from vitamin A, which are present in the retina of the eye. Rhodopsin is found in the retinal cells responsible for night vision, and three iodopsins (sensitive to red, yellow, and blue wavelengths) regulate colour vision during daylight. These four forms of vitamin A are isomers of *retinal*, an active (aldehyde) form of the vitamin.[85] Poor adaptation to changes in light intensity and poor night vision are indicative of a low vitamin A status. In developed countries, vitamin A deficiency usually results from malabsorption; supplementation induces a rapid restoration of vision.[86] Beta-carotene, once converted into the active form of vitamin A by oxidative cleavage via the enzyme beta-carotene monooxygenase, also contributes to the chemistry of vision.[87]

People who eat foods rich in lutein and zeaxanthin (including broccoli, collard, kale, spinach, and turnip greens) are much less likely to suffer from age-related cataracts* than those who do not. These carotenoid pigments are also effective in reducing the incidence of macular degeneration,† likely a consequence of their ability to quench oxidative damage within the eye. Recent studies show that these auxiliary photosynthetic pigments may also slow down age-related increases in lens density.[88]

Low circulating levels of vitamins C, E, and beta-carotene are implicated in the development of cataracts in the eye;[89] conversely, high serum levels have been shown to reduce the prevalence of cataract formation.[90, 91] Beta-carotene also acts as a natural biological solar filter, protecting against light-induced UV damage to the eye.[92] There is substantial evidence that, when used in combination, the actions of these antioxidant partners are synergistic in nature, providing a level of protection that strikingly exceeds the sum of their individual contributions.[93]

The Bottom Line

Accordingly, supplementation with vitamin C, E, and A, and the carotenoids, beta-carotene, lutein, and zeaxanthin, at levels deemed suitable for optimal nutritional health by our cited nutritional authorities, is included as an important component of our product-rating criteria.

The criterion for Ocular Health poses the following question:

Does the product contain the antioxidants, vitamin C, vitamin E (including alpha and gamma tocopherol, or mixed tocopherols), vitamin A (including beta-carotene) and the carotenoids, lutein and zeaxanthin, at potencies up to 100% of the potencies for these nutrients in the Blended Standard?

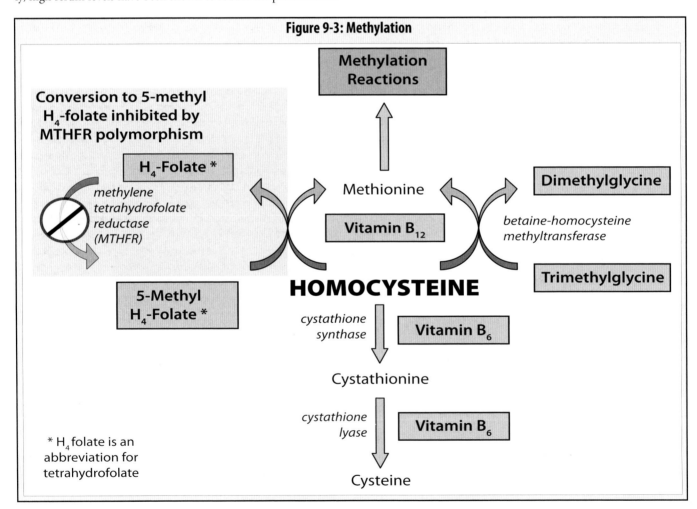

Figure 9-3: Methylation

---

* A cataract is a clouding of the eye's natural lens, which focuses light onto the retina at the back of the eye. The lens is mostly made of water and protein, with the protein fibers arranged in a precise way to keep the lens clear and transparent. Oxidative damage to these proteins causes them to clump together and start to cloud the lens. This is known as a cataract. In time, the cataract may grow larger and cloud more of the lens, making it translucent or milky. The consequence is blurred and darkened vision.

† Macular degeneration is the development of blurred or distorted central vision due to degeneration of the macula of the eye. This small area in the center of the retina makes sharp-detail vision possible from the central portion of the eye.

12. Methylation Support

Over 40 major clinical studies confirm that homocysteine levels are a predictive marker for heart disease, stroke, and peripheral artery disease. A powerful oxidizing agent, homocysteine is now believed to be responsible for the initial damage to the inner walls of the arteries and the subsequent initiation of atherosclerotic plaque formation. Twenty to 40% of patients with heart disease have elevated levels of homocysteine.[94, 95] Deficiencies in vitamin B_6, vitamin B_{12}, and folic acid can increase circulating levels of homocysteine; conversely, together, these nutrients reduce circulating homocysteine levels by helping to convert it to methionine, a harmless amino acid used by the cell for other functions. For more information on homocysteine metabolism and the particular biochemical functions of these nutrients, please refer to the discussion in Chapter 6 or log on to www.NutriSearch.ca.

Most individuals with high levels of homocysteine respond well to supplementation with vitamins B_6, B_{12}, and folic acid; however, a significant proportion of the population is resistant to this nutritional intervention. Persons with homocysteine resistance often suffer from a common genetic defect (polymorphism) that impairs the enzyme, methylene tetrahydrofolate reductase (MTHFR). A defect in the MTHFR enzyme creates a metabolic bottleneck that limits the conversion of homocysteine to methionine and results in elevated levels of homocysteine in the blood (see Figure 6-2, Chapter 6; and Figure 9-3, Chapter 9). Supplementing with vitamins B_6, B_{12}, and folic acid cannot effectively alleviate this bottleneck; however, studies show that the defective enzyme *is* sensitive to riboflavin deficiency.[96] Consequently, it has been suggested by the Ames group of Berkeley that mega-dose therapy with riboflavin, the precursor vitamin to the flavin adenine dinucleotide (FAD) coenzyme required by the defective enzyme, would prove beneficial (see Figure 6-2, Chapter 6).[97]

When provided as a dietary supplement, trimethylglycine (TMG), commonly known as betaine, can also address homocysteine resistance, which is experienced in about 15% to 20% of the population. Supplementation with TMG creates a bypass to the MTHFR bottleneck, providing an alternate route for the methylation of homocysteine. By donating one of its three methyl (CH_3-) groups to homocysteine in a process mediated by the enzyme, betaine-homocysteine methyltransferase, TMG effectively regenerates methionine and lowers homocysteine levels (see Figure 9-3).[98] The subsequent decrease in blood homocysteine can be maintained as long as the supplement is taken.[99]

The Bottom Line

A high level of homocysteine in the blood is a primary risk factor for cardiovascular disease and warrants supplementation with vitamins B_2, B_6, B_{12}, and folic acid as a prudent preventive measure. This is particularly so for the elderly, with respect to noted age-related declines of vitamin B_{12}. Accordingly, supplementation with these nutrients at levels deemed suitable for optimal nutritional health by our cited nutritional authorities is included as an important component in our product rating criteria.

The criterion for Methylation Support poses the following question:

Does the product contain vitamin B_2, vitamin B_6, vitamin B_{12}, folic acid, and trimethylglycine at potencies up to 100% of the potencies for these nutrients in the Blended Standard?

13. Lipotropic Factors

In our toxic world, we are exposed to ever-increasing levels of contaminants and harmful chemicals that, once ingested, accumulate in fatty deposits within the body. The liver and the brain are two primary targets for the bioaccumulation of lipid-soluble toxins, such as pesticides and metals. Vitamins C, E, and beta-carotene, the water-soluble B-complex vitamins, and some of the trace minerals consumed in the diet play important roles in protecting these tissues from the damage caused by oxidative assault from such toxins.[100, 101] However, it is the liver—the body's toxic filtration and purification unit—that does most of the heavy lifting. First in line to deal with the contaminants consumed in our foods and drinking water, the liver is subject to a daily onslaught of noxious challenges. In addition to the external toxic load (a function of lifestyle and environment), the liver must also deal with a range of endogenous (internal) toxins produced by the metabolic processes of our body. Normally, the liver can cope quite handily; however, when things go wrong—a result of chronic nutritional deficiencies, disease, or overuse of over-the-counter drugs such as acetaminophen—the workload for the liver can increase dramatically.

Fortunately, proper diet, nutritional supplementation, and treatment with herbal remedies can fortify the liver to withstand this toxic stress. Within the liver, choline and inositol assist with the elimination of toxins, helping to mobilize the fatty tissue and remove metals and other noxious compounds. Such agents are known as *lipotropic* (fat-moving) factors because of their ability to mobilize fats and bile (a secretion from the liver that helps emulsify fats during the digestive process). Lipotropic factors have a long history of use within the naturopathic community, helping to restore and enhance liver function and treat a number of common liver ailments. Dietary lipotropic factors work by increasing the levels of s-adenosyl methionine (SAMe), the liver's in-house lipotropic agent, and glutathione, the premier detoxicant in the body. They have been used preferentially because, until recently, dietary SAMe has not been widely available and because oral glutathione is not well absorbed in the digestive tract.

The Bottom Line

Our selected nutritional authorities recognize the lipotropic factors, choline and inositol, as essential because of the pivotal roles these nutrients play in lipid mobilization and detoxification within the liver. Eight out of our twelve cited authors recommend daily supplementation with choline at a median level of 94 mg/day and nine out of the twelve recommend inositol at a median intake of 125 mg/day. Lecithin (phosphatidylcholine), which converts to choline during the digestive process, is recommended at 350 mg/day. Accordingly, supplementation with these nutrients, at the levels deemed suitable for optimal nutritional health by our cited authorities, is included as an important component in our product rating criteria. For further details on the scientific evidence supporting the use of each of these nutrients, please log on to www.NutriSearch.ca.

The criterion for Lipotropic Factors poses the following question:

Does the product contain the important lipotropic factors, choline or lecithin (phosphatidylcholine), and inositol at potencies up to 100% of the potencies for these nutrients in the Blended Standard?

14. Inflammation Control

Chronic inflammation, frequently induced by uncontrolled oxidative stress, is a principal mechanism by which degenerative disease takes root. Reducing oxidative stress and changing the balance within the body to favour the production of anti-inflammatory chemical messengers is, therefore, important in lowering the levels of inflammation. This can be attained through conscious changes to diet and lifestyle, including appropriate supplementation.

Consuming foods rich in the omega-3 essential fatty acids, eicosapentaenoic acid (EPA), and docosahexaenoic acid (DHA), derived from fish oil, has a profound impact on reducing inflammation. When an appropriate balance of omega-3 to omega-6 essential fats is consumed, production of anti-inflammatory prostaglandins* is favoured and inflammation is kept in check.[102] Increasing the consumption of foods rich in omega-3 fats, such as salmon and other cold-water fish, or supplementing with a high quality, ultra-refined fish oil, suppresses the formation of harmful prostaglandin E-2 (PG-E2) while promoting the synthesis of beneficial prostaglandins (PG-E1 and PG-E3).[103, 104] Because the modern North American diet contains 10 to 20 times the amount of omega-6 oils that we need, the most sensible dietary approach is to reduce sources of omega-6 oils and supplement with high-dose omega-3 oils to bring us back to an optimal 4:1 ratio of omega-6:omega-3.[105]

Supplementing with flaxseed oil is another effective means of optimizing your omega-6:omega-3 ratio. Anti-inflammatory EPA can be manufactured in the body via the enzymatic conversion of alpha-linolenic acid that is prevalent in flaxseed oil. Supplementation with the oil, along with restriction of omega-6 fatty acid intake, raises tissue EPA levels to those comparable to fish oil supplementation. In fact, flaxseed oil contains more than twice the omega-3 fats as fish oil. Alpha-linolenic acid can be found in a variety of other plant sources, such as pumpkin seeds, walnuts, and other nuts; however, flaxseed—by far the richest source of this important omega-3 oil—contains a whopping 58% by weight.[105]

Gamma tocopherol is another nutrient that plays a pivotal role in quenching inflammation.[106] Acting through a mechanism unavailable to alpha tocopherol, gamma tocopherol reacts with

Green tea polyphenols are believed to be neuroprotective, invoking a spectrum of cellular mechanisms, including the chelation of metals, scavenging of free radicals, activation of anti-inflammation signalling pathways, and modulation of mitochondrial function in nervous tissues.

and expunges toxic reactive nitrogen oxide (RNO) radicals, subduing inflammation.[107] gamma tocopherol can also reduce inflammation by inhibiting cyclooxygenase-2 (COX-2), an enzyme central to the inflammatory process. COX-2 controls the synthesis of inflammatory prostaglandin E2 (see Figure 4-2, Chapter 4). Administration of gamma tocopherol has been found to reduce several other powerful inflammatory protagonists at the site of inflammation—strong evidence that this form of vitamin E exhibits potent anti-inflammatory properties that have important implications for human disease prevention and therapy.[108]

Lipoic acid (LA) is both a water-soluble and fat-soluble antioxidant. Capable of preventing oxidative damage in the cytosol (the fluid portion) of the cell and within the cell's membranous structures, LA is able to neutralize reactive nitrogen oxide and oxygen species, including one of the most damaging free radicals of all—the hydroxyl (OH) radical.[109] While all antioxidants possess some anti-inflammatory properties, LA's aptitude as an anti-inflammatory agent is highly regarded. LA is a potent inhibitor of nuclear factor kappa beta (NFkB), the nuclear transcription factor activated in response to oxidative stress. As we learned in Chapter 4, NFkB, once activated, switches on genes that manufacture several proinflammatory cytokines. For that reason, the presence of LA is critical to the cell's ability to reduce inflammation.[110] Very recently, researchers investigating the use of LA as a therapeutic agent against bone loss associated with systemic inflammation found that the antioxidant can also reduce the production of proinflammatory PG-E2 via inhibition of cyclooxygenase-2 enzyme.[111]

There is substantial evidence from human trials and animal-model studies that supplementation with physiological doses (doses in the range provided in a normal diet) of vitamin C can depress clinical markers of inflammation, including tumor necrosis factor-beta (TNF-beta)[112] and C-reactive protein.[113] In an investigation of the effect of antioxidant therapy in the recurrence of atrial fibrillation, vitamin C dramatically lowered the rate of recurrence from 36.3% to 4.5% and attenuated the associated low-level inflammatory response.[114] Importantly, intracellular vitamin C can inhibit the activation of NFkB.[115] High-dose supplementation with vitamin C can also reduce dysfunction of the endothelial lining of blood vessels, caused by acute inflammation,[116] and suppress apoptosis (cell death) of endothelial cells damaged from an inflammatory response.[117]

New research has revealed that flavonoids and other polyphenols not only serve as effective antioxidants, they also modulate cell-signalling processes that direct inflammatory events and may, themselves, serve as signalling agents to attenuate such events.[118] Several recent studies reveal that, as a group, flavonoids possess remarkable anti-inflammatory abilities, including the capacity to inhibit the expression of cellular adhesion molecules and the ability to subdue the generation of prostaglandin E-2.[119-121] Numerous studies also report that flavonoids inhibit the activity of the inflammation-promoting enzyme cyclooxygenase-2,[120, 122] attenu-

---

* Prostaglandins belong to a large class of oxygenated fatty acids, called the eicosanoids. They are derived from the essential fatty acids supplied through our diet. Eicosanoids are actually primitive hormones from our evolutionary past that act as localized cellular signalling molecules.

ate activation of the inflammation-signalling molecule, NFkB, and inhibit the synthesis of the inflammatory mediator, nitric oxide (NO).[123] Resveratrol, a type of polyphenol found in grapes, has been shown to inhibit the expression of inflammatory cytokines* *in vivo* (within the body)[124] and block the activation of other cell-signalling molecules, including NFkB and activator protein-1† (AP-1).[125] Through its ability to inhibit NFkB activation, resveratrol, along with other flavonoids, can effectively choke off inflammation at a critical control point, thereby influencing a wide variety of inflammatory pathways. In a study on experimental colitis, resveratrol significantly reduced the degree of colonic injury and suppressed the expression of the proinflammatory COX-2 enzyme.[126]

Similar to resveratrol, green tea polyphenols can also inhibit the activation of NFkB and, through this mechanism, control a wide variety of inflammatory pathways. They are also believed to be neuroprotective, invoking a spectrum of cellular mechanisms, including the chelation of metals, scavenging of free radicals, activation of anti-inflammation signalling pathways, and modulation of mitochondrial function in nervous tissues.[127] Green tea polyphenols are now being considered as therapeutic agents to alter brain processes and to serve as neuroprotective agents in progressive neurodegenerative disorders, such as Alzheimer's and Parkinson's disease.[128]

A recent review by Bengmark (2006) shows that almost 1500 papers dealing with curcumin have been published in recent years—an indication of the level of interest this simple herb is attracting within the scientific community.[129] Curcumin is completely non-toxic, possesses potent antioxidant activity, and has been shown to inhibit such mediators of inflammation as NFkB, phospholipase, cyclooxygenase-2 (COX-2), lipoxygenase (LOX), and inducible nitric oxide synthase (iNOS). Moreover, studies show that a number of inflammation-signalling cytokines (proteins) are also inhibited by curcumin.

Recent studies have examined the anti-inflammatory nature of virgin olive oil and of the olive vegetation water expressed from the processing of the oil. The findings show that, similar to the polyphenols found in green tea, grapes, and turmeric, olive oil phenols can reduce the expression of a key inflammatory cytokine, tumor necrosis factor alpha (TNF-alpha), and decrease the production of the inflammation-promoting enzyme, inducible nitric oxide synthase (iNOS).[130] In several recent studies, olive oil phenols have demonstrated protective anti-inflammatory effects by reducing atherosclerotic lesions,[131] improving major risk factors for cardiovascular disease (including endothelial function),[132] and lowering the expression of inflammation-signalling molecules in human inflammatory bowel disease.[133] Several researchers consider the consumption of virgin olive oil and olive extracts a valued strategy in the prevention of inflammation.

The Bottom Line

There are, indeed, a wide variety of nutrients that are involved in fighting systemic inflammation, and we have included these in our Inflammation Control criterion. These nutrients and nutrient categories include eicosapentaenoic and docosahexaenoic acids; linolenic acid; gamma tocopherol; alpha-lipoic acid; vitamin C; flavonoids; procyanidolic oligomers; and the phenolic compounds found in green tea, turmeric (curcumin), and olive extracts. All are proven inflammation antagonists. Together, these nutrients and nutrient categories, at potencies prescribed in the *Blended Standard,* comprise the Inflammation Control criterion.

The criterion for Inflammation Control poses the following question:

> *Does the product contain eicosapentaenoic and docosahexaenoic acids, linolenic acid, gamma tocopherol, alpha-lipoic acid, vitamin C, flavonoids, procyanidolic oligomers, and the phenolic compounds from green tea, olive, and turmeric extracts, at potencies up to 100% of the potencies for these nutrients or nutrient categories in the* Blended Standard?

Due to the technical challenges, including tableting, stability, and shelf-life involved in the addition of high levels of essential fatty acids (fish oils and plant seed oils) in tableted products, the levels of these nutrient categories are only included in the Inflammation criterion for those products categorized as Combination Products.

15. Glycation Control

Aging—the outcome of the conflict between chemistry and biology in living systems—introduces chronic, cumulative chemical modifications that compromise the structure and function of important biomolecules within our cells. We now know that changes to these molecular structures, driven by unrelenting oxidative stress, can render them dysfunctional. Their accumulation, the detritus of an ongoing oxidative war within the cell, is a hallmark of the aging process.

Proteins with long life spans serve as molecular repositories for cumulative oxidative damage, which is detectable in the form of advanced glycation and lipoxidation end-products (AGEs and ALEs).[134] A telltale sign of protein oxidation is the addition of carbonyl groups ($>C=O$) to particular amino acids within a protein's structure. Carbonylation is an irreversible process;[135] just as you cannot unscramble an egg, carbonylated proteins, once formed, must be destroyed and expunged from the cell. Normally, they are marked for degradation by the cell's proteolytic enzymes; however—depending on the vitality of the cell's removal processes—they can escape to form aggregates that accumulate with age. Carbonylation of proteins occurs through direct oxidative attack from free radicals and metal ions, from reactions with oxidized sugars and lipid peroxides (oxidized fats), and through the process of glycation.[136]

Glycation (also called glycosylation) is the complexing of a protein with a sugar to form a molecular arrangement that irreversibly alters the structure of the protein and destroys its functionality. The effects of glycation can be seen in the brown-

---

*   Cytokines are proteinaceous signalling compounds, similar to hormones and neurotransmitters, which are used extensively for localized inter-cellular communication.

†   AP-1 is a proinflammatory cytokine that acts as a transcription factor, controlling the transfer of genetic information from the cell's DNA to molecules of messenger RNA (mRNA), which subsequently direct the manufacture of other inflammatory proteins.

ing of a glazed ham or turkey during the cooking process. Essentially, the same things happen in the body, which acts much like a low-temperature oven (37°C) with a 76-year cooking cycle.[137] Over time, non-enzymatic reactions between sugars and proteins generate a "browning" of our cells with a consequent accumulation of dysfunctional glycosylated proteins. Excessive glycation is a common occurrence in diabetes. Fuelled by high blood-sugar levels, glycation is responsible for much of the damage to tissues and organs that is a hallmark of the disease, including disruption of the transport of blood gases, development of cataracts and diabetic retinopathy, destruction of the myelin sheath of nerve cells, and the development of diabetic neuropathy. For the diabetic, the consequences of uncontrolled glycation can prove deadly, indeed.

The buildup of glycosylated proteins also leads to molecular cross linking and further oxidative modifications, resulting in the formation of AGE deposits. These high-molecular-weight aggregates can become cytotoxic.[138] A growing body of evidence suggests that AGEs and similar toxic rubble from lipid peroxidation (ALEs) contribute to the progress of several degenerative diseases, including Parkinson's disease, Alzheimer's disease, and cancer. [134, 139-142]

Carnosine

Carnosine, a simple dipeptide of the amino acids, beta-alanine and l-histidine, has emerged as the most promising broad-spectrum shield to date against the oxidative modification of proteins.[143] In multiple studies, the peptide has been shown to inhibit lipid peroxidation, free radical-induced oxidative damage, protein glycation, AGE formation, and protein-protein cross linking.[144-147] As an antioxidant, it reduces carbonylation; as a chelator of metal ions, it interrupts their ability to catalyze other forms of oxidative protein modification. Carnosine acts as a natural scavenger of toxic reactive aldehydes produced from the degradation of fats, sugars, and proteins. As well, carnosine inhibits the cross linking of proteins that leads to the formation of AGEs.[145] Senile plaque formation of amyloid-beta protein is stimulated in the presence of metal ions, such as copper and zinc; as a chelator of transition metals, carnosine can prevent the cross linking of these proteins that leads to such plaque formation.

Most importantly, carnosine shields normal proteins from the toxic reach of AGEs already present in the cell.[148] By offering itself as a sacrificial target and binding preferentially to glucose, carnosine spares important cellular proteins from oxidative degradation.[149] In the process, carnosine, itself, becomes glycosylated, forming a non-mutagenic derivative that can be safely degraded by the cell.[150] Some researchers have observed that carnosine's ability to address the challenges of protein modification fit the bill so well, it appears that the molecule was designed by Nature's hand to address this unique need.[143]

While carnosine is available in the US market, it is restricted in products manufactured for the Canadian market. Regardless of this, our Health Support criteria are evidence-based and do not

consider the regulatory question. Consequently, we have included carnosine as a critical component of our Glycation Control criterion. We recognize that this places Canadian products at a very slight disadvantage in the final product rankings. This is unfortunate; Health Canada will, hopefully, see reason to allow this important anti-aging nutrient to be made available in Canada in the near future.

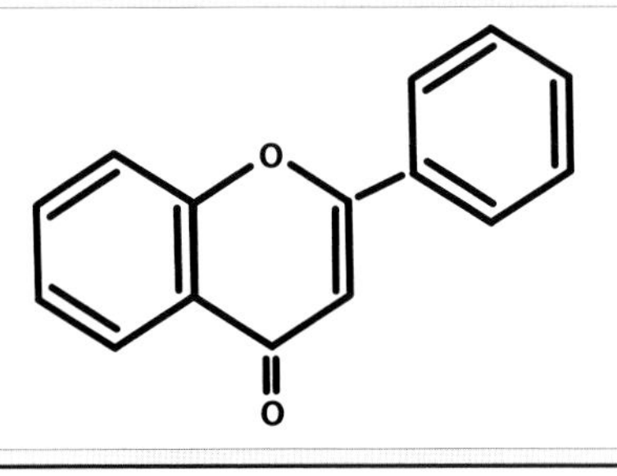

Other Nutrients

High doses of vitamin C and E, both powerful antioxidants in their own right, separately and in combination have been found to confer protection against glycation.[151, 152] The combination of vitamins C and E was found to block the formation of protein cross links and delay collagen aging in young mice,[153] and to reduce levels of glycosylated haemoglobin and low-density lipoproteins in diabetic animals.[154] A cross-sectional study investigating the association of diet and lifestyle with levels of glycated blood proteins in non-diabetic, middle-aged adults demonstrated that a high intake of these antioxidants correlated with a reduced level of glycation.[155]

In animal-model studies, alpha-lipoic acid has been found to reduce hypertension and hyperglycemia.[156] Other studies have demonstrated the antioxidant's ability to prevent glycation and inactivation of proteins.[157] It has been proposed that supplementation with alpha-lipoic acid and vitamin E may directly strengthen the anti-glycation defense mechanisms in the brain to protect against AD.[158] When human blood cells are treated with alpha-lipoic acid, they demonstrate a marked reduction in lipid peroxide levels. This finding is supported by a recent animal-model study. Laboratory rats given intraperitoneal injections of alpha-lipoic acid, at 35mg/kg of body weight, had significantly less glycation and accretion of AGEs in their diaphragm muscles than did control animals. According to the authors, the findings provide strong evidence for the therapeutic utility of alpha-lipoic acid in reducing protein glycation.[159]

The Bottom Line

Glycation and other processes of protein degradation, including oxidative carbonylation and AGE formation, are principal pathways for the onset of degenerative disease. Carnosine, a simple dipeptide of beta-alanine and histidine, has emerged as an effective and natural means of reducing such protein damage and guarding against age-related proteolytic decline, which retards the removal of damaged proteins. Supplementation with carnosine provides the added benefit of cellular rejuvenation—the reason it has been dubbed as Nature's "pluripotent life extension agent." Carnosine, along with vitamins E and C, and alpha-lipoic acid, demonstrate powerful antioxidant and anti-glycation effects. These four important nutrients, at doses recommended in the *Blended Standard*, comprise our Glycation Control criterion.

The criterion for Glycation Control poses the following question:

Does the product contain l-carnosine, vitamin E (including alpha tocopherol and gamma tocopherol, or

Figure 9-4: Flavone Ring Skeleton

mixed tocopherols), vitamin C, and alpha-lipoic acid at potencies up to 100% of the potencies for those nutrients or nutrient categories listed in the Blended Standard?

16. Bioflavonoid Profile

Polyphenols are a diverse class of compounds found naturally in the leaves, bark, roots, flowers, and seeds of plants. Citrus fruits, grapes, olives, tea leaves, bark, vegetables, dark berries, whole grains, and nuts are particularly rich sources of these natural antioxidants. Polyphenol pigments are largely responsible for the brightly coloured hues of ripened fruits and vegetables. Within the plant, they guard the cells from disease, filter out harmful ultraviolet light, and protect the delicate plant seeds until germination. When consumed in the diet, polyphenols become prodigious free radical scavengers, conferring numerous health benefits. There is evidence that some phenolic compounds also help detoxify the body by chelating with metals and facilitating their removal.[160, 161]

There are two major groups of polyphenols, differentiated on the basis of their structural formula: the *flavonoids* and the *phenolic compounds* (derived from phenolic acids). The flavonoids are known as "nature's biological response modifiers" because of their ability to alter the body's reactions to allergens, viruses and carcinogens, and to protect cellular tissues against oxidative attack. Flavonoids, found in the edible pulp of many fruits and vegetables, impart a bitter taste when isolated. Citrus fruits, such as oranges, lemons, limes, grapefruit, and kiwi, are particularly rich sources of flavonoids. Rose hips, cherries, black currents, grapes, green peppers, broccoli, onions, and tomatoes are also high in these compounds, as are many herbs, including bilberry, ginkgo, yarrow, hawthorn, and milk thistle. Other flavonoid compounds are found in the leaves, bark, and seeds of various plant species. The leaves of *Camellia sinensis* (dried to make green and black tea), the bark of the maritime (*Landes*) pine, and the seeds of ripened grapes are excellent sources of a variety of flavonoid compounds. As well, soybeans, nuts, and whole grains are replete with a class of flavonoids known as isoflavones.

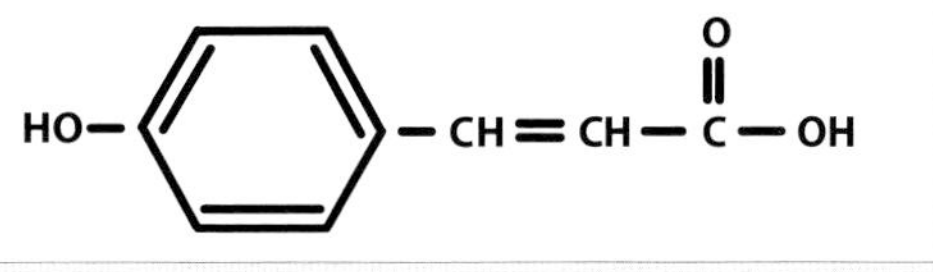

Flavonoids are important for the health and integrity of blood vessels. Through their ability to decrease permeability, flavonoids can reduce microvascular haemorrhaging and enhance capillary strength. The flavonoids confer cardio-protective benefits specifically through their ability to prevent oxidation of cholesterol. This ability is reported to be similar to, and possibly more potent than, the antioxidant powers of vitamins C and E. The scientific literature is filled with studies reporting the beneficial effects of dietary flavonoids in human health. Flavonoids, along with beta-carotene, vitamin C, and vitamin E, may be the cell's principal cancer chemopreventive agents. Their abundance in fruit and vegetables underlies the strong correlation between high fruit and vegetable consumption and reduced cancer risk.[162, 163]

Citrus flavonoids, also called *bioflavonoids,* are, perhaps, the largest of the flavonoid groups. Studies indicate they can relax smooth muscles in the arteries, reduce vascular permeability, and enhance the strength of capillaries, thereby lowering blood pressure and improving circulation. As well as possessing anti-inflammatory properties, citrus flavonoids exhibit powerful antioxidant properties and protect the cardiovascular system from harmful lipid peroxidation. Quercetin, one of the most biologically active of the flavonoids, serves as the backbone for many of the citrus flavonoids. Quercetin is indicated in the prevention of diabetes, due to its ability to enhance insulin production, protect the insulin-producing beta-cells in the pancreas, and inhibit platelet aggregation (a principle cause of blood clotting in diabetics).[164] In animal studies, quercetin has proved effective against a wide variety of cancers.[165] Unfortunately, there is little human research available to assess its efficacy. Other important citrus flavonoids, including rutin, quercitrin, and hesperidin, are derivatives of quercetin. The subtle differences in the chemistry of these compounds are a consequence of the various sugar molecules attached to the quercetin backbone.

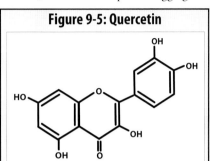

Figure 9-5: Quercetin

According to Bagchi,[166] the flavonoids found in grape seed extract (GSE) are highly bioavailable. Proanthocyanidins, the active components of GSE, form a complex of bioflavonoid compounds, known as *procyanidolic oligomers* (PCOs). This unique group of flavonoids appears to confer the cardio-protective benefits noted in consumers of red wine. PCO compounds also exhibit cytotoxicity (cell-killing ability) against several types of cancer cells, increase intracellular levels of vitamin C, enhance capillary stability, and inhibit the destruction of collagen.[167, 168]

The antioxidant actions of flavonoids appear to protect blood lipids from oxidative damage by quenching lipid peroxidation.[169, 170] These properties complement and enhance the antioxidant powers of vitamin C, vitamin E, and the carotenoids. Flavonoids also possess several other important pharmacological properties: they are antibacterial, antiviral, anti-inflammatory, antiallergic, antihemorrhagic, and vasodilatory.[171-175] All in all, not bad for a day's work!

The Bottom Line

Accordingly, the bioflavonoids (citrus flavonoids, soy isoflavones, quercetin, quercitrin, hesperidin, rutin, bilberry, and assorted berry extracts) are combined with the procyanidolic oligomers (including resveratrol, grape seed and pine bark extracts) to form an important component of our product rating criteria, listed collectively under the category of Mixed Bioflavonoids.

The criterion for the Bioflavonoid Profile poses the following question:

Does the product contain a mixture of bioflavonoids (cit-

Figure 9-6: *p*-Hydroxycinnamic Acid

rus flavonoids, soy isoflavones, quercetin, quercitrin, hes-peridin, rutin, bilberry, and assorted berry extracts) and PCOs (including resveratrol, grape seed, and pine bark extracts) at potencies up to 100% of the recommended potencies for mixed bioflavonoids and PCOs in the Blended Standard?

17. Phenolic Compounds Profile

Phenolic compounds are derivatives of the phenolic acids, hydroxycinnamic acid and hydroxybenzoic acid. These compounds differ from the flavonoids in that they are composed of a single six-carbon ring, known as an aromatic or cyclic ring, which provides them with a strong electron-donating ability. The many different phenolic compounds found in nature are variations of these basic structures, with a wide variety of structures attached to this basic hydrocarbon skeleton. The difference in the ring structure in the phenolic compounds, compared to the flavonoids, provides for a slightly different (but equally valuable) chemical nature.

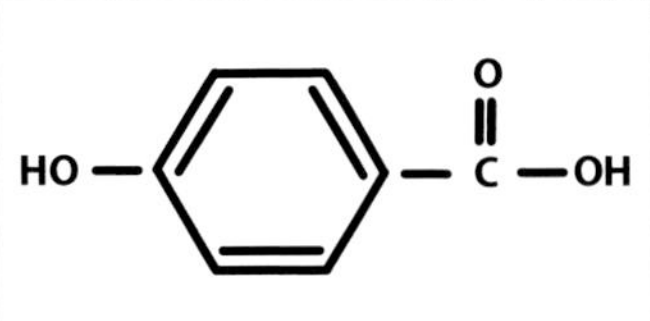

The most intensely studied of the phenolic compounds include:

✔ turmeric, a perennial herb of the ginger family and a major ingredient in curry. Long used in Chinese and Ayurvedic (Indian) medicine as an anti-inflammatory, it is an effective antioxidant, anticarcinogenic, cardiovascular, and hepatic agent.

✔ green tea, a rich source of a class of polyphenolic compounds called catechins. These antioxidant compounds possess powerful antimutagenic properties, protecting cellular DNA from oxidative damage.[176]

✔ olive extracts containing tyrosol, hydroxytyrosol, and the oleuropeine glycosides, found in the fruit of the olive tree. *Extra Virgin* olive oil, extracted from the first cold press of the olive, derives its unique aroma, pungent taste, and high thermal stability from these complex aromatic compounds.[161]

The weight of scientific evidence supporting the health benefits of the dietary consumption of polyphenols is immense. Their power as free radical antagonists, their recognized efficacy in reducing cardiovascular and cancer risks, and their demonstrated

Figure 9-7: p-Hydroxybenzoic Acid

pharmacologic properties as anti-inflammatory, antiviral, antibacterial, antiallergic, antihemorrhagic, and immuno-enhancing agents, make an exceptionally strong case for their inclusion in nutritional supplementation. The *International Consensus Statement*, issued recently by the European Commission, promoting the adoption of the Mediterranean diet, echoes the scientific findings: the consumption of olive oil and the phenolic compounds derived from such a diet confers profound health benefits. For further information on the scientific evidence supporting the use of each of these nutrients and nutrient categories, please log on to www.NutriSearch.ca.

The Bottom Line

The biochemistry of polyphenols is an emerging area of nutritional research; because of its novel nature, there is not yet a quantitative consensus among our cited nutritional authorities with respect to daily intake. While it is recognized that supplementation with polyphenols is highly desireable, no *median* recommended daily intake specific to phenolic compounds is yet available. For this reason, we have turned to the emergent scientific literature (Visioli et al)[160,177] in order to establish a recommended daily intake of 25 mg of phenolic compounds as the basis for our *Blended Standard*.

Accordingly, the phenolic compounds include the olive-based phenolic compounds and the phenolic-acid derivatives, curcumin and green tea catechins. Together, they form another important component of our product rating criteria, listed under the Phenolic Compounds Profile.

The criterion for the Phenolic Compounds Profile poses the following question:

Does the product contain phenolic compounds (polyphenolic acids and their derivatives, which include olive, curcumin, and the green tea extracts) at the potency for this nutrient category established in the Blended Standard?

18. Potential Toxicities

In order to optimize preventive benefits, the strategy of nutritional supplementation is to encourage long-term use. Consequently, there exists a potential for cumulative toxicity of particular nutrients. It would be folly, indeed, to supplement with high levels of certain nutrients, only to find down the road that your investment, instead of promoting wellbeing, has jeopardized your health. Most nutrients used in nutritional supplements have a high degree of safety; however, some nutrients require a degree of prudence when it comes to long-term use.

Vitamin A (retinol), because of its solubility in fatty tissues, can become toxic when taken in high doses over a long period. As well, chronic iron overload can significantly increase the level of oxidative damage to cells. Accidental overdose of iron-containing supplements is, in fact, a leading cause of fatal poisoning in children (see Table 5-1, Chapter 5). This is not to say that vitamin A and iron are not important to the health of our cells; both nutri-

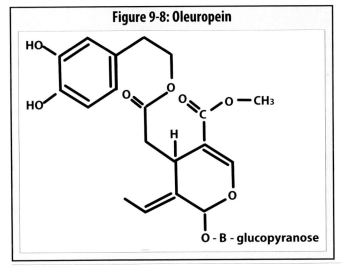

Figure 9-8: Oleuropein

O - B - glucopyranose

ents play crucial roles in cellular metabolism. However, it is important to be aware that there exist safe and effective alternatives for meeting the daily requirements for these nutrients *without* compromising one's health through imprudent use. Because of their importance in cellular health and their potential for cumulative damage, either too much or too little vitamin A and iron is problematic.

Vitamin A

Despite the prevalence of vitamin A deficiency, retinol toxicity is a common occurrence. As many as 5% of those who supplement with vitamin A unknowingly suffer from toxicity symptoms.[178] Supplementation at 5,000-10,000 IU per day of pre-formed vitamin A—a dose well within the range offered in many popular vitamin supplements—may lead to a *cumulative* toxic overdose.[179] As well, accidental ingestion of a single, large dose of vitamin A can produce acute toxicity in children. One large study of over 22,000 pregnant women who supplemented with vitamin A during early pregnancy found that among the babies born to women who took more than 10,000 IU of preformed vitamin A per day in the form of supplements, about 1 infant in 57 had a malformation attributable to the supplement.[180, 181]

Consumption of more than 10,000 IU of vitamin A carries a five-fold greater risk of birth defects than does consumption of less than 5,000 IU per day. Rothman and co-workers[181] found that the prevalence of birth defects appears greatest in those women who consume high levels of the pre-formed vitamin within the first seven weeks of their pregnancy. The authors conclude that women who *might* become pregnant should limit their retinol intake to below 5,000 IU, or—better yet—supplement with beta-carotene.

Beta-carotene, the orange/yellow-coloured pigment found in many garden vegetables, is a retinol precursor. The body easily converts beta-carotene into vitamin A by cleaving the carotene molecule into two molecules of retinol *as needed*, thereby avoiding the toxic accumulation of pre-formed vitamin A. Once transformed into active retinol, beta-carotene confers the same beneficial effects. Other than occasional loose stools or slight discoloration of the skin, even high doses of beta-carotene do not exhibit toxicity. As an added benefit, beta-carotene is a much more potent antioxidant than retinol and provides even greater protection against oxidative challenge. If you take too much beta-carotene you might turn orange like a carrot—but provided you're not around any large rabbits, you'll be just fine!

Iron

Iron plays an important role in the physiology of the body. As a central part of the haemoglobin and myoglobin molecules, iron is indispensable to the body's ability to transport gases into and out of the cell. It is also needed in several important enzymes involved in energy production, metabolism, and DNA synthesis. Some iron is lost through the breakdown of red blood cells and excretion in the bile. However, due to its importance, the body conserves iron at all costs; the kidneys do not eliminate the metal.

It would be folly, indeed, to supplement with high levels of certain nutrients, only to find down the road that your investment, instead of promoting wellbeing, has jeopardized your health.

The dark side of iron supplementation arises when it is consumed in amounts excessive to the body's needs. While unbound (non-heme) iron is more likely to generate oxidative challenges through free radical generation, excessive iron supplementation in *any* form can create profound problems for the cell. Iron overload can cause deterioration of the gut lining, vomiting and diarrhoea, abdominal and joint pain, liver damage, loss of weight, and intense fatigue.[182] Acute doses as low as 3 g can cause death in children.

Approximately one out of every 250 North Americans suffers from haemochromatosis, a genetic defect common in those of northern European descent. The disorder causes the body to accumulate and store abnormally high levels of iron. People with haemochromatosis store twice as much iron as others, placing themselves at increased risk for iron-related diseases. Symptoms generally occur after 50 years of age and include fatigue, abdominal pain, achy joints, impotence, and symptoms that mimic diabetes. Evidence from several studies suggests that high levels of iron contribute to a noticeable increase in the risk for cardiovascular disease, likely due to non-haeme iron's aggressive pro-oxidant nature. Serum ferritin (iron) levels are, in fact, one of the strongest biochemical markers for the progression of atherosclerosis, a consequence of dramatically increased oxidation of LDL cholesterol.[183] A 1995 study, conducted on Finnish men, found that those with high body stores of iron had a substantially increased risk of heart attack. Men with the highest levels of stored iron showed a level of risk three times that of men with the lowest levels.[184]

Iron accumulation disorders contribute to a variety of other disease states, all of which are degenerative in nature. Studies reveal that chronic iron overload contributes to increased infections, cancer, arthritis, osteoporosis, diabetes, and various cognitive dysfunctions.[185, 186] Data obtained from the first National Health and Nutrition Examination Survey (NHANES I), linking body-stores of iron and cancer, found an elevated risk was associated with high iron levels.[187] Unless you are a woman with regular menses (menstrual periods), the only way to remove excess iron is through blood letting. That is why, for men, iron overload can prove quite problematic to resolve. Very recent research has found that long-term supplementation with iron at doses less than 5 mg/day can lead to iron-overload toxicity.[1] Consequently, this guide has adopted an upper limit of iron intake at 5 mg/day when considering a product's rating. Any product containing iron at a daily dose greater than this limit is penalized in this rating criterion.

The Bottom Line

The majority of nutrients used in supplementation have a large measure of safety; however, the use of vitamin A and iron warrants prudence and caution, particularly when consumed by children or pregnant women. Accordingly, the level of vitamin A in excess of the upper limit of intake (UL) presribed by the Food and Nutrition Board of the Institute of Medicine (page 78) and the level of iron in excess of 5 mg/day forms the final criterion in the 18-point product rating used in this guide. This criterion penalizes any product whose daily dose of either vitamin A or iron exceeds these established limits.

The criterion for Potential Toxicities poses the following questions:

> *Does the nutritional supplement contain vitamin A and iron (which is no longer included in the* Blended Standard*)? Does the potency of vitamin A exceed 100% of the upper limit of intake (UL) prescribed by the US Food and Nutrition Board? Does the potency of iron exceed 5 mg/day?*

Summary

From these 18 criteria, a five-star rating, based on half-star increments, is determined. A five-star rating highlights those products whose characteristics for optimal nutrition are clearly superior to the majority of products on the market and that approach or meet the pooled recommendations of the *Blended Standard.* Conversely, a one-star rating or less represents products possessing few, if any, of the characteristics for optimal nutrition reflected in the *Blended Standard.* We believe that this five-star scale, divisible in half-star increments, provides an intuitive means by which the consumer can compare products, based on product content.

Comparisons were completed for 1,612 products; however, because of the sheer volume, not every product is graphically displayed. To maximize the number of manufacturers represented in our analysis, the highest-ranking product (rating three stars or above) from each manufacturer was selected. In some cases, where a manufacturer has both a Canadian and a US product, or produces gender-specific products, the manufacturer may have more than one product represented in the graphs. All graphical comparisons are found in Section V.

New to this edition of the *Comparative Guide*, we have included combination products, described earlier in this chapter, as a separate category. With the exception of the criteria for completeness, potency, and inflammation control (which must take into account the difficulties in manufacturing a tableted product containing essential fatty acids), combination products are evaluated using the same criteria as stand-alone products.

Because of these differences, and for convenience of the reader, stand-alone products and combination products have been rated and listed separately within Section V of this guide.

Quality means doing it right when no one is looking.
— Henry Ford (1863-1947)

CHAPTER TEN

MEDALS OF ACHIEVEMENT

Products that reach five stars are eligible to participate in the *NutriSearch Medal of Achievement Program,*™ which awards **GOLD**, **SILVER**, or **BRONZE** medals based on an assessment of the type of Good Manufacturing Practice (GMP) used to manufacture the product, and on third-party laboratory verification of the product's formulation.

To reach **BRONZE** status, the manufacturer must demonstrate compliance with a nationally recognized certification program for GMP based on a food model. Manufacturers that have completed and can document a current and valid "A" rating for GMP compliance with the Natural Products Association (NPA) [formerly the National Nutritional Foods Association (NNFA)] GMP Certification Program will receive the **NutriSearch BRONZE Medal of Achievement**™ for the selected product. To meet the standard of evidence, the manufacturer must supply written documentation of both the successful completion of the NPA audit and current good standing with the NPA program.

To reach **SILVER** status, the manufacturer must demonstrate compliance with a nationally recognized certification program for natural health product (NHP)-model GMP (Canada), medicinal product-model GMP (Australia), or pharmaceutical-model GMP (US). Manufacturers that have completed and can document a current and valid audit for GMP compliance with the *NSF International Dietary Supplement Verification Program*, the United States Pharmacopoeia (USP) Dietary Supplement Verification Program, Canadian Natural Health Products Directorate (NHPD)* site licensing, or Australian Therapeutic Goods Administration (TGA)† site licensing receive the **NutriSearch SILVER Medal of Achievement**™ for the selected product. To meet the standard of evidence, NutriSearch will accept written documentation of the successful completion of the NSF or USP audits and current good standing with either program, a current Canadian Drug Identification Number (DIN), a current Canadian Natural Product Number (NPN), or a current listing in the Australian Register of Therapeutic Goods.

GOLD medal status requires two elements: GMP certification and laboratory verification of the product's formulation, including identity and potency. Manufacturers that qualify for **SILVER** status (based on GMP compliance) and that provide written documentation of the successful completion of a recognized, third-party laboratory analysis of product content will receive a **NutriSearch GOLD Medal of Achievement**.™ To meet the standard of evidence, NutriSearch will accept notarized certificates of analysis from either the *NSF International Dietary Supplement Verification Program*, or the *USP Dietary Supplement Verification Program*. NutriSearch will also recognize as an acceptable standard of evidence a notarized certificate of analysis from an independent third-party laboratory that meets current ISO 17025 standards.

All manufacturers who wish to receive GOLD *Medal recognition MUST submit their product(s) to a comprehensive laboratory analysis of active ingredients, using their choice of one of the three above-mentioned independent procedures.*

How the Program Works

For those products receiving a five-star rating in the initial product assessment, NutriSearch contacts each manufacturer and invites them to participate in the *NutriSearch Medal of Achievement Program.*™ A manufacturer may then choose to apply to one of the above-noted agencies for a GMP audit and/or finished product analysis. Those manufacturers deciding not to participate in the *NutriSearch Medal of Achievement Program*™ forfeit their opportunity to demonstrate superior product quality and receive no further recognition beyond their five-star rating.

Upon successful completion of GMP and/or product verification, the manufacturer is required to submit notarized documentation of such to NutriSearch. Once this documentation has been reviewed and accepted, NutriSearch will ensure that the manufacturer's product is appropriately displayed in the

---

* In Canada, nutritional supplements—including vitamins, minerals, and herbal products sold in dosage form—are classified as natural health products and are federally regulated by Health Canada's Natural Health Products Directorate (NHPD). These products bear either a Drug Identity Number (DIN) or a Natural Health Product Number (NPN). Conversely, in the United States, such products are commonly known as dietary supplements and are regulated like foods.

† In Australia, dietary supplements are classified as Listed Medicinal Products and are regulated under the Australian Therapeutic Goods Authority. These products bear a numerical identifier (Aust-L) and are listed in the Australian Register of Therapeutic Goods.

next edition of the *NutriSearch Comparative Guide to Nutritional Supplements.*™ The five-star rating will be highlighted in colours relating to the level of compliance (Gold, Silver, or Bronze) with the product's Medal of Achievement prominently displayed in the manufacturer's profile.

There are no fees for the *NutriSearch Medal of Achievement Program,*™ other than those incurred through each of the independent agencies for the site audit and laboratory verification of product content.

Beyond the Stars: Proof of Quality

Whether talking about pharmaceutical products or dietary supplements, adherence to pharmaceutical-model GMP and laboratory-based verification of the identity, potency, and purity of the finished product is the **Gold Standard of proof** for product quality and safety.

The Government of Canada requires that all manufacturers of natural health products sold in or into Canada comply with federally mandated GMP and product-quality standards for natural health products. These standards are established by Health Canada's NHPD and may require site inspections of the manufacturing plant and an assessment of the finished product as a pre-market requirement for site licensing and product licensing. The new Canadian GMP standards for natural health products approach GMP standards modelled for pharmaceutical products. Consequently, Canada (along with Australia) is one of the strictest regulatory environments for natural health products in the developed world.

Unfortunately, this is not the case in the United States, where compliance with pharmaceutical-model GMP and quality standards for finished products are currently voluntary. The US Dietary Supplement Health and Education Act (1994) places nutritional supplements in a special category, regulated by the US Food and Drug Authority (FDA). In this category, the language regarding GMP compliance is modelled after food-processing practices. Under the Act, the manufacturer is responsible for determining that the supplements it makes are safe and that any claims made about the products are substantiated. There are no regulations that establish minimum standards of practice (GMP)—the manufacturer is solely responsible for establishing its own manufacturing practices and quality control measures, and for ensuring that those practices are met. The burden of proof for unsafe or adulterated products and false or misleading labelling, however, lies wholly with the FDA and not with the manufacturer. Consequently, the US market for dietary supplements is one where, according to some authorities, the majority of US dietary supplements fail to meet label claims. Simply put, although regulations exist, the enforcement and burden of proof is such that the reliability of supplements manufactured in the US is, indeed, questionable.

Assessing Product Quality

The previous edition of this guide attempted to provide evidence of standards of quality and GMP compliance in the company profiles of some of our top-rated products; however, until now it has not been possible to provide such evidence as an integral component in our product ratings. **In this edition of the guide, NutriSearch introduces a new level of product assessment** that incorporates GMP compliance and product-content verification as critical components of our product ratings.

This higher standard of evidence incurs considerable cost and effort on the part of the selected manufacturers; consequently, it is offered only to those manufacturers whose products merit a five-star rating, based upon our initial content analysis. For these top-rated products, each manufacturer must provide notarized certification showing:

✔ the level of GMP compliance (food-to-pharmaceutical model); and

✔ third-party laboratory verification of product identity and potency according to label claim.

Most experts in the field of nutritional supplementation believe that these two additional criteria are every bit as important as the particular nuances concerning the nutrient content of a given product—a sentiment with which NutriSearch wholeheartedly agrees. Together, GMP certification and laboratory-based content analysis provide assurance to the consumer that the product meets established standards for manufacturing safety and product quality, and that what is on the label is really in the bottle.

Currently, in the United States there are three independent non-government programs available for the evaluation of GMP compliance for nutritional (dietary) supplements. Each program has its own standard of GMP compliance, which varies based on how it is modelled (food-to-pharmaceutical).

These programs are:

✔ the *NPA GMP Certification Program*;

✔ the *NSF International Dietary Supplement Verification Program*; and

✔ the *USP Dietary Supplement Verification Program.*

For US companies who also sell dietary supplements into Canada or Australia, two additional standards of evidence are accepted. Both Health Canada's NHPD and the Australian TGA will licence US-based manufacturers in accordance with their respective national standards. NutriSearch will accept evidence of compliance with either of these standards as verification of GMP compliance for both US and Canadian products. Such products will bear a Health Canada Drug Identification Number (DIN), a Health Canada Natural Product Number (NPN), or will be listed in the Australian Register of Therapeutic Goods.

Certification Programs Overview

The following discussion will provide the reader with an overview of the various government and non-government programs available in the United States and Canada that provide certification for dietary (nutritional) supplements. The levels of certification range form food-model to pharmaceutical-model GMP and finished product standards.

Natural Products Association Certification

The Natural Products Association (NPA) offers both a GMP certification program and a separate product verification (TruLabel) program.

NPA GMP Certification Program

The NPA developed its standards in concert with member manufacturers, other trade associations, and the FDA. As with all facility audits for GMP compliance, the NPA's auditors examine many aspects of manufacturing, including: personnel; plant and grounds; sanitation; equipment; quality control; production and process controls; and warehouse, distribution, and post-distribution practices. Third parties selected by the NPA conduct audits of the manufacturing facilities. There are three levels of compliance:

An 'A' rating means the member "has excellent compliance with NPA GMPs, with few deficiencies noted." An 'A' rating is required to apply for certification and the right to display the NPA GMP certification logo.

A 'B' rating means the member "has good compliance with NPA GMPs, but several significant deficiencies were noted." Members may apply for 'A' status with written verification of correction of the noted deficiencies.

A 'C' rating means the member "has fair or poor compliance with NPA GMPs." Many deficiencies are noted and a re-audit of the facility is required.

NPA members also have the right to appeal a compliance rating, and the NPA will work with both the member and the auditor to resolve any outstanding issues. **NPA GMP certification does not include any laboratory verification of the label claims of the finished product.**

NutriSearch considers the NPA GMP Certification Program a food-model GMP standard, which is less stringent than a pharmaceutical standard. Products manufactured under this program are awarded a NutriSearch BRONZE Medal of Achievement.™

NPA TruLabel Program

The NPA product certification (TruLabel) program is completely separate from its GMP certification. The TruLabel program involves randomized testing of products registered with the program. It is important to note that a product registered with the TruLabel program may *never* be tested; instead, products are randomly chosen for verification each year. Consequently, not every product bearing a TruLabel mark has undergone an actual laboratory verification of label claim—something consumers might well be led to expect. NutriSearch will therefore not accept TruLabel compliance as evidence of product verification. For further information on NPA GMP certification and the TruLabel program, contact:

Natural Products Association
1773 T Street, NW
Washington, DC 20009
USA

or call (202) 223-0101. You can also e-mail your inquiry to natural@naturalproductsassoc.org, or log on to www.naturalproductsassoc.org.

Because the NPA TruLabel program involves randomized testing of products—that is, the NPA does not test every product that participates in the program and, in fact, may never test a given product—an NPA-certified TruLabel manufacturer cannot make the claim that their product underwent a comprehensive laboratory analysis for identity and potency. Consequently, the TruLabel program does not qualify as an

acceptable standard of evidence for the NutriSearch GOLD Medal of Achievement.™

NSF Dietary Supplements Certification

The NSF Dietary Supplements Certification Program includes both facility audits and laboratory-based product verification; each step of the program uses third-party agents selected by NSF. When a manufacturer or supplier contacts the NSF Dietary Supplements Certification Program Office, an NSF representative will assist the manufacturer through a five-step certification process. This process includes application, formulation review, facility audit, product testing, and documentation-report registration and certification. The certification process begins when a completed application is returned to NSF. NSF then provides a confidential review of product formulations and labels and determines appropriate testing. Initial facility inspections for certification are conducted by trained NSF field auditors and include a GMP audit and assessment of conformity to NSF policies. Products are then tested at NSF laboratories to verify conformity to the NSF Dietary Supplement Standard - NSF 173-2001.

Product assessment includes testing of raw materials as well as the finished product. Testing includes identity, quantity, consistency, and purity, where analytical criteria can be established. Tolerances for purity of ingredients and contamination standards are adopted from several sources, including the World Health Organization, the NSF International Standards, USP, British Pharmacopeia, European Pharmacopeia, and Health Canada. Certification is awarded after all of the requirements for listing have been successfully completed. Annual audits and product tests are conducted to ensure ongoing compliance.

NutriSearch considers the NSF Dietary Supplements Certification Program a dietary supplement-model GMP that approaches the rigours of a pharmaceutical-model GMP. **However, NSF has chosen to accept products into its program that have received only NPA-GMP (food-model) certification. NutriSearch is of the opinion that the qualification of products manufactured to food-model GMP *without* the need for an NSF-GMP audit compromises the rigour of the NSF certification criteria. Consequently, for such products, NutriSearch treats the NPA-GMP certification as a food-model standard. Hence, products bearing an NSF-GMP certification will only be awarded a *NutriSearch BRONZE Medal of Achievement*™ unless the manufacturer can verify that the product was subjected to a full NSF facility audit for GMP.**

Products awarded an NSF-GMP certification, through an NSF facility audit, qualify for a NutriSearch SILVER Medal of Achievement.™ *Silver medal recipients, in turn, are eligible for a* NutriSearch GOLD Medal of Achievement™ *once the manufacturer completes a third-party laboratory analysis of product content.*

About NSF

The NSF Dietary Supplements Certification Program standards are more stringent than the NPA standards, and include a full laboratory analysis of each product submitted for certification.

NSF has developed over 50 voluntary American National Standards under the scope of public health and safety. NSF/ANSI standards are developed through involvement of those who are directly affected by the standard. The process ensures input from industry representatives, public health/regulatory officials, and consumers. NSF is accredited by the American National Standards Institute (ANSI) to develop American National Standards. ANSI is a central repository for organizations setting standards for many consumer products and processes. Their accreditation verifies that NSF develops standards in a manner that ensures openness and due process. NSF/ANSI Standards are constantly being reviewed and revised to ensure that the standards are up to date and technically sound.

For further information regarding the NSF International Dietary Certification Program, contact:

NSF International
PO Box 130140, 789 N. Dixboro Road
Ann Arbor, MI 48113-0140
USA

Alternatively, call 1-800-NSF-MARK, or e-mail info@nsf.org, or log on to www.nsf.org.

NHPD and TGA Certification

Health Canada's NHPD oversees the manufacture, distribution, and sale of natural health products (dietary and herbal supplements), including vitamin, mineral, and herbal supplements. Until recently, nutritional supplements sold in Canada were treated the same as prescription drugs, requiring pharmaceutical standards for ingredients, processing, and distribution. Health Canada's former Therapeutic Products Program issued a Drug Identification Number (DIN), which still applies to pharmaceutical products, to accepted natural health products. Awarding a DIN required manufacturers to comply with site-licensing and product-licensing requirements before receiving pre-market product approval.

Responsibility for site and product licensing for the sale of natural health products was transferred to the new Natural Health Products Directorate (NHPD) on January 1, 2004. As in the past, all natural health products sold in Canada under the new NHPD regulations continue to be subject to rigorous levels of compliance. Pre-market site and product licensing continue to be mandatory prior to the awarding of a Natural Product Number (NPN). Not only must the product formulator meet Health Canada's GMP for natural health products, so, too, must the label printers, distributors, packagers, importers, and ingredient manufacturers.

Unfortunately, Health Canada does not necessarily conduct a physical audit of the manufacturing plant or a laboratory analysis of product content before issuing GMP and product approval, relying instead on extensive documentation to demonstrate compliance. Because the Canadian marketplace is still in transition from pharmaceutical regulations to natural health product (NHP) regulations, some products sold in Canada still bear a DIN rather than the new NPN. It is illegal to offer for sale in Canada a natural health product that does not bear a current DIN or NPN. Products sold in or into Canada, which bear either a Health Canada DIN or NPN, are recognized by NutriSearch as providing sufficient evidence of compliance with Canadian NHP-model GMP.

Widely considered one of the toughest regulators in the world, Australia's TGA is responsible for controlling the manufactur-

ing, distribution, and sale of vitamin and mineral products in that country. TGA-approved supplements, which are classified in Australia as Listed Medicinal Products and bear an AUST-L numerical identifier, must meet pharmaceutical-model GMP. The TGA strictly regulates not only the specific ingredients in nutritional supplements, but also the source, amounts, and forms of those ingredients. TGA regulations require all manufacturing facilities to pass a GMP audit based on the Australian Code of Good Manufacturing Practice for Medicinal Products. In addition, pre-market evaluation of a product includes a close look at potential toxicity, product dosage, potential side effects, long-term effects, and more. The TGA continues to monitor products long after they enter the Australian market, requiring ongoing compliance with its strict regulations and GMP requirements.

NutriSearch considers both the Canadian NHPD and Australian TGA approvals to be an acceptable level of GMP compliance because they include both product-manufacturing and site-licensing procedures. Products approved for sale in those countries and that bear the respective DIN or NPN (Canada) or are listed in the Australian Register of Therapeutic Goods, will receive a NutriSearch SILVER Medal of Achievement.™

Silver medal recipients are eligible for a NutriSearch GOLD Medal of Achievement™ once the manufacturer completes a third-party laboratory analysis of product content.

USP Dietary Supplement Verification Program

The USP Dietary Supplement Verification Program (DSVP) sets GMP standards that approach pharmaceutical-model GMP. Although the organization does not claim to address all safety issues, USP will not accept a supplement into its program that contains an ingredient with known safety concerns.

Even before USP begins its verification of a product, the applicant must pass three criteria:
✔ detailed checklist for USP GMP compliance;
✔ verification of validated analytical methodologies for each ingredient in the product; and
✔ validation of finished product shelf-life.

Once a supplement has been accepted, USP conducts a three-day site audit based on its GMP model for dietary supplements, published in its General Chapter 2750 Manufacturing Practices for Dietary Supplements. The detailed audit examines personnel, document management, equipment, facilities, component control, maintenance, record keeping, laboratory controls, label control, quality control, and performance reviews. The applicant has only 20 days to respond to reported deficiencies with a corrective action plan in order to continue in the program. Proof of compliance with the action plan is required during a later self-audit.

Product verification includes laboratory testing for ingredient identity and potency. Testing for contamination with microbes, heavy metals, pesticides, and other toxins is also conducted. The USP product verification program tests all active ingredients in a product. Product performance characteristics, including dissolution and disintegration, weight variation, and content uniformity, are also examined.

Upon completion of testing, the DSVP report will include recommended actions for compliance.

✔ *Action Level 1* issues involve changes to the current quality system and must be adequately resolved prior to certification;

✔ *Action Level 2* issues do not involve changes to the quality system, but must still be adequately resolved prior to certification; and

✔ *Action Level 3* issues can be resolved by supplying additional information or making requested changes, but will not delay certification of the product.

Market surveillance, self-audits, and mandatory reporting of changes to the product or production process are all part of the ongoing participation in the DSVP. If critical product deficiencies are detected, USP may recommend a recall of the product or demand removal of the DSVP certification mark.

For further information on the USP Dietary Supplement Certification Program, contact:

United States Pharmacopoeia
12601 Twinbrook Parkway
Rockville, Maryland 20852-1790
USA

You can also contact the program by calling 1-301-816-8273 or by e-mail at uspverified@usp.org.

NutriSearch considers the USP DSVP to be the definitive standard for both facility and product verification. Upon submission of notarized documentation, products manufactured in compliance with USP-GMP standards are awarded a NutriSearch SILVER Medal of Achievement.™

If the finished product has also been certified under the USP DSVP and can provide a notarized certificate of analysis, it is awarded a NutriSearch GOLD Medal of Achievement.™

Independent ISO 17025 Verification

In order to facilitate the protracted process of laboratory verification currently experienced by companies attempting to verify their products, manufacturers may also use an independent, third-party laboratory that is ISO/IEC-17025-certified to provide verification of the finished product according to label claim. ISO 17025 certification ensures that the laboratory chosen to conduct the analysis follows accepted calibration and analytical procedures.

ISO, the International Standards Organization, is best known for its ISO 9000 certifications. These management protocols ensure that all aspects of a company's practices are documented. ISO certification is recognized around the world as an assurance of quality. Laboratories must ensure that management practices meet a rigorous quality standard and that their procedures, such as equipment calibration and measurement protocols, also meet the highest standards. The ISO/IEC-17025 standard is the laboratory equivalent of ISO 9000. It applies to any organization that wants to assure its customers of precision, accuracy, and reproducibility of results.

Supplement manufacturers that demonstrate GMP compliance using a method that does not include product verification in a laboratory (as can be the case with the NSF and USP certification programs) may choose a third-party ISO-certified laboratory to provide evidence of product verification.

NutriSearch will accept, as a standard of evidence, a notarized certificate of analysis of active ingredients from the ISO-certified laboratory that performed the analysis. The certificate of analysis must show identity and potency of active ingredients.

Summary

Products that reach five stars are eligible to participate in the *NutriSearch Medal of Achievement Program*,™ which awards **GOLD**, **SILVER**, or **BRONZE** medals based on an assessment of the type of Good Manufacturing Practice (GMP) used to manufacture the product, and on third-party laboratory verification of the product's formulation. This program is voluntary and the expense for GMP audit and product verification is borne by the product's manufacturer. Those manufacturers who successfully complete the program of their choice (as described above) and provide proof of GMP compliance, and those who furnish laboratory verification of product content according to label claim, are awarded the appropriate Medal of Achievement and are featured, along with an individual profile of the company and its products, in the following chapter.

Those manufacturers having more than one five-star product and who have provided a certificate of analysis for at least one of these products are awarded a *NutriSearch GOLD Medal of Achievement*™ for all five-star products, providing these products have been manufactured in the same facility.

Section IV

Top Products

This section provides the reader with an in-depth look at:

■ Top-rated Products
■ Company Profiles of NutriSearch GOLD Medal of Achievement™ Recipients

A brief review of the scope of the research leads to a listing of the top-rated products within each product category (stand-alone products and combination products). Those select few companies awarded a NutriSearch Medal of Achievement™ are highlighted. Company profiles of the NutriSearch Medal Recipients, with information of interest to the consumer on each company, its product line, and how to order products, are provided.

The preservation of health is a duty.
Few seem conscious that there is such a thing as physical morality.
—*Herbert Spencer (1820-1903)*

CHAPTER ELEVEN

TOP-RATED PRODUCTS

In conducting the research for this edition of the Comparative Guide, we examined approximately 2,000 nutritional supplements from throughout the United States and Canada. From this, 1,612 products qualified as multiple vitamin/mineral supplements, representing 394 manufacturers. Twenty-one of these products were eliminated because they exceeded the Upper Limits of safety for three or more nutrients. The remaining 1,591 were further evaluated using the Blended Standard (described in Chapter 8), and the Health Support Profile (described in Chapter 9).

Graphical comparisons were completed for 163 products. Because of the sheer volume of products, not every product was graphically analyzed; to maximize the number of manufacturers represented in our analysis, the highest-ranking product from each manufacturer rating three stars or above was selected. In some cases, where a manufacturer has both a Canadian and a US product, or produces gender-specific products, the manufacturer may have more than one product represented in the graphs. All graphical comparisons are found in Section V.

Top-rated Stand-alone Products

Table 11-1 on the following page lists the stand-alone products that achieved a five-star rating. These are nutritional products of less than three separate capsules or tablets taken in a single serving, which contain vitamins, minerals, and antioxidants, and which may also contain a variety of other nutrients.

Headlining the list are those product that also earned the NutriSearch Gold Medal of Achievement.™ These products represent the "best of the best" within the Stand-alone Products category—having attained an unsurpassed five-star rating, having demonstrated compliance with current Good Manufacturing Practices (cGMP), and having verified, through independent laboratory analysis, that what is on the label is in the bottle.

Of the 1,433 stand-alone products evaluated in this edition of the Comparative Guide, the products of only four manufacturers, representing a miniscule 0.6% of the products evaluated, were awarded this honour.

Top-rated Combination Products

Table 11-2 lists the top-rated combination products. These are nutritional products of three or more separate capsules or tablets taken in a single serving, which contain vitamins, minerals, and antioxidants, and which may also contain a variety of other nutri-ents, including fatty acids not normally found in a stand-alone product.

Headlining the list are those select few combination products that have earned the NutriSearch Gold Medal of Acievement.™ These award-winning combination products are the "best of the best" within the Combination Products category—having attained an unsurpassed five-star rating, having demonstrated compliance with cGMP, and having verified, through independent laboratory analysis, that what is on the label is really in the bottle.

Of the 179 combination products evaluated in this edition of the Comparative Guide, the products of only three manufacturers, representing a mere 3.3% of the products evaluated, were awarded this honour.

Going for the Gold

To reach a five-star product rating is a significant accomplishment for a nutritional manufacturer; nevertheless, it does not tell the whole story. With any dietary supplement, the single most important factor is quality: quality research, quality formulations, and quality manufacturing. These considerations are, in turn, a reflection of the quality-control practices (GMP) employed in a product's manufacture and in the testing and verification of identity and potency of ingredients, right from the raw materials to the finished goods. When it comes to consumer safety there is simply no room for compromise.

Manufacturers of products awarded the NutriSearch Gold Medal of Achievement™ have, at considerable expense, gone that extra mile to demonstrate their commitment to the highest standards of quality in the industry. They have met and exceeded the most stringent of manufacturing standards that are the consumer's guarantee of product quality and safety, and they have further demonstrated that commitment to quality through independent laboratory verification of identity and potency of the ingredients in the finished product, according to product label. To provide the consumer with more information about these companies, on pages 74 through 77 we have invited each manufacturer to "tell their story" in their own words.

For a complete listing of all products and their ratings, please refer to Section VI, where products are listed alphabetically by product name and alphabetically by five-star rating.

Table 11-1: Top Products STAND-ALONE

Creating Wellness Alliance

Vitalize Men's Formula

VItalize Women's Formula

Vitalize Senior Women's Gold Formula

Douglas Laboratories

Ultra Preventive IX

Ultra Preventive IX
with vitamin K

Ultra Preventive X

TrueStar Health

TrueBASIC

USANA Health Sciences

CA Essentials

US Essentials

Remaining Five-Star Rated STAND-ALONE Products

Allergy Research Group Wholly Immune	US	Rejuvenation Science Maximum Vitality	US
HealthyWize Vital Nutrients	US	Source Naturals Élan Vitàl	US
Life Extension Foundation Life Extension Mix	US	Source Naturals Life Force Multiple	US
NSI (Neutraceutical Sciences Institute)		Swanson Lee Swanson Signature Line Longevital	US
Synergy Men's Version 2	US	Vitamin Research Products Optimum 18	US

Table 11-2: Top Products COMBINATION

Douglas Laboratories

Daily Core Essentials

Longevity Support Pack

TrueStar Health

TrueBASICS Plus for Men

TrueBASICS Plus for Women

USANA Health Sciences

CA HealthPak 100

US HealthPak 100

Remaining Five-Star Rated COMBINATION Products

Colgan Institute Men's Pak	US	NSI (Neutraceutical Sciences Institute)	
Colgan Institute Men's+ 50 Pak	US	Synergy Max	US
Colgan Institute Sports Pak	US	NSI (Neutraceutical Sciences Institute)	
Colgan Institute Women's 50+ Pak	US	Synergy Ultra	US
Colgan Institute Women's Active Pak	US	Ortho Molecular Products Alpha Base	
Colgan Institute Women's Pak	US	Ultimate Pak	US

CREATING WELLNESS ALLIANCE

Five-Star Gold Medal-winning Products:

✔ **Vitalize Men's Formula**
✔ **Vitalize Women's Formula**
✔ **Vitalize Senior Women's Gold Formula**

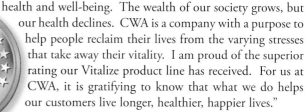

Dr Patrick Gentempo, Jr., the Chief Executive Officer and co-founder of Creating Wellness Alliance, LLC (CWA), is a world-renowned chiropractor and wellness expert. He has inspired audiences throughout the world, some as large as 8,000 people, with his vision of worldwide wellness.

Dr Gentempo's mission throughout his career has been to improve the human condition with the development of a wellness model using knowledge, technology, and a sound nutritional and lifestyle philosophy. Gentempo states that, "We live in a culture that bombards us with advertisements for things that rob us of our

health and well-being. The wealth of our society grows, but our health declines. CWA is a company with a purpose to help people reclaim their lives from the varying stresses that take away their vitality. I am proud of the superior rating our Vitalize product line has received. For us at CWA, it is gratifying to know that what we do helps our customers live longer, healthier, happier lives."

CWA has created a substantial wellness brand in part by developing "Best-of-class" wellness products—such as the Vitalize supplement line featured here—and by offering a breakthrough comprehensive lifestyle wellness program called the Creating Wellness System, offered through affiliated Creating Wellness Centers. Presently, there are hundreds of Creating Wellness Centers operating in the United States, Canada, and New Zealand.

CWA sells lifestyle products under the Creating Wellness brand and, in addition to multiple vitamin and mineral products, produces a Weight Management product—Metabolize—and a Joint Support product named Mobilize. The Vitalize brand of products, in just its first year on the market, has achieved the highest rating available—the Five Star, Gold Medal rating—in the fourth Edition of the *NutriSearch Comparative Guide to Nutritional Supplements.*™

CWA's NSF certified manufacturing facility prides itself in consistently maintaining the highest standards in the industry by striving in all manufacturing practices and procedures to retain, not only the respected GMP (Good Manufacturing Practices) for pharmaceutical-grade products and USP certifications, but also the highly acclaimed international TGA (Therapeutic Goods Association) and NPA (Natural Products Association) certifications. CWA uses all natural nutrients of the finest quality. Analytical, chemical and physical testing is performed on all nutrients by a highly trained—and well-staffed—on-sight quality control/quality assurance department. An independent third party lab for nutrient potency verification additionally analyzes CWA products.

CWA also offers customized wellness programs for corporations, governmental bodies, and other entities that desire and, in many cases, need to develop a wellness culture amongst their workforce. Dr Gentempo states, "The solution to the economic crisis facing our government and corporations relative to healthcare costs is shifting the workplace culture from a sick care model to a wellness model. Creating Wellness is the agent to help these entities make that change and chart a new and better course."

Creating Wellness Alliance, LLC
One International Blvd., Suite 750,
Mahwah, NJ 07495
Phone: (888) 589-WELL (9355)
Order Line: (888) 589-9355, ext. 138
Web Site: www.creatingwellness.com

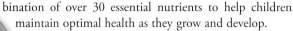

NUTRISEARCH GOLD MEDAL OF ACHIEVEMENT RECIPIENT:

TRUESTAR HEALTH

Five-Star Gold Medal-winning Products:

✔ **TrueBASIC**
✔ **TrueBASICS Plus for Men**
✔ **TrueBASICS Plus for Women**

After: 137 lbs.

Before: 166 lbs.

Founded in 2001 by CEO Tim Mulcahy, Truestar Health embraces a comprehensive approach to optimal wellness that pinpoints five key areas of health: Vitamins, Nutrition, Exercise, Sleep and Attitude.

The Truestar Health philosophy centers on the belief that a weakness in one of these areas can adversely affect a person's overall health. The harmonization of these five aspects of health translates into a proprietary total health system called the Synergistic Personal Training System. By teaching each person to balance these priorities, Truestar Health aims to bring men, women and children of all ages to their healthy lifestyle goals.

Disappointed by the quality of supplements available in the health and fitness industry, the Truestar Health team of medical experts developed Truestar Professional Series vitamins and supplements to complement their treatment philosophy. Formulated by a team of naturopathic and medical doctors, Truestar Professional Series supplements are designed to work synergistically for optimal results.

All Truestar Professional Series supplements are manufactured to stringent specifications in ISO 9001 and ISO 17025 accredited laboratories. Truestar Health currently has supplement programs to support more than 500 medical conditions and lifestyle concerns.

The five focus points of the Truestar Health program are reinforced by Truestar Health's immense online resource, truestarhealth.com, where users complete an in-depth profile to receive personalized programs in each of the key areas. Users are guided daily on their exercise regimen, supplement intake, diet, sleep habits and stress management. Leading experts in the fields of physical and mental health contribute articles and information backed by scientific research and independent studies.

Supported by a cutting-edge weight loss program, Truestar Health is the world's most comprehensive nutrition, fitness and healthy lifestyle resource serving the Canadian fitness and health industries. Truestar Health's mission is to develop the highest quality products and provide the most up-to-date information relating to personal health.

With its head offices in Toronto, Ontario, Truestar Health is rapidly becoming an international company. Truestar Professional Series supplements are being promoted in health and fitness clubs worldwide.

Truestar™
HEALTH

Nutrition

Exercise

Vitamins

Attitude

Sleep

www.truestar.com • 1 888 448 TRUE (8783)

NUTRISEARCH GOLD MEDAL OF ACHIEVEMENT RECIPIENT:

USANA HEALTH SCIENCES

Five-Star Gold Medal-winning Products:

✔ **Essentials**
✔ **HealthPak 100**

Microbiologist and immunologist Dr Myron Wentz established USANA Health Sciences in 1992 to create products that provide antioxidant protection and over-all cellular nutrition for the body. A world-renowned pioneer in cell-culture technology, Dr Wentz is committed to continued research and development. He has ensured that USANA's scientific staff includes experts on human nutrition, cellular biology, biochemistry, natural product chemistry, and clinical research. As a result, USANA scientists have developed a line of world-class nutritional products and received two patents for a unique olive-fruit extract, Olivol®.

The primary focus of the company is to develop and market scientifically advanced nutritional products to promote optimal health—products people can trust. USANA® products are helping to improve the lives of its Independent Associates and their customers throughout the United States, Canada, Mexico, Australia, New Zealand, the United Kingdom, the Netherlands, the Caribbean, Puerto Rico, Hong Kong, Singapore, Japan, Korea, Taiwan, and Malaysia.

To ensure that the high-quality formulas developed in its laboratories are produced safely and consistently, USANA manufactures most products in its own state-of-the-art facility. In the United States, USANA voluntarily follows GMP for pharmaceuticals as the basis for its quality assurance program, meaning USANA treats nutritional supplements with the same care that goes into the manufacturing of pharmaceutical products. To adhere to these exacting standards, USANA's quality assurance program includes several quality control tests on each product during manufacturing, including testing the raw ingredients when they are received, testing again during manufacturing, and then final product testing for purity and potency once more before packaging.

Recently, USANA's Salt Lake City, Utah, manufacturing facility has been certified to be in compliance with dietary supplement GMP requirements set forth in NSF/ANSI Standard 173-2006, Dietary Supplements by NSF International, which is an independent, not-for-profit organization that helps protect consumers by certifying products and writing standards for food, water, air and consumer goods. As an Australian suppler, USANA is also regularly inspected and audited by the Therapeutic Goods Association (TGA) to ensure it meets GMP standards.

Guaranteed to meet USP specifications for quality, potency, and disintegration, where applicable, every dietary supplement produced by USANA carries a potency guarantee, which ensures that what is stated on the label is actually contained in the product. The Essentials™ (Mega Antioxidant and Chelated Mineral), Proflavanol® 90, and the HealthPak 100™ AM/PM packs have all been exhaustively tested by the NSF and have been found to contain all ingredients at the labeled amounts.

USANA is proud to be the official nutritional supplement supplier to many recognized athletic teams such as the Sony Ericsson WTA Tour, the premier women's tennis association. The Company believes in the quality and purity of its nutritional products so strongly that it offers a pioneering athlete guarantee, in which USANA and select athletes enter into agreements that should the athlete test positive for a banned substance included in the World Anti-Doping Agency list as a result of taking USANA nutritional products, USANA will compensate the athlete two times their earnings, up to $1 million. This confident stance strengthens USANA's leading position in the industry and affirms its commitment to providing "Nutritionals You Can Trust."

USANA)
HEALTH SCIENCES

3838 W. Parkway Blvd., Salt Lake City, Utah 84120
Phone: 801-954-7100 Order Line: 888-950-9595
Web site: www.usana.com

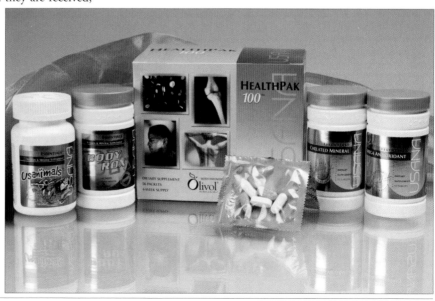

Table 11-3: Table of Recommended Daily Intakes (Blended Standard)

Nutritional Components	Amt	Atkins Average	Balch/Balch Average	Colgan Average	Higdon/LPI Average	Grossman/Kurzweil Average	Miller/LEF Average	Mindell Average	Murray Average	Passwater Average	Perricone Average	Strand Average	Whitaker Average	Blended Standard Median	NOTES	Upper Limits (UL)
Vitamins																
Vitamin A	IU	2,250	7,500	6,250	5,000	5,000	5,000	NR	5,000	17,500		NR	5,000	5,000		10,000 IU
Vitamin D	IU	135	400	400	600	1,300	400	300	250	650		625	250	400		2000 IU
Vitamin K	ug		300	75	no amt	105	7,500		180	75		75	180	180		ND
B-Complex Vitamins																
Biotin	ug	338	600	500	30		300	200	200	63		650	200	250		ND
Folic Acid	ug	3,000	600	400	400	600	800	350	400	600		900	300	600		1000 ug
Vitamin B1 (thiamin)	mg	45	75	50	2	105	100	38	55	63		25	55	55		ND
Vitamin B2 (riboflavin)	mg	36	33	45	2	55	50	63	30	63		38	55	45		ND
Vitamin B3 (niacin)	mg	23	33	50	20	60	50	63	55	150		53	20	[28]		35 mg
Vitamin B3 (niacinamide)	mg	45	75	80			150		20					60		ND
Vitamin B5 (Pantethine)	mg	113												ID		ND
Vitamin B5 (Pantothenic acid)	mg	113	75	150	10		400		63	150		140	63	75		100 mg
Vitamin B6 (pyridoxine)	mg	45	75	50	2	75	50	100	63	63		38	63	63		100 mg
Vitamin B6 (pyridoxyl-5-phosphate)	mg	9												ID		ND
Vitamin B12 (cobalamin)	ug	210	300	100	18	18	100	550	400	88		175	300	175		ND
Antioxidant Vitamins and Nutrients																
Coenzyme Q10	mg		65	30		130	125	60	100	35	30	25		60		ND
alpha-Lipoic acid	mg			100		150	375		35		28	23		100		ND
Para-Aminobenzoic Acid	mg	450	30		300		50			63				NR		ND
Vitamin C	mg	750	2,000	2,000	200	1,250	3,000	2,000	1,000	7,000		1,500		1,500		2000 mg
Vitamin E (as alpha-tocopherol)	IU	225	500	400	200	600	1,000	400	600	700		600	175	600		1467 IU (1000 mg)
Vitamin E (as gamma-tocopherol or mixed tocopherols)	mg			200	299			400					600	200	^^^	ND
Bioflavonoid Complex																
Bioflavonoids (mixed/citrus)	mg	525	350	350				no amt	4,000					540	!	ND
Hesperidin	mg		75											ID		ND
Phenolic compounds (see comment in legend)	mg			900										25	^^	ND
Pinus Epicatechins	mg			10					350			no amt		ID		ND
Procyanidolic Oligomers	mg		105	185					50	100		100		100		ND
Quercetin	mg					150			900			no amt		ID		ND
Resveratrol (3,4',5-trihydroxystilbene)	mg													ID		ND
Rutin	mg		25			400						no amt		ID		ND
Carotenoids																
Astaxanthin (marine carotenoid)	mg										3			ID		ND
beta-Carotene	IU	4,500	15,000	11,250	750		15,000	6,250	15,000	17,500		12,500	15,000	13,750	***	ND
carotenoids (mixed)	IU		0				5,000	6,250				542		5,625		ND
Lutein/Zeaxanthin	mg			6		6	150				500	4	55	5		ND
Lycopene	mg			15		20	50				500	2	55	15		ND
Glutathione Complex																
Acetyl-L-cysteine	mg	90	300	50				no amt		150		63		76		ND
Cysteine	mg		75						6,000		2,500			ID		ND
Glutathione	mg	23		100					2,000			15		NR		ND
Lipid Metabolism																
Acetyl-l-Carnitine	mg										500			500		ND
Carnitine	mg	450	300					750		138	500	150	55	500		3500 mg
Choline	mg	360	500				150	63	55	63		200	55	94	* <	ND
Inositol	mg		125	200				200	55	63				125		ND
Lecithin	mg		125	250						2,500				350		ND
alpha-Linolenic Acid (an omega-3 essential fatty acid)	mg		350			3,350								3,125		ND
Conjugated linoleic acid (CLA)	mg		no amt											ID		ND
Linoleic Acid (an omega-6 essential fatty acid)	mg		150	150			1,304							ID		ND
gamma-Linolenic Acid (GLA)	mg		25	25							300			ID		ND
Omega-3 fish oil (EPA/DHA)	mg								300	360	978			1,141	*	ND
Phosphatidylcholine	mg		200											ID		ND
Phosphatidylserine	mg		180											ID	* <	ND

Table 11-3: Table of Recommended Daily Intakes (Blended Standard) [continued]

	Units													Standard	UL
Minerals																
Boron	mg	300	5	3		2	3	4	3	3	3	2		3	20
Calcium	mg	225	1,750	800	1,100	1,250	1,000	600	750	350	1,150	500	2	800	2500 mg
Chromium (trivalent)	ug	1	275	200	120	160	200	300	300	300	250	300	2	238	ND
Copper	mg		3	1	1	2	2	3	2	2	2	2		2	10 mg
Fluoride (as fluoride)	mg				NR								100	ID	10 mg
Iodine	ug		163	100	100	150	150	100	100	150	150	100	100	100	1100 ug
Iron	mg	75	NR	10	NR	!!!	NR	NR	23	15	NR	23		NR **	45 mg
Magnesium	mg	18	875	600	100	500	500	525	375	400	650	375		[280] !!	350 mg
Manganese	mg	45	7	6	2	20	4	10	13	4	5	13		7	11 mg
Molybdenum	ug		65	60	75	150			18	150	75	18		65	2000 ug
Potassium	mg		300	100		99			350	130	75	350		215	ND
Selenium	ug	180	150	250	128	200	175	200	38	150	200	150		150	400 ug
Silicon	mg									53	3	1		8	ND
Vanadium	ug	68	600					113		75	65	75		75	ND
Zinc	mg	36	40	13	15	40	23	13	30	28	25	23		25	40 mg
Other Nutritional Factors																
Arginine	mg						7,500							ID	ND
Betaine (trimethylglycine or TMG)	mg	no amt						no amt				350		350	ND
Bromelaine (digestive enzymes)	mg										no amt			ID	ND
Carnosine	mg					1,000		1,000						1,000	ND
Dimethylglycine (DMG)	mg													ID	ND
Dimethylaminoethanol (DMAE)	mg										75			ID	ND
Garlic extract (standardized)	mg			80		1,600								ID	ND
Gingko Biloba	mg													ID	ND
Glucosamine	mg							1,500		no amt				ID	ND
Glutamine	mg				200					no amt	0.5 tsp			ID	ND
Indole-3-Carbinol	mg													ID	ND
Lysine	mg		75											ID	ND
Melatonin	mg						2		3		2			ID	ND
Methionine	mg		75											ID	ND
Octacosanol	ug	675												ID	ND
Taurine	mg		300							50				ID	ND
Tyrosine	mg		500							50				ID	ND
Vinpocetine	mg										75			ID	ND

Upper Limits (UL) - The upper level of intake considered safe for use by adults, incorporating a safety factor, Food and Nutrition Board of the Institute of Medicine

Table Codes

* Colgan: lecithin specified in form of phosphatidyl-choline
** Balch: only if an iron deficiency exists
*** Strand: conversion from mg to IU provided by Murray MT, Encyclopedia of Nutritional Supplements, page 25
^ Passwater: 1-2 caps estimated at 1000 mg/cap as lecithin
^^ Recommended level of Phenolic Acids adapted from: Visioli F et al. Atherosclerosis 1995, 117: 25-32.
^^^ based on the recommended 2:1 ratio of alpha-tocopherol to gamma-tocopherol (see Chapter Nine) also see Helzlsouer KJ et al. J Nat Canc Inst. 2000;92(24):2018-2023
! also includes values for hesperedin, quercetin, rutin, and pinus epicatechins
!! 350 mg represents the Upper Limit for a pharmacological agent only
!!! Pre-menopausal women only
ID Insufficient Data
ND Not Determined
NR Not Recommended
no amt while recommended, no amount has been specified
[number] daily recommended intake truncated at 80% of Upper Safe Limit for that nutrient

References by author

Balch, PA. *Prescription for Nutritional Healing*, Avery Books, New York, NY, 2002.
Colgan, M. *Hormonal Health*, Apple Publishing, Vancouver, BC, 1996.
Mindell, E. *What You Should Know about Creating Your Personal Vitamin Plan*, Keats Pub, New Canaan, CT, 1996.
Murray, M and Pizzorino J. *Encyclopedia of Natural Medicine*, Prima Publishing, Rocklin, CA, 1998.
Murray, M. *Encyclopedia of Nutritional Supplements*, Prima Publishing, Rocklin, CA, 1996.
Passwater, RA. *The New Supernutrition*, Simon and Schuster Inc. New York, NY, 1991.
Strand, R. *What Your Doctor Doesn't Know about Nutritional Medicine May Be Killing You*, Thomas Nelson Inc. Nashville TN, 2002.
Whitaker, J. *Dr. Whitaker's Guide to Natural Healing*, Prima Publishing, Rocklin CA, 1996.
Perricone, N. *The Perricone Weight-loss Diet*, Ballantine Books, New York, 2005.
Kurzweil, R and Grossman, T. *Fantastic Voyage*, Holtzbrinck Publishers, 2004.
Atkins RC. *Dr. Atkins' Vita-nutrient Solution*, Fireside Printers, New York, 1999.
Miller, PL. and the Life Extension Foundation, *The Life Extension Revolution*, Bantam Dell, New York, 2005.
Higdon J. and the Linus Pauling Institute. *An Evidence-based Approach to Vitamins and Minerals*, Thieme Publishers, New York, 2003.

Figure 11-1

Eighteen Important Health Support Criteria

Completeness: looks to see if the product contains all the Blended Standard nutrients.

Potency: looks to see how much of each nutrient the product contains compared to the Blended Standard amounts.

Antioxidant Support: examines the nutrients that help to prevent or repair cellular damage caused by oxidation, including vitamin C, vitamin E, vitamin A, beta-carotene, alpha-lipoic acid, lycopene, coenzyme Q10, and selenium.

Bioactivity of Vitamin E: looks to see if the vitamin E is the natural or synthetic form. Natural forms include *d*-alpha tocopherol, while synthetic vitamin E, only half as effective, is usually in the form of *d,l*-alpha tocopherol.

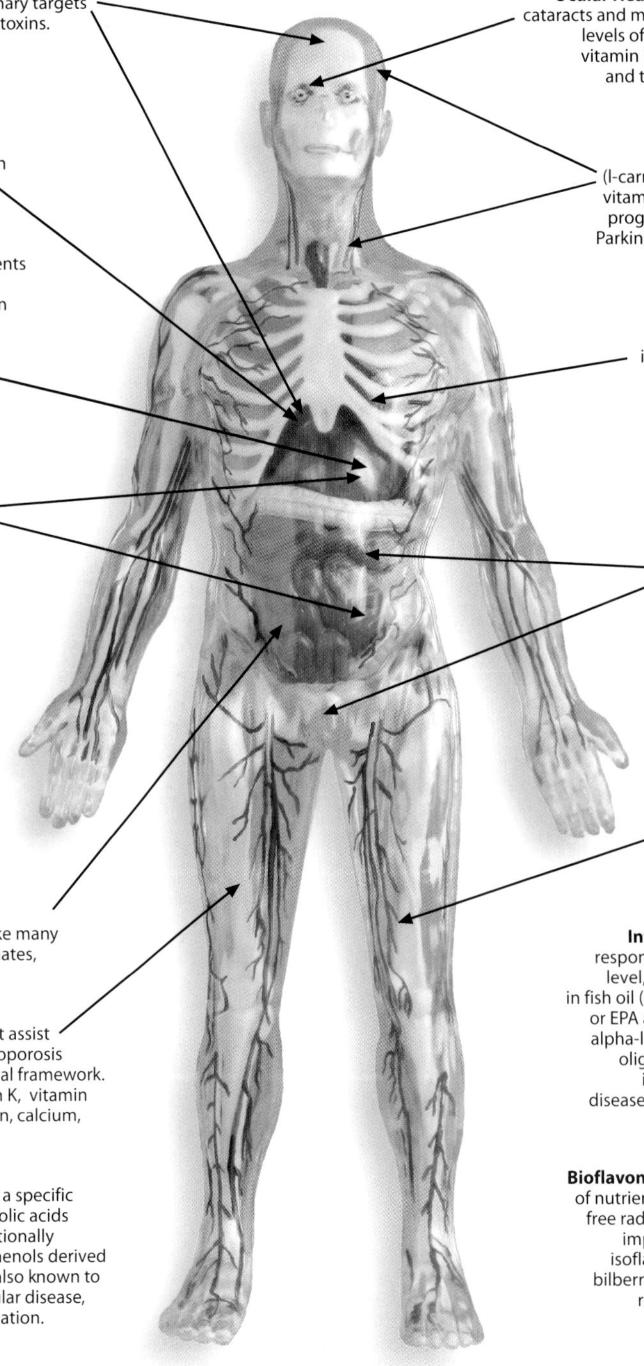

Lipotropic Factors: examines those nutrients, including choline, lecithin, and inositol, that help remove toxins, including heavy metals like lead. The liver and the brain are two primary targets for the accumulation of fat-soluble toxins.

Ocular Health: Good eyesight and prevention of cataracts and macular degeneration require adequate levels of several nutrients, including vitamin C, vitamin E, vitamin A (including beta-carotene), and the carotenoids, lutein and zeaxanthin.

Liver Health: examines those nutrients (including vitamin C, cysteine and n-acetyl-cysteine, selenium, vitamin B2, and vitamin B3) that enhance liver function and optimize levels of glutathione, which helps cells fight off toxic challenges.

Glycation Control: examines those nutrients (l-carnosine, alpha-tocopherol, gamma-tocopherol, vitamin C, and alpha-lipoic acid) that help slow the progress of many degenerative diseases, including Parkinson's disease, Alzheimer's disease, and cancer.

Metabolic Health: examines those nutrients that help the body handle its daily sugar load, keeping systems responsive to insulin and restoring lost insulin sensitivity. These nutrients include vitamin B3 , vitamin B6, vitamin B12, vitamin C, vitamin E , biotin, coenzyme Q10, chromium, magnesium, manganese, and zinc.

Heart Health: examines nutrients that help protect the heart and cardiovascular system, including vitamin E, beta-carotene, coenzyme Q10, calcium, magnesium, l-carnitine or acetyl-l-carnitine, procyanidolic oligomers (PCOs), phenolic compounds, and lycopene.

Potential Toxicities: examines those nutrients that can build up in the body, possibly leading to toxic levels with long-term intake. This includes vitamin A and iron. Accidental overdose of iron-containing supplements is, in fact, a leading cause of fatal poisoning in children. Vitamin A is available, safely, as beta-carotene, while adequate iron is easily obtainable for most people from foods.

Gamma Tocopherol: checks to see if the product includes the gamma form of vitamin E. Studies show that gamma-tocopherol reduces chronic inflammation and protects against cancers of the colon and prostate. High-dose supplementation with alpha tocopherol alone can reduce the level of gamma tocopherol in body tissues.

Mineral Forms: examines the molecules that minerals are bound with to help them cross into the bloodstream. Amino acid chelates and organic acid complexes (such as citrates and gluconates) mimic the natural mineral chelates that form during the digestive process. Chelated minerals also appear not to block other minerals from being absorbed, unlike many of the less expensive mineral salts (carbonates, sulphates, and chlorides).

Methylation Support: looks at those nutrients, including vitamin B2, vitamin B6, vitamin B12, folic acid, and trimethylglycine, required for the body to produce methyl donor molecules. Methyl donors help reduce homocysteine levels in the blood, protecting the arteries and nerve fibres.

Inflammation Control: examines the nutrients responsible for reducing inflammation at the cellular level, such as omega-3 oils—including those found in fish oil (eicosapentaenoic and docosahexaenoic acids, or EPA and DHA)—linolenic acid, gamma-tocopherol, alpha-lipoic acid, vitamin C, flavonoids, procyanidolic oligomers, and the phenolic compounds. Chronic inflammation can lead to serious degenerative disease, including heart disease, cancers and arthritis.

Bone Health: examines the nutrients that assist in bone remodeling, vital to ward off osteoporosis and other diseases that weaken the skeletal framework. These nutrients include vitamin D, vitamin K, vitamin C, vitamin B6, vitamin B12, folic acid, boron, calcium, magnesium, silicon, and zinc.

Phenolic Compounds Profile: examines a specific group of phenolic compounds (polyphenolic acids and their derivatives), known to be exceptionally potent defenders against free radicals. Phenols derived from olives, green tea, and curcumin are also known to improve major risk factors for cardiovascular disease, including lowering the impact of inflammation.

Bioflavonoid Profile: examines the bioflavonoid family of nutrients, which work throughout the body to attack free radicals and support many bodily fuctions. These important nutrients include citrus flavonoids, soy isoflavones, quercetin, quercitin, hesperidin, rutin, bilberry, assorted berry extracts, and PCOs (including resveratrol, grape seed, and pine bark extracts).

Section V

Graphical Comparisons: Stand-alone and Combination Products

This section provides the reader with a graphical look at:

- ■ Top-rated Products (three-star and above)
- ■ Product comparison to the Blended Standard
- ■ Individual Product Health Support Profiles

To be included in the graphs, products must attain a Final Product Rating *of three stars or above. Each qualifying manufacturer's highest-rating product is graphically analyzed by two measures:*
- • *the nutrient content of each product is compared to the recommendations for daily intake derived from the* Blended Standard; *and*
- • *each product is assessed against 18* Health Support Profile *criteria, which are used to rank the product according to a five-star scale.*

Star rankings are prominently displayed below the two graphs for each product.

Nutrient Profile

Health Support Profile

Nutrient Profile Legend

1	Vitamin A	5000 IU	25	n-acetyl-l-Cysteine	56	mg
2	Vitamin D	400 IU	26	acetyl-l-Carnitine	500	mg
3	Vitamin K	180 ug	27	Carnitine	500	mg
4	Biotin	250 ug	28	Choline	94	mg
5	Folic Acid	600 ug	29	Inositol	125	mg
6	Vitamin B1 (Thiamin)	55 mg	30	Lecithin	350	mg
7	Vitamin B2 (Riboflavin)	45 mg	31	alpha-Linolenic Acid	3125	mg
8	Vitamin B3 (Niacin)	28 mg	32	Omega-3 Fish Oil (EPA/DHA)	1141	mg
9	Vitamin B3 (Niacinamide)	60 mg	33	Boron	3	mg
10	Vitamin B5 (Pantothenic Acid)	75 mg	34	Calcium	800	mg
11	Vitamin B6 (Pyridoxine)	63 mg	35	Chromium	238	ug
12	Vitamin B12 (Cobalamin)	175 ug	36	Copper	2	mg
13	Coenzyme Q10	60 mg	37	Iodine	100	ug
14	alpha-Lipoic Acid	100 mg	38	Magnesium	280	mg
15	Vitamin C	1500 mg	39	Manganese	7	mg
16	Vitamin E (alpha tocopherol)	600 IU	40	Molybdenum	65	ug
17	Vitamin E (gamma/mixed)	200 mg	41	Potassium	215	mg
18	Bioflavonoids (mixed)	540 mg	42	Selenium	150	ug
19	Procyanidolic Oligomers (PCOs)	100 mg	43	Silicon	8	mg
20	Phenolic Compounds	25 mg	44	Vanadium	75	ug
21	beta-Carotene	13750 IU	45	Zinc	25	mg
22	Carotenoids (mixed)	5625 IU	46	Trimethylglycine (TMG/Betaine)	350	mg
23	Lutein/Zeaxanthin	5 mg	47	Carnosine	1000	mg
24	Lycopene	15 mg	48	Iron (NOT recommended)	5	mg

Health Support Profile Legend

1. Completeness	10. Metabolic Health
2. Potency	11. Ocular Health
3. Mineral Forms	12. Methylation Support
4. Bioactivity of Vitamin E	13. Lipotropic Factors
5. Gamma Tocopherol	14. Inflammation Control
6. Antioxidant Support	15. Glycation Control
7. Bone Health	16. Bioflavonoid Profile
8. Heart Health	17. Phenolic Compounds
9. Liver Health	18. Potential Toxicities

4Life RiteStart Men

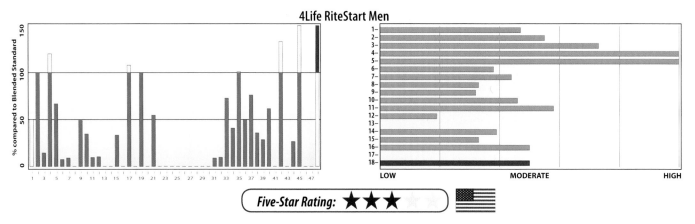

Five-Star Rating: ★ ★ ★

4Life RiteStart Women

Five-Star Rating: ★ ★ ★

Advanced Nutritional Innovations (ANI) CORALadvantage Bone & Joint Multi

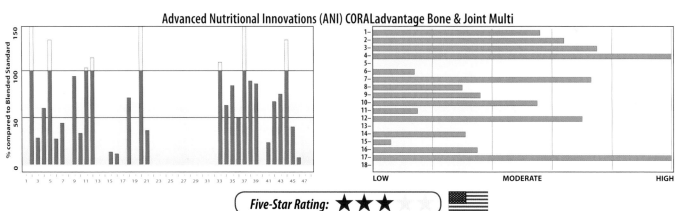

Five-Star Rating: ★ ★ ★

Nutrient Profile

Health Support Profile

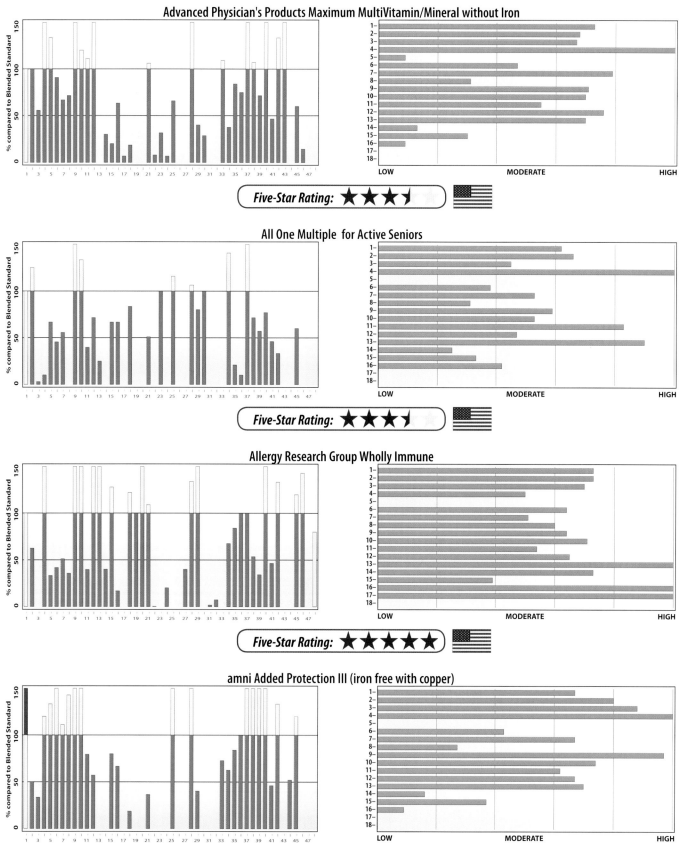

Advanced Physician's Products Maximum MultiVitamin/Mineral without Iron

Five-Star Rating: ★★★★↲

All One Multiple for Active Seniors

Five-Star Rating: ★★★★↲

Allergy Research Group Wholly Immune

Five-Star Rating: ★★★★★

amni Added Protection III (iron free with copper)

Five-Star Rating: ★★★★

Nutrient Profile

Health Support Profile

Nutrient Profile Legend

1	Vitamin A	5000	IU	25	n-acetyl-l-Cysteine	56	mg
2	Vitamin D	400	IU	26	acetyl-l-Carnitine	500	mg
3	Vitamin K	180	ug	27	Carnitine	500	mg
4	Biotin	250	ug	28	Choline	94	mg
5	Folic Acid	600	ug	29	Inositol	125	mg
6	Vitamin B1 (Thiamin)	55	mg	30	Lecithin	350	mg
7	Vitamin B2 (Riboflavin)	45	mg	31	alpha-Linolenic Acid	3125	mg
8	Vitamin B3 (Niacin)	28	mg	32	Omega-3 Fish Oil (EPA/DHA)	1141	mg
9	Vitamin B3 (Niacinamide)	60	mg	33	Boron	3	mg
10	Vitamin B5 (Pantothenic Acid)	75	mg	34	Calcium	800	mg
11	Vitamin B6 (Pyridoxine)	63	mg	35	Chromium	238	ug
12	Vitamin B12 (Cobalamin)	175	ug	36	Copper	2	mg
13	Coenzyme Q10	60	mg	37	Iodine	100	ug
14	alpha-Lipoic Acid	100	mg	38	Magnesium	280	mg
15	Vitamin C	1500	mg	39	Manganese	7	mg
16	Vitamin E (alpha tocopherol)	600	IU	40	Molybdenum	65	ug
17	Vitamin E (gamma/mixed)	200	mg	41	Potassium	215	mg
18	Bioflavonoids (mixed)	540	mg	42	Selenium	150	ug
19	Procyanidolic Oligomers (PCOs)	100	mg	43	Silicon	8	mg
20	Phenolic Compounds	25	mg	44	Vanadium	75	ug
21	beta-Carotene	13750	IU	45	Zinc	25	mg
22	Carotenoids (mixed)	5625	IU	46	Trimethylglycine (TMG/Betaine)	350	mg
23	Lutein/Zeaxanthin	5	mg	47	Carnosine	1000	mg
24	Lycopene	15	mg	48	Iron (NOT recommended)	5	mg

Health Support Profile Legend

1. Completeness	10. Metabolic Health
2. Potency	11. Ocular Health
3. Mineral Forms	12. Methylation Support
4. Bioactivity of Vitamin E	13. Lipotropic Factors
5. Gamma Tocopherol	14. Inflammation Control
6. Antioxidant Support	15. Glycation Control
7. Bone Health	16. Bioflavonoid Profile
8. Heart Health	17. Phenolic Compounds
9. Liver Health	18. Potential Toxicities

AOR Ortho-Core

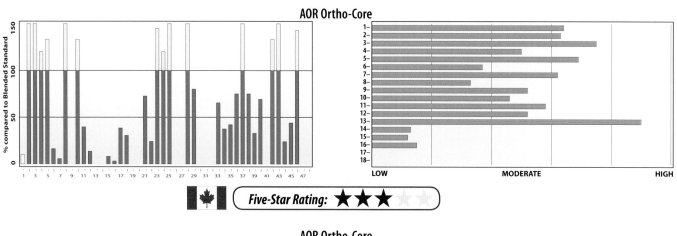

Five-Star Rating: ★★★☆☆

AOR Ortho-Core

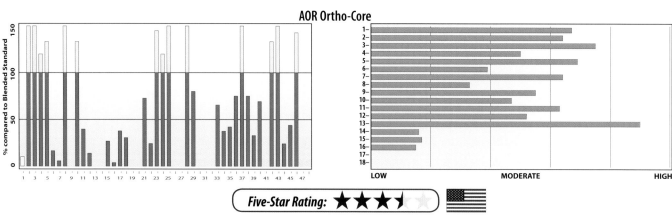

Five-Star Rating: ★★★⯪☆

Biogenesis Nutraceuticals UltraGenesis without iron

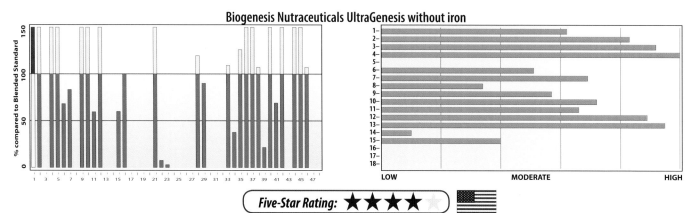

Five-Star Rating: ★★★★☆

Nutrient Profile

Health Support Profile

Bluebonnet Super Vita-CoQ10 Formula

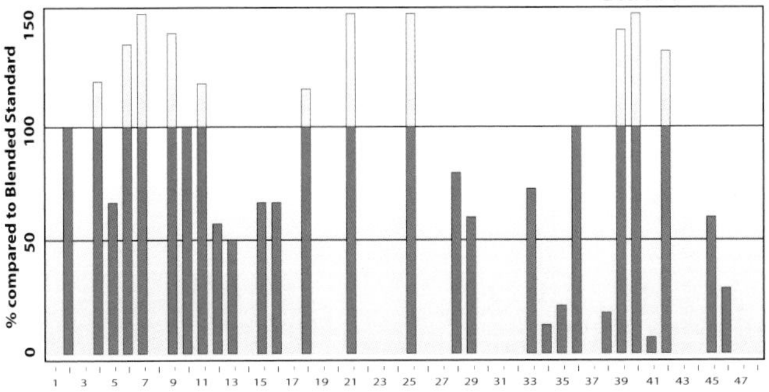

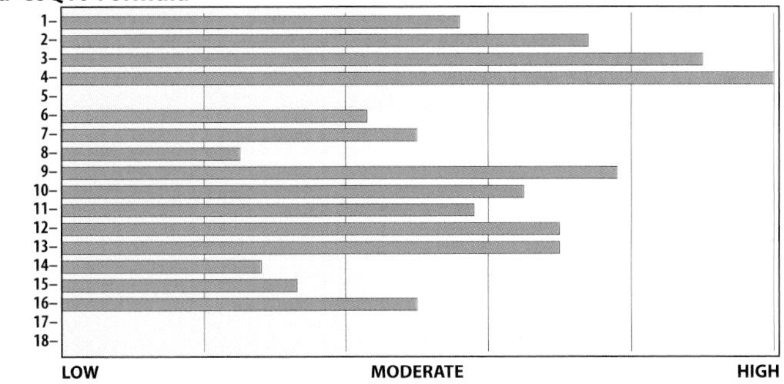

Five-Star Rating: ★★★★⭒

Body Wise Right Choice A.M. + P.M. Formulas

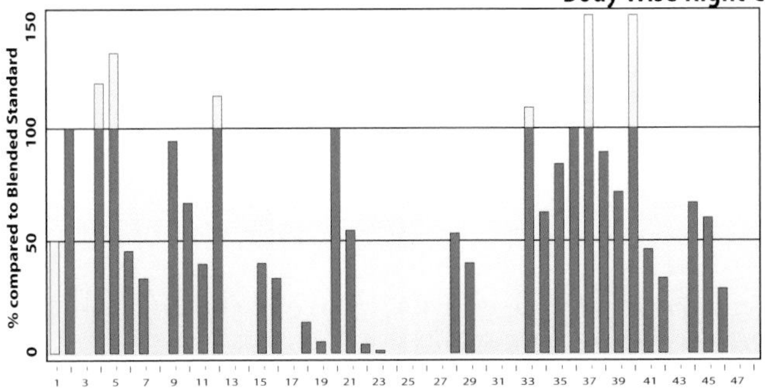

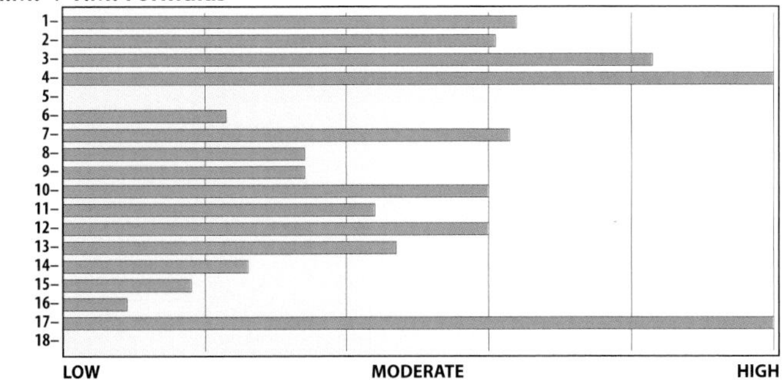

Five-Star Rating: ★★★★⭒

Bronson Laboratories Vegi Source

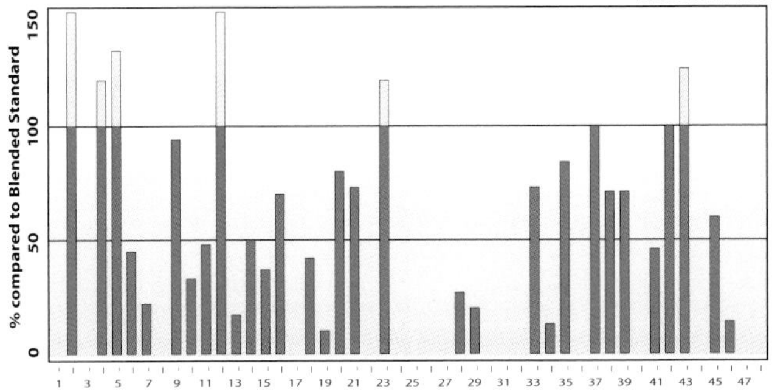

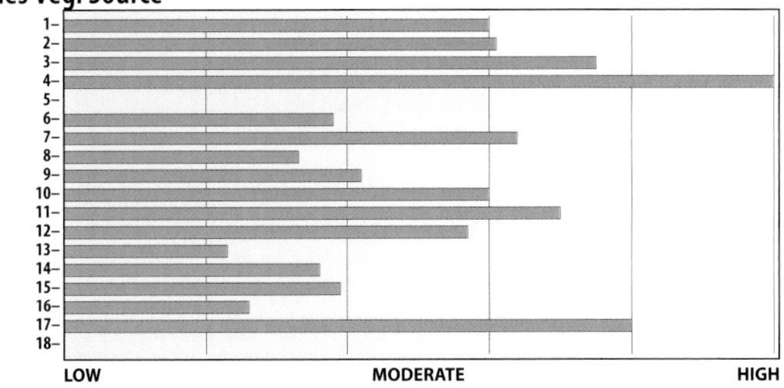

Five-Star Rating: ★★★★⭒

CanPrev Immuno-Pro Formula

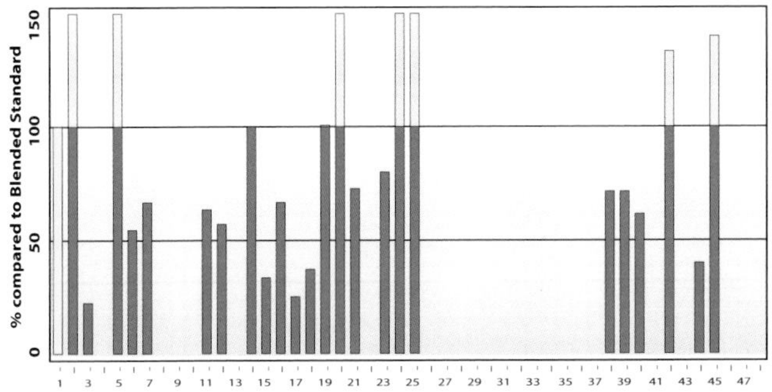

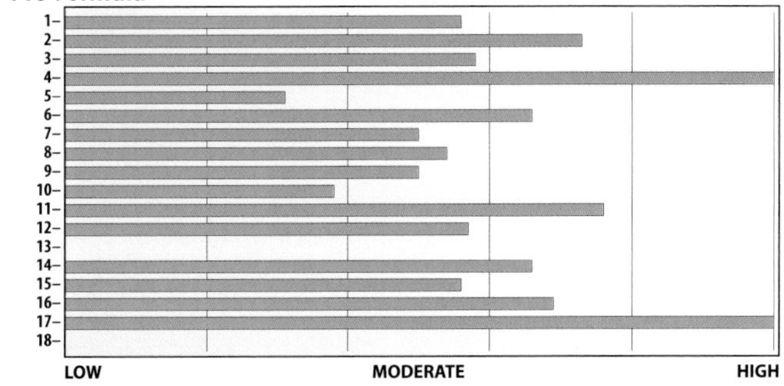

Five-Star Rating: ★★★★⭒

Nutrient Profile

Health Support Profile

Nutrient Profile Legend					
1	Vitamin A	5000	IU	25 n-acetyl-l-Cysteine	56 mg
2	Vitamin D	400	IU	26 acetyl-l-Carnitine	500 mg
3	Vitamin K	180	ug	27 Carnitine	500 mg
4	Biotin	250	ug	28 Choline	94 mg
5	Folic Acid	600	ug	29 Inositol	125 mg
6	Vitamin B1 (Thiamin)	55	mg	30 Lecithin	350 mg
7	Vitamin B2 (Riboflavin)	45	mg	31 alpha-Linolenic Acid	3125 mg
8	Vitamin B3 (Niacin)	28	mg	32 Omega-3 Fish Oil (EPA/DHA)	1141 mg
9	Vitamin B3 (Niacinamide)	60	mg	33 Boron	3 mg
10	Vitamin B5 (Pantothenic Acid)	75	mg	34 Calcium	800 mg
11	Vitamin B6 (Pyridoxine)	63	mg	35 Chromium	238 ug
12	Vitamin B12 (Cobalamin)	175	ug	36 Copper	2 mg
13	Coenzyme Q10	60	mg	37 Iodine	100 ug
14	alpha-Lipoic Acid	100	mg	38 Magnesium	280 mg
15	Vitamin C	1500	mg	39 Manganese	7 mg
16	Vitamin E (alpha tocopherol)	600	IU	40 Molybdenum	65 ug
17	Vitamin E (gamma/mixed)	200	mg	41 Potassium	215 mg
18	Bioflavonoids (mixed)	540	mg	42 Selenium	150 ug
19	Procyanidolic Oligomers (PCOs)	100	mg	43 Silicon	8 mg
20	Phenolic Compounds	25	mg	44 Vanadium	75 ug
21	beta-Carotene	13750	IU	45 Zinc	25 mg
22	Carotenoids (mixed)	5625	IU	46 Trimethylglycine (TMG/Betaine)	350 mg
23	Lutein/Zeaxanthin	5	mg	47 Carnosine	1000 mg
24	Lycopene	15	mg	48 Iron (NOT recommended)	5 mg

Health Support Profile Legend	
1. Completeness	10. Metabolic Health
2. Potency	11. Ocular Health
3. Mineral Forms	12. Methylation Support
4. Bioactivity of Vitamin E	13. Lipotropic Factors
5. Gamma Tocopherol	14. Inflammation Control
6. Antioxidant Support	15. Glycation Control
7. Bone Health	16. Bioflavonoid Profile
8. Heart Health	17. Phenolic Compounds
9. Liver Health	18. Potential Toxicities

CNC (Creative Nutrition Canada) Vitamost Plus Formula

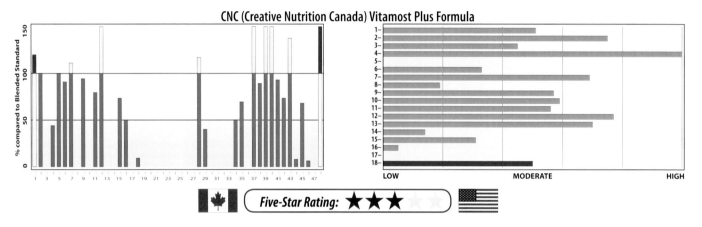

Five-Star Rating: ★★★☆☆

Colgan Institute First Defense Multi

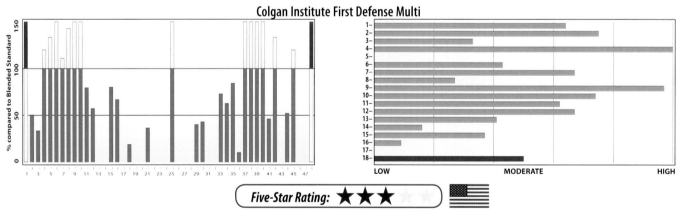

Five-Star Rating: ★★★☆☆

Country Life Superior

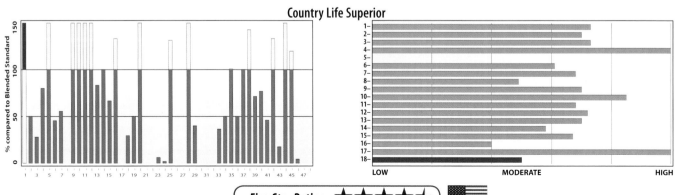

Five-Star Rating: ★★★★⯨

Nutrient Profile

Health Support Profile

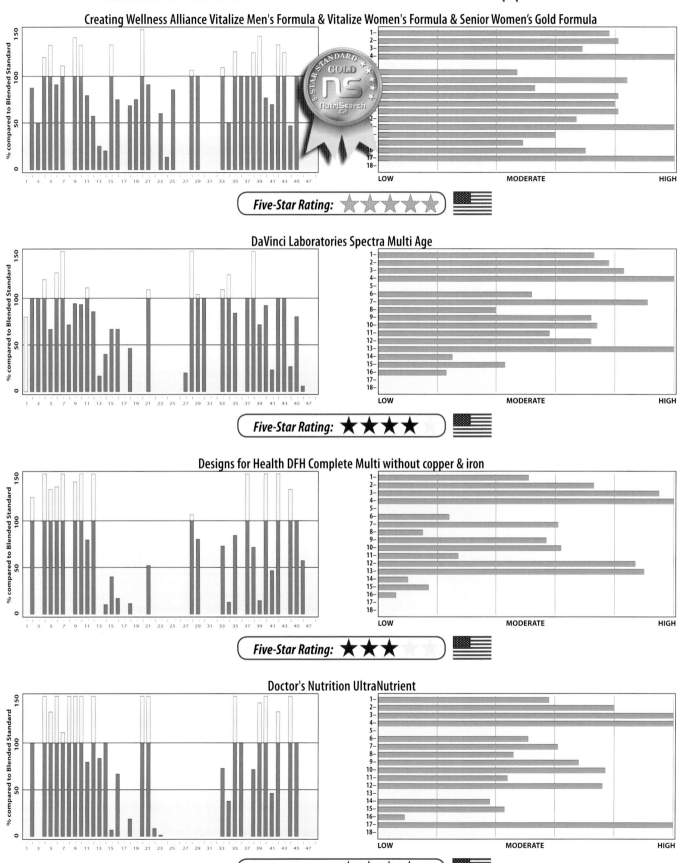

Creating Wellness Alliance Vitalize Men's Formula & Vitalize Women's Formula & Senior Women's Gold Formula

Five-Star Rating: ⭐⭐⭐⭐⭐

DaVinci Laboratories Spectra Multi Age

Five-Star Rating: ★★★★

Designs for Health DFH Complete Multi without copper & iron

Five-Star Rating: ★★★

Doctor's Nutrition UltraNutrient

Five-Star Rating: ★★★★

Nutrient Profile

Nutrient Profile Legend					
1	Vitamin A	5000 IU	25	n-acetyl-l-Cysteine	56 mg
2	Vitamin D	400 IU	26	acetyl-l-Carnitine	500 mg
3	Vitamin K	180 ug	27	Carnitine	500 mg
4	Biotin	250 ug	28	Choline	94 mg
5	Folic Acid	600 ug	29	Inositol	125 mg
6	Vitamin B1 (Thiamin)	55 mg	30	Lecithin	350 mg
7	Vitamin B2 (Riboflavin)	45 mg	31	alpha-Linolenic Acid	3125 mg
8	Vitamin B3 (Niacin)	28 mg	32	Omega-3 Fish Oil (EPA/DHA)	1141 mg
9	Vitamin B3 (Niacinamide)	60 mg	33	Boron	3 mg
10	Vitamin B5 (Pantothenic Acid)	75 mg	34	Calcium	800 mg
11	Vitamin B6 (Pyridoxine)	63 mg	35	Chromium	238 ug
12	Vitamin B12 (Cobalamin)	175 ug	36	Copper	2 mg
13	Coenzyme Q10	60 mg	37	Iodine	100 ug
14	alpha-Lipoic Acid	100 mg	38	Magnesium	280 mg
15	Vitamin C	1500 mg	39	Manganese	7 mg
16	Vitamin E (alpha tocopherol)	600 IU	40	Molybdenum	65 ug
17	Vitamin E (gamma/mixed)	200 mg	41	Potassium	215 mg
18	Bioflavonoids (mixed)	540 mg	42	Selenium	150 ug
19	Procyanidolic Oligomers (PCOs)	100 mg	43	Silicon	8 mg
20	Phenolic Compounds	25 mg	44	Vanadium	75 ug
21	beta-Carotene	13750 IU	45	Zinc	25 mg
22	Carotenoids (mixed)	5625 IU	46	Trimethylglycine (TMG/Betaine)	350 mg
23	Lutein/Zeaxanthin	5 mg	47	Carnosine	1000 mg
24	Lycopene	15 mg	48	Iron (NOT recommended)	5 mg

Health Support Profile

Health Support Profile Legend	
1. Completeness	10. Metabolic Health
2. Potency	11. Ocular Health
3. Mineral Forms	12. Methylation Support
4. Bioactivity of Vitamin E	13. Lipotropic Factors
5. Gamma Tocopherol	14. Inflammation Control
6. Antioxidant Support	15. Glycation Control
7. Bone Health	16. Bioflavonoid Profile
8. Heart Health	17. Phenolic Compounds
9. Liver Health	18. Potential Toxicities

Don Lemmon's All Natural Balanced Multi-Nutrient

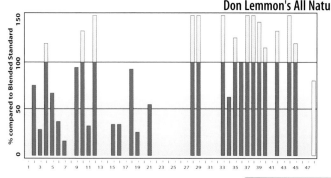

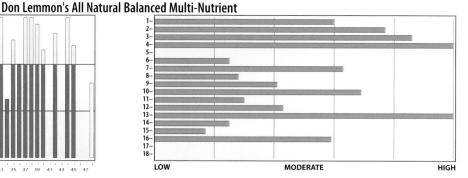

Five-Star Rating: ★★★☆

Douglas Laboratories Ultra Preventive X

Five-Star Rating: ★★★★★

Dr. Cranton's PrimeNutrients

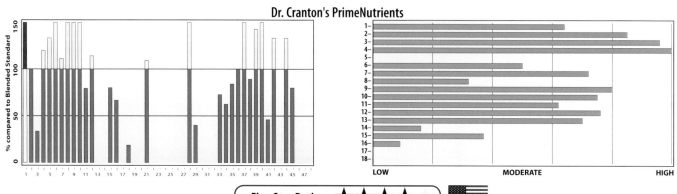

Five-Star Rating: ★★★★

Nutrient Profile

Health Support Profile

Eclectic Institute Opti Gyn Formula

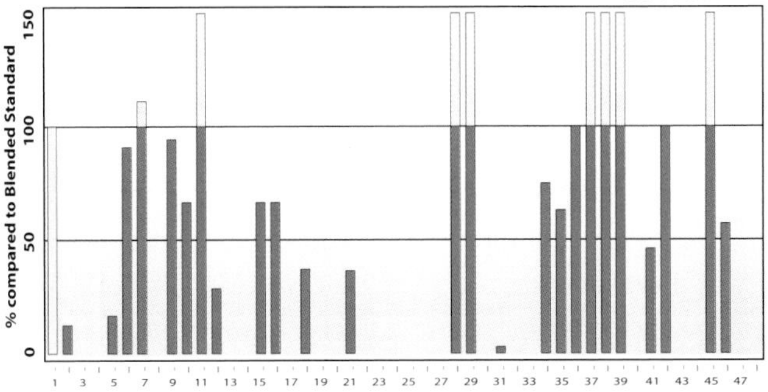

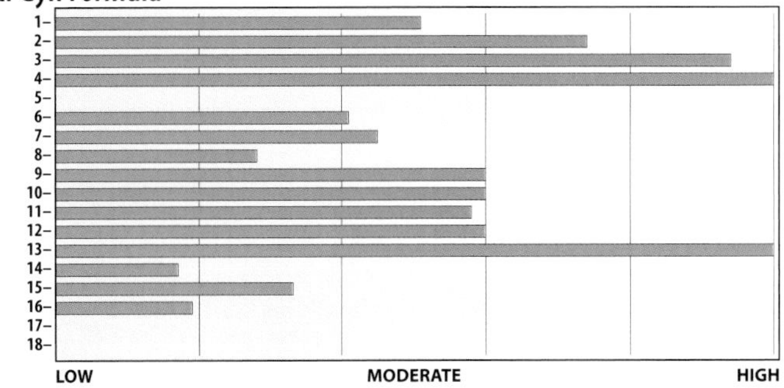

Five-Star Rating: ★ ★ ★ ⭐

Enzymatic Therapy Doctor's Choice for 45-Plus Women

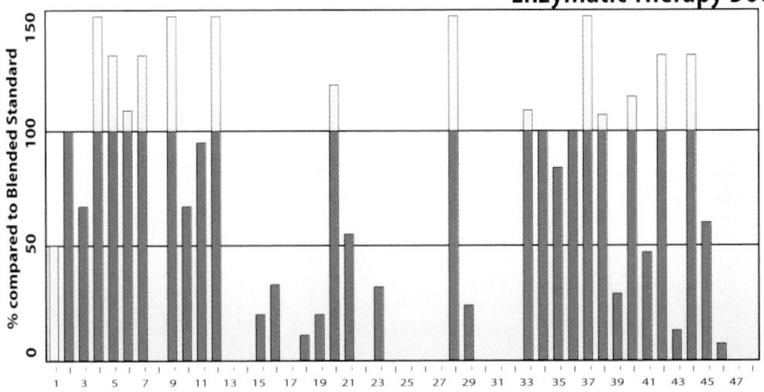

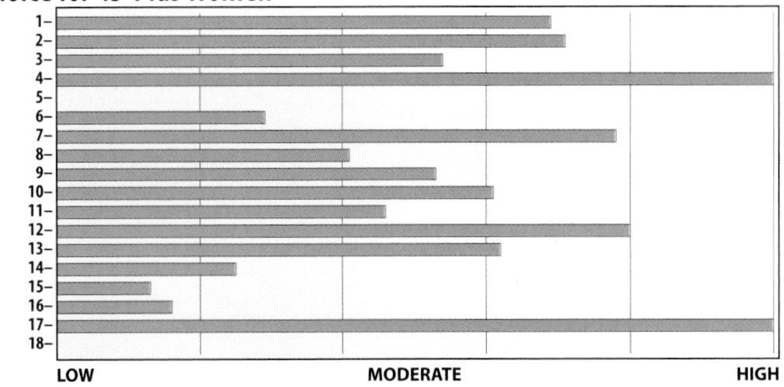

Five-Star Rating: ★ ★ ★ ⭐

Enzymatic Therapy Doctor's Choice for 50-Plus Men

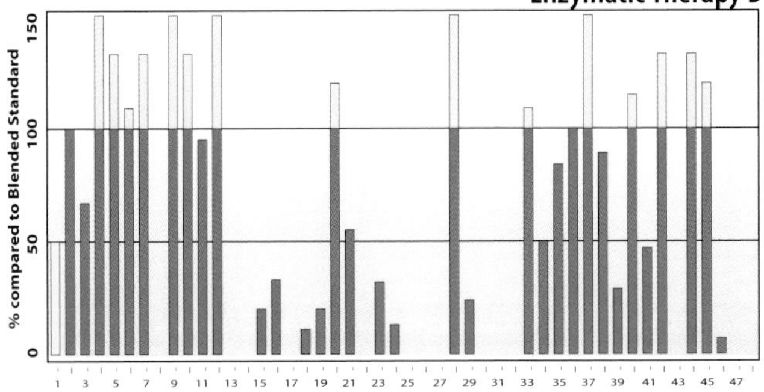

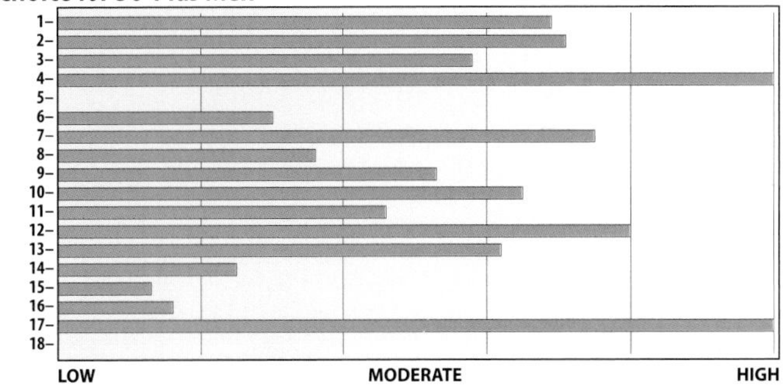

Five-Star Rating: ★ ★ ★ ★

FoodScience of Vermont Superior Multi Age

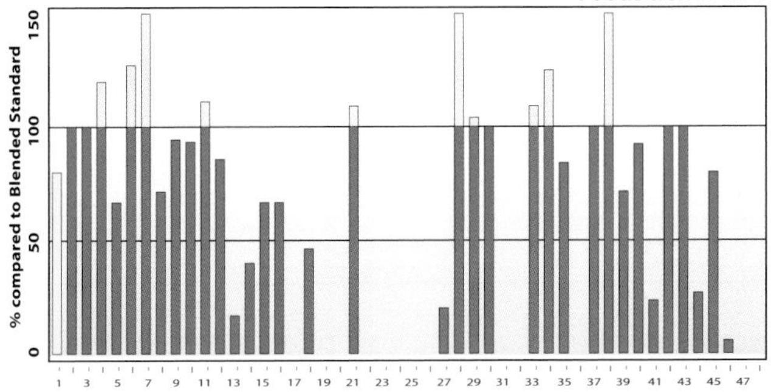

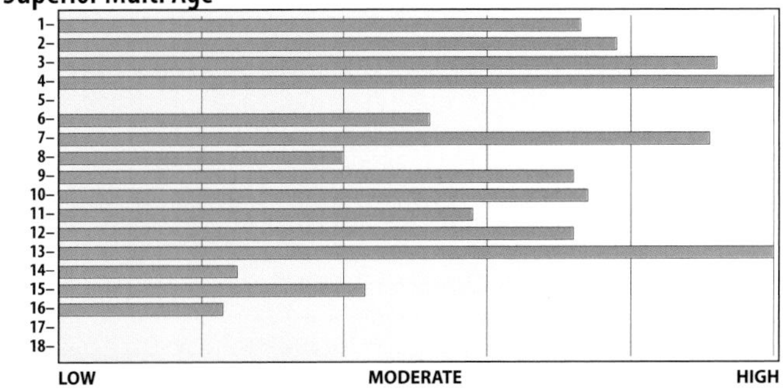

Five-Star Rating: ★ ★ ★ ★

Nutrient Profile

Health Support Profile

Nutrient Profile Legend

1	Vitamin A	5000 IU	25	n-acetyl-l-Cysteine	56	mg
2	Vitamin D	400 IU	26	acetyl-l-Carnitine	500	mg
3	Vitamin K	180 ug	27	Carnitine	500	mg
4	Biotin	250 ug	28	Choline	94	mg
5	Folic Acid	600 ug	29	Inositol	125	mg
6	Vitamin B1 (Thiamin)	55 mg	30	Lecithin	350	mg
7	Vitamin B2 (Riboflavin)	45 mg	31	alpha-Linolenic Acid	3125	mg
8	Vitamin B3 (Niacin)	28 mg	32	Omega-3 Fish Oil (EPA/DHA)	1141	mg
9	Vitamin B3 (Niacinamide)	60 mg	33	Boron	3	mg
10	Vitamin B5 (Pantothenic Acid)	75 mg	34	Calcium	800	mg
11	Vitamin B6 (Pyridoxine)	63 mg	35	Chromium	238	ug
12	Vitamin B12 (Cobalamin)	175 ug	36	Copper	2	mg
13	Coenzyme Q10	60 mg	37	Iodine	100	ug
14	alpha-Lipoic Acid	100 mg	38	Magnesium	280	mg
15	Vitamin C	1500 mg	39	Manganese	7	mg
16	Vitamin E (alpha tocopherol)	600 IU	40	Molybdenum	65	ug
17	Vitamin E (gamma/mixed)	200 mg	41	Potassium	215	mg
18	Bioflavonoids (mixed)	540 mg	42	Selenium	150	ug
19	Procyanidolic Oligomers (PCOs)	100 mg	43	Silicon	8	mg
20	Phenolic Compounds	25 mg	44	Vanadium	75	ug
21	beta-Carotene	13750 IU	45	Zinc	25	mg
22	Carotenoids (mixed)	5625 IU	46	Trimethylglycine (TMG/Betaine)	350	mg
23	Lutein/Zeaxanthin	5 mg	47	Carnosine	1000	mg
24	Lycopene	15 mg	48	Iron (NOT recommended)	5	mg

Health Support Profile Legend

1. Completeness	10. Metabolic Health
2. Potency	11. Ocular Health
3. Mineral Forms	12. Methylation Support
4. Bioactivity of Vitamin E	13. Lipotropic Factors
5. Gamma Tocopherol	14. Inflammation Control
6. Antioxidant Support	15. Glycation Control
7. Bone Health	16. Bioflavonoid Profile
8. Heart Health	17. Phenolic Compounds
9. Liver Health	18. Potential Toxicities

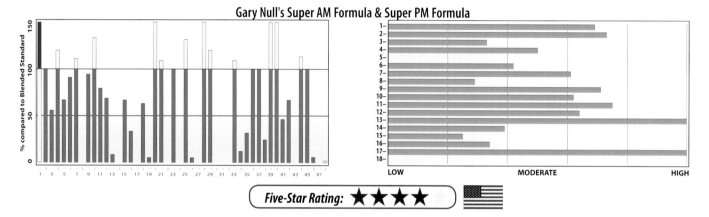

Gary Null's Super AM Formula & Super PM Formula

Five-Star Rating: ★ ★ ★ ★

Genesis Today 4 Total Nutrition

Five-Star Rating: ★ ★ ★

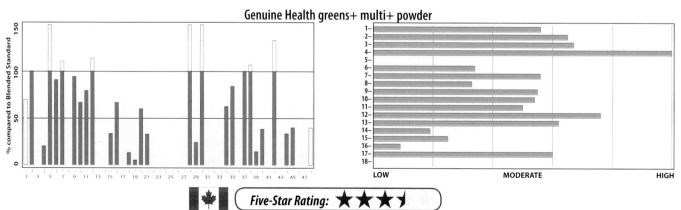

Genuine Health greens+ multi+ powder

Five-Star Rating: ★ ★ ★ ★ ⯪

Nutrient Profile

Health Support Profile

GNC Multi Liquid Ultra Mega

Five-Star Rating: ★★★☆☆

Great Earth TNT Extra Strength Timed Release

Five-Star Rating: ★★★★⯪

HealthyWize Vital Nutrients

Five-Star Rating: ★★★★★

Highland Laboratories Energy with Whole Food Concentrates

Five-Star Rating: ★★★☆☆

Nutrient Profile

Health Support Profile

Nutrient Profile Legend

#	Nutrient	Amount	Unit	#	Nutrient	Amount	Unit
1	Vitamin A	5000	IU	25	n-acetyl-l-Cysteine	56	mg
2	Vitamin D	400	IU	26	acetyl-l-Carnitine	500	mg
3	Vitamin K	180	ug	27	Carnitine	500	mg
4	Biotin	250	ug	28	Choline	94	mg
5	Folic Acid	600	ug	29	Inositol	125	mg
6	Vitamin B1 (Thiamin)	55	mg	30	Lecithin	350	mg
7	Vitamin B2 (Riboflavin)	45	mg	31	alpha-Linolenic Acid	3125	mg
8	Vitamin B3 (Niacin)	28	mg	32	Omega-3 Fish Oil (EPA/DHA)	1141	mg
9	Vitamin B3 (Niacinamide)	60	mg	33	Boron	3	mg
10	Vitamin B5 (Pantothenic Acid)	75	mg	34	Calcium	800	mg
11	Vitamin B6 (Pyridoxine)	63	mg	35	Chromium	238	ug
12	Vitamin B12 (Cobalamin)	175	ug	36	Copper	2	mg
13	Coenzyme Q10	60	mg	37	Iodine	100	ug
14	alpha-Lipoic Acid	100	mg	38	Magnesium	280	mg
15	Vitamin C	1500	mg	39	Manganese	7	mg
16	Vitamin E (alpha tocopherol)	600	IU	40	Molybdenum	65	ug
17	Vitamin E (gamma/mixed)	200	mg	41	Potassium	215	mg
18	Bioflavonoids (mixed)	540	mg	42	Selenium	150	ug
19	Procyanidolic Oligomers (PCOs)	100	mg	43	Silicon	8	mg
20	Phenolic Compounds	25	mg	44	Vanadium	75	ug
21	beta-Carotene	13750	IU	45	Zinc	25	mg
22	Carotenoids (mixed)	5625	IU	46	Trimethylglycine (TMG/Betaine)	350	mg
23	Lutein/Zeaxanthin	5	mg	47	Carnosine	1000	mg
24	Lycopene	15	mg	48	Iron (NOT recommended)	5	mg

Health Support Profile Legend

1. Completeness
2. Potency
3. Mineral Forms
4. Bioactivity of Vitamin E
5. Gamma Tocopherol
6. Antioxidant Support
7. Bone Health
8. Heart Health
9. Liver Health
10. Metabolic Health
11. Ocular Health
12. Methylation Support
13. Lipotropic Factors
14. Inflammation Control
15. Glycation Control
16. Bioflavonoid Profile
17. Phenolic Compounds
18. Potential Toxicities

Intensive Nutrition Multi-VM

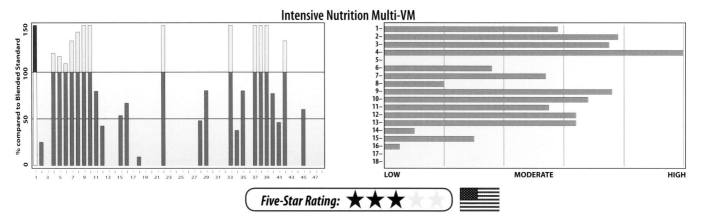

Five-Star Rating: ★★★☆☆

Jarrow Formulas Longevity Multi

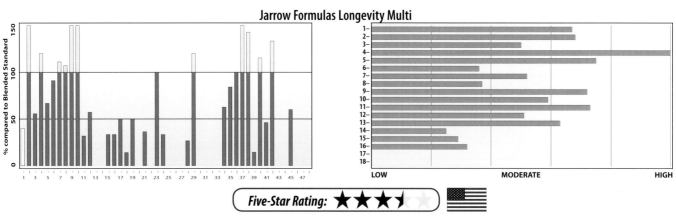

Five-Star Rating: ★★★★⯨

Jean Carper's Stop Aging Now! **OR** Stop Aging Now! PLUS

Five-Star Rating: ★★★★☆

Nutrient Profile

Health Support Profile

Julian Whitaker, M.D. Forward Multi-Nutrient

Five-Star Rating: ★★★☆☆

Kal Enhanced Energy

Five-Star Rating: ★★★☆☆

Karuna Maxxum 4

Five-Star Rating: ★★★⯪☆

Life Extension Foundation Life Extension Mix

Five-Star Rating: ★★★★★

Nutrient Profile

Health Support Profile

Nutrient Profile Legend

1	Vitamin A	5000	IU	25	n-acetyl-l-Cysteine	56	mg
2	Vitamin D	400	IU	26	acetyl-l-Carnitine	500	mg
3	Vitamin K	180	ug	27	Carnitine	500	mg
4	Biotin	250	ug	28	Choline	94	mg
5	Folic Acid	600	ug	29	Inositol	125	mg
6	Vitamin B1 (Thiamin)	55	mg	30	Lecithin	350	mg
7	Vitamin B2 (Riboflavin)	45	mg	31	alpha-Linolenic Acid	3125	mg
8	Vitamin B3 (Niacin)	28	mg	32	Omega-3 Fish Oil (EPA/DHA)	1141	mg
9	Vitamin B3 (Niacinamide)	60	mg	33	Boron	3	mg
10	Vitamin B5 (Pantothenic Acid)	75	mg	34	Calcium	800	mg
11	Vitamin B6 (Pyridoxine)	63	mg	35	Chromium	238	ug
12	Vitamin B12 (Cobalamin)	175	ug	36	Copper	2	mg
13	Coenzyme Q10	60	mg	37	Iodine	100	ug
14	alpha-Lipoic Acid	100	mg	38	Magnesium	280	mg
15	Vitamin C	1500	mg	39	Manganese	7	mg
16	Vitamin E (alpha tocopherol)	600	IU	40	Molybdenum	65	ug
17	Vitamin E (gamma/mixed)	200	mg	41	Potassium	215	mg
18	Bioflavonoids (mixed)	540	mg	42	Selenium	150	ug
19	Procyanidolic Oligomers (PCOs)	100	mg	43	Silicon	8	mg
20	Phenolic Compounds	25	mg	44	Vanadium	75	ug
21	beta-Carotene	13750	IU	45	Zinc	25	mg
22	Carotenoids (mixed)	5625	IU	46	Trimethylglycine (TMG/Betaine)	350	mg
23	Lutein/Zeaxanthin	5	mg	47	Carnosine	1000	mg
24	Lycopene	15	mg	48	Iron (NOT recommended)	5	mg

Health Support Profile Legend

1. Completeness
2. Potency
3. Mineral Forms
4. Bioactivity of Vitamin E
5. Gamma Tocopherol
6. Antioxidant Support
7. Bone Health
8. Heart Health
9. Liver Health
10. Metabolic Health
11. Ocular Health
12. Methylation Support
13. Lipotropic Factors
14. Inflammation Control
15. Glycation Control
16. Bioflavonoid Profile
17. Phenolic Compounds
18. Potential Toxicities

Longevity Science Revitalize

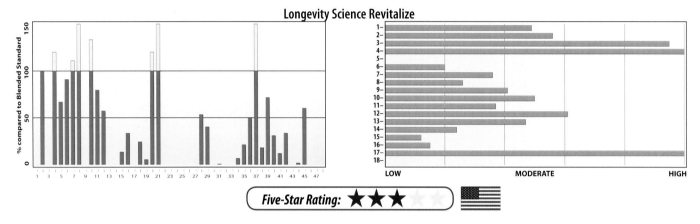

Five-Star Rating: ★★★☆☆

Majestic Earth Ultimate Classic

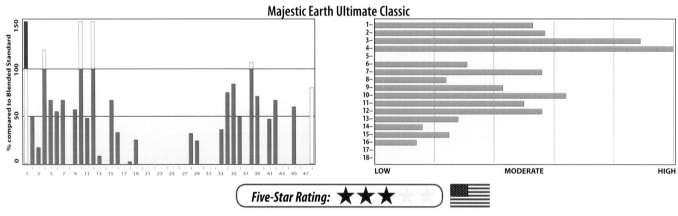

Five-Star Rating: ★★★☆☆

MaxiVision Whole Body Formula

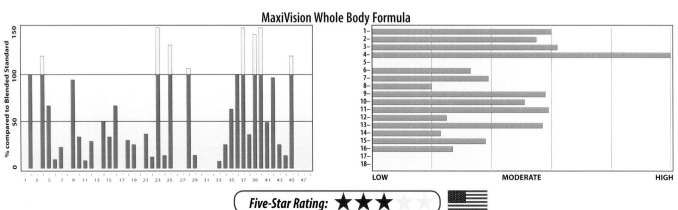

Five-Star Rating: ★★★☆☆

Nutrient Profile

Health Support Profile

MD's Choice Complete Formula for Men OR Complete Formula for Mature Women OR Complete Formula for Young Women

Five-Star Rating: ★ ★ ★ ☆ ☆

MegaFood Maximum Life

Five-Star Rating: ★ ★ ★ ☆ ☆

Metagenics Multigenics Intensive Care (without iron)

Five-Star Rating: ★ ★ ★ ☆

MMS Pro Preventamins Iron Free

Five-Star Rating: ★ ★ ★ ☆

Nutrient Profile

Health Support Profile

Nutrient Profile Legend

1	Vitamin A	5000 IU	25	n-acetyl-l-Cysteine	56	mg
2	Vitamin D	400 IU	26	acetyl-l-Carnitine	500	mg
3	Vitamin K	180 ug	27	Carnitine	500	mg
4	Biotin	250 ug	28	Choline	94	mg
5	Folic Acid	600 ug	29	Inositol	125	mg
6	Vitamin B1 (Thiamin)	55 mg	30	Lecithin	350	mg
7	Vitamin B2 (Riboflavin)	45 mg	31	alpha-Linolenic Acid	3125	mg
8	Vitamin B3 (Niacin)	28 mg	32	Omega-3 Fish Oil (EPA/DHA)	1141	mg
9	Vitamin B3 (Niacinamide)	60 mg	33	Boron	3	mg
10	Vitamin B5 (Pantothenic Acid)	75 mg	34	Calcium	800	mg
11	Vitamin B6 (Pyridoxine)	63 mg	35	Chromium	238	ug
12	Vitamin B12 (Cobalamin)	175 ug	36	Copper	2	mg
13	Coenzyme Q10	60 mg	37	Iodine	100	ug
14	alpha-Lipoic Acid	100 mg	38	Magnesium	280	mg
15	Vitamin C	1500 mg	39	Manganese	7	mg
16	Vitamin E (alpha tocopherol)	600 IU	40	Molybdenum	65	ug
17	Vitamin E (gamma/mixed)	200 mg	41	Potassium	215	mg
18	Bioflavonoids (mixed)	540 mg	42	Selenium	150	ug
19	Procyanidolic Oligomers (PCOs)	100 mg	43	Silicon	8	mg
20	Phenolic Compounds	25 mg	44	Vanadium	75	ug
21	beta-Carotene	13750 IU	45	Zinc	25	mg
22	Carotenoids (mixed)	5625 IU	46	Trimethylglycine (TMG/Betaine)	350	mg
23	Lutein/Zeaxanthin	5 mg	47	Carnosine	1000	mg
24	Lycopene	15 mg	48	Iron (NOT recommended)	5	mg

Health Support Profile Legend

1. Completeness	10. Metabolic Health
2. Potency	11. Ocular Health
3. Mineral Forms	12. Methylation Support
4. Bioactivity of Vitamin E	13. Lipotropic Factors
5. Gamma Tocopherol	14. Inflammation Control
6. Antioxidant Support	15. Glycation Control
7. Bone Health	16. Bioflavonoid Profile
8. Heart Health	17. Phenolic Compounds
9. Liver Health	18. Potential Toxicities

More than a Multiple for Men

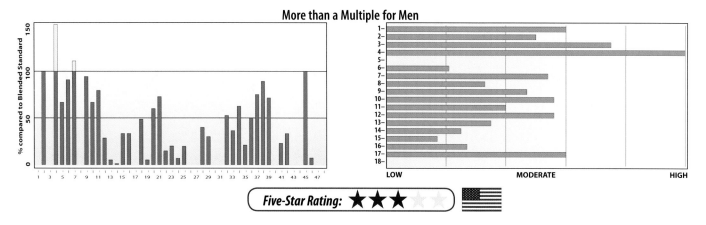

Five-Star Rating: ★★★☆☆

Mountain Naturals of Vermont Superior Multi Age Powder

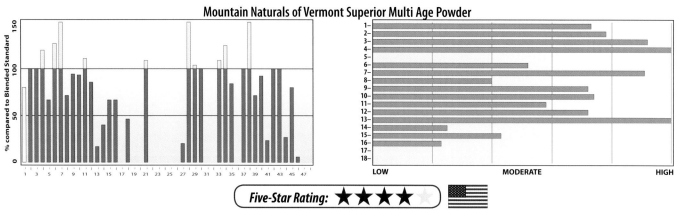

Five-Star Rating: ★★★★☆

Mountain Peak Nutritionals Ultra High

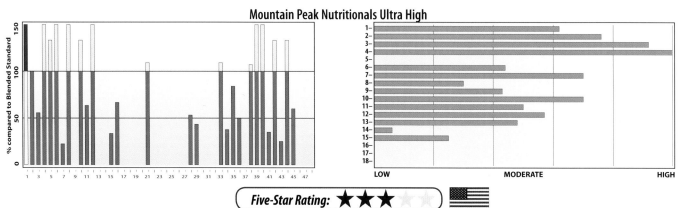

Five-Star Rating: ★★★☆☆

Nutrient Profile

Health Support Profile

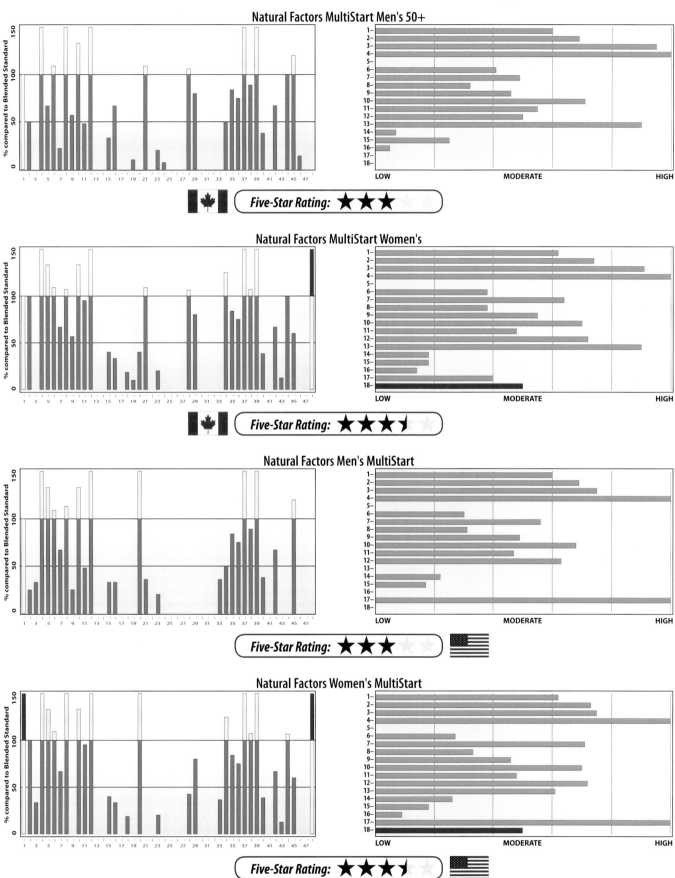

Natural Factors MultiStart Men's 50+

Five-Star Rating: ★★★☆☆

Natural Factors MultiStart Women's

Five-Star Rating: ★★★☆☆

Natural Factors Men's MultiStart

Five-Star Rating: ★★★☆☆

Natural Factors Women's MultiStart

Five-Star Rating: ★★★☆☆

Nutrient Profile

Health Support Profile

Nutrient Profile Legend

1	Vitamin A	5000	IU	25	n-acetyl-l-Cysteine	56	mg
2	Vitamin D	400	IU	26	acetyl-l-Carnitine	500	mg
3	Vitamin K	180	ug	27	Carnitine	500	mg
4	Biotin	250	ug	28	Choline	94	mg
5	Folic Acid	600	ug	29	Inositol	125	mg
6	Vitamin B1 (Thiamin)	55	mg	30	Lecithin	350	mg
7	Vitamin B2 (Riboflavin)	45	mg	31	alpha-Linolenic Acid	3125	mg
8	Vitamin B3 (Niacin)	28	mg	32	Omega-3 Fish Oil (EPA/DHA)	1141	mg
9	Vitamin B3 (Niacinamide)	60	mg	33	Boron	3	mg
10	Vitamin B5 (Pantothenic Acid)	75	mg	34	Calcium	800	mg
11	Vitamin B6 (Pyridoxine)	63	mg	35	Chromium	238	ug
12	Vitamin B12 (Cobalamin)	175	ug	36	Copper	2	mg
13	Coenzyme Q10	60	mg	37	Iodine	100	ug
14	alpha-Lipoic Acid	100	mg	38	Magnesium	280	mg
15	Vitamin C	1500	mg	39	Manganese	7	mg
16	Vitamin E (alpha tocopherol)	600	IU	40	Molybdenum	65	ug
17	Vitamin E (gamma/mixed)	200	mg	41	Potassium	215	mg
18	Bioflavonoids (mixed)	540	mg	42	Selenium	150	ug
19	Procyanidolic Oligomers (PCOs)	100	mg	43	Silicon	8	mg
20	Phenolic Compounds	25	mg	44	Vanadium	75	ug
21	beta-Carotene	13750	IU	45	Zinc	25	mg
22	Carotenoids (mixed)	5625	IU	46	Trimethylglycine (TMG/Betaine)	350	mg
23	Lutein/Zeaxanthin	5	mg	47	Carnosine	1000	mg
24	Lycopene	15	mg	48	Iron (NOT recommended)	5	mg

Health Support Profile Legend

1. Completeness	10. Metabolic Health
2. Potency	11. Ocular Health
3. Mineral Forms	12. Methylation Support
4. Bioactivity of Vitamin E	13. Lipotropic Factors
5. Gamma Tocopherol	14. Inflammation Control
6. Antioxidant Support	15. Glycation Control
7. Bone Health	16. Bioflavonoid Profile
8. Heart Health	17. Phenolic Compounds
9. Liver Health	18. Potential Toxicities

Nature's Life Full Spectrum Antioxidant Soft Multi

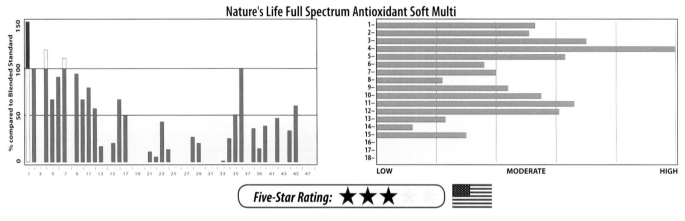

Five-Star Rating: ★★★

Nature's Plus ReGeneration Soft Gels

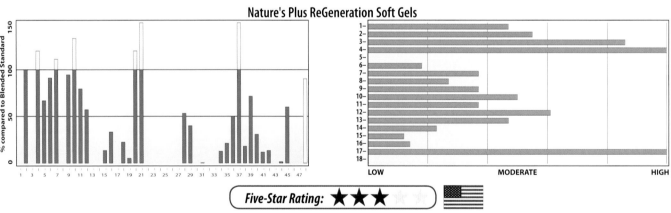

Five-Star Rating: ★★★

Nature's Way Multi Vitamin Iron-Free

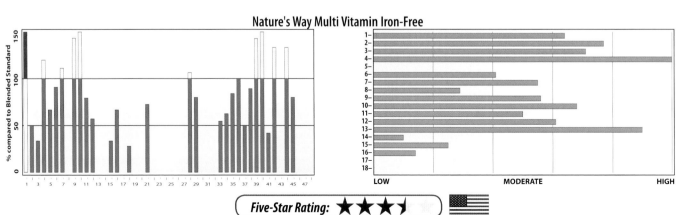

Five-Star Rating: ★★★★⟩

Nutrient Profile

Health Support Profile

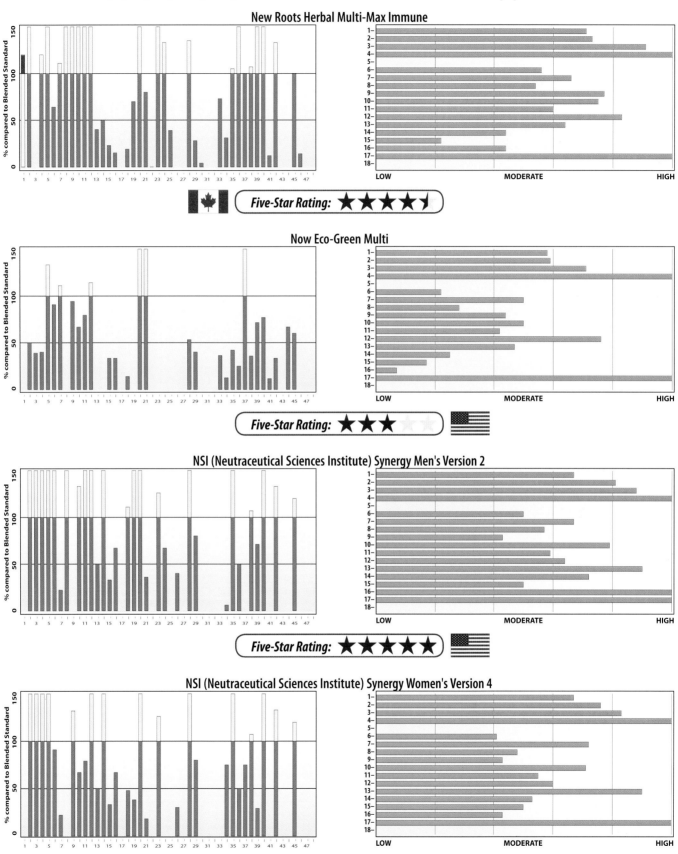

New Roots Herbal Multi-Max Immune

Five-Star Rating: ★★★★⯪

Now Eco-Green Multi

Five-Star Rating: ★★★

NSI (Neutraceutical Sciences Institute) Synergy Men's Version 2

Five-Star Rating: ★★★★★

NSI (Neutraceutical Sciences Institute) Synergy Women's Version 4

Five-Star Rating: ★★★★⯪

Nutrient Profile

Health Support Profile

Nutrient Profile Legend

1	Vitamin A	5000 IU	25	n-acetyl-l-Cysteine	56	mg
2	Vitamin D	400 IU	26	acetyl-l-Carnitine	500	mg
3	Vitamin K	180 ug	27	Carnitine	500	mg
4	Biotin	250 ug	28	Choline	94	mg
5	Folic Acid	600 ug	29	Inositol	125	mg
6	Vitamin B1 (Thiamin)	55 mg	30	Lecithin	350	mg
7	Vitamin B2 (Riboflavin)	45 mg	31	alpha-Linolenic Acid	3125	mg
8	Vitamin B3 (Niacin)	28 mg	32	Omega-3 Fish Oil (EPA/DHA)	1141	mg
9	Vitamin B3 (Niacinamide)	60 mg	33	Boron	3	mg
10	Vitamin B5 (Pantothenic Acid)	75 mg	34	Calcium	800	mg
11	Vitamin B6 (Pyridoxine)	63 mg	35	Chromium	238	ug
12	Vitamin B12 (Cobalamin)	175 mg	36	Copper	2	mg
13	Coenzyme Q10	60 mg	37	Iodine	100	ug
14	alpha-Lipoic Acid	100 mg	38	Magnesium	280	mg
15	Vitamin C	1500 mg	39	Manganese	7	mg
16	Vitamin E (alpha tocopherol)	600 IU	40	Molybdenum	65	ug
17	Vitamin E (gamma/mixed)	200 mg	41	Potassium	215	mg
18	Bioflavonoids (mixed)	540 mg	42	Selenium	150	ug
19	Procyanidolic Oligomers (PCOs)	100 mg	43	Silicon	8	mg
20	Phenolic Compounds	25 mg	44	Vanadium	75	ug
21	beta-Carotene	13750 IU	45	Zinc	25	mg
22	Carotenoids (mixed)	5625 IU	46	Trimethylglycine (TMG/Betaine)	350	mg
23	Lutein/Zeaxanthin	5 mg	47	Carnosine	1000	mg
24	Lycopene	15 mg	48	Iron (NOT recommended)	5	mg

Health Support Profile Legend

1. Completeness	10. Metabolic Health
2. Potency	11. Ocular Health
3. Mineral Forms	12. Methylation Support
4. Bioactivity of Vitamin E	13. Lipotropic Factors
5. Gamma Tocopherol	14. Inflammation Control
6. Antioxidant Support	15. Glycation Control
7. Bone Health	16. Bioflavonoid Profile
8. Heart Health	17. Phenolic Compounds
9. Liver Health	18. Potential Toxicities

NutriCare NutriDaily

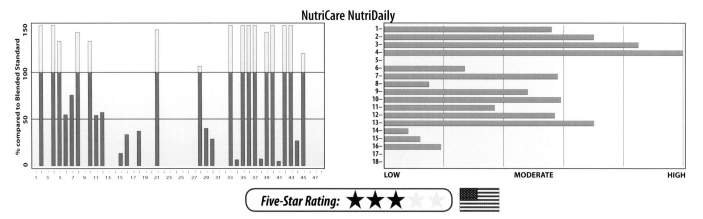

Five-Star Rating: ★★★☆☆

Nutriex Sport

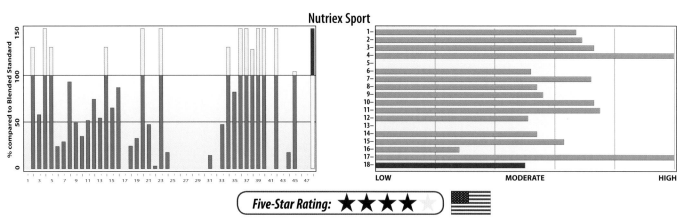

Five-Star Rating: ★★★★☆

Nutrition Dynamics Day Start & Day End Essentials

Five-Star Rating: ★★★★⯪

Nutrient Profile

Health Support Profile

NuTriVene-D Full Spectrum Formula

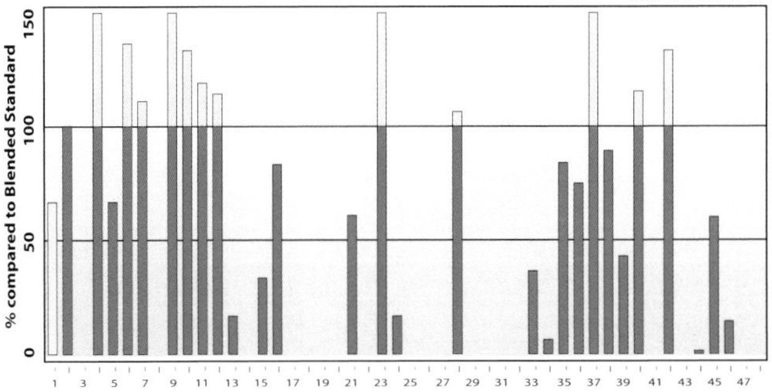

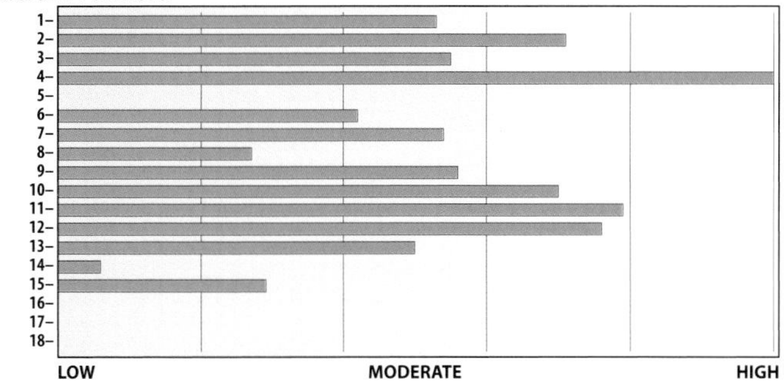

Five-Star Rating: ★★★☆☆

Ola Loa Super Multi (Orange)

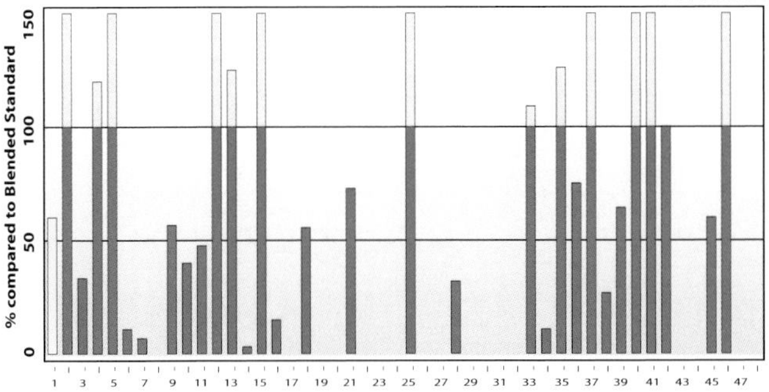

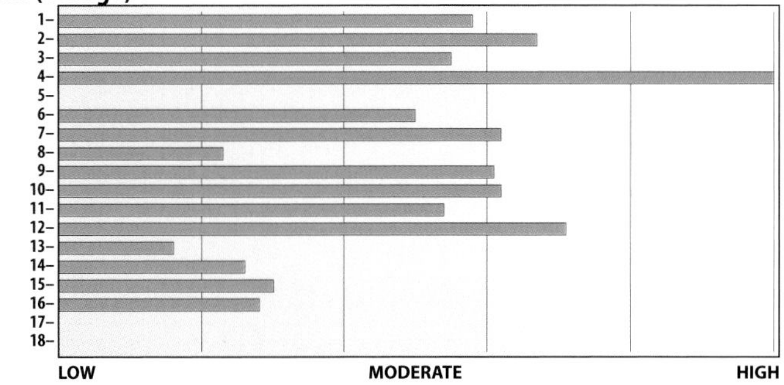

Five-Star Rating: ★★★☆☆

Optimox Androvite for Men

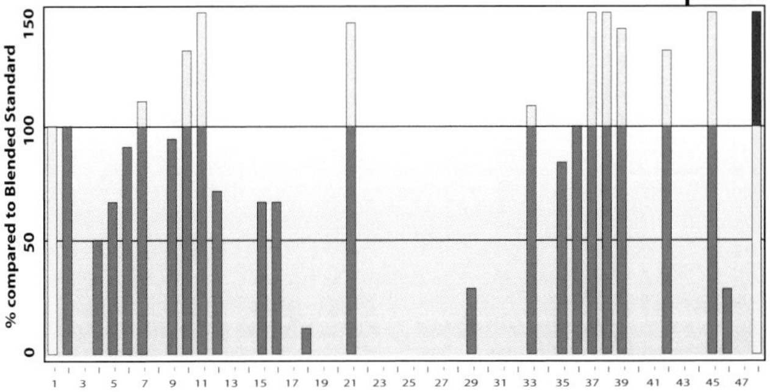

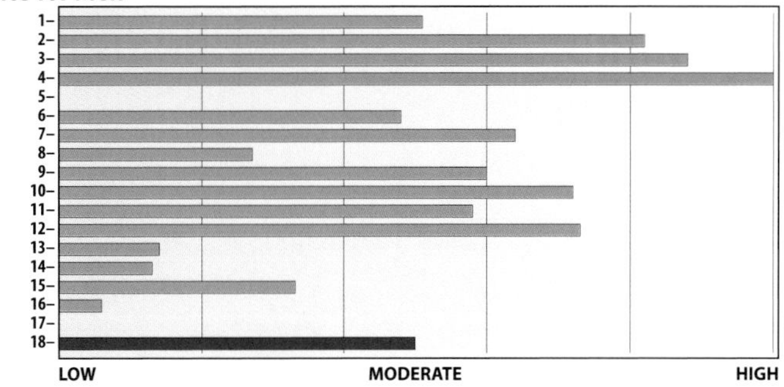

Five-Star Rating: ★★★☆☆

Oregon Health Multi-GuarD with CoQ10

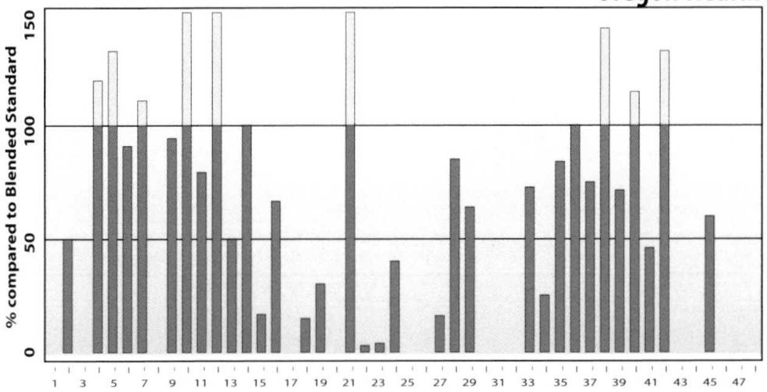

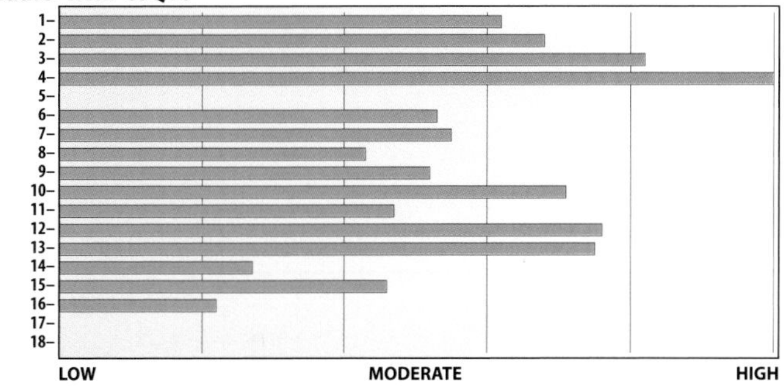

Five-Star Rating: ★★★★⯪☆

Nutrient Profile

Health Support Profile

Nutrient Profile Legend

1	Vitamin A	5000 IU	25	n-acetyl-l-Cysteine	56	mg
2	Vitamin D	400 IU	26	acetyl-l-Carnitine	500	mg
3	Vitamin K	180 ug	27	Carnitine	500	mg
4	Biotin	250 ug	28	Choline	94	mg
5	Folic Acid	600 ug	29	Inositol	125	mg
6	Vitamin B1 (Thiamin)	55 mg	30	Lecithin	350	mg
7	Vitamin B2 (Riboflavin)	45 mg	31	alpha-Linolenic Acid	3125	mg
8	Vitamin B3 (Niacin)	28 mg	32	Omega-3 Fish Oil (EPA/DHA)	1141	mg
9	Vitamin B3 (Niacinamide)	60 mg	33	Boron	3	mg
10	Vitamin B5 (Pantothenic Acid)	75 mg	34	Calcium	800	mg
11	Vitamin B6 (Pyridoxine)	63 mg	35	Chromium	238	ug
12	Vitamin B12 (Cobalamin)	175 ug	36	Copper	2	mg
13	Coenzyme Q10	60 mg	37	Iodine	100	ug
14	alpha-Lipoic Acid	100 mg	38	Magnesium	280	mg
15	Vitamin C	1500 mg	39	Manganese	7	mg
16	Vitamin E (alpha tocopherol)	600 IU	40	Molybdenum	65	ug
17	Vitamin E (gamma/mixed)	200 mg	41	Potassium	215	mg
18	Bioflavonoids (mixed)	540 mg	42	Selenium	150	ug
19	Procyanidolic Oligomers (PCOs)	100 mg	43	Silicon	8	mg
20	Phenolic Compounds	25 mg	44	Vanadium	75	ug
21	beta-Carotene	13750 IU	45	Zinc	25	mg
22	Carotenoids (mixed)	5625 IU	46	Trimethylglycine (TMG/Betaine)	350	mg
23	Lutein/Zeaxanthin	5 mg	47	Carnosine	1000	mg
24	Lycopene	15 mg	48	Iron (NOT recommended)	5	mg

Health Support Profile Legend

1. Completeness	10. Metabolic Health
2. Potency	11. Ocular Health
3. Mineral Forms	12. Methylation Support
4. Bioactivity of Vitamin E	13. Lipotropic Factors
5. Gamma Tocopherol	14. Inflammation Control
6. Antioxidant Support	15. Glycation Control
7. Bone Health	16. Bioflavonoid Profile
8. Heart Health	17. Phenolic Compounds
9. Liver Health	18. Potential Toxicities

Ortho Molecular Products Alpha Base Tablets OR Alpha Base Capsules without Iron

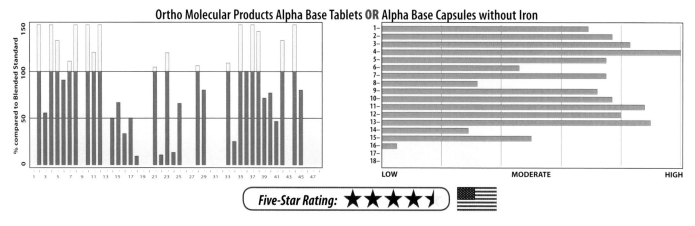

Five-Star Rating: ★★★★⯨

Pharmacist's Ultimate Health Man's Ultimate Formula

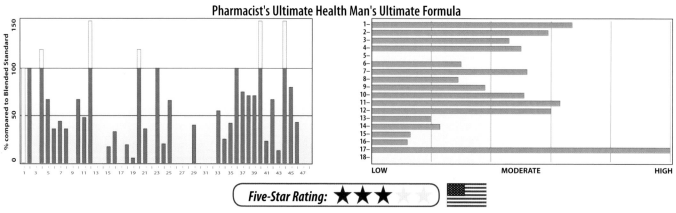

Five-Star Rating: ★★★

Pharmacist's Ultimate Health Woman's Ultimate Formula

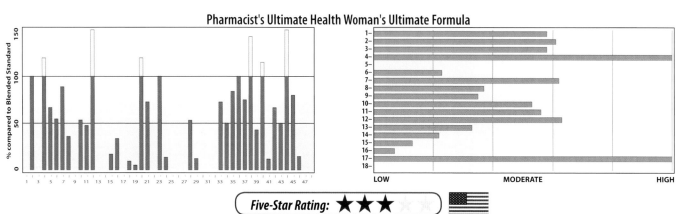

Five-Star Rating: ★★★

Nutrient Profile

Health Support Profile

PhytoPharmica Clinical Nutrients for 50-Plus Men

Five-Star Rating: ★ ★ ★ ★

PhytoPharmica Clinical Nutrients for 45-Plus Women

Five-Star Rating: ★ ★ ★ ★ ✧

Pioneer Vegetarian 1+ Vitamin Mineral

Five-Star Rating: ★ ★ ★

Platinum Super EasyMulti Plus for Men 45+

Five-Star Rating: ★ ★ ★

Nutrient Profile

Health Support Profile

```
┌─────────────────────────────────────────────────────────┐
│              Nutrient Profile Legend                    │
├─────────────────────────────────────────────────────────┤
│  1 Vitamin A                5000  IU  │ 25 n-acetyl-l-Cysteine           56  mg │
│  2 Vitamin D                 400  IU  │ 26 acetyl-l-Carnitine           500  mg │
│  3 Vitamin K                 180  ug  │ 27 Carnitine                    500  mg │
│  4 Biotin                    250  ug  │ 28 Choline                       94  mg │
│  5 Folic Acid                600  ug  │ 29 Inositol                     125  mg │
│  6 Vitamin B1 (Thiamin)       55  mg  │ 30 Lecithin                     350  mg │
│  7 Vitamin B2 (Riboflavin)    45  mg  │ 31 alpha-Linolenic Acid        3125  mg │
│  8 Vitamin B3 (Niacin)        28  mg  │ 32 Omega-3 Fish Oil (EPA/DHA)  1141  mg │
│  9 Vitamin B3 (Niacinamide)   60  mg  │ 33 Boron                          3  mg │
│ 10 Vitamin B5 (Pantothenic Acid) 75 mg│ 34 Calcium                      800  mg │
│ 11 Vitamin B6 (Pyridoxine)    63  mg  │ 35 Chromium                     238  ug │
│ 12 Vitamin B12 (Cobalamin)   175  ug  │ 36 Copper                         2  mg │
│ 13 Coenzyme Q10               60  mg  │ 37 Iodine                       100  ug │
│ 14 alpha-Lipoic Acid         100  mg  │ 38 Magnesium                    280  mg │
│ 15 Vitamin C                1500  mg  │ 39 Manganese                      7  mg │
│ 16 Vitamin E (alpha tocopherol) 600 IU│ 40 Molybdenum                    65  ug │
│ 17 Vitamin E (gamma/mixed)   200  mg  │ 41 Potassium                    215  mg │
│ 18 Bioflavonoids (mixed)     540  mg  │ 42 Selenium                     150  ug │
│ 19 Procyanidolic Oligomers (PCOs) 100 mg│ 43 Silicon                      8  mg │
│ 20 Phenolic Compounds         25  mg  │ 44 Vanadium                      75  ug │
│ 21 beta-Carotene           13750  IU  │ 45 Zinc                          25  mg │
│ 22 Carotenoids (mixed)      5625  IU  │ 46 Trimethylglycine (TMG/Betaine) 350 mg │
│ 23 Lutein/Zeaxanthin           5  mg  │ 47 Carnosine                   1000  mg │
│ 24 Lycopene                   15  mg  │ 48 Iron (NOT recommended)         5  mg │
└─────────────────────────────────────────────────────────┘
```

```
┌─────────────────────────────────────────────────────────┐
│            Health Support Profile Legend                │
├─────────────────────────────────────────────────────────┤
│  1. Completeness            10. Metabolic Health        │
│  2. Potency                 11. Ocular Health           │
│  3. Mineral Forms           12. Methylation Support     │
│  4. Bioactivity of Vitamin E 13. Lipotropic Factors     │
│  5. Gamma Tocopherol        14. Inflammation Control    │
│  6. Antioxidant Support     15. Glycation Control       │
│  7. Bone Health             16. Bioflavonoid Profile    │
│  8. Heart Health            17. Phenolic Compounds      │
│  9. Liver Health            18. Potential Toxicities    │
└─────────────────────────────────────────────────────────┘
```

Platinum Super EasyMulti Plus for Women 45+

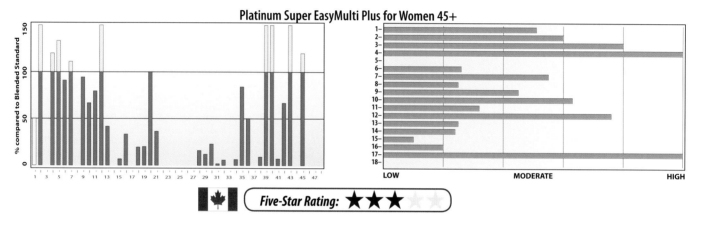

Five-Star Rating: ★★★☆☆

Prairie Naturals Multi-Force

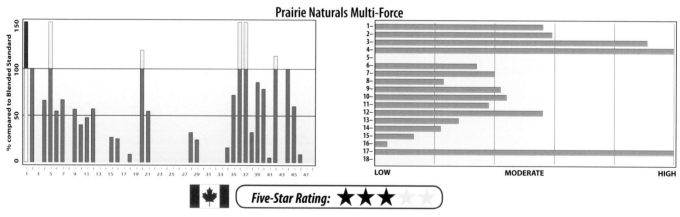

Five-Star Rating: ★★★☆☆

Pro Health Super Multiple without Iron

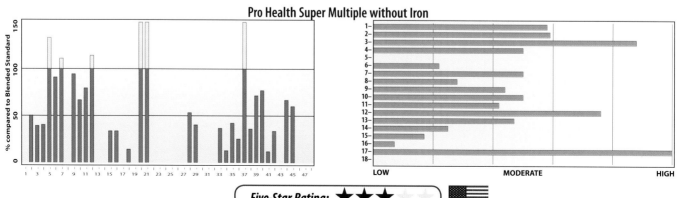

Five-Star Rating: ★★★☆☆

Nutrient Profile

Health Support Profile

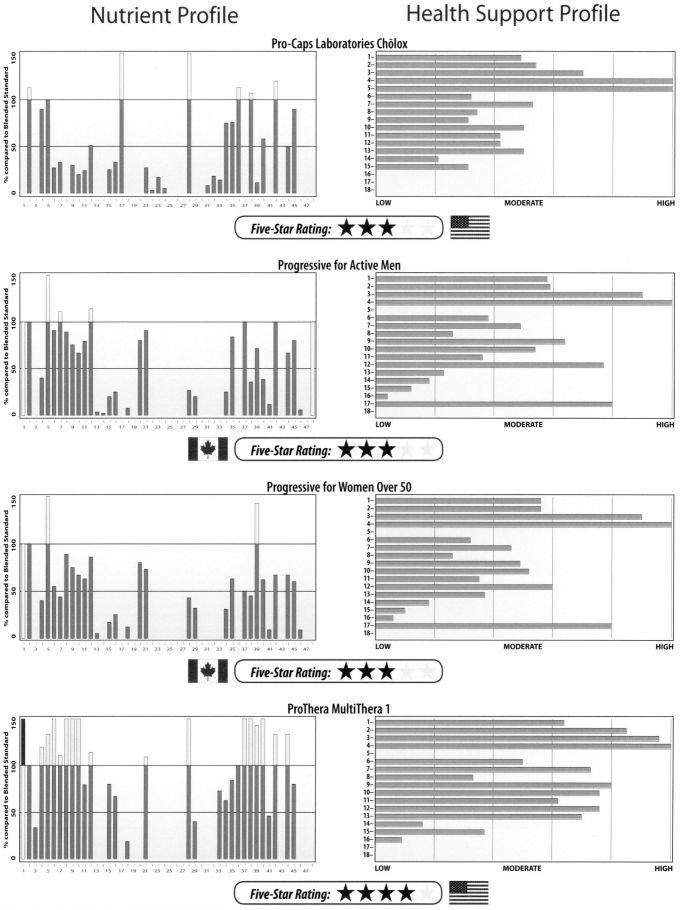

Pro-Caps Laboratories Chōlox

Five-Star Rating: ★ ★ ★ ☆ ☆

Progressive for Active Men

Five-Star Rating: ★ ★ ★ ☆ ☆

Progressive for Women Over 50

Five-Star Rating: ★ ★ ★ ☆ ☆

ProThera MultiThera 1

Five-Star Rating: ★ ★ ★ ★ ☆

Nutrient Profile

Health Support Profile

Nutrient Profile Legend		
1 Vitamin A	5000 IU	25 n-acetyl-l-Cysteine 56 mg
2 Vitamin D	400 IU	26 acetyl-l-Carnitine 500 mg
3 Vitamin K	180 ug	27 Carnitine 500 mg
4 Biotin	250 ug	28 Choline 94 mg
5 Folic Acid	600 ug	29 Inositol 125 mg
6 Vitamin B1 (Thiamin)	55 mg	30 Lecithin 350 mg
7 Vitamin B2 (Riboflavin)	45 mg	31 alpha-Linolenic Acid 3125 mg
8 Vitamin B3 (Niacin)	28 mg	32 Omega-3 Fish Oil (EPA/DHA) 1141 mg
9 Vitamin B3 (Niacinamide)	60 mg	33 Boron 3 mg
10 Vitamin B5 (Pantothenic Acid)	75 mg	34 Calcium 800 mg
11 Vitamin B6 (Pyridoxine)	63 mg	35 Chromium 238 ug
12 Vitamin B12 (Cobalamin)	175 mg	36 Copper 2 mg
13 Coenzyme Q10	60 mg	37 Iodine 100 ug
14 alpha-Lipoic Acid	100 mg	38 Magnesium 280 mg
15 Vitamin C	1500 mg	39 Manganese 7 mg
16 Vitamin E (alpha tocopherol)	600 IU	40 Molybdenum 65 ug
17 Vitamin E (gamma/mixed)	200 mg	41 Potassium 215 mg
18 Bioflavonoids (mixed)	540 mg	42 Selenium 150 ug
19 Procyanidolic Oligomers (PCOs)	100 mg	43 Silicon 8 mg
20 Phenolic Compounds	25 mg	44 Vanadium 75 ug
21 beta-Carotene	13750 IU	45 Zinc 25 mg
22 Carotenoids (mixed)	5625 IU	46 Trimethylglycine (TMG/Betaine) 350 mg
23 Lutein/Zeaxanthin	5 mg	47 Carnosine 1000 mg
24 Lycopene	15 mg	48 Iron (NOT recommended) 5 mg

Health Support Profile Legend	
1. Completeness	10. Metabolic Health
2. Potency	11. Ocular Health
3. Mineral Forms	12. Methylation Support
4. Bioactivity of Vitamin E	13. Lipotropic Factors
5. Gamma Tocopherol	14. Inflammation Control
6. Antioxidant Support	15. Glycation Control
7. Bone Health	16. Bioflavonoid Profile
8. Heart Health	17. Phenolic Compounds
9. Liver Health	18. Potential Toxicities

Pure Encapsulations UltraNutrient

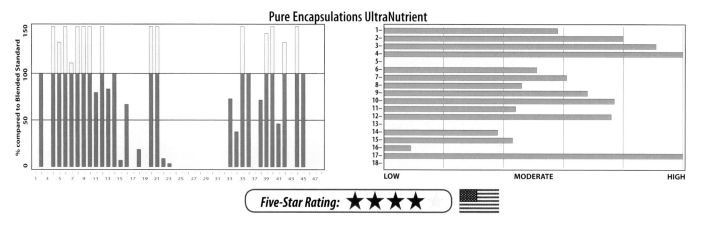

Five-Star Rating: ★★★★

Pure Essence Labs Life Essence Powder

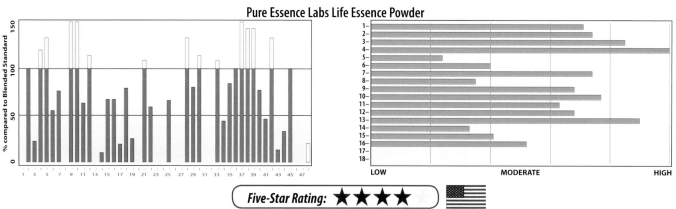

Five-Star Rating: ★★★★

Puritan's Pride Ultra Man 75

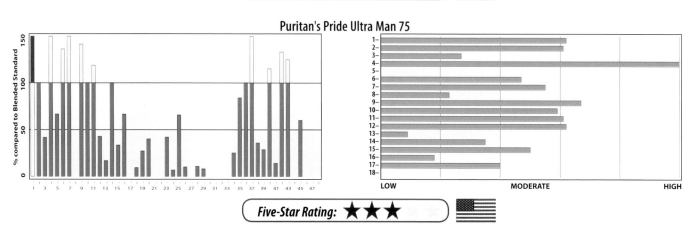

Five-Star Rating: ★★★

Nutrient Profile

Health Support Profile

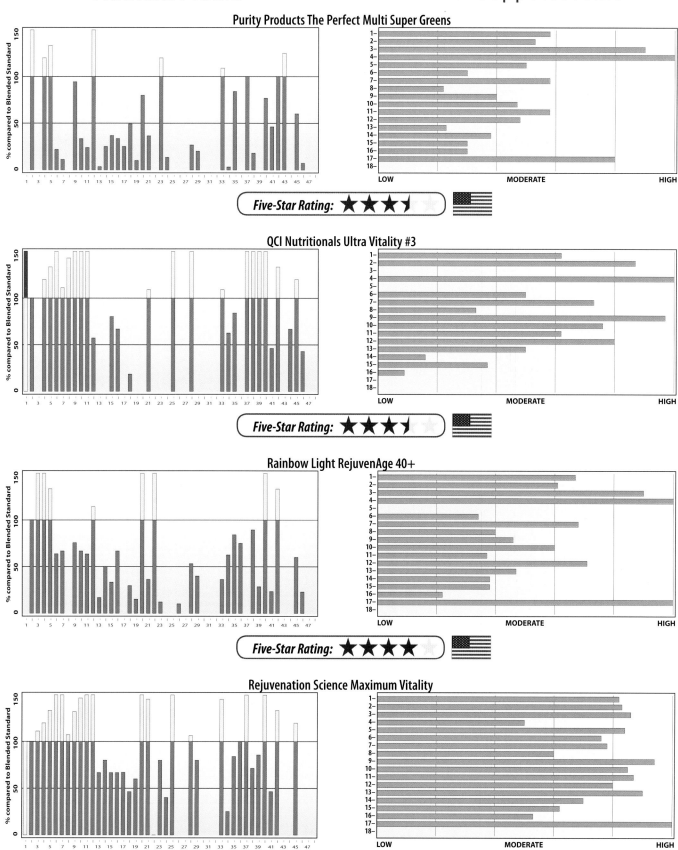

Purity Products The Perfect Multi Super Greens

Five-Star Rating: ★★★★⌐

QCI Nutritionals Ultra Vitality #3

Five-Star Rating: ★★★★⌐

Rainbow Light RejuvenAge 40+

Five-Star Rating: ★★★★

Rejuvenation Science Maximum Vitality

Five-Star Rating: ★★★★★

Nutrient Profile

Health Support Profile

Nutrient Profile Legend

1	Vitamin A	5000	IU	25	n-acetyl-l-Cysteine	56	mg
2	Vitamin D	400	IU	26	acetyl-l-Carnitine	500	mg
3	Vitamin K	180	ug	27	Carnitine	500	mg
4	Biotin	250	ug	28	Choline	94	mg
5	Folic Acid	600	ug	29	Inositol	125	mg
6	Vitamin B1 (Thiamin)	55	mg	30	Lecithin	350	mg
7	Vitamin B2 (Riboflavin)	45	mg	31	alpha-Linolenic Acid	3125	mg
8	Vitamin B3 (Niacin)	28	mg	32	Omega-3 Fish Oil (EPA/DHA)	1141	mg
9	Vitamin B3 (Niacinamide)	60	mg	33	Boron	3	mg
10	Vitamin B5 (Pantothenic Acid)	75	mg	34	Calcium	800	mg
11	Vitamin B6 (Pyridoxine)	63	mg	35	Chromium	238	ug
12	Vitamin B12 (Cobalamin)	175	ug	36	Copper	2	mg
13	Coenzyme Q10	60	mg	37	Iodine	100	ug
14	alpha-Lipoic Acid	100	mg	38	Magnesium	280	mg
15	Vitamin C	1500	mg	39	Manganese	7	mg
16	Vitamin E (alpha tocopherol)	600	IU	40	Molybdenum	65	ug
17	Vitamin E (gamma/mixed)	200	mg	41	Potassium	215	mg
18	Bioflavonoids (mixed)	540	mg	42	Selenium	150	ug
19	Procyanidolic Oligomers (PCOs)	100	mg	43	Silicon	8	mg
20	Phenolic Compounds	25	mg	44	Vanadium	75	ug
21	beta-Carotene	13750	IU	45	Zinc	25	mg
22	Carotenoids (mixed)	5625	IU	46	Trimethylglycine (TMG/Betaine)	350	mg
23	Lutein/Zeaxanthin	5	mg	47	Carnosine	1000	mg
24	Lycopene	15	mg	48	Iron (NOT recommended)	5	mg

Health Support Profile Legend

1. Completeness
2. Potency
3. Mineral Forms
4. Bioactivity of Vitamin E
5. Gamma Tocopherol
6. Antioxidant Support
7. Bone Health
8. Heart Health
9. Liver Health

10. Metabolic Health
11. Ocular Health
12. Methylation Support
13. Lipotropic Factors
14. Inflammation Control
15. Glycation Control
16. Bioflavonoid Profile
17. Phenolic Compounds
18. Potential Toxicities

Rx Vitamins Revitalize without Iron

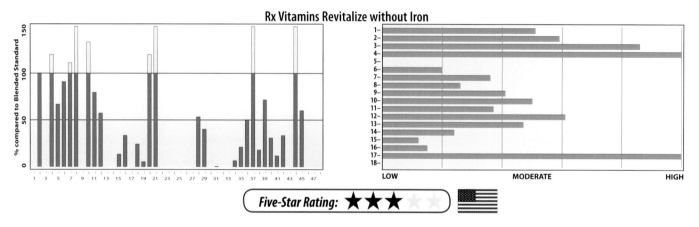

Five-Star Rating: ★★★☆☆

Schwarzbein Institute Ultra Preventive III (tablets)

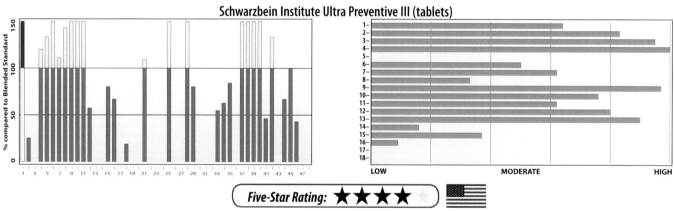

Five-Star Rating: ★★★★☆

Selekta Selekta-Clear

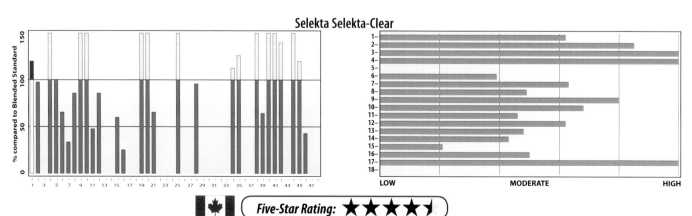

Five-Star Rating: ★★★★✦

Nutrient Profile

Health Support Profile

Solaray Spectro 3 Iron Free

Five-Star Rating: ★★★☆☆

Solgar Female Multiple

Five-Star Rating: ★★★☆☆

Solgar Male Multiple

Five-Star Rating: ★★★⯪☆

Source Naturals Life Force Multiple

Five-Star Rating: ★★★★★

Nutrient Profile

Health Support Profile

Nutrient Profile Legend

1	Vitamin A	5000	IU	25	n-acetyl-l-Cysteine	56	mg
2	Vitamin D	400	IU	26	acetyl-l-Carnitine	500	mg
3	Vitamin K	180	ug	27	Carnitine	500	mg
4	Biotin	250	ug	28	Choline	94	mg
5	Folic Acid	600	ug	29	Inositol	125	mg
6	Vitamin B1 (Thiamin)	55	mg	30	Lecithin	350	mg
7	Vitamin B2 (Riboflavin)	45	mg	31	alpha-Linolenic Acid	3125	mg
8	Vitamin B3 (Niacin)	28	mg	32	Omega-3 Fish Oil (EPA/DHA)	1141	mg
9	Vitamin B3 (Niacinamide)	60	mg	33	Boron	3	mg
10	Vitamin B5 (Pantothenic Acid)	75	mg	34	Calcium	800	mg
11	Vitamin B6 (Pyridoxine)	63	mg	35	Chromium	238	ug
12	Vitamin B12 (Cobalamin)	175	ug	36	Copper	2	mg
13	Coenzyme Q10	60	mg	37	Iodine	100	ug
14	alpha-Lipoic Acid	100	mg	38	Magnesium	280	mg
15	Vitamin C	1500	mg	39	Manganese	7	mg
16	Vitamin E (alpha tocopherol)	600	IU	40	Molybdenum	65	ug
17	Vitamin E (gamma/mixed)	200	mg	41	Potassium	215	mg
18	Bioflavonoids (mixed)	540	mg	42	Selenium	150	ug
19	Procyanidolic Oligomers (PCOs)	100	mg	43	Silicon	8	mg
20	Phenolic Compounds	25	mg	44	Vanadium	75	ug
21	beta-Carotene	13750	IU	45	Zinc	25	mg
22	Carotenoids (mixed)	5625	IU	46	Trimethylglycine (TMG/Betaine)	350	mg
23	Lutein/Zeaxanthin	5	mg	47	Carnosine	1000	mg
24	Lycopene	15	mg	48	Iron (NOT recommended)	5	mg

Health Support Profile Legend

1. Completeness	10. Metabolic Health
2. Potency	11. Ocular Health
3. Mineral Forms	12. Methylation Support
4. Bioactivity of Vitamin E	13. Lipotropic Factors
5. Gamma Tocopherol	14. Inflammation Control
6. Antioxidant Support	15. Glycation Control
7. Bone Health	16. Bioflavonoid Profile
8. Heart Health	17. Phenolic Compounds
9. Liver Health	18. Potential Toxicities

SuperNutrition Men's Blend

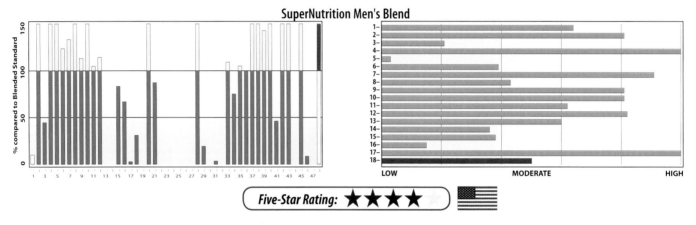

Five-Star Rating: ★ ★ ★ ★

SupraLife Ultra Body Toddy with Cell Shield

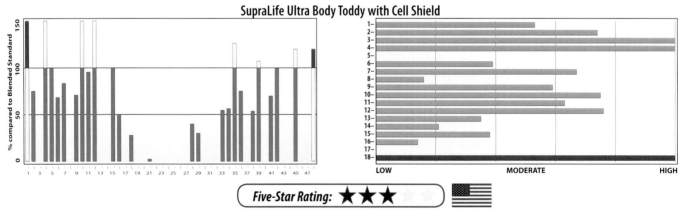

Five-Star Rating: ★ ★ ★

Swanson Lee Swanson Signature Line Longevital

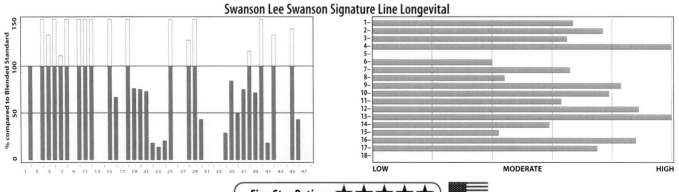

Five-Star Rating: ★ ★ ★ ★ ★

Nutrient Profile

Health Support Profile

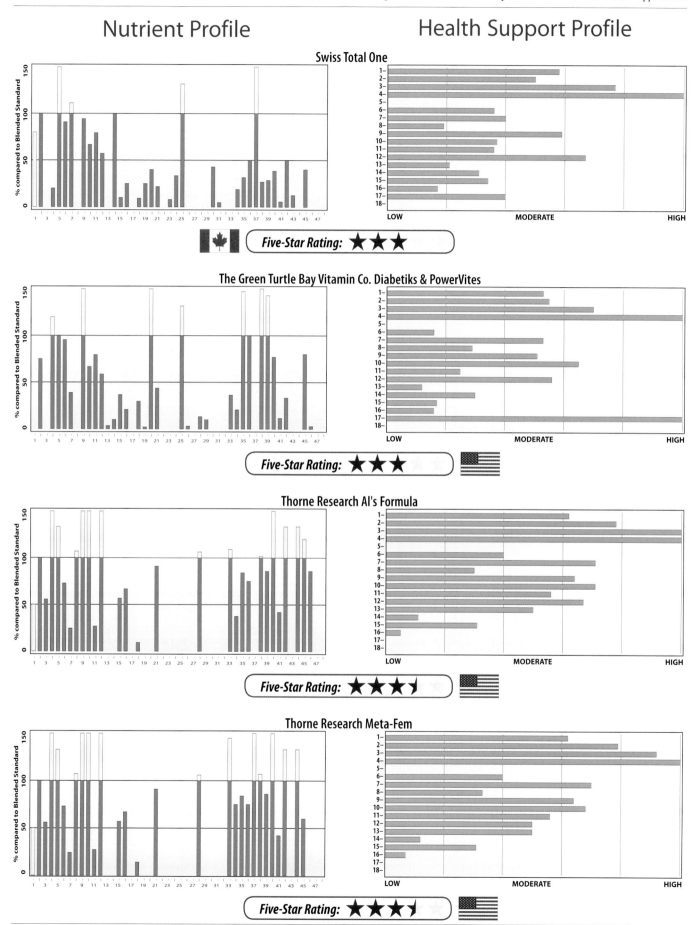

Swiss Total One

Five-Star Rating: ★★★

The Green Turtle Bay Vitamin Co. Diabetiks & PowerVites

Five-Star Rating: ★★★

Thorne Research Al's Formula

Five-Star Rating: ★★★★⌐

Thorne Research Meta-Fem

Five-Star Rating: ★★★★⌐

Nutrient Profile

Health Support Profile

Nutrient Profile Legend			
1 Vitamin A	5000 IU	25 n-acetyl-l-Cysteine	56 mg
2 Vitamin D	400 IU	26 acetyl-l-Carnitine	500 mg
3 Vitamin K	180 ug	27 Carnitine	500 mg
4 Biotin	250 ug	28 Choline	94 mg
5 Folic Acid	600 ug	29 Inositol	125 mg
6 Vitamin B1 (Thiamin)	55 mg	30 Lecithin	350 mg
7 Vitamin B2 (Riboflavin)	45 mg	31 alpha-Linolenic Acid	3125 mg
8 Vitamin B3 (Niacin)	28 mg	32 Omega-3 Fish Oil (EPA/DHA)	1141 mg
9 Vitamin B3 (Niacinamide)	60 mg	33 Boron	3 mg
10 Vitamin B5 (Pantothenic Acid)	75 mg	34 Calcium	800 mg
11 Vitamin B6 (Pyridoxine)	63 mg	35 Chromium	238 ug
12 Vitamin B12 (Cobalamin)	175 ug	36 Copper	2 mg
13 Coenzyme Q10	60 mg	37 Iodine	100 ug
14 alpha-Lipoic Acid	100 mg	38 Magnesium	280 mg
15 Vitamin C	1500 mg	39 Manganese	7 mg
16 Vitamin E (alpha tocopherol)	600 IU	40 Molybdenum	65 ug
17 Vitamin E (gamma/mixed)	200 mg	41 Potassium	215 mg
18 Bioflavonoids (mixed)	540 mg	42 Selenium	150 ug
19 Procyanidolic Oligomers (PCOs)	100 mg	43 Silicon	8 mg
20 Phenolic Compounds	25 mg	44 Vanadium	75 ug
21 beta-Carotene	13750 IU	45 Zinc	25 mg
22 Carotenoids (mixed)	5625 IU	46 Trimethylglycine (TMG/Betaine)	350 mg
23 Lutein/Zeaxanthin	5 mg	47 Carnosine	1000 mg
24 Lycopene	15 mg	48 Iron (NOT recommended)	5 mg

Health Support Profile Legend	
1. Completeness	10. Metabolic Health
2. Potency	11. Ocular Health
3. Mineral Forms	12. Methylation Support
4. Bioactivity of Vitamin E	13. Lipotropic Factors
5. Gamma Tocopherol	14. Inflammation Control
6. Antioxidant Support	15. Glycation Control
7. Bone Health	16. Bioflavonoid Profile
8. Heart Health	17. Phenolic Compounds
9. Liver Health	18. Potential Toxicities

Trophic Complete

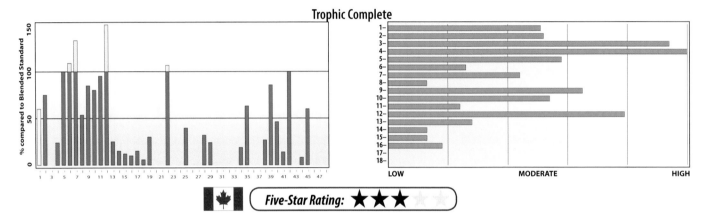

Five-Star Rating: ★★★☆☆

Truestar Health TrueBASIC

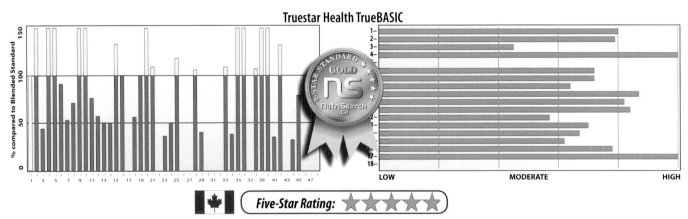

Five-Star Rating: ★★★★★

Ultimate Nutrition Super Complete

Five-Star Rating: ★★★☆☆

Nutrient Profile

Health Support Profile

USANA Health Sciences Essentials

Five-Star Rating: ⭐⭐⭐⭐⭐

USANA Health Sciences Essentials

Five-Star Rating: ⭐⭐⭐⭐⭐

VegLife Iron Free MultiVeg Energy

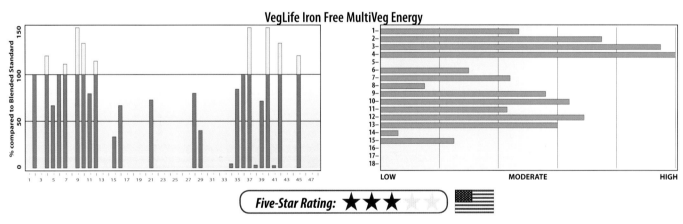

Five-Star Rating: ★★★☆☆

Vital Nutrients Multi-Nutrients No Iron or Iodine

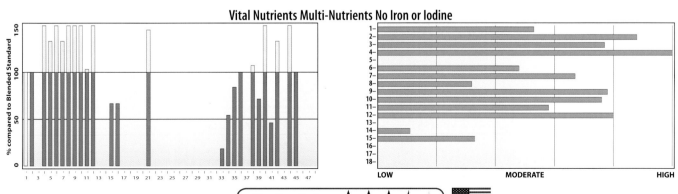

Five-Star Rating: ★★★★⯪

Nutrient Profile

Health Support Profile

Nutrient Profile Legend					
1 Vitamin A	5000	IU	25 n-acetyl-l-Cysteine	56	mg
2 Vitamin D	400	IU	26 acetyl-l-Carnitine	500	mg
3 Vitamin K	180	ug	27 Carnitine	500	mg
4 Biotin	250	ug	28 Choline	94	mg
5 Folic Acid	600	ug	29 Inositol	125	mg
6 Vitamin B1 (Thiamin)	55	mg	30 Lecithin	350	mg
7 Vitamin B2 (Riboflavin)	45	mg	31 alpha-Linolenic Acid	3125	mg
8 Vitamin B3 (Niacin)	28	mg	32 Omega-3 Fish Oil (EPA/DHA)	1141	mg
9 Vitamin B3 (Niacinamide)	60	mg	33 Boron	3	mg
10 Vitamin B5 (Pantothenic Acid)	75	mg	34 Calcium	800	mg
11 Vitamin B6 (Pyridoxine)	63	mg	35 Chromium	238	ug
12 Vitamin B12 (Cobalamin)	175	ug	36 Copper	2	mg
13 Coenzyme Q10	60	mg	37 Iodine	100	ug
14 alpha-Lipoic Acid	100	mg	38 Magnesium	280	mg
15 Vitamin C	1500	mg	39 Manganese	7	mg
16 Vitamin E (alpha tocopherol)	600	IU	40 Molybdenum	65	ug
17 Vitamin E (gamma/mixed)	200	mg	41 Potassium	215	mg
18 Bioflavonoids (mixed)	540	mg	42 Selenium	150	ug
19 Procyanidolic Oligomers (PCOs)	100	mg	43 Silicon	8	mg
20 Phenolic Compounds	25	mg	44 Vanadium	75	ug
21 beta-Carotene	13750	IU	45 Zinc	25	mg
22 Carotenoids (mixed)	5625	IU	46 Trimethylglycine (TMG/Betaine)	350	mg
23 Lutein/Zeaxanthin	5	mg	47 Carnosine	1000	mg
24 Lycopene	15	mg	48 Iron (NOT recommended)	5	mg

Health Support Profile Legend	
1. Completeness	10. Metabolic Health
2. Potency	11. Ocular Health
3. Mineral Forms	12. Methylation Support
4. Bioactivity of Vitamin E	13. Lipotropic Factors
5. Gamma Tocopherol	14. Inflammation Control
6. Antioxidant Support	15. Glycation Control
7. Bone Health	16. Bioflavonoid Profile
8. Heart Health	17. Phenolic Compounds
9. Liver Health	18. Potential Toxicities

Vitamin Research Products Optimum 18

Five-Star Rating: ★★★★★

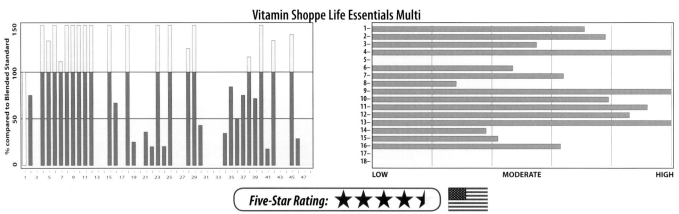

Vitamin Shoppe Life Essentials Multi

Five-Star Rating: ★★★★⯪

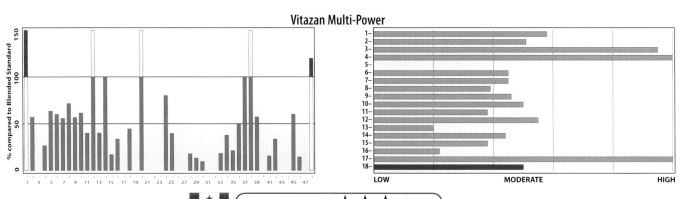

Vitazan Multi-Power

Five-Star Rating: ★★★

Nutrient Profile

Health Support Profile

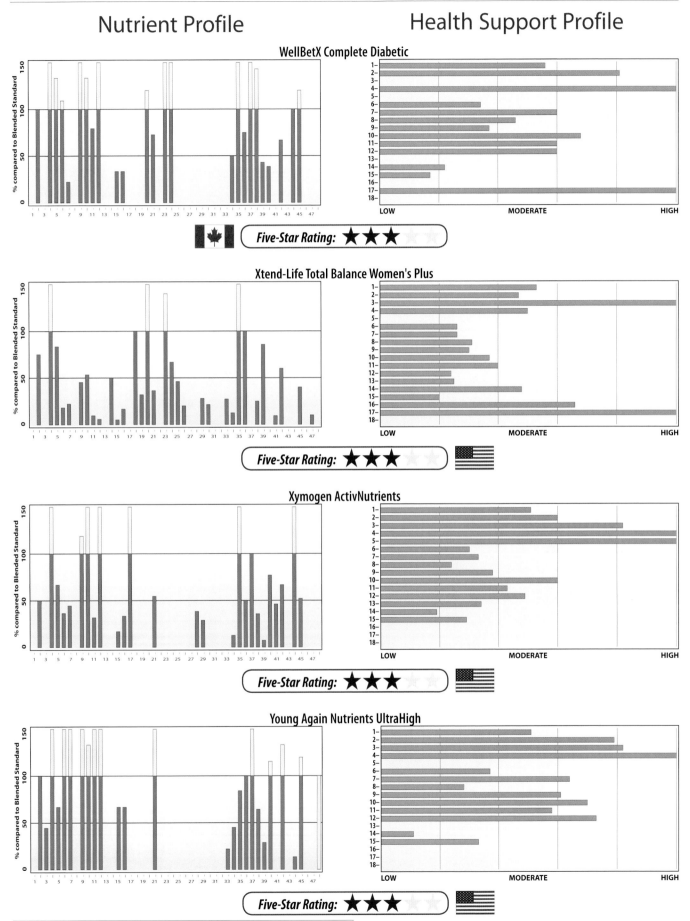

WellBetX Complete Diabetic

Five-Star Rating: ★★★☆☆

Xtend-Life Total Balance Women's Plus

Five-Star Rating: ★★★☆☆

Xymogen ActivNutrients

Five-Star Rating: ★★★☆☆

Young Again Nutrients UltraHigh

Five-Star Rating: ★★★☆☆

Nutrient Profile

Nutrient Profile Legend				
1 Vitamin A	5000 IU	25 n-acetyl-l-Cysteine	56 mg
2 Vitamin D	400 IU	26 acetyl-l-Carnitine	500 mg
3 Vitamin K	180 ug	27 Carnitine	500 mg
4 Biotin	250 ug	28 Choline	94 mg
5 Folic Acid	600 ug	29 Inositol	125 mg
6 Vitamin B1 (Thiamin)	55 mg	30 Lecithin	350 mg
7 Vitamin B2 (Riboflavin)	45 mg	31 alpha-Linolenic Acid	3125 mg
8 Vitamin B3 (Niacin)	28 mg	32 Omega-3 Fish Oil (EPA/DHA)	1141 mg
9 Vitamin B3 (Niacinamide)	60 mg	33 Boron	3 mg
10 Vitamin B5 (Pantothenic Acid)	75 mg	34 Calcium	800 mg
11 Vitamin B6 (Pyridoxine)	63 mg	35 Chromium	238 ug
12 Vitamin B12 (Cobalamin)	175 ug	36 Copper	2 mg
13 Coenzyme Q10	60 mg	37 Iodine	100 ug
14 alpha-Lipoic Acid	100 mg	38 Magnesium	280 mg
15 Vitamin C	1500 mg	39 Manganese	7 mg
16 Vitamin E (alpha tocopherol)	600 IU	40 Molybdenum	65 ug
17 Vitamin E (gamma/mixed)	200 mg	41 Potassium	215 mg
18 Bioflavonoids (mixed)	540 mg	42 Selenium	150 ug
19 Procyanidolic Oligomers (PCOs)	100 mg	43 Silicon	8 mg
20 Phenolic Compounds	25 mg	44 Vanadium	75 ug
21 beta-Carotene	13750 IU	45 Zinc	25 mg
22 Carotenoids (mixed)	5625 IU	46 Trimethylglycine (TMG/Betaine)	350 mg
23 Lutein/Zeaxanthin	5 mg	47 Carnosine	1000 mg
24 Lycopene	15 mg	48 Iron (NOT recommended)	5 mg

Health Support Profile

Health Support Profile Legend	
1. Completeness	10. Metabolic Health
2. Potency	11. Ocular Health
3. Mineral Forms	12. Methylation Support
4. Bioactivity of Vitamin E	13. Lipotropic Factors
5. Gamma Tocopherol	14. Inflammation Control
6. Antioxidant Support	15. Glycation Control
7. Bone Health	16. Bioflavonoid Profile
8. Heart Health	17. Phenolic Compounds
9. Liver Health	18. Potential Toxicities

BioX Multi Vitamin Pack

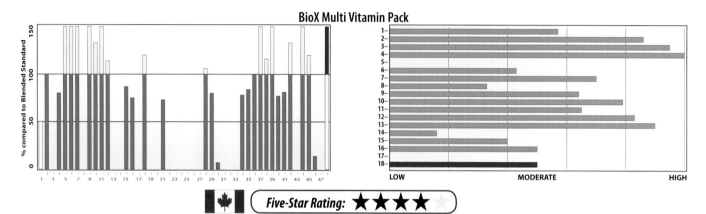

Five-Star Rating: ★★★★☆

Colgan Institute Men's Active Pak

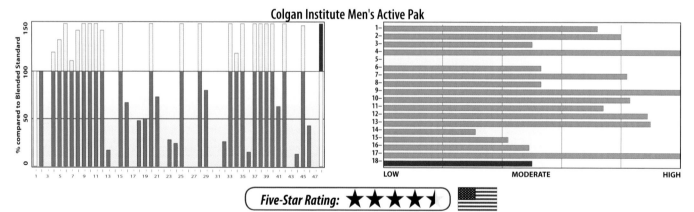

Five-Star Rating: ★★★★⯪

Colgan Institute Women's Active Pak

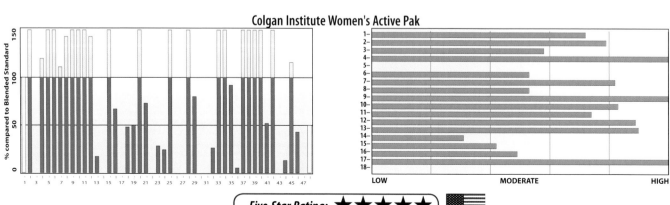

Five-Star Rating: ★★★★★

Nutrient Profile

Health Support Profile

CVC 4 Health Unit Pac Ultimate

Five-Star Rating: ★★★ ☆☆

dc (Dee Cee Laboratories) Mega Vita-Min

Five-Star Rating: ★★★ ☆☆

Douglas Laboratories Daily Core Essentials

Five-Star Rating: ★★★★★

Douglas Laboratories Longevity Support Pack

Five-Star Rating: ★★★★★

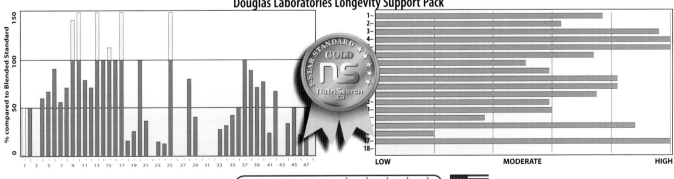

Nutrient Profile

Health Support Profile

Nutrient Profile Legend						
1 Vitamin A	5000	IU	25 n-acetyl-l-Cysteine	56	mg
2 Vitamin D	400	IU	26 acetyl-l-Carnitine	500	mg
3 Vitamin K	180	ug	27 Carnitine	500	mg
4 Biotin	250	ug	28 Choline	94	mg
5 Folic Acid	600	ug	29 Inositol	125	mg
6 Vitamin B1 (Thiamin)	55	mg	30 Lecithin	350	mg
7 Vitamin B2 (Riboflavin)	45	mg	31 alpha-Linolenic Acid	3125	mg
8 Vitamin B3 (Niacin)	28	mg	32 Omega-3 Fish Oil (EPA/DHA)	1141	mg
9 Vitamin B3 (Niacinamide)	60	mg	33 Boron	3	mg
10 Vitamin B5 (Pantothenic Acid)	75	mg	34 Calcium	800	mg
11 Vitamin B6 (Pyridoxine)	63	mg	35 Chromium	238	ug
12 Vitamin B12 (Cobalamin)	175	ug	36 Copper	2	mg
13 Coenzyme Q10	60	mg	37 Iodine	100	ug
14 alpha-Lipoic Acid	100	mg	38 Magnesium	280	mg
15 Vitamin C	1500	mg	39 Manganese	7	mg
16 Vitamin E (alpha tocopherol)	600	IU	40 Molybdenum	65	ug
17 Vitamin E (gamma/mixed)	200	mg	41 Potassium	215	mg
18 Bioflavonoids (mixed)	540	mg	42 Selenium	150	ug
19 Procyanidolic Oligomers (PCOs)	100	mg	43 Silicon	8	mg
20 Phenolic Compounds	25	mg	44 Vanadium	75	ug
21 beta-Carotene	13750	IU	45 Zinc	25	mg
22 Carotenoids (mixed)	5625	IU	46 Trimethylglycine (TMG/Betaine)	350	mg
23 Lutein/Zeaxanthin	5	mg	47 Carnosine	1000	mg
24 Lycopene	15	mg	48 Iron (NOT recommended)	5	mg

Health Support Profile Legend	
1. Completeness	10. Metabolic Health
2. Potency	11. Ocular Health
3. Mineral Forms	12. Methylation Support
4. Bioactivity of Vitamin E	13. Lipotropic Factors
5. Gamma Tocopherol	14. Inflammation Control
6. Antioxidant Support	15. Glycation Control
7. Bone Health	16. Bioflavonoid Profile
8. Heart Health	17. Phenolic Compounds
9. Liver Health	18. Potential Toxicities

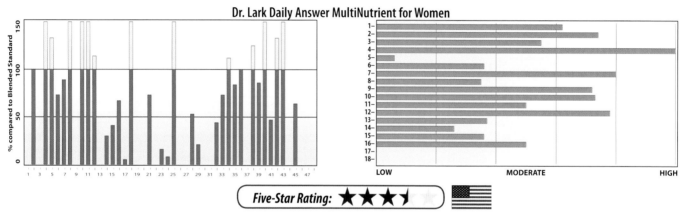

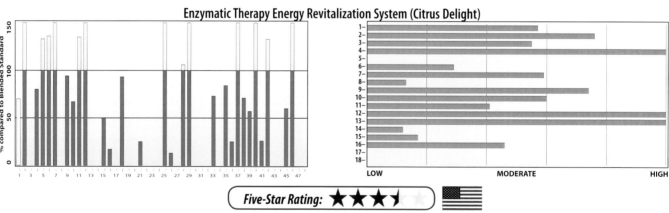

Nutrient Profile

Health Support Profile

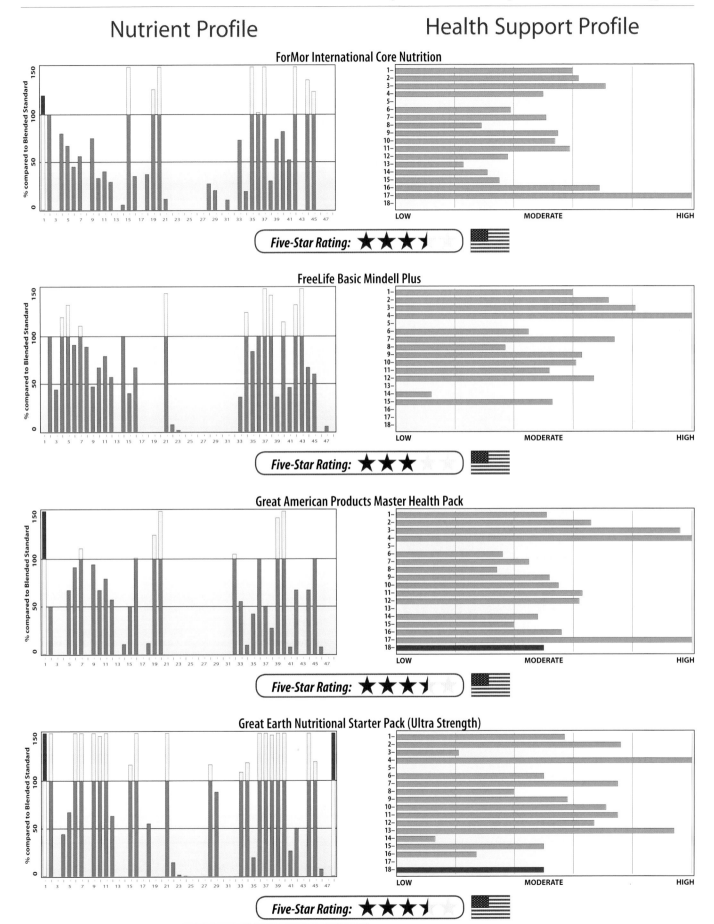

ForMor International Core Nutrition

Five-Star Rating: ★ ★ ★ ⤙

FreeLife Basic Mindell Plus

Five-Star Rating: ★ ★ ★

Great American Products Master Health Pack

Five-Star Rating: ★ ★ ★ ⤙

Great Earth Nutritional Starter Pack (Ultra Strength)

Five-Star Rating: ★ ★ ★ ⤙

Nutrient Profile

Health Support Profile

Nutrient Profile Legend					
1 Vitamin A	5000	IU	25 n-acetyl-l-Cysteine	56	mg
2 Vitamin D	400	IU	26 acetyl-l-Carnitine	500	mg
3 Vitamin K	180	ug	27 Carnitine	500	mg
4 Biotin	250	ug	28 Choline	94	mg
5 Folic Acid	600	ug	29 Inositol	125	mg
6 Vitamin B1 (Thiamin)	55	mg	30 Lecithin	350	mg
7 Vitamin B2 (Riboflavin)	45	mg	31 alpha-Linolenic Acid	3125	mg
8 Vitamin B3 (Niacin)	28	mg	32 Omega-3 Fish Oil (EPA/DHA)	1141	mg
9 Vitamin B3 (Niacinamide)	60	mg	33 Boron	3	mg
10 Vitamin B5 (Pantothenic Acid)	75	mg	34 Calcium	800	mg
11 Vitamin B6 (Pyridoxine)	63	mg	35 Chromium	238	ug
12 Vitamin B12 (Cobalamin)	175	ug	36 Copper	2	mg
13 Coenzyme Q10	60	mg	37 Iodine	100	ug
14 alpha-Lipoic Acid	100	mg	38 Magnesium	280	mg
15 Vitamin C	1500	mg	39 Manganese	7	mg
16 Vitamin E (alpha tocopherol)	600	IU	40 Molybdenum	65	ug
17 Vitamin E (gamma/mixed)	200	mg	41 Potassium	215	mg
18 Bioflavonoids (mixed)	540	mg	42 Selenium	150	ug
19 Procyanidolic Oligomers (PCOs)	100	mg	43 Silicon	8	mg
20 Phenolic Compounds	25	mg	44 Vanadium	75	ug
21 beta-Carotene	13750	IU	45 Zinc	25	mg
22 Carotenoids (mixed)	5625	IU	46 Trimethylglycine (TMG/Betaine)	350	mg
23 Lutein/Zeaxanthin	5	mg	47 Carnosine	1000	mg
24 Lycopene	15	mg	48 Iron (NOT recommended)	5	mg

Health Support Profile Legend	
1. Completeness	10. Metabolic Health
2. Potency	11. Ocular Health
3. Mineral Forms	12. Methylation Support
4. Bioactivity of Vitamin E	13. Lipotropic Factors
5. Gamma Tocopherol	14. Inflammation Control
6. Antioxidant Support	15. Glycation Control
7. Bone Health	16. Bioflavonoid Profile
8. Heart Health	17. Phenolic Compounds
9. Liver Health	18. Potential Toxicities

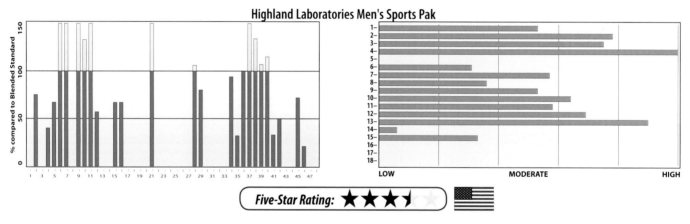

Highland Laboratories Men's Sports Pak

Five-Star Rating: ★★★★⯪

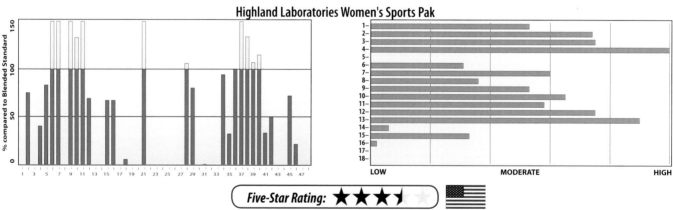

Highland Laboratories Women's Sports Pak

Five-Star Rating: ★★★★⯪

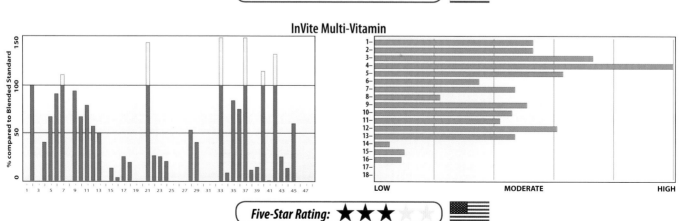

InVite Multi-Vitamin

Five-Star Rating: ★★★

Nutrient Profile

Health Support Profile

Jarrow Formulas All Capsule Health Pak

Five-Star Rating: ★ ★ ★ ★

Jean Carper's Stop Aging Now! Anti-Aging Power-Pak

Five-Star Rating: ★ ★ ★ ★ ⭒

Julian Whitaker, M.D. Forward Plus Daily Regimen

Five-Star Rating: ★ ★ ★ ★

Julian Whitaker, M.D. Forward Plus Daily Regimen

Five-Star Rating: ★ ★ ★ ★ ⭒

Nutrient Profile

Health Support Profile

Nutrient Profile Legend					
1 Vitamin A	5000	IU	25 n-acetyl-l-Cysteine	56	mg
2 Vitamin D	400	IU	26 acetyl-l-Carnitine	500	mg
3 Vitamin K	180	ug	27 Carnitine	500	mg
4 Biotin	250	ug	28 Choline	94	mg
5 Folic Acid	600	ug	29 Inositol	125	mg
6 Vitamin B1 (Thiamin)	55	mg	30 Lecithin	350	mg
7 Vitamin B2 (Riboflavin)	45	mg	31 alpha-Linolenic Acid	3125	mg
8 Vitamin B3 (Niacin)	28	mg	32 Omega-3 Fish Oil (EPA/DHA)	1141	mg
9 Vitamin B3 (Niacinamide)	60	mg	33 Boron	3	mg
10 Vitamin B5 (Pantothenic Acid)	75	mg	34 Calcium	800	mg
11 Vitamin B6 (Pyridoxine)	63	mg	35 Chromium	238	ug
12 Vitamin B12 (Cobalamin)	175	ug	36 Copper	2	mg
13 Coenzyme Q10	60	mg	37 Iodine	100	ug
14 alpha-Lipoic Acid	100	mg	38 Magnesium	280	mg
15 Vitamin C	1500	mg	39 Manganese	7	mg
16 Vitamin E (alpha tocopherol)	600	IU	40 Molybdenum	65	ug
17 Vitamin E (gamma/mixed)	200	mg	41 Potassium	215	mg
18 Bioflavonoids (mixed)	540	mg	42 Selenium	150	ug
19 Procyanidolic Oligomers (PCOs)	100	mg	43 Silicon	8	mg
20 Phenolic Compounds	25	mg	44 Vanadium	75	ug
21 beta-Carotene	13750	IU	45 Zinc	25	mg
22 Carotenoids (mixed)	5625	IU	46 Trimethylglycine (TMG/Betaine)	350	mg
23 Lutein/Zeaxanthin	5	mg	47 Carnosine	1000	mg
24 Lycopene	15	mg	48 Iron (NOT recommended)	5	mg

Health Support Profile Legend

1. Completeness
2. Potency
3. Mineral Forms
4. Bioactivity of Vitamin E
5. Gamma Tocopherol
6. Antioxidant Support
7. Bone Health
8. Heart Health
9. Liver Health

10. Metabolic Health
11. Ocular Health
12. Methylation Support
13. Lipotropic Factors
14. Inflammation Control
15. Glycation Control
16. Bioflavonoid Profile
17. Phenolic Compounds
18. Potential Toxicities

Life-Line Total Health Formula

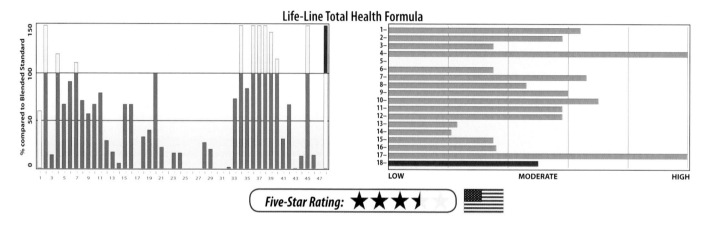

Five-Star Rating: ★★★☆

Lorna Vanderhaeghe FemmEssentials

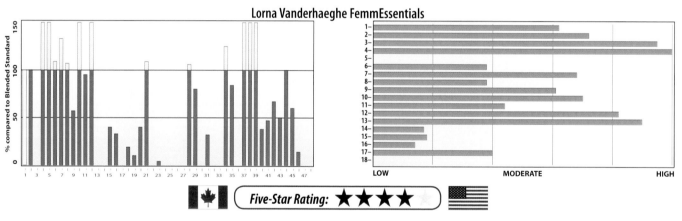

Five-Star Rating: ★★★★

Metagenics Wellness Essentials

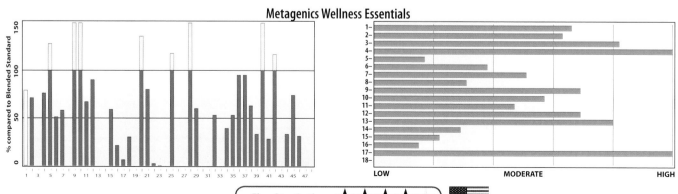

Five-Star Rating: ★★★★

Nutrient Profile

Health Support Profile

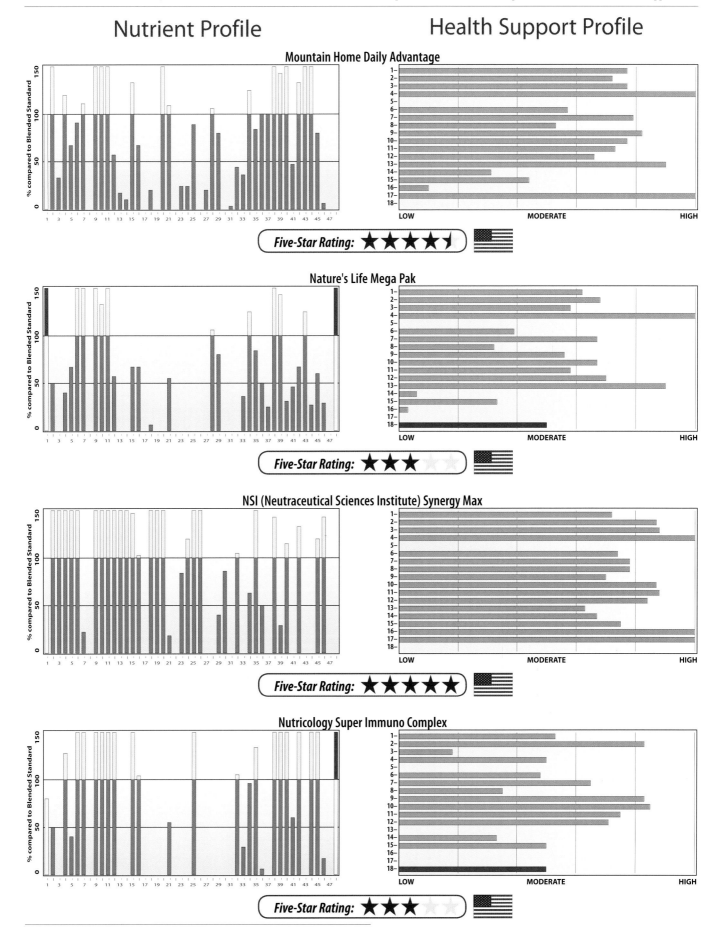

Mountain Home Daily Advantage

Five-Star Rating: ★★★★✦

Nature's Life Mega Pak

Five-Star Rating: ★★★☆☆

NSI (Neutraceutical Sciences Institute) Synergy Max

Five-Star Rating: ★★★★★

Nutricology Super Immuno Complex

Five-Star Rating: ★★★☆☆

Nutrient Profile

Health Support Profile

Nutrient Profile Legend

1	Vitamin A	5000 IU	25	n-acetyl-l-Cysteine	56	mg
2	Vitamin D	400 IU	26	acetyl-l-Carnitine	500	mg
3	Vitamin K	180 ug	27	Carnitine	500	mg
4	Biotin	250 ug	28	Choline	94	mg
5	Folic Acid	600 ug	29	Inositol	125	mg
6	Vitamin B1 (Thiamin)	55 mg	30	Lecithin	350	mg
7	Vitamin B2 (Riboflavin)	45 mg	31	alpha-Linolenic Acid	3125	mg
8	Vitamin B3 (Niacin)	28 mg	32	Omega-3 Fish Oil (EPA/DHA)	1141	mg
9	Vitamin B3 (Niacinamide)	60 mg	33	Boron	3	mg
10	Vitamin B5 (Pantothenic Acid)	75 mg	34	Calcium	800	mg
11	Vitamin B6 (Pyridoxine)	63 mg	35	Chromium	238	ug
12	Vitamin B12 (Cobalamin)	175 ug	36	Copper	2	mg
13	Coenzyme Q10	60 mg	37	Iodine	100	ug
14	alpha-Lipoic Acid	100 mg	38	Magnesium	280	mg
15	Vitamin C	1500 mg	39	Manganese	7	mg
16	Vitamin E (alpha tocopherol)	600 IU	40	Molybdenum	65	ug
17	Vitamin E (gamma/mixed)	200 mg	41	Potassium	215	mg
18	Bioflavonoids (mixed)	540 mg	42	Selenium	150	ug
19	Procyanidolic Oligomers (PCOs)	100 mg	43	Silicon	8	mg
20	Phenolic Compounds	25 mg	44	Vanadium	75	ug
21	beta-Carotene	13750 IU	45	Zinc	25	mg
22	Carotenoids (mixed)	5625 IU	46	Trimethylglycine (TMG/Betaine)	350	mg
23	Lutein/Zeaxanthin	5 mg	47	Carnosine	1000	mg
24	Lycopene	15 mg	48	Iron (NOT recommended)	5	mg

Health Support Profile Legend

1. Completeness	10. Metabolic Health
2. Potency	11. Ocular Health
3. Mineral Forms	12. Methylation Support
4. Bioactivity of Vitamin E	13. Lipotropic Factors
5. Gamma Tocopherol	14. Inflammation Control
6. Antioxidant Support	15. Glycation Control
7. Bone Health	16. Bioflavonoid Profile
8. Heart Health	17. Phenolic Compounds
9. Liver Health	18. Potential Toxicities

Nutrilite Perfect Health Pack

Five-Star Rating: ★★★★☆

Nutristart Nutri-Pods

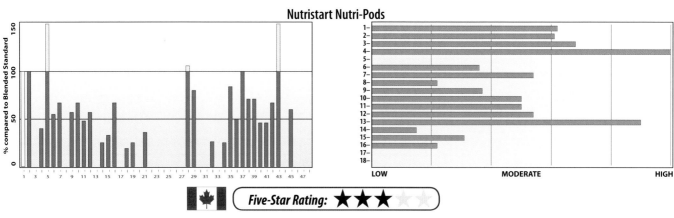

Five-Star Rating: ★★★☆☆

Nutrition Dynamics Just For Dad

Five-Star Rating: ★★★★⯪

Nutrient Profile

Health Support Profile

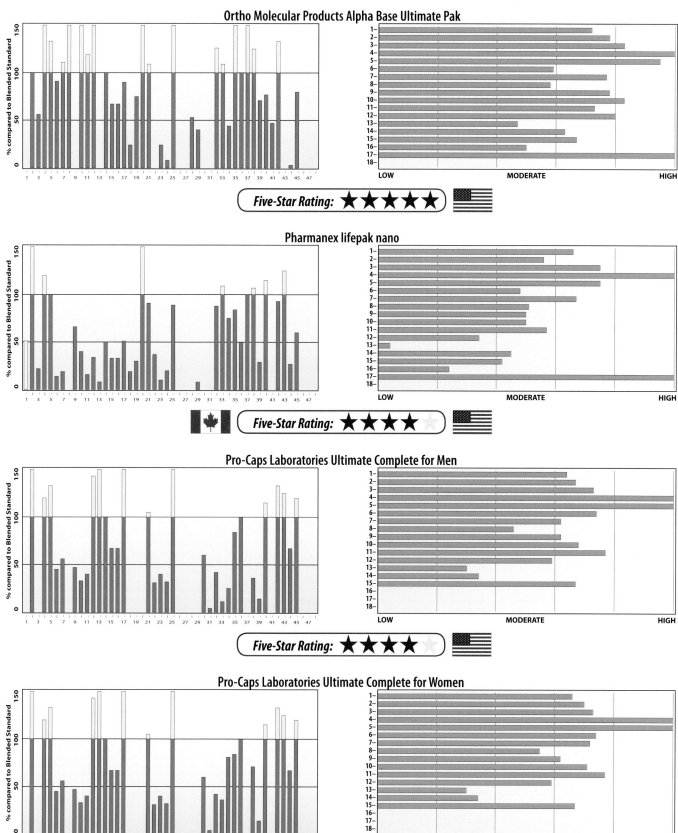

Ortho Molecular Products Alpha Base Ultimate Pak

Five-Star Rating: ★ ★ ★ ★ ★

Pharmanex lifepak nano

Five-Star Rating: ★ ★ ★ ★ ☆

Pro-Caps Laboratories Ultimate Complete for Men

Five-Star Rating: ★ ★ ★ ★ ☆

Pro-Caps Laboratories Ultimate Complete for Women

Five-Star Rating: ★ ★ ★ ★ ⯪

Nutrient Profile

Health Support Profile

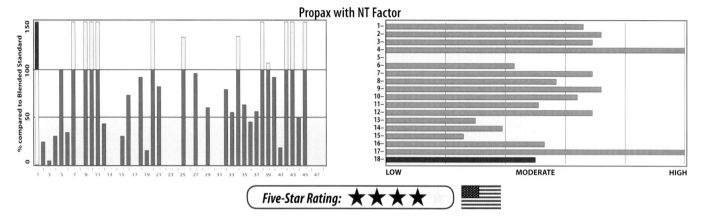

Nutrient Profile Legend					
1 Vitamin A	5000	IU	25 n-acetyl-l-Cysteine	56	mg
2 Vitamin D	400	IU	26 acetyl-l-Carnitine	500	mg
3 Vitamin K	180	ug	27 Carnitine	500	mg
4 Biotin	250	ug	28 Choline	94	mg
5 Folic Acid	600	ug	29 Inositol	125	mg
6 Vitamin B1 (Thiamin)	55	mg	30 Lecithin	350	mg
7 Vitamin B2 (Riboflavin)	45	mg	31 alpha-Linolenic Acid	3125	mg
8 Vitamin B3 (Niacin)	28	mg	32 Omega-3 Fish Oil (EPA/DHA)	1141	mg
9 Vitamin B3 (Niacinamide)	60	mg	33 Boron	3	mg
10 Vitamin B5 (Pantothenic Acid)	75	mg	34 Calcium	800	mg
11 Vitamin B6 (Pyridoxine)	63	mg	35 Chromium	238	ug
12 Vitamin B12 (Cobalamin)	175	ug	36 Copper	2	mg
13 Coenzyme Q10	60	mg	37 Iodine	100	ug
14 alpha-Lipoic Acid	100	mg	38 Magnesium	280	mg
15 Vitamin C	1500	mg	39 Manganese	7	mg
16 Vitamin E (alpha tocopherol)	600	IU	40 Molybdenum	65	ug
17 Vitamin E (gamma/mixed)	200	mg	41 Potassium	215	mg
18 Bioflavonoids (mixed)	540	mg	42 Selenium	150	ug
19 Procyanidolic Oligomers (PCOs)	100	mg	43 Silicon	8	mg
20 Phenolic Compounds	25	mg	44 Vanadium	75	ug
21 beta-Carotene	13750	IU	45 Zinc	25	mg
22 Carotenoids (mixed)	5625	IU	46 Trimethylglycine (TMG/Betaine)	350	mg
23 Lutein/Zeaxanthin	5	mg	47 Carnosine	1000	mg
24 Lycopene	15	mg	48 Iron (NOT recommended)	5	mg

Health Support Profile Legend	
1. Completeness	10. Metabolic Health
2. Potency	11. Ocular Health
3. Mineral Forms	12. Methylation Support
4. Bioactivity of Vitamin E	13. Lipotropic Factors
5. Gamma Tocopherol	14. Inflammation Control
6. Antioxidant Support	15. Glycation Control
7. Bone Health	16. Bioflavonoid Profile
8. Heart Health	17. Phenolic Compounds
9. Liver Health	18. Potential Toxicities

Propax with NT Factor

Five-Star Rating: ★★★★☆

R Garden Essential Nutrition Pack OR Essential Nutrition Plus

Five-Star Rating: ★★★☆☆

TrueStar Health TrueBASICS Plus for Men OR TrueBASICS Plus for Women

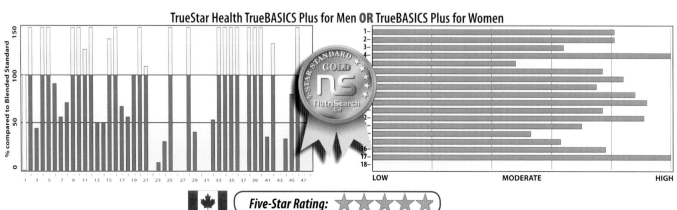

Five-Star Rating: ★★★★★

Nutrient Profile

Health Support Profile

USANA Health Sciences HealthPak 100

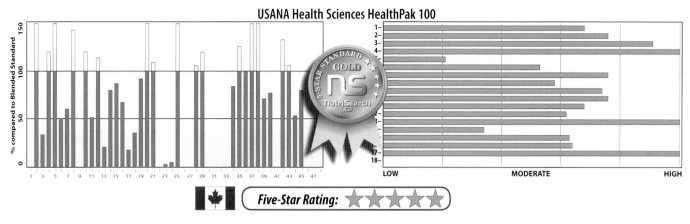

Five-Star Rating: ★★★★★

USANA Health Sciences HealthPak 100

Five-Star Rating: ★★★★★

ViSalus Vi-PAK

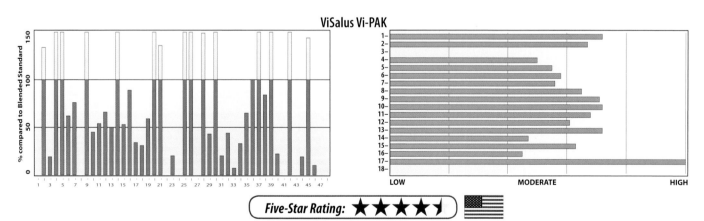

Five-Star Rating: ★★★★⯪

Vitamin Shoppe Multi-Vitamin Pack

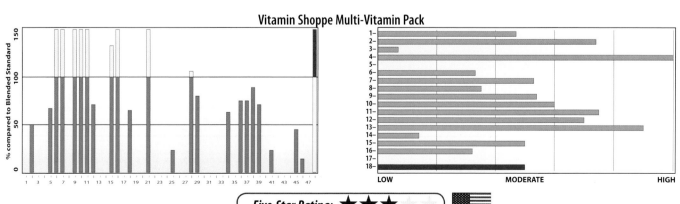

Five-Star Rating: ★★★

Nutrient Profile

Health Support Profile

Nutrient Profile Legend					
1 Vitamin A	5000 IU		25 n-acetyl-l-Cysteine	56	mg
2 Vitamin D	400 IU		26 acetyl-l-Carnitine	500	mg
3 Vitamin K	180 ug		27 Carnitine	500	mg
4 Biotin	250 ug		28 Choline	94	mg
5 Folic Acid	600 ug		29 Inositol	125	mg
6 Vitamin B1 (Thiamin)	55 mg		30 Lecithin	350	mg
7 Vitamin B2 (Riboflavin)	45 mg		31 alpha-Linolenic Acid	3125	mg
8 Vitamin B3 (Niacin)	28 mg		32 Omega-3 Fish Oil (EPA/DHA)	1141	mg
9 Vitamin B3 (Niacinamide)	60 mg		33 Boron	3	mg
10 Vitamin B5 (Pantothenic Acid)	75 mg		34 Calcium	800	mg
11 Vitamin B6 (Pyridoxine)	63 mg		35 Chromium	238	ug
12 Vitamin B12 (Cobalamin)	175 ug		36 Copper	2	mg
13 Coenzyme Q10	60 mg		37 Iodine	100	ug
14 alpha-Lipoic Acid	100 mg		38 Magnesium	280	mg
15 Vitamin C	1500 mg		39 Manganese	7	mg
16 Vitamin E (alpha tocopherol)	600 IU		40 Molybdenum	65	ug
17 Vitamin E (gamma/mixed)	200 mg		41 Potassium	215	mg
18 Bioflavonoids (mixed)	540 mg		42 Selenium	150	ug
19 Procyanidolic Oligomers (PCOs)	100 mg		43 Silicon	8	mg
20 Phenolic Compounds	25 mg		44 Vanadium	75	ug
21 beta-Carotene	13750 IU		45 Zinc	25	mg
22 Carotenoids (mixed)	5625 IU		46 Trimethylglycine (TMG/Betaine)	350	mg
23 Lutein/Zeaxanthin	5 mg		47 Carnosine	1000	mg
24 Lycopene	15 mg		48 Iron (NOT recommended)	5	mg

Health Support Profile Legend	
1. Completeness	10. Metabolic Health
2. Potency	11. Ocular Health
3. Mineral Forms	12. Methylation Support
4. Bioactivity of Vitamin E	13. Lipotropic Factors
5. Gamma Tocopherol	14. Inflammation Control
6. Antioxidant Support	15. Glycation Control
7. Bone Health	16. Bioflavonoid Profile
8. Heart Health	17. Phenolic Compounds
9. Liver Health	18. Potential Toxicities

Weil Complete Daily Pack

Five-Star Rating: ★★★☆☆

Weil Complete Daily Pack

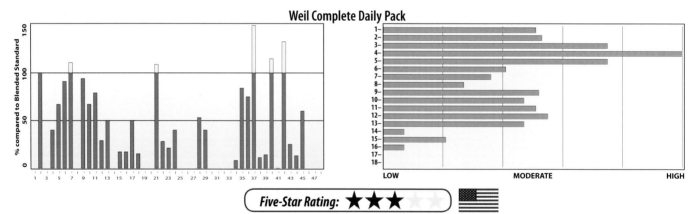

Five-Star Rating: ★★★☆☆

Section VI

Product Ratings

This section provides the reader with:

■ A listing in alphabetical order
  of all products reviewed
■ A listing by product rating
  of all products reviewed
■ Chapter references and Index of Terms

All products reviewed have been catalogued alphabetically by product name, along with their product rating and pertinent information regarding their formulation.

Products are also listed by their five-star ratings, with products of equal rank categorized alphabetically. Complete chapter references are provided.

Appendix A: Stand-alone Products Alphabetically

Manufacturer & Product Name	Country	# of Stars	Dosages and Considerations
21st Century Mega Multi for Men	US	1.5	
21st Century Mega Multi for Women	US	2.0	
21st Century One Daily Active	US	0.5	
21st Century One Daily Adults 50+	US	1.0	
21st Century One Daily CarbHealth	US	1.0	
21st Century One Daily Women's	US	-	
4Life MultiPlex	CA/US	1.5	dosage derived
4Life RiteStart Men	US	3.0	additional nutrient amounts not specified
4Life RiteStart Women	US	3.0	additional nutrient amounts not specified
4Life Start Plus	US	2.0	dosage derived
Action Labs Action Man Multi Once Daily	US	2.0	
Action Labs Action-Tabs Made for Men	US	1.0	
Adrien Gagnon Feminex Multi	CA	1.0	
Adrien Gagnon Sélect Multi	CA	1.0	
Advanced Nutritional Innovations (ANI) CORALadvantage	US	1.0	
Advanced Nutritional Innovations (ANI) CORALadvantage Bone & Joint Multi	US	3.0	
Advanced Physician's Products Complete MultiVitamin/Mineral without iron	US	2.5	
Advanced Physician's Products Maximum MultiVitamin/Mineral without Iron	US	3.5	
Advocare CorePlex	US	2.0	
agel Min	US	1.5	
agel Min	CA	1.5	
Alacer Super-Gram III	US	1.5	
Albi Imports Rocky Mountain Multiple	CA	2.0	DPD data; 2003 data
Albi Imports Super One a Day	CA	1.5	DPD data; 2003 data
Alive Vitamins Super One Plus	CA	2.0	DPD data; 2003 data
All One Multiple for Active Seniors	US	3.5	
All One Multiple Green Phyto Base	US	3.0	
All One Multiple Original Formula	US	3.0	
All One Multiple Rice Base	US	3.0	
Allergy Research Group Multi-Vi-Min	US	1.5	
Allergy Research Group Multi-Vi-Min without Copper & Iron	US	2.0	
Allergy Research Group Steady On	US	4.0	
Allergy Research Group Wholly Immune	US	5.0	
alpha betic Once-A-Day Multi-Vitamin	US	1.0	
American Health Nutri Mega	US	2.0	
American Nutrition Ultra VM-T	US	2.0	
amni Added Protection III (copper and iron free)	US	3.5	
amni Added Protection III (copper free with iron)	US	3.5	
amni Added Protection III (iron free with copper)	US	4.0	
amni Added Protection III (with copper & iron)	US	3.5	
amni Basic Preventive 1	US	3.5	
amni Basic Preventive 2	US	3.5	
amni Basic Preventive 3	US	3.5	
amni Basic Preventive 4	US	3.5	
amni Basic Preventive 5	US	3.5	
amni Basic Preventive 5 Plus Extra Vitamin D	US	4.0	
amni Essential Basics	US	3.0	
Anabolic Laboratories Aved-Digest Multi	US	2.0	
Anabolic Laboratories Aved-Multi	US	1.5	
Anabolic Laboratories Aved-Multi Iron Free	US	2.0	
Anabolic Laboratories Multigel Caps	US	2.0	
AOR Essential Mix	CA/US	3.0	additional nutrient amounts not specified
AOR Ortho-Core	US	3.5	
AOR Ortho-Core	CA	3.0	
Apex Fitness FIT 50 Plus	US	1.0	
Apex Fitness FIT Performance	US	1.0	
Apex Fitness FIT Vegan/High Carb	US	0.5	
Arbonne Complete Essentials for Men	US	1.5	
Arbonne Complete Essentials for Women I	US	1.0	
Arbonne Complete Essentials for Women II	US	1.0	
Atkins Basic 3	CA	2.0	
Atkins Basic 3	US	1.5	
AuMed Coremed	US	2.0	dosage derived; additional nutrient amounts not specified
Avena Originals Vitamin Supreme	CA	2.5	additional nutrient amounts not specified
Awareness Life Daily Complete	US	1.5	additional nutrient amounts not specified
Bio-Actif Phytobec	CA	0.5	
Biogenesis Nutraceuticals BioFocus	US	1.5	
Biogenesis Nutraceuticals UltraGenesis	US	3.5	dosage derived
Biogenesis Nutraceuticals UltraGenesis without iron	US	4.0	
Bio-lumin Essence Daily Essence	US	1.5	dosage derived
Biotics Research Corporation Bio-Multi Plus	US	1.0	
Biotics Research Corporation Bio-Multi Plus Iron & Copper Free	US	1.5	
Biotics Research Corporation Bio-Multi Plus Iron-Free	US	1.5	
BioX Ultimate Once A Day	CA	2.5	dosage derived
Bluebonnet Iron Free Multi One	US	2.0	
Bluebonnet Maxi One	US	2.0	

Product	Country	Rating	Notes
Bluebonnet Maxi Two	US	2.5	
Bluebonnet Multi One	US	1.5	
Bluebonnet Multi-Vita Softgels	US	2.5	
Bluebonnet Super Earth Iron-Free	US	3.0	
Bluebonnet Super Earth mini-caplets	US	2.5	
Bluebonnet Super Earth with Iron	US	2.5	
Bluebonnet Super Vita-CoQ10 Formula	US	3.5	
Body Guard Antioxidant Formula	CA/US	2.0	
Body Rewards Daily Multiple	US	1.5	
Body Wise Right Choice A.M. + P.M. Formulas	CA/US	3.5	
Botanic Choice Complete Assurance for Men	US	2.0	
Botanic Choice Complete Assurance for Women	US	2.0	
Botanic Choice High Potency Vitamin & Mineral	US	0.5	
Botanic Choice Senior Multi-Vitamin	US	1.5	
Botanic Choice Whole Foods Power Multi	US	1.5	
Bronson Laboratories Fortified Vitamin & Mineral Insurance Formula	US	1.5	
Bronson Laboratories Mega Multi Softcaps	US	2.0	
Bronson Laboratories Men's Complete Formula with 7-Keto	US	2.0	
Bronson Laboratories Multi Formula with Lutein	US	1.5	
Bronson Laboratories Performance Edge for Men	US	2.0	
Bronson Laboratories Performance Edge for Women	US	2.0	
Bronson Laboratories The Bronson Formula	US	1.0	
Bronson Laboratories Therapeutic Vitamin & Mineral Formula	US	0.5	
Bronson Laboratories Therapeutic Vitamin & Mineral Formula - without iron	US	1.0	
Bronson Laboratories Vegi Source	US	3.5	
Bronson Laboratories Vitamin & Mineral Insurance Formula	US	2.0	
Burns Drugs Multi-Max	US	0.5	
Burns Drugs Super-T	US	-	
Canadian Sun Formula Flow	CA	1.5	
Canadian Sun One Plus	CA	2.0	
Canadian Sun Seniors Only	CA	1.0	
CanPrev Immuno-Pro Formula	CA	4.0	
Carlson Multi-Gel	US	2.5	
Carlson Super 1 Daily	US	1.5	
Carlson Super 2 Daily	US	2.5	
Carlson Super-75	US	2.0	
Cell Tech International Alpha Sun	US	-	
Cell Tech International Omega Sun	US	-	
Centrum	CA	-	
Centrum	US	-	
Centrum Forte	CA	-	
Centrum Advantage	CA	1.0	
Centrum Carb Assist	US	0.5	
Centrum Chewables	US	-	
Centrum Liquid	US	-	
Centrum Performance	US	0.5	
Centrum Performance	CA	-	
Centrum Protegra	CA	0.5	
Centrum Select	CA	0.5	
Centrum Silver	US	0.5	
Centrum Silver Chewables	US	0.5	
Clinician's Formula Vitality Multivite	US	1.5	additional nutrient amounts not specified
Club Vitamin Best	CA	0.5	dosage derived
CNC (Creative Nutrition Canada) Vitamost Plus Formula	CA/US	3.0	dosage derived
CNC (Creative Nutrition Canada) Vitamost Prime Formula	CA	2.5	dosage derived
CNC (Creative Nutrition Canada) Vitamost RTRE Formula	CA/US	2.5	
Colgan Institute First Defense Multi	US	3.0	
Colorado Nutrition Ultimate Men's Formula	US	1.5	
Colorado Nutrition Ultimate One	US	1.0	
Colorado Nutrition Ultimate Women's Formula	US	1.5	
Comprehensive Formula Men's	US	1.5	2003 data
Comprehensive Formula Women's	US	1.0	2003 data
Cooper Complete Basic One Iron Free	US	1.0	
Cooper Complete Basic One with Iron	US	1.0	
Cooper Complete Iron Free	US	2.5	
Cooper Complete with Iron	US	2.5	
Country Life Adult Multi	US	1.0	
Country Life Beyond Food	US	3.0	
Country Life Daily Total One	US	1.5	
Country Life Enhanced QM-1	US	1.5	
Country Life Esssential Life	US	2.5	
Country Life Green Edge II	US	1.5	dosage derived
Country Life Max for Men	US	3.0	
Country Life Maxine for Women	US	2.5	
Country Life Maxine for Women Iron-Free	US	3.0	
Country Life Maxine for Women Vegetarian Caps	US	2.5	
Country Life Multi-100	US	2.0	
Country Life Seniority	US	1.5	
Country Life Superior	US	4.5	
Country Life Vegetarian Support	US	2.0	
Creating Wellness Alliance Vitalize Men's Formula	US	5.0	**NutriSearch GOLD Medal of Achievement Recipient**

Creating Wellness Alliance Vitalize Women's Formula	US	5.0	**NutriSearch GOLD Medal of Achievement Recipient**
Creating Wellness Alliance Vitalize Senior Women's Gold Formula	US	5.0	**NutriSearch GOLD Medal of Achievement Recipient**
Curves Complete	US	1.5	
Curves Complete Biomultiple	US	1.5	
Curves Multivitamin	CA	2.0	
Curves Protein Drink	US	-	new data unavailable, 2004 data
CVS Pharmacy Daily Multiple 50 Plus	US	0.5	
CVS Pharmacy Daily Multiple for Men	US	0.5	
CVS Pharmacy Daily Multiple for Women	US	-	
CVS Pharmacy Mega Multi	US	2.0	
CVS Pharmacy Multivitamin & Minerals	US	-	
CVS Pharmacy Spectravite	US	-	
CVS Pharmacy Spectravite Performance	US	0.5	
CVS Pharmacy Spectravite Senior	US	0.5	
CVS Pharmacy Spectravite Senior Chewables	US	0.5	
CVS Pharmacy Thera Plus	US	0.5	
CVS Pharmacy Today's Life Men's	US	1.0	
CVS Pharmacy Today's Life Women's	US	1.5	
CVS Pharmacy Today's Life 50+	US	0.5	
CVS Pharmacy Today's Life Active+	US	0.5	
CVS Pharmacy Weight Sharp	US	1.0	
Cyto Charge Life Assurance	US	2.5	
DaVinci Laboratories Daily Best	US	2.0	
DaVinci Laboratories GENEssentials Spectra SNP	US	3.5	
DaVinci Laboratories Omni	US	1.5	
DaVinci Laboratories Spectra	US	3.5	
DaVinci Laboratories Spectra Man	US	3.5	
DaVinci Laboratories Spectra Multi Age	US	4.0	
DaVinci Laboratories Spectra Senior	US	3.5	
DaVinci Laboratories Spectra without Copper & Iron	US	3.5	
DaVinci Laboratories Spectra Woman	US	3.5	
dc (Dee Cee Laboratories) 6BG+	US	0.5	
dc (Dee Cee Laboratories) Formula 19	US	0.5	
dc (Dee Cee Laboratories) Formula 249 Iron Free	US	1.0	
dc (Dee Cee Laboratories) Formula 360	US	0.5	
dc (Dee Cee Laboratories) Formula 75	US	1.5	
dc (Dee Cee Laboratories) Formula 784	US	-	
dc (Dee Cee Laboratories) Formula 814	US	0.5	
dc (Dee Cee Laboratories) Ultra VM	US	1.5	
dc (Dee Cee Laboratories) Vidoplex-ML	US	0.5	
Designs for Health DFH Complete Multi	US	3.0	
Designs for Health DFH Complete Multi without copper & iron	US	3.0	
Doctor's Nutrition Mega Vites Man	US	3.5	
Doctor's Nutrition Mega Vites Senior	US	3.0	
Doctor's Nutrition Mega Vites without Copper & Iron	US	3.5	
Doctor's Nutrition Mega Vites Woman	US	3.5	
Doctor's Nutrition UltraNutrient	US	4.0	
Don Lemmon's All Natural Balanced Multi-Nutrient	US	3.5	
Douglas Laboratories Added Protection III	US	3.5	
Douglas Laboratories Added Protection III Copper & Iron Free	US	3.5	
Douglas Laboratories Added Protection III Copper Free	US	3.5	
Douglas Laboratories Added Protection III Iron Free	US	4.0	
Douglas Laboratories Basic Preventive 1	US	3.5	
Douglas Laboratories Basic Preventive 2	US	3.5	
Douglas Laboratories Basic Preventive 3	US	3.5	
Douglas Laboratories Basic Preventive 4	CA	3.5	
Douglas Laboratories Basic Preventive 5	US	3.5	
Douglas Laboratories Basic Preventive 5 Plus Extra Vitamin D	US	4.0	
Douglas Laboratories Essential Basics	US	3.0	
Douglas Laboratories Geri-Vite 25	US	1.0	
Douglas Laboratories Multivite	US	-	
Douglas Laboratories Nutri-Smart Formula	US	2.5	
Douglas Laboratories Ultra Balance III (capsules)	CA	2.5	
Douglas Laboratories Ultra Balance III (tablets)	CA	4.0	
Douglas Laboratories Ultra Balance III with Iron (tablets)	CA	3.5	
Douglas Laboratories Ultra Fem	US	3.0	
Douglas Laboratories Ultra Preventive Beta	US	3.5	
Douglas Laboratories Ultra Preventive Beta with Copper	US	3.5	
Douglas Laboratories Ultra Preventive Beta with Copper & Iron	US	3.5	
Douglas Laboratories Ultra Preventive D	US	3.5	
Douglas Laboratories Ultra Preventive D with Copper	US	4.0	
Douglas Laboratories Ultra Preventive D with Copper & Iron	US	3.5	
Douglas Laboratories Ultra Preventive III (capsules)	US	3.0	
Douglas Laboratories Ultra Preventive III (tablets)	US	4.0	
Douglas Laboratories Ultra Preventive III with Copper & Iron (tablets)	US	3.5	
Douglas Laboratories Ultra Preventive III with Copper (capsules)	US	2.5	
Douglas Laboratories Ultra Preventive III with Copper (tablets)	US	4.0	
Douglas Laboratories Ultra Preventive III with Iron (tablets)	US	3.0	
Douglas Laboratories Ultra Preventive III with Zinc Picolinate (tablets)	US	3.0	
Douglas Laboratories Ultra Preventive IX	US	5.0	**NutriSearch GOLD Medal of Achievement Recipient**
Douglas Laboratories Ultra Preventive IX with Vitamin K	US	5.0	**NutriSearch GOLD Medal of Achievement Recipient**

Douglas Laboratories Ultra Preventive X	CA/US	5.0	**NutriSearch GOLD Medal of Achievement Recipient**
Douglas Laboratories Ultra Vite 75 II	US	1.0	
Douglas Laboratories Ultra-AM & Ultra-PM	US	4.0	
Douglas Laboratories Vita-Chel-Plus	US	2.5	
Douglas Laboratories Vitaworx	US	3.5	
Dr. Cranton's PrimeNutrients	US	4.0	
Dr. Donsbach's Ora-Flo	US	2.5	
Dr. Fuhrman's Gentle Care Formula	US	1.0	dosage derived
Dr. Rath's Vitacor Plus	US	1.0	
Dr. Rath's Women's Health Program	US	2.0	
Drinkables Multi Vitamins for Seniors	US	0.5	
Drucker Labs intraMAX	US	2.5	additional nutrient amounts not specified
Eclectic Institute Opti Gyn Formula	CA/US	3.5	
Eclectic Institute Vital Force	US	3.0	
EcoNugenics Men's Longevity Essentials Plus	US	1.5	
EcoNugenics Women's Longevity Rhythms	US	2.0	
EcoNugenics Women's Longevity Rhythms Gold	US	2.0	
Endurance Products Endur-VM	US	0.5	
Endurance Products Endur-VM without Iron	US	0.5	
Enerex Sona	CA	2.0	
Enerex Sona Rx	CA	2.5	
Eniva Essential Phytamins & Cell-Ready Minerals (Cranberry-Grapefruit Blend)	US	1.5	
Eniva Essential Phytamins and Cell-Ready Minerals (original formula)	US	1.5	additional nutrient amounts not specified
Eniva Vibe	US	1.5	additional nutrient amounts not specified
Enzymatic Therapy Doctor's Choice for 45-Plus Women	US	3.5	
Enzymatic Therapy Doctor's Choice for 50-Plus Men	US	4.0	
Enzymatic Therapy Doctor's Choice for Men	CA	3.5	
Enzymatic Therapy Doctor's Choice for Men	US	3.5	
Enzymatic Therapy Doctor's Choice for Women	US	3.5	
Enzyme Labs Nutraceuticals Multi-Life	US	1.5	additional nutrient amounts not specified
epic4health Physician's Multi Vitamin Formula	US	2.0	
Equaline Central-Vite	US	-	
Equaline Central-Vite Carb Dieter Formula	US	0.5	
Equaline Central-Vite Performance	US	0.5	
Equaline Central-Vite Select	US	0.5	
Equaline One Daily 50 Plus	US	0.5	
Equaline One Daily Active	US	0.5	
Equaline One Daily Dieter's Support Formula	US	1.0	
Equaline One Daily Maximum	US	-	
Equaline One Daily Men's Health Formula	US	0.5	
Equaline One Daily Women's	US	-	
Equate Century Complete	CA	-	
Equate Century Perform	CA	-	
Equate Century Plus	CA	-	
Equate Century Premium	CA	0.5	
Equate Century Silver	CA	0.5	
Equate Century Silver Chewable	CA	0.5	
Equate Complete	US	-	
Equate Complete Mature	US	0.5	
Equate One Daily Men's	CA	0.5	
Equate One Daily Men's	US	0.5	
Equate One Daily Women's	US	-	
Equate One Tablet Daily	CA	0.5	
Equate One Tablet Daily Adults	CA	-	
Equate One Tablet Daily Adults 50+	CA	0.5	
Equate One Tablet Daily Women's	CA	-	
Essence-of-Life Liquid Nutrition Plus/Essence	US	2.0	dosage derived
Essence-of-Life Only One Cell-Ready Nutrition	US	1.0	additional nutrient amounts not specified
Exact Essentra Balance	CA	-	
Exact Essentra Elite	CA	0.5	
Exact Essentra Forte	CA	-	
Exact Essentra Platinum	CA	0.5	
Exact for Adults over 50	CA	-	
Exact Multi Max 1	CA	2.0	
Exact Vital One Men's Formula	CA	0.5	
Exact Vital-Fem 1	CA	-	
First Organics Daily Multiple	US	1.0	
Flora Multi Vitamins	CA	2.0	
FoodScience of Vermont Daily Best	US	2.0	
FoodScience of Vermont Men's Superior	US	3.5	
FoodScience of Vermont Senior's Superior	US	3.5	
FoodScience of Vermont Superior Care	US	3.0	
FoodScience of Vermont Superior Care without Copper and Iron	US	3.5	
FoodScience of Vermont Superior Multi Age	US	4.0	
FoodScience of Vermont Total Care	US	1.5	
FoodScience of Vermont Women's Superior	US	3.5	
ForMor International AnOx	US	2.0	dosage derived
Freeda MonoCaps	US	0.5	dosage derived
Freeda Quintabs-M	US	1.0	
Freeda Quintabs-M Iron-Free	US	1.5	
Freeda Ultra Freeda, A-Free	US	2.0	

Freeda Ultra Freeda, Iron-Free	US	2.5	
Freeda Ultra Freeda, with Iron	US	2.5	
Future Formulations Advance (Iron Free)	CA	1.5	
FutureBiotics Hi Energy Multi for Men	US	2.0	
FutureBiotics MultiVitamin Energy Plus for Women	US	1.5	
FutureBiotics Vegetarian Super Multi	US	2.0	
Garden of Life Living Multi	CA	1.5	
Garden of Life Living Multi	US	2.0	
Garden of Life Living Multi Iron Free	CA	2.0	
Garden of Life Living Multi Men's Formula	CA/US	2.0	
Garden of Life Living Multi Optimal Women's Formula	CA	1.5	
Garden of Life Living Multi Optimal Women's Formula	US	1.5	
Gary Null's Super AM Formula	US	2.0	
Gary Null's Super AM Formula & Super PM Formula	US	4.0	
Gary Null's Super PM Formula	US	1.5	
Genesis Today 4 Total Nutrition	US	3.0	
Genuine Health greens+ multi+	CA	3.0	dosage derived
Genuine Health greens+ multi+ powder	CA	3.5	
Genuine Health greens+ multi+ tablets	CA	2.5	
Genuine Health multi+ complete	CA	3.0	dosage derived
Genuine Health multi+ daily trim	CA	2.0	
Geritol Complete	US	-	
Global Health Trax (GHT) Daily Vita Plus & Mega Minerals Plus	US	2.0	dosage derived
GNC Chewable Solotron	US	0.5	
GNC Mega Men	CA	1.5	
GNC Mega Men	US	2.5	
GNC Mega Men 50 Plus	US	2.0	
GNC Multi Liquid Ultra Mega	US	3.0	
GNC Multi Preventron	US	1.0	
GNC Multi Solotron	CA	1.0	
GNC Multi Solotron	US	1.0	
GNC Multi Solotron Platinum	US	1.0	
GNC Multi Solotron without iron	US	1.5	
GNC Multi Ultra Mega	CA	1.5	
GNC Multi Ultra Mega	US	1.5	
GNC Multi Ultra Mega Gold	US	2.5	
GNC Multi Ultra Mega Gold without Iron	US	2.5	
GNC Multi Ultra Mega Green	US	2.0	
GNC Multi Ultra Mega Softgels	CA	2.0	
GNC Multi-Gel	US	1.5	dosage derived
GNC Platinum Years	CA	1.0	
GNC Preventive Nutrition Men's Multiple	US	1.5	
GNC Preventive Nutrition Premium One without Iron	US	1.5	
GNC Preventive Nutrition Women's Multiple	US	1.5	
GNC Women's Ultra Mega	CA	2.0	
GNC Women's Ultra Mega without iron	CA	2.0	
GNC Women's Women's Ultra Mega	US	2.0	
GNC Women's Women's Ultra Mega Bone Density	US	2.0	
GNLD International Formula IV	US	1.0	
GNLD International Formula IV Plus	US	1.5	
GNLD International Vegetarian Multi	US	1.0	
Goldshield Centural Silver	US	0.5	
Goldshield Total Multivitamin & Mineral Formula	US	2.0	
Good Neighbor Pharmacy Century	US	-	
Good Neighbor Pharmacy Century Advantage	US	0.5	
Good Neighbor Pharmacy Century Senior	US	0.5	
Good Neighbor Pharmacy Maximum One Daily	US	0.5	
Good Neighbor Pharmacy One Daily Carb-Vantage	US	0.5	
Good Neighbor Pharmacy Therapeutic-M Complete	US	0.5	
Good Neighbor Pharmacy Women's One Daily	US	-	
Great American Products Master Green Multi	US	2.5	
Great Earth Super Hy-Vites Extra Strength	US	2.0	dosage derived
Great Earth Super Hy-Vites Regular Strength	US	1.5	dosage derived
Great Earth Super Hy-Vites Ultra Strength	US	2.5	dosage derived
Great Earth TNT Extra Strength Timed Release	US	3.5	dosage derived
greens+ greens+ powder	US	1.5	
Health First Iron Free Multi-First	CA	2.0	
Health First Multi-First	CA	1.5	
HealthyWize Vital Greens	US	4.5	
HealthyWize Vital Nutrients	US	5.0	
Heaven Sent Naturals Balanced Essentials	US	1.0	
H-E-B Complete	US	-	
H-E-B Complete Advantage	US	0.5	
H-E-B Complete Senior	US	0.5	
H-E-B Multiple Vitamins Men's	US	0.5	
H-E-B Multiple Vitamins 50 Plus	US	0.5	
H-E-B Multiple Vitamins Maximum	US	-	
H-E-B Therapeutic-M	US	0.5	
Henry's Farmer's Market 75 Complete	US	2.0	
Henry's Farmer's Market Basic Multi	US	0.5	
Henry's Farmer's Market Iron Free Basic Multi	US	0.5	

Henry's Farmer's Market Iron Free Multi Caps	US	2.0	
Henry's Farmer's Market Iron Free Ultimate One	US	2.0	
Henry's Farmer's Market Life Multi Complete	US	2.0	
Henry's Farmer's Market Softgel Multi	US	2.0	
Henry's Farmer's Market Ultimate Capsule	US	1.5	
Henry's Farmer's Market Ultimate One	US	2.0	
Henry's Farmer's Market Ultimate Two	US	2.0	
Henry's Farmer's Market Ultimate Vegetarian Multi	US	2.0	
Henry's Marketplace Ultimate Senior Multi	US	1.5	
Herbalife ShapeWorks Garden 7	US	1.0	
Herbalife Shapeworks Multivitamin Complex (Formula 2)	US	1.0	additional nutrient amounts not specified
HerbaSway Laboratories MultiVitamin Magic & MultiMineral Magic	US	1.5	
Highland Laboratories Energy with Whole Food Concentrates	US	3.0	
Highland Laboratories Mega I Daily	US	1.5	
Highland Laboratories Mega I Daily Iron-free	US	1.5	
Highland Laboratories Mega II Daily	US	2.0	
Highland Laboratories Mega II Daily Iron-free	US	2.0	
Highland Laboratories Men's 30 Plus Multi	US	2.5	
Highland Laboratories Nature's Daily	US	1.0	
Highland Laboratories OMNI	US	2.5	
Highland Laboratories Women's 30 Plus Multi	US	2.5	
Hillestad Pharmaceuticals Sterling	US	2.0	dosage derived
Hillestad Pharmaceuticals Summit Gold	US	1.5	dosage derived
Hillestad Pharmaceuticals Summit Gold Special Formula	US	2.0	dosage derived
Hillestad Pharmaceuticals Vitamin/Mineral Complex Unit A	US	1.0	dosage derived
Holista Advanz	US	1.5	
Holista Advanz Iron Free	US	1.5	
Immunotec Research Vitamin/Mineral Supplement	CA	0.5	dosage derived
Immuvit Original Swiss Formula	US	0.5	
Innate Response Formulas BioMax Food Multi III	US	0.5	
Innate Response Formulas Food Multi II	US	1.0	
Innate Response Formulas Food Multi IV	US	2.5	
Innate Response Formulas Men Over 40	US	2.5	
Innate Response Formulas Men's Multi	US	1.0	
Innate Response Formulas Men's Multi Without Iron	US	1.5	
Innate Response Formulas Men's One Daily	US	0.5	
Innate Response Formulas One Daily I	US	0.5	
Innate Response Formulas One Daily II	US	0.5	
Innate Response Formulas Women Over 40	US	2.0	
Innate Response Formulas Women's Multi	US	1.0	
Innate Response Formulas Women's One Daily	US	0.5	
Inno-Vite Formula H.H.	CA	1.5	
Inno-Vite Total NRG Lift	CA	1.5	2003 data; additional nutrient amounts not specified
Intelligent Nutrients NutriBase	US	2.0	dosage derived; additional nutrient amounts not specified
Intensive Nutrition Mega-VM	US	2.5	
Intensive Nutrition Multi-VM	US	3.0	
Isagenix Essentials for Men	CA	1.5	dosage derived
Isagenix Essentials for Men	US	1.5	dosage derived; additional nutrient amounts not specified
Isagenix Essentials for Women	US	1.5	dosage derived; additional nutrient amounts not specified
Isagenix Women's Essentials	CA	1.5	dosage derived
Isotonix Champion Blend	US	2.0	
Isotonix MultiTech	US	1.0	dosage derived
Isotonix MultiTech with Iron	US	0.5	dosage derived
Jamieson Power Vitamins for Men	CA	1.5	
Jamieson Regular Vita-Vim	CA	1.0	
Jamieson Stamina	CA	0.5	
Jamieson Super Vita-Vim	CA	1.5	
Jamieson Vita Slim	CA	1.5	
Jamieson Vita-Vim Adult 50+	CA	1.0	
Jamieson Vita-Vim Adult Chewable	CA	0.5	
Jarrow Formulas Longevity Multi	US	3.5	
Jarrow Formulas Multi 1-to-3	US	2.5	
Jarrow Formulas Multi Easy Powder	CA/US	2.5	
Jarrow Formulas Women's Multi	CA/US	2.0	
Jean Carper's Stop Aging Now!	US	4.0	
Jean Carper's Stop Aging Now! PLUS	US	4.0	
Julian Whitaker, M.D. Forward Multi-Nutrient	US	3.0	dosage derived
Juvio Rejuvionate Green Perfection	CA/US	1.5	dosage derived; additional nutrient amounts not specified
Kal Enhanced Energy	US	3.0	
Kal Enhanced-75	US	2.0	
Kal High Potency Soft Multiple Iron Free	US	2.0	
Kal Mega Vita-Min	US	2.0	
Kal Multi-Active	US	3.0	
Kal Multi-Four+	US	2.5	
Kal Multi-Max 1	US	2.0	
Kal Multiple Energy	US	2.5	
Kal SoftOne Multi with Lutein	US	1.5	
Kal Vitality for Women	US	2.0	
Karuna HIM	US	3.0	
Karuna Maxxum 1	US	3.0	
Karuna Maxxum 2	US	3.0	

Karuna Maxxum 3	US	3.0	
Karuna Maxxum 4	US	3.5	
Kirkland Daily Multi	US	0.5	
Kirkland Formula Forte	CA	-	
Kirkland Premium Performance Multivitamin	US	0.5	
Kirkman EveryDay	US	0.5	
Kirkman EveryDay & NuThera EveryDay Companion Capsules	US	1.5	
Kirkman Nu-Thera without Vitamins A & D	US	1.0	
Kirkman Super Nu-Thera	US	1.0	
Klamath Blue Green Algae	US	0.5	
Klamath Power 3	US	0.5	
Kroger Complete	US	-	dosage derived
Kroger Fortify	US	0.5	
Kroger Men	US	1.5	
Kroger One Daily Maximum	US	-	
Kroger One Daily Men's Health Formula	US	0.5	
Kroger One Daily Women's Health	US	-	
Kroger Thera Plus	US	0.5	
LA Weight Loss Centers Vita-Max	CA	1.0	dosage derived
Leader Century	US	-	
Leader Century Senior	US	0.5	
Leader Men's One Daily	US	0.5	
Leader Women's One Daily	US	-	
Levity+Plus Multivitamin for Women	US	2.0	
Life Adult	CA	-	
Life Chewable Tablets	CA	0.5	
Life Daily-One 50+	CA	0.5	
Life Daily-One Adult	CA	-	
Life Daily-One Carb Sense	CA	0.5	
Life Daily-One for Women	CA	-	
Life Daily-One Men's Formula	CA	0.5	
Life Daily-One Weight Sense	CA	1.0	
Life Extension Foundation Life Extension Mix	US	5.0	
Life For People over 50	CA	-	
Life Optimum	CA	0.5	
Life Optimum 50+	CA	0.5	
Life Plus Daily BioBasics	US	2.5	
Life Solutions Super Multi Vitamins and Minerals	US	2.5	
Life Spectrum	CA	-	
Life Spectrum Gold	CA	0.5	
Life Spectrum Performa	CA	0.5	
Life Spectrum with Beta Carotene	CA	1.5	
Life-Line Daily Plus 50	US	0.5	
Life-Line Maximum Daily Greens	US	2.0	
Life-Line Theravits 100	US	2.5	
LifeScript Daily Essentials, plus Calcium Complete	US	1.0	
LifeSource Nutrition Liquid Multi Vitamin & Immune Booster	US	1.5	additional nutrient amounts not specified
LifeSource Nutrition Multi Vitamin & Minerals	US	2.5	
Lifestyles Lifecycles for Mature Men	CA/US	1.0	2003 data
Lifestyles Lifecycles for Mature Women	CA/US	1.0	2003 data
Lifestyles Lifecycles for Men	CA/US	1.0	2003 data
Lifestyles Lifecycles for Women	CA/US	1.0	2003 data
LifeTime Adult Vit-Mins	US	1.0	
LifeTime Life's Basics	US	2.0	
LifeTime Multi-Vitamin & Mineral Soft Gels	US	2.0	
LifeTime Nutrilife Soft Gels	CA	1.0	
Liquid Health Daily Multiple	US	0.5	
LiquiMax Complete Nutrition	US	1.0	additional nutrient amounts not specified
London Drugs Multi Complete	CA	-	
London Drugs Multi Plus	CA	0.5	
London Drugs Multi Premium	CA	1.0	
London Drugs Multi Silver	CA	1.0	
London Drugs Multi Vitamin & Minerals	CA	0.5	
London Drugs One Adults 50+	CA	1.0	
London Drugs One Tablet Daily Adults	CA	0.5	
London Drugs Women's Formula	CA	-	
London Naturals Iron-Free	CA	2.0	
London Naturals Premier	CA	2.0	
Longevity Science Revitalize	US	3.0	
Longs Advanced Formula Central Vite	US	-	
Longs Central Vite Carb Dieter Formula	US	0.5	
Longs Central Vite Performance	US	0.5	
Longs Central Vite Select	US	0.5	
Longs Men's Multivitamin/Mineral Supplement with Herbs	US	2.0	
Longs One Daily Dieter's Support Formula	US	1.0	
Longs One Daily Men's Health Formula	US	0.5	
Longs One Daily Women's	US	-	
Longs Thera Plus	US	-	
Longs Wellness High Potency Multi Vitamin & Mineral	US	-	
Longs Women's Multivitamin/Multimineral/Herbs	US	1.0	
Majestic Earth Ultimate Classic	US	3.0	dosage derived

Majestic Earth Ultimate Daily	US	1.5	
Mannatech Glycentials	US	2.5	
Mannatech Glycentials	CA	2.0	additional nutrient amounts not specified
Mason Daily Multiple Vitamins with Minerals	US	-	
Mason Super Multiple	US	1.0	
Mason VitaTrum Complete	US	-	
Mason VitaTrum Endurance	US	0.5	
Mason Vitrum Senior	US	0.5	
Matol MegaVitamins	CA	2.0	
Matol MegaVitamins	US	2.0	
Maxion Formula F-L-W	CA	1.5	
Maxion Nutrition Artr-E-Clnz	US	1.5	
Maxion Nutrition Max Multi Liquid Vitamin	CA/US	1.0	
MaxiVision Whole Body Formula	US	3.0	
MD Healthline Ad-ditions	US	1.0	
MD Healthline Advanced Green Multi Formula	US	-	additional nutrient amounts not specified
MD's Choice Complete Formula for Mature Women	US	3.0	dosage derived
MD's Choice Complete Formula for Men	US	3.0	dosage derived
MD's Choice Complete Formula for Young Women	US	3.0	dosage derived
MegaFood Alpha DailyFoods	US	1.5	
MegaFood Essentials FoodBased Mini's	US	2.5	
MegaFood Essentials for Menopause	US	2.5	
MegaFood Essentials Iron Free One Daily	US	1.5	
MegaFood Essentials One Daily	US	1.5	
MegaFood Iron Free One Daily	US	0.5	
MegaFood LifeStyle DailyFoods	US	2.0	
MegaFood Maximum Life	US	3.0	
MegaFood Maximum Man	US	2.0	
MegaFood Maximum Man One Daily	US	1.0	
MegaFood Maximum Woman	US	2.0	
MegaFood Maximum Woman One Daily	US	1.0	
MegaFood Medi-Safe DailyFoods	US	0.5	
MegaFood Men Over 40 DailyFoods	US	2.0	
MegaFood Men's DailyFoods	US	0.5	
MegaFood Men's One Daily DailyFoods	US	-	
MegaFood One Daily DailyFoods	US	0.5	
MegaFood Optimum Foods	US	1.5	
MegaFood Women Over 40 DailyFoods	US	2.0	
MegaFood Women's DailyFoods	US	1.0	
MegaFood Women's One Daily DailyFoods	US	-	
Melaleuca Vitality for Men	US	1.0	dosage derived; additional nutrient amounts not specified
Melaleuca Vitality for Women	US	1.0	dosage derived; additional nutrient amounts not specified
Melaleuca Vitality Gold for Men	US	2.0	dosage derived; additional nutrient amounts not specified
Melaleuca Vitality Gold for Women	US	2.0	dosage derived; additional nutrient amounts not specified
Melaleuca Vitality Pack for Men	US	1.0	dosage derived; additional nutrient amounts not specified
Melaleuca Vitality Pack for Women	US	1.0	dosage derived; additional nutrient amounts not specified
Member's Mark Complete Multi	US	-	
Member's Mark Mature Multi	US	0.5	
Metabolic Maintenance Basic Maintenance with Iron	US	1.5	
Metabolic Maintenance Basic Maintenance without Iron	US	2.0	
Metabolic Maintenance Men's Maintenance	US	2.5	
Metabolic Maintenance Multi-Vitamin Powder	US	1.5	
Metabolic Maintenance The Big One with Iron	US	1.5	
Metabolic Maintenance The Big One without Iron	US	2.0	
Metabolic Maintenance Women's Maintenance with Iron	US	2.0	
Metabolic Maintenance Women's Maintenance without Iron	US	2.5	
Metagenics Multigenics	US	3.0	
Metagenics Multigenics Intensive Care	US	3.5	
Metagenics Multigenics Intensive Care (without iron)	US	3.5	
Metagenics Multigenics without iron	US	3.5	
MHP Activite Sport	US	2.5	additional nutrient amounts not specified
Michael's Active Senior Tabs	US	2.5	dosage derived; additional nutrient amounts not specified
Michael's For Men	US	2.5	dosage derived
Michael's For Women	CA/US	2.5	dosage derived
Michael's Just One	US	2.0	dosage derived; additional nutrient amounts not specified
Miracle 2000 Total Body Nutrition	US	2.0	dosage derived
MMS Pro Preventamins Iron Free	US	3.5	
Moducare Multi-mune	US	1.0	
Molecular Biologics Allervimin	US	1.5	
Molecular Biologics Bio-Naturalvite	US	1.0	dosage derived
Molecular Biologics Derma-Vites	US	1.5	dosage derived
Molecular Biologics Fruit Colloidal Mineral & Vitamin Elixir	US	1.0	
Molecular Biologics Liqui-Vimin	US	0.5	
More than a Multiple	US	2.5	
More than a Multiple for Men	US	3.0	
More than a Multiple for Women	US	2.5	
More than a Multiple Iron Free/Vegetarian	US	3.0	
Mountain Naturals of Vermont Men's Superior	US	3.5	
Mountain Naturals of Vermont Senior Superior	US	3.5	
Mountain Naturals of Vermont Superior Multi Age Powder	US	4.0	
Mountain Naturals of Vermont Women's Superior	US	3.5	

Mountain Peak Nutritionals Energy Formula	US	2.5	dosage derived
Mountain Peak Nutritionals Ultra High	US	3.0	
MultiSure for Men	CA	2.0	
MultiSure for Men 50+	CA	2.0	
MultiSure for Women	CA	2.0	
MultiSure for Women 50+	CA	2.5	
Myadec Professional Formula	US	-	
N.V. Perricone, M.D. Physician's Super Antioxidant	US	1.5	
Natrol My Favorite Multiple (original)	US	2.5	
Natrol My Favorite Multiple Energizer	US	1.0	
Natura Select Adult Food-Based Multivitamin	CA/US	1.0	dosage derived
Natura Select Basic Adult Multi	CA/US	0.5	dosage derived
Natura Select Food Based Men's Multi	CA/US	1.5	
Natura Select Food Based Women's Multi	CA/US	1.5	dosage derived
Natural Factors Hi Potency Multi	CA	2.0	
Natural Factors Men's MultiStart	US	3.0	
Natural Factors Multi Flow Oral Chelation Formula	CA	3.5	
Natural Factors MultiStart	CA	1.5	
Natural Factors MultiStart Men's 50+	CA	3.0	
Natural Factors MultiStart Women's	CA	3.5	
Natural Factors MultiStart Women's 45+	CA	3.5	
Natural Factors Super Multi Iron Free	CA	1.5	
Natural Factors Super Multi Plus Iron	CA	1.5	
Natural Factors Ultra Multi Plus	CA	2.0	
Natural Factors WellBetX	CA	3.0	
Natural Factors Women's MultiStart	US	3.5	
Natural Factors Women's Plus MultiStart	US	3.0	
Natural Nutrition Active Men's	US	2.5	
Natural Nutrition Active Woman's	US	2.5	
Natural Nutrition Life Essentials	US	2.5	
Natural Nutrition Ultra VMT	US	2.5	
Natural Nutrition Vi-Min	US	2.5	
Natural Nutrition Vita Super	US	1.5	
Natural Nutrition Vita-Min 75	US	2.5	
Natural Nutrition Vita-Min 75 No Iron	US	2.5	
Naturally Preferred 75 Complete	US	2.0	
Naturally Preferred Life Multi Complete	US	2.0	
Naturally Preferred Men's Multi	US	2.5	
Naturally Preferred Nutri-Max	US	2.0	
Naturally Preferred One Daily Multi	US	0.5	
Naturally Preferred Vita Max	US	2.0	
Naturally Preferred Women's Multi	US	2.0	
Nature Made Adult Multivitamin Chewable	US	0.5	
Nature Made Essential 50+	US	0.5	
Nature Made Essential Balance	US	-	
Nature Made Essential Daily	US	-	
Nature Made Essential Man	US	0.5	
Nature Made Essential Mega	US	1.0	
Nature Made Essential Woman	US	0.5	
Nature Made Multi 50+	US	0.5	
Nature Made Multi Complete	US	-	
Nature Made Multi Daily	US	-	
Nature Made Multi For Her	US	-	
Nature Made Multi For Her 50+	US	0.5	
Nature Made Multi For Him	US	0.5	
Nature Made Multi For Him 50+	US	0.5	
Nature Made Multi Max	US	1.0	
Nature's Answer Liquid Multiple Vitamins & Liquid Multiple Minerals	US	2.0	
Nature's Best TR Mega 100	US	2.0	dosage derived
Nature's Best TR Mega 50	US	1.5	dosage derived
Nature's Blend Mega Multivitamin with Minerals	US	1.0	
Nature's Blend Multi-Vitamin with Minerals	US	-	
Nature's Blend Theratrum Complete	US	-	
Nature's Bounty Multi-Day Womens	US	-	
Nature's Bounty Ultra Man	US	2.0	dosage derived
Nature's Bounty Ultra Woman	US	2.0	dosage derived
Nature's Bounty Weight Trim	US	0.5	
Nature's Harmony Adult Chewable	CA	1.0	
Nature's Harmony High Potency One Per Day	CA	2.0	
Nature's Harmony Superior One Per Day Iron Free	CA	1.0	
Nature's Life E-Z Vite Multiple	US	1.0	dosage derived; additional nutrient amounts not specified
Nature's Life Full Spectrum Antioxidant Soft Multi	US	3.0	dosage derived
Nature's Life Green Multi	US	2.0	
Nature's Life One Daily Multiple	US	1.5	
Nature's Life Soft Gelatin Multiple	US	2.0	dosage derived
Nature's Life Ultra Mega Vite	US	2.0	
Nature's Life Vegetarian Green Multi	US	2.0	dosage derived
Nature's Life Vegetarian Mega-Vita-Min	US	1.5	
Nature's Life Vegetarian Super Mega Vite	US	1.5	dosage derived
Nature's Plus Adult's Chewable	US	1.0	
Nature's Plus Nutri-Genic	US	2.0	

Nature's Plus ReGeneration Liquid Sunshine	US	2.0	dosage derived
Nature's Plus ReGeneration Soft Gels	US	3.0	
Nature's Plus Source of Life Adult's Chewable Wafers	US	1.5	dosage derived
Nature's Plus Source of Life Liquid	US	2.0	dosage derived
Nature's Plus Source of Life Men Liquid	US	2.5	
Nature's Plus Source of Life Tablets/Capsules	US	2.0	
Nature's Plus Source of Life Women	US	2.5	
Nature's Plus Source of Life Women Liquid	US	2.5	
Nature's Plus Ultra I	US	2.0	
Nature's Plus Ultra II	US	2.0	
Nature's Plus Ultra Juice	US	1.0	
Nature's Plus Ultra Source of Life	US	2.5	additional nutrient amounts not specified
Nature's Plus Ultra Source of Life No Iron	US	2.5	additional nutrient amounts not specified
Nature's Sunshine Super Supplemental without Iron	US	2.0	
Nature's Sunshine VitaWave	US	2.0	additional nutrient amounts not specified
Nature's Valley Women's Formula	US	2.0	dosage derived
Nature's Way Alive! Drink Mix Powder	US	3.0	dosage derived
Nature's Way Alive! Tablets with Iron	US	2.5	
Nature's Way Alive! Vcaps/Tablets, no Iron added	US	3.0	
Nature's Way Completia Energy	CA	1.5	
Nature's Way Completia Energy Plus Iron	CA	1.0	
Nature's Way Completia Ultra Energy (Iron-Free)	US	2.0	
Nature's Way Completia Ultra Energy Multivitamin	US	2.0	
Nature's Way Daily Two Multi Iron Free	US	3.0	
Nature's Way Multi Vitamin Iron-Free	US	3.5	
Nature's Way Multi Vitamin with Iron	US	3.0	
Nature's Way Once Daily Multi	US	2.0	
New Roots Herbal Multi-Max	CA	3.0	
New Roots Herbal Multi-Max Immune	CA	4.5	
New Roots Herbal Phytomax	CA	1.5	
New Vision JuicePower Fruit/Vegetable Caps	US	1.0	
Neways Maximol Solutions	US	-	
Neways ProZinger	US	1.5	
NewChapter Every Man	CA	1.5	
NewChapter Everyone's Multiple	CA	1.0	dosage derived
NewChapter Only One	CA	1.0	
NewChapter Organics Every Man	US	1.5	
NewChapter Organics Every Man II	US	1.5	
NewChapter Organics Every Man II	CA	1.5	
NewChapter Organics Every Man's One Daily	CA	1.0	
NewChapter Organics Every Woman	US	1.0	
NewChapter Organics Every Woman II	US	1.0	
NewChapter Organics Every Woman's One Daily	CA	1.0	
NewChapter Organics Every Woman's One Daily	US	1.0	
NewChapter Organics Only One	US	1.0	
NewChapter Organics Tiny Tabs Multi	US	0.5	
NewChapter Tiny Tabs Multiple	CA	0.5	
NF Formulas, Inc. Women's Formula	US	2.5	
NF Formulas, Inc. Women's Formula without iron	US	2.5	
NHK Laboratories Multi-Vitamin and Mineral	US	0.5	dosage derived
NHK Laboratories Multi-Vitamin and Mineral with Lutein	US	0.5	dosage derived
NHK Laboratories Senior Multi-Vitamin and Mineral	US	0.5	dosage derived
Nikken Kenzen	US	2.0	
North American Pharmacal Polyvite A & Phytocal A	US	2.0	dosage derived
North American Pharmacal Polyvite AB & Phytocal AB	US	2.0	dosage derived
North American Pharmacal Polyvite B & Phytocal B	US	1.5	dosage derived
North American Pharmacal Polyvite O & Phytocal O	US	1.5	dosage derived
Now Adam	US	2.5	
Now Daily Vits	US	1.0	
Now Eco-Green Multi	US	3.0	
Now Eve	US	2.5	
Now Special One	US	1.5	
Now Special Two	CA/US	2.0	
Now Vit-Min 100	US	2.5	
Now Vit-Min 75+ Iron Free	US	2.0	
Now Vit-Min Caps	US	2.5	
NSI (Neutraceutical Sciences Institute) Synergy Basic Version 2	US	3.0	additional nutrient amounts not specified
NSI (Neutraceutical Sciences Institute) Synergy Men's Version 2	US	5.0	
NSI (Neutraceutical Sciences Institute) Synergy Version 9	US	4.5	
NSI (Neutraceutical Sciences Institute) Synergy Women's Version 4	US	4.5	
Nu-Life Gourmet Chewables Multiple	CA	1.5	
Nu-Life The Legend	CA	2.5	
Nu-Life The Legend High Stress/Activity for Men	CA	2.5	additional nutrient amounts not specified
Nu-Life The Legend High Stress/Activity for Women	CA	2.0	additional nutrient amounts not specified
Nu-Life The Legend Max Stress/Activity for Men	CA	2.5	additional nutrient amounts not specified
Nu-Life The Legend Max Stress/Activity for Women	CA	2.5	additional nutrient amounts not specified
Nu-Life Ultimate One for Men 50 Plus	CA	2.0	additional nutrient amounts not specified
Nu-Life Ultimate One for Men Active	CA	2.5	additional nutrient amounts not specified
Nu-Life Ultimate One for Men Adult	CA	2.0	additional nutrient amounts not specified
Nu-Life Ultimate One for Women 50 Plus	CA	2.0	additional nutrient amounts not specified
Nu-Life Ultimate One for Women Active	CA	2.0	additional nutrient amounts not specified

Nu-Life Ultimate One Right Weight	CA	2.5	additional nutrient amounts not specified
Nu-Life Ultimate One Women Adult	CA	2.0	additional nutrient amounts not specified
Nutra Perfect VitaPerfect	US	1.5	
Nutra Therapeutics All-In-One	CA/US	2.0	
nutraMetrix MultiVitamins & MultiMinerals with Iron	US	1.0	
nutraMetrix MultiVitamins & MultiMinerals without Iron	US	1.0	
Nutri-Betics Nutra Balance For Men	CA	2.5	additional nutrient amounts not specified
NutriCare NutriDaily	US	3.0	
NutriCare Prime Greens	US	0.5	additional nutrient amounts not specified
NutriCare Prime Greens Capsules	US	0.5	additional nutrient amounts not specified
NutriCology Multi-Vi-Min	US	1.5	
NutriCology Multi-Vi-Min without Copper & Iron	US	2.0	
Nutriex Health	US	3.5	
Nutriex Sport	US	4.0	
Nutrilite Daily	US	0.5	
Nutrina Athlete Formula	US	2.0	dosage derived
Nutrina Champion Formula	US	2.5	dosage derived
Nutrina Marathon Formula	US	2.5	
Nutrina Mega Greens	US	2.0	
Nutrina Vitamax Powder	US	2.0	dosage derived
Nutrina Vitamax Tablets	US	1.5	dosage derived
Nutrition Dynamics Balanced Vita-Plus-Min	US	3.0	
Nutrition Dynamics Day Start & Day End Essentials	US	3.5	
Nutrition Dynamics Iodine Free "Vegi" Formula	US	2.5	
Nutrition Dynamics Multi-vitasorb	US	-	
Nutrition Dynamics Ultra Fem	US	3.0	
Nutrition Dynamics Ultra Vitaplex	US	1.5	
Nutrition House Men's Multi Extra	CA	2.5	
Nutrition House Multi-Vitamin Extra	CA	1.5	
Nutrition House Multi-Vitamin Extra Iron Free	CA	2.0	
Nutrition House Women's Multi Extra	CA	2.5	
Nutrition Now Adult Formula	US	-	
Nutrition Now Multi Earth Force	US	2.5	
NuTriVene-D Advanced Formula Daily Supplement	US	2.5	
NuTriVene-D Full Spectrum Formula	US	3.0	
Nutri-West Core Level Health Reserve	US	2.5	
Nutri-West Multi Complex	US	1.0	
Nutri-West Multibalance for Men	US	1.5	
Nutri-West Multibalance for Women	US	1.5	
Nutri-West Total Female	US	-	
Nutri-West Total Male	US	0.5	
Ola Loa Super Multi (Tropical)	US	3.0	
Ola Loa Super Multi (Orange)	US	3.0	
Olay Complete 50+ Multivitamin	US	0.5	
Olay Complete Multivitamin	US	0.5	
Olay Complete Woman's Multivitamin	US	0.5	
Olay Complete Woman's Multivitamin 50+	US	0.5	
Olympian Labs Vita Vitamin	US	2.5	dosage derived
Olympian Labs Vita-One	US	2.5	dosage derived
Omnilife Magnus	US	0.5	
Omnitrition Omni IV	US	0.5	additional nutrient amounts not specified
Omnitrition Shield Antioxidant	US	1.5	
One A Day 50 Plus	US	0.5	
One A Day Active	US	0.5	
One A Day Adults	CA	-	
One A Day Adults 50+	CA	0.5	
One A Day CarbSmart	US	0.5	
One A Day Cholesterol Plus	US	0.5	
One A Day Maximum	US	-	
One A Day Men's	CA	0.5	
One A Day Men's Health Formula	US	0.5	
One A Day Weight Smart	CA	1.0	
One A Day Weight Smart	US	1.0	
One A Day Women's	CA	-	
One A Day Women's	US	-	
OneSource 50 Plus	US	0.5	
OneSource Advanced Formula	US	0.5	
OneSource Men's	US	2.0	
OneSource Micro	US	0.5	
OneSource Pure Performance	US	0.5	
OneSource Women's	US	2.0	
Optimox Androvite for Men	US	3.0	
Optimox Gynovite Plus	US	2.0	
Optimox Optivite PMT for Women	US	2.5	
Oregon Health Multi-GuarD with CoQ10	US	3.5	
Oregon Health Women's Multiple	US	3.0	
Organika One Daily	CA	1.5	
Origin Complete Multi-Vitamin & Mineral	US	-	
Original Medicine NutraSyn	US	2.0	
Ortho Molecular Products Alpha Base Capsules	US	4.0	
Ortho Molecular Products Alpha Base Capsules without Iron	US	4.5	

Ortho Molecular Products Alpha Base Capsules without Iron or Copper	US	4.5	
Ortho Molecular Products Alpha Base Tablets	US	4.5	
Pataki USA 2001 Formula	· US	1.5	dosage derived; additional nutrient amounts not specified
Pataki USA 2101 Formula	US	1.0	dosage derived; additional nutrient amounts not specified
Performance Labs Vitalert	US	0.5	
Personnelle Complete	CA	-	
Personnelle Forte	CA	-	
Personnelle Natura Senior	CA	0.5	
Personnelle Senior	CA	0.5	
Personnelle Superia	CA	0.5	
Peter Gillham's Natural Vitality Liquid Organic life Vitamins	US	2.0	
Pharmacist's Ultimate Health Man's Ultimate Formula	US	3.0	
Pharmacist's Ultimate Health Woman's Ultimate Formula	US	3.0	
Pharmanex Life Essentials	CA	1.0	
Pharmanex Life Essentials	US	1.0	
PharmAssure Men's Biomultiple	US	1.5	
PharmAssure Women's Biomultiple	US	1.5	
Pharmaton Ginsana Gold Formula	US	0.5	
Physician Formulas MultiVit-Rx	US	2.0	
Phytobec	CA	0.5	
PhytoPharmica Clinical Nutrients for 45-Plus Women	US	4.0	
PhytoPharmica Clinical Nutrients for 50-Plus Men	US	4.0	
PhytoPharmica Clinical Nutrients for Men	US	3.5	
PhytoPharmica Clinical Nutrients for Women	US	3.5	
Pioneer Chewable	US	2.5	
Pioneer Vegetarian 1+ Vitamin Mineral	US	3.0	
Plante Gummi 50+	CA/US	0.5	
Platinum Active EasyMulti Plus for Men	CA	3.0	
Platinum Active EasyMulti Plus for Women	CA	3.0	
Platinum EasyMulti	CA	1.0	
Platinum MegaVita Minerals with Hempseed Oil	CA	0.5	
Platinum Super EasyMulti Plus for Men 45+	CA	3.0	
Platinum Super EasyMulti Plus for Women 45+	CA	3.0	
Prairie Naturals Multi-Force Powder	CA	2.0	
Prairie Naturals Multi-Force	CA	3.0	
Prevention Diabetic Support	US	2.0	
Prevention Dieter's Complete	CA	2.5	
Prevention Dieter's Complete	US	2.0	
Prevention for Men	CA/US	2.5	
Prevention for Men 50 Plus	CA	2.5	
Prevention for Men 50 Plus	US	2.5	
Prevention for Women	CA	2.5	
Prevention for Women	US	2.5	
Prevention for Women 50 Plus	CA	2.5	
Prevention for Women 50 Plus	US	2.5	
Pro Health Multiple One	US	2.5	
Pro Health Super Multiple II	US	2.0	
Pro Health Super Multiple without Iron	US	3.0	
Pro Image Pro Vitamin Complete	US	-	dosage derived; additional ingredient amounts not specified
Pro-Caps Laboratories Cholox	US	3.0	
Professional Health Products Multidyn	CA	1.5	
Professional Health Products Multi-Pro	CA	2.5	
Progressive for Active Men	CA	3.0	
Progressive for Active Women	CA	3.0	
Progressive for Adult Men	CA	2.5	
Progressive for Adult Women	CA	2.5	
Progressive for Men Over 50	CA	3.0	
Progressive for Women Over 50	CA	3.0	
ProThera LDA Multi-Vitamin & LDA Trace Mineral Complex	US	2.5	
ProThera MultiThera 1	US	4.0	
ProThera MultiThera 2	US	3.5	
ProThera VItaPrime	US	2.5	
Pure Advantage Womens Multiple	US	2.0	
Pure Encapsulations Nutrient 280	US	1.5	
Pure Encapsulations Nutrient 950	US	3.0	
Pure Encapsulations Nutrient 950 with NAC	US	3.0	
Pure Encapsulations Nutrient 950 without copper & iron	US	3.0	
Pure Encapsulations Nutrient 950 without copper, iron & iodine	US	3.5	
Pure Encapsulations Nutrient 950 without iron	US	3.5	
Pure Encapsulations UltraNutrient	US	4.0	
Pure Essence Labs Life Essence Powder	US	4.0	
Pure Essence Labs Life Essence Tablets	US	4.0	
Pure Essence Labs One'n'Only	US	2.0	additional nutrient amounts not specified
Puritan's Pride Daily 3 Caps	US	2.5	
Puritan's Pride Formula 100	US	2.0	
Puritan's Pride Green Source	US	2.0	additional nutrient amounts not specified
Puritan's Pride Green Source Iron Free	US	2.5	
Puritan's Pride Mega Vita Gel	US	2.0	
Puritan's Pride Mega Vita Min	US	2.0	
Puritan's Pride Mega Vita Min for Seniors	US	2.0	
Puritan's Pride Mega Vita Min for Women	US	2.0	

Puritan's Pride Mega Vita Min for Women Iron Free	US	2.0	
Puritan's Pride Mega Vita Min Iron Free	US	2.0	
Puritan's Pride Multi-Day Plus Minerals	US	-	
Puritan's Pride Potent 75 Super VM	US	1.5	
Puritan's Pride Puritron	US	1.0	
Puritan's Pride Theravim-M	US	-	
Puritan's Pride Ultra Man 75	US	3.0	
Puritan's Pride Ultra Vita Man	US	2.0	
Puritan's Pride Ultra Vita-Min	US	1.0	
Puritan's Pride Ultra Vita-Min Iron Free	US	1.0	
Puritan's Pride Women's Exclusive Formula	US	1.5	
Purity Products Fizz-5 Formula	US	1.0	
Purity Products The Perfect Multi	US	3.5	
Purity Products The Perfect Multi Super Greens	US	3.5	
QCI Nutritionals Daily Preventive #1	US	3.5	
QCI Nutritionals Ultra Vitality #2	US	3.0	
QCI Nutritionals Ultra Vitality #3	US	3.5	
QCI Nutritionals Ultra Vitality Elite	US	3.5	
Quest Adults	CA	1.0	
Quest Extra Once a Day	CA	1.0	
Quest Maximum Once A Day	CA	2.5	
Quest Premium Multi-Cap	CA	1.0	
Quest Premium Multi-One	CA	1.5	
Quest Super Once A Day	CA	1.5	
Radiance Green Source Iron Free	US	2.5	
Radiance Mega Vita Gel	US	2.0	
Radiance Mega Vita-Min Iron Free	US	2.0	dosage derived
Rainbow Light Advanced Nutritional System	US	3.0	additional nutrient amounts not specified
Rainbow Light Advanced Nutritional System Iron-Free	US	3.5	additional nutrient amounts not specified
Rainbow Light Complete Nutritional System	US	2.5	
Rainbow Light Just Once	US	1.0	
Rainbow Light Just Once Active Senior	US	2.0	
Rainbow Light Just Once Iron-Free	US	1.0	
Rainbow Light Just Once Men's Energy	US	1.5	
Rainbow Light Just Once Men's One	US	1.5	
Rainbow Light Just Once Women's One	US	1.5	
Rainbow Light Master Nutrient System Plus	US	1.5	
Rainbow Light RejuvenAge 40+	US	4.0	
Rainbow Light Women's Nutritional System	US	2.5	
RBC Life Sciences 24Seven Life Essentials	CA/US	1.5	additional nutrient amounts not specified
Rejuvenation Science Maximum Vitality	US	5.0	
Reliv Classic	CA	1.0	
Reliv Classic	US	1.0	
Reliv Now	CA	1.0	additional nutrient amounts not specified
Reliv Now	US	1.0	
Resource Optisource	US	1.5	
Resurgex	US	1.5	
Resurgex Plus	US	1.5	
Resurgex Select	US	1.0	dosage derived
Revival Firm Foundation	US	1.0	
Rexall Complete	CA	-	
Rexall Complete for Adults 50+	CA	0.5	
Rexall Complete Forte	CA	-	
Rexall Multiple Vitamins & Minerals	CA	-	
Rexall Multivitamin + Multimineral Forte	CA	-	additional nutrient amounts not specified
Rexall One Tablet Daily Adult	CA	-	
Rexall One Tablet Daily Adults 50+	CA	0.5	
Rexall One Tablet Daily Women's	CA	-	
Rexall One Weigh	CA	1.0	
R-Garden Vitamin Mineral Formula	US	1.5	
Ripple Creek Mega-100	US	2.5	
Ripple Creek Mega-Caps 2	US	2.0	
Ripple Creek Mega-One 75	US	1.5	
Rite Aid Central-Vite	US	-	
Rite Aid Central-Vite Select	US	0.5	
Rite Aid High Potency Multi	US	-	
Rite Aid One Daily	US	-	
Rite Aid One Daily Low Carb Support	US	0.5	
Rite Aid One Daily Men's Multi	US	0.5	
Rite Aid One Daily Women's	US	-	
Rite Aid Therapeutic M	US	-	
Rite Aid Trim Support	US	0.5	
Rite Aid Whole Source	US	0.5	
Rite Aid Whole Source Complete Formula for Women	US	1.5	
Rite Aid Whole Source Mature Adult	US	1.0	
Rite Aid Whole Source Men	US	1.0	
Rite Aid Whole Source Women	US	1.0	
Rx Vitamins Revitalize	US	3.0	
Rx Vitamins Revitalize without Iron	US	3.0	
Safeway Select Central-Vite	US	-	
Safeway Select Central-Vite Performance	US	0.5	

Safeway Select Central-Vite Senior Formula	US	0.5	
Safeway Select Formula Forte	CA	-	
Safeway Select Formula Forte Senior	CA	0.5	
Safeway Select Formule pour 50+	CA	0.5	
Safeway Select Formule pour hommes	CA	0.5	
Safeway Select Formule Régulière	CA	-	
Safeway Select Maximum One Tablet Daily	US	-	
Safeway Select Multivitamin & Mineral	US	-	
Safeway Select One Tablet Daily Dieter's Support Formula	US	1.0	
Safeway Select One Tablet Daily Men's Health	US	0.5	
Safeway Select One Tablet Daily Women's	US	-	
Safeway Select Super Men's Multivitamin	US	1.5	
Safeway Select Super Women's Multivitamin	US	2.0	
Safeway Select Weight-Conscious	CA	1.0	
Safeway Select Women's Formula	CA	-	
Sangster's Choice Apex	CA	0.5	
Sangster's Choice Apex	US	0.5	dosage derived
Sangster's Daily Choice	CA/US	1.0	
Sangster's Men's Choice	US	2.5	dosage derived
Sangster's Multi Vitamin	CA	1.5	
Sangster's Multi Vitamin	US	1.5	
Sangster's Senior's Choice	US	2.0	dosage derived
Sangster's Vege Choice	US	2.0	dosage derived
Sangster's Women's Choice	US	2.0	dosage derived
Sav-on Osco One Daily Maximum	US	-	
Schiff Prime Years	US	1.0	
Schiff Single Day	US	2.0	
Schiff Vegetarian Multiple	US	0.5	
Schwarzbein Institute Ultra Preventive III (capsules)	US	3.0	
Schwarzbein Institute Ultra Preventive III (tablets)	US	4.0	
Selekta Multi II's with Copper & Iron	CA	2.0	
Selekta Multi's without Copper & Iron	CA	2.0	
Selekta Selekta-Clear	CA	4.5	
Seroyal Super Orti Vite	CA	2.5	2003 data
Shaklee Advanced Formula Vita-Lea	CA	1.0	
Shaklee Vita-Lea Gold with Vitamin K	US	1.5	
Shaklee Vita-Lea Gold without Vitamin K	US	1.5	
Shaklee Vita-Lea with Iron	US	1.0	
Shaklee Vita-Lea without Iron	US	1.0	
SISU Mini Vits	CA	1.5	
SISU Multi Active	CA	2.0	
SISU Multi Active Woman	CA	2.0	
SISU Multi-Vi-Min	CA	1.0	
SISU Only One	CA	1.5	
SISU Only One Iron Free	CA	1.5	
SISU Vegi Mins	CA	2.5	
Solaray Men's Golden Multi-Vita-Min	US	2.0	
Solaray Multi-Vita Mega Mineral Multi-Vita-Min	US	2.5	
Solaray Once Daily High Energy	US	1.5	
Solaray Once Daily High Energy Iron Free	US	1.5	
Solaray Once Daily High Energy Softgel	CA	1.5	
Solaray Once Daily Iron Free	US	1.0	
Solaray Provide	US	2.0	
Solaray Provide Iron Free	US	2.5	
Solaray Spectro 3	US	3.0	
Solaray Spectro 3 Iron Free	US	3.0	
Solaray Spectro Multi-Vita-Min	US	3.0	
Solaray Spectro Multi-Vita-Min	CA	2.0	
Solaray Spectro Multi-Vita-Min Iron Free	US	2.5	
Solaray Spectro Multi-Vita-Min Iron Free	CA	2.5	
Solaray Spectro Smoothie Once Daily	US	3.0	
Solaray Three Daily Super Energy	US	2.5	
Solaray Three Daily Super Energy Iron Free	US	3.0	
Solaray Twice Daily Iron Free	US	2.5	
Solaray Twice Daily Multi Energy	US	2.0	
Solaray Twice Daily Multi Energy Iron Free	US	2.5	
Solaray Vegetarian Spectro Multi-Vita-Min	US	3.0	
Solaray VitaPrime for Men	US	2.5	
Solaray VitaPrime for Women	US	2.5	
Solaray Women's Golden Multi-Vita-Min	US	2.5	
Solgar Earth Source Multi-Nutrient	US	2.0	
Solgar Female Multiple	US	3.0	dosage derived
Solgar Formula VM-2000	US	2.0	dosage derived
Solgar Formula VM-75	US	2.0	
Solgar Formula VM-75 Iron-Free	US	2.0	
Solgar Formula VM-Prime	US	2.0	
Solgar Male Multiple	US	3.5	dosage derived
Solgar Naturvite	US	1.5	dosage derived
Solgar Omnium	US	3.0	dosage derived
Solgar Omnium Iron-Free	US	3.5	
Solgar Solovite Iron Free	US	1.0	

Product	Region	Rating	Notes
Solgar Vegetarian Multiple	US	1.5	
SomaLife SomaVit Plus	CA/US	2.5	
Sonergy Mega Plan	US	1.5	
Sonergy One Daily Multiple with Iron	US	-	
Source Naturals Élan Vitàl Multiple	US	5.0	
Source Naturals Life Defense	US	3.0	additional nutrient amounts not specified
Source Naturals Life Force Multiple	US	5.0	
Source Naturals Ultra Multiple	US	2.0	additional nutrient amounts not specified
Source Naturals Wellness Multiple	US	4.0	
Spring Valley Naturally Complete Multivitamin	US	0.5	
Spring Valley Sentury-Vite	US	0.5	
Standard Process Catalyn	US	-	
Standard Process Immunoplex	US	0.5	
Sundown Complete 50+	US	0.5	
Sundown Complete Daily	US	0.5	
Sundown Complete Multi 50+	US	0.5	
Sundown Complete Ultra	US	1.0	
Sundown Complete Women's	US	0.5	
Sundown SunVite	US	-	
Sunmark Complete Advanced	US	-	
Sunmark Complete Senior	US	0.5	
SunMark Multiple Vitamins Women's	US	-	
Sunmark Therapeutic-M	US	0.5	
SuperNutrition Longevity	US	2.0	
SuperNutrition Men's Blend	US	4.0	
SuperNutrition Multi Vitamin & Mineral	CA	2.0	
SuperNutrition Perfect Blend	US	3.5	
SuperNutrition Simply One	US	2.0	
SuperNutrition Simply One Men	US	2.0	additional nutrient amounts not specified
SuperNutrition Simply One Women	US	2.0	additional nutrient amounts not specified
SupraLife Formula Plus	US	2.5	
SupraLife Maxum Essentials	US	2.5	
SupraLife Total Toddy	US	2.0	dosage based on 150 lb. body weight
SupraLife Ultra Body Toddy with Cell Shield	US	3.0	dosage based on 150 lb. body weight; additional nutrient amounts not specified
Swanson Active One	US	1.5	
Swanson Active One without Iron	US	2.0	
Swanson All-Day Complete	US	2.5	
Swanson All-Day Complete for Seniors without Iron	US	3.0	
Swanson Century Formula without Iron	US	1.0	
Swanson High Potency Soft Multiple	US	2.0	
Swanson High Potency Soft Multiple Iron Free	US	2.5	
Swanson Lee Swanson Signature Line Longevital	US	5.0	
Swanson Ultra Whole Food	US	2.5	
Swiss Adult Multi One Formula	CA	2.0	
Swiss Hi Potency Swiss One "80"	CA	2.0	
Swiss Mega Swiss One "25"	CA	1.0	
Swiss Slim Essentials	CA	2.0	
Swiss Super Adult	CA	1.5	
Swiss Super Swiss One "50"	CA	1.5	
Swiss Swiss One	CA	0.5	
Swiss Swiss Total One Men	CA	3.0	
Swiss Swiss Total One Women	CA	2.5	
Swiss Total One	CA	3.0	
Swiss Vege Multivitamin and Mineral	CA	2.0	
Symmetry Ultra Vitality	US	1.0	additional nutrient amounts not specified
Synergy Multiple Vitamin/Mineral	US	0.5	
Target Adult Multivitamin/Multimineral	US	-	
Target Men's Daily Multivitamin	US	0.5	
Target Multivitamin/Multimineral	US	-	
Target Multivitamin/Multimineral for Adults 50+	US	0.5	
Target Weight Sense	US	1.0	
Target Women's Daily Multivitamin	US	-	
The Greatest Vitamin in the World	US	2.0	
The Green Turtle Bay Co. PowerVites	US	1.5	
The Green Turtle Bay Vitamin Co. Diabetiks & PowerVites	US	3.0	
The Green Turtle Bay Vitamin Co. Maple Melts	US	1.0	
The Synergy Company Vita Synergy for Men	US	2.5	dosage derived
The Synergy Company Vita Synergy for Women	US	2.5	dosage derived
Theragran-M Advanced Formula	US	0.5	
Theragran-M Premier	US	0.5	
Theragran-M Premier 50 Plus	US	0.5	
Thompson Adult-Plex	US	2.0	
Thompson Coach's Formula	US	2.0	
Thompson Mega 80	US	2.0	
Thompson Multi Formula for Women	US	0.5	
Thompson Multi-Vitamins	US	0.5	
Thompson Nuplex	US	0.5	
Thompson Super Maxicaps	US	1.5	
Thorne Research Al's Formula	US	3.5	
Thorne Research Basic Nutrients I	US	3.0	
Thorne Research Basic Nutrients II	US	3.0	

Product	Country	Rating	Notes
Thorne Research Basic Nutrients III	US	3.0	
Thorne Research Basic Nutrients III without Copper & Iron	US	3.0	
Thorne Research Basic Nutrients IV	US	3.0	
Thorne Research Basic Nutrients V	US	3.0	
Thorne Research Extra Nutrients	US	3.5	
Thorne Research Meta-Fem	US	3.5	
Thorne Research Nutri-Fem	US	3.0	
Top Care Complete	US	-	
Top Care Complete Advantage	US	0.5	dosage derived
Top Care Complete Senior	US	0.5	
Top Care Multi for Women	US	-	
Top Care One Daily 50+	US	0.5	
Top Care One Daily Dieter's Support Formula	US	-	
Top Care One Daily Maximum	US	-	
Top Care One Daily Men's	US	0.5	
Top Care One Daily Women's	US	-	
Total Multivitamin	US	0.5	
TotalOne SuperMulti	US	0.5	
Trace Minerals Complete Foods Multi	US	2.5	
Trace Minerals Electro-Vita-Min	US	1.5	
Trace Minerals Electro-Vita-Min (New & Improved)	US	1.5	
Trace Minerals ImmunoMax	US	0.5	
Trace Minerals Liquid Multi Vita-Mineral	US	2.0	
Trace Minerals Maxi Multi	US	1.0	
TRC Nutritional Laboratories Female Basic Multiple	US	1.0	
TRC Nutritional Laboratories Liquid Life	US	2.5	
TRC Nutritional Laboratories Male Basic Multiple	US	1.5	
TRC Nutritional Laboratories Vast Vitality	US	1.5	
TriVita Daily Men	US	1.5	additional nutrient amounts not specified
TriVita Daily Women	US	1.5	additional nutrient amounts not specified
TriVita VitaDaily AM/PM	US	2.0	
Trophic Complete	CA	3.0	
Trophic Multiple Vitamins & Minerals	CA	1.0	
Trophic Select	CA	2.0	
Tropical Oasis Multiple Vitamin/Mineral	US	0.5	
Tropical Oasis Tropical Plus	US	1.5	dosage derived
Truestar Health TrueBASIC	CA	5.0	**NutriSearch GOLD Medal of Achievement Recipient**
Truly Century Plus	CA	-	
Truly Century Premium	CA	0.5	
Truly Century Silver	CA	0.5	
Truly Weight One	CA	1.0	
Twinlab Daily One Caps with Iron	US	1.5	
Twinlab Daily One Caps without Iron	US	1.5	
Twinlab Dualtabs	US	2.0	dosage derived
Twinlab Food-Based Ultra Daily	US	1.0	additional nutrient amounts not specified
Twinlab Men's Ultra Daily	US	2.5	
Twinlab Women's Ultra Daily	US	2.5	
Ultima For Men	US	1.0	
Ultima For Women	US	0.5	
Ultimate Nutrition Super Complete	US	3.5	
Unicap M Dietary Supplement	US	-	
Unicap Sr. Dietary Supplement	US	-	
Unicity Bios Life 2 Original	US	-	
Unicity CoreHealth for Men	US	2.0	
Unicity CoreHealth for Women	US	2.0	
Unicity LifeHealth on the go	US	1.0	dosage derived
Universal Nutrition Genesis	CA	2.0	
Universal Nutrition Mega Edge	CA	2.0	
USANA Health Sciences Essentials	CA	5.0	**NutriSearch GOLD Medal of Achievement Recipient**
USANA Health Sciences Essentials	US	5.0	**NutriSearch GOLD Medal of Achievement Recipient**
Växa Daily Essentials	US	2.0	dosage derived
VegLife Iron Free MultiVeg Energy	US	3.0	
VegLife Spectro Veg High Energy	US	2.5	
VegLife Vegan One Multiple	CA/US	2.0	
Viactiv Multi-Vitamin	US	-	dosage derived
Vicon-C High Potency Multivitamin/Mineral	US	-	
VirtuVites Iron-Free Vita-Min 75	US	2.5	
ViSalus Nutri-One	US	1.5	
Vision for Life Body Force	US	2.0	additional nutrient amounts not specified
Vita-Complete AA (Anti-Aging)	CA/US	0.5	
Vita-Complete Vita-Complete 29	CA/US	-	dosage derived
Vital Nutrients Minimal and Essential	US	2.0	
Vital Nutrients Multi Nutrients V	US	2.5	
Vital Nutrients Multi-Nutrients II	US	3.0	
Vital Nutrients Multi-Nutrients III	US	3.0	
Vital Nutrients Multi-Nutrients IV	US	2.5	
Vital Nutrients Multi-Nutrients No Iron or Iodine	US	3.5	
Vital Nutrients Multi-Nutrients Veg Caps No Iron or Iodine	US	3.0	
Vital Nutrients Multi-Nutrients with Iron and Iodine	US	3.0	
Vitalert	US	0.5	
Vitality New Generation	US	2.0	

Product	Country	Rating	Notes
Vitality Products Multi-Vitamins and Minerals	US	2.0	
Vitality Products Two-A-Day	US	1.5	
Vitamin Power Mega Multiple 85	US	1.0	dosage derived
Vitamin Power Power Source 100	US	2.0	dosage derived
Vitamin Power SuperFem Multiple	US	1.5	
Vitamin Power Super-Vite	US	1.0	
Vitamin Power Ultra Multi 90 Plus	US	2.0	
Vitamin Power Vita-Max	US	1.0	dosage derived
Vitamin Research Products Extend Core	US	3.0	
Vitamin Research Products Extend Liquid	US	2.5	
Vitamin Research Products Extend One	US	2.0	
Vitamin Research Products Extend Plus	US	4.5	
Vitamin Research Products Optimum 18	US	5.0	
Vitamin Research Products Optimum 6	US	4.0	
Vitamin Research Products Optimum D	US	3.5	
Vitamin Research Products Optimum Silver	US	3.0	
Vitamin Research Products Women's Essentials	US	3.0	
Vitamin Shoppe Daily 3 Complete	US	3.0	
Vitamin Shoppe From the Earth (without Iron)	US	2.5	
Vitamin Shoppe Life Essentials Multi	US	4.5	
Vitamin Shoppe Mega-Vites 75	US	2.0	
Vitamin Shoppe One Daily	US	1.5	
Vitamin Shoppe Ultimate Man	US	2.0	
Vitamin Shoppe Ultimate Woman	US	2.0	
Vitamin Shoppe Ultimate Woman No Iron	US	2.0	
Vitamin World ABC Plus	US	-	
Vitamin World Daily 3 Caps	US	2.5	
Vitamin World Green Source	US	2.5	
Vitamin World Mega Vita Gel	US	2.0	
Vitamin World Mega Vita Min for Seniors	US	2.0	
Vitamin World Mega Vita Min for Women	US	2.0	
Vitamin World Mega Vita Min for Women with Iron	US	2.0	
Vitamin World Mega Vita-Min	US	2.0	
Vitamin World Mega Vita-Min Iron Free	US	2.0	
Vitamin World Nutri-100 Gold	US	2.0	
Vitamin World Theravim-M	US	-	
Vitamin World Ultra Vita Man	US	2.0	
Vitamin World Ultra Vita-Min	US	0.5	
Vitamin World Ultra Vita-Min Iron Free	US	1.0	
Vitaminerals Combadult	US	1.0	
Vitaminerals Combadult M	US	1.0	
Vitaplen Complete	US	0.5	additional nutrient amounts not specified
Vitaplex Total One Daily	CA	2.0	
Vitasmart Advanced Formula Complete	US	-	
Vitasmart Carb-Vantage	US	0.5	
Vitasmart Century Advantage	US	0.5	
Vitasmart Complete Senior	US	0.5	
Vitasmart Daily Diet Support	US	1.0	
Vitasmart Hi Potency Complete	US	-	
Vitasmart Maximum	US	-	
Vitasmart Men's Health Formula	US	0.5	
Vitasmart Men's Premium Multivitamin	US	1.5	
Vitasmart Select Men's Multi	US	2.0	
Vitasmart Select Super Multi 50+	US	0.5	
Vitasmart Select Women's Multi	US	1.5	
Vitasmart Women's	US	-	
Vitazan Multi-Power	CA	3.0	dosage derived
Vitosophy	US	1.0	additional nutrient amounts not specified
VIVA Life Science DailyGuard	US	2.0	
VIVA Life Science LiquiGuard	US	2.5	additional nutrient amounts not specified
VIVA Life Science VIVA for Life	US	1.0	
Walgreens A thru Z	US	-	
Walgreens A thru Z Advantage	US	0.5	
Walgreens A thru Z Select	US	0.5	
Walgreens One Daily 50 Plus	US	0.5	
Walgreens One Daily Men's	US	0.5	
Walgreens One Daily Women's	US	-	
Walgreens One Daily Women's 50 Plus	US	0.5	
Walgreens Super Aytinal for Active Adults	US	-	
Walgreens Super Aytinal for Adults 50 Plus	US	0.5	
Walgreens Therapeutic M	US	0.5	
Walgreens UltraChoice Adult	US	0.5	
Walgreens UltraChoice Mature	US	1.0	dosage derived
Wampole Adult Chewable	CA	0.5	
Wampole HSN Formula Women's	CA	0.5	
Watkins Super Multi	CA	1.5	
Watkins Superfood Multiple	US	1.5	
Weil Daily Multivitamin for Optimum Health	US	2.0	
Weil Daily Multivitamin Formula	CA	2.0	
WellBetX Complete Diabetic	CA	3.0	
Wellness International Network Phyto-Vite	US	2.5	

Wellness Resources Daily Energy	US	2.5	
Westcoast Naturals Multi-Plus	CA	0.5	
Western Family Active Women 50+	US	0.5	
Western Family Complete Advanced	US	-	
Western Family Complete Premium	US	0.5	
Western Family Complete Senior Formula	US	0.5	
Western Family Daily Diet Support	US	1.0	
Western Family Multi Vitamins with Minerals	CA	0.5	
Western Family Multra	CA	0.5	
Western Family Multra 50+	CA	1.0	
Western Family Multra with Iron	CA	0.5	additional nutrient amounts not specified
Western Family One Daily Maximum	US	-	
Western Family One Daily Women's	US	-	
Western Family Therapeutic M	US	0.5	
Wheaties Multivitamin	US	1.0	dosage derived
Wild Oats Basic Multi	US	0.5	
Wild Oats Food Origins Men's Prime Plus Multi-Vitamin	US	1.5	dosage derived
Wild Oats Food Origins Multi-Vitamin One	US	0.5	
Wild Oats Food Origins Women's Prime Plus Multi-Vitamin	US	1.5	dosage derived
Wild Oats Iron Free Multi Caps	US	2.0	dosage derived
Wild Oats Iron Free Ultimate One	US	2.0	
Wild Oats Life Multi Complete	US	2.0	dosage derived
Wild Oats Multi-Vitamin One	US	-	
Wild Oats Ultimate One	US	2.0	
Wild Oats Ultimate Two	US	2.0	
Wild Oats Ultimate Vegetarian Multi	US	2.0	
Win Fuel Men's formula	US	0.5	
Win Fuel Women's formula	US	-	
Women's International Pharmacy Nutri-Woman	US	2.5	
Women's International Pharmacy OsteoEmphasis	US	2.5	
Xtend-Life Total Balance Men's Plus	NZ/US	2.5	
Xtend-Life Total Balance Unisex	NZ/US	2.5	
Xtend-Life Total Balance Women's Plus	NZ/US	3.0	
Xymogen ActivNutrients	US	3.0	
Xymogen ActivNutrients Women (with Iron)	US	2.0	
Xymogen ActivNutrients Women (without iron)	US	2.0	
Xymogen InsuLean Rice	US	1.0	dosage derived
Xymogen InsuLean Soy	US	2.0	
Young Again Nutrients Complete One	US	2.0	
Young Again Nutrients UltraHigh	US	3.0	
Young Again Nutrients UltraMan	US	2.5	
Young Again Nutrients UltraWoman	US	2.0	
Zand Herbal Formulas Zanergy	US	2.0	dosage derived
Ziquin Mind & Body Tonic	US	1.5	additional nutrient amounts not specified

Appendix B: Stand-alone Products Alphabetically by Star Rating

Manufacturer & Product Name	Country	# of Stars	Dosages and Considerations
Creating Wellness Alliance Vitalize Men's Formula	US	5.0	NutriSearch GOLD Medal of Achievement Recipient
Creating Wellness Alliance Vitalize Women's Formula	US	5.0	**NutriSearch GOLD Medal of Achievement Recipient**
Creating Wellness Alliance Vitalize Senior Women's Gold Formula	US	5.0	NutriSearch GOLD Medal of Achievement Recipient
Douglas Laboratories Ultra Preventive IX	US	5.0	NutriSearch GOLD Medal of Achievement Recipient
Douglas Laboratories Ultra Preventive IX with Vitamin K	US	5.0	NutriSearch GOLD Medal of Achievement Recipient
Douglas Laboratories Ultra Preventive X	CA/US	5.0	**NutriSearch GOLD Medal of Achievement Recipient**
Truestar Health TrueBASIC	CA	5.0	NutriSearch GOLD Medal of Achievement Recipient
USANA Health Sciences Essentials	US	5.0	NutriSearch GOLD Medal of Achievement Recipient
USANA Health Sciences Essentials	CA	5.0	NutriSearch GOLD Medal of Achievement Recipient
Allergy Research Group Wholly Immune	US	5.0	
HealthyWize Vital Nutrients	US	5.0	
Life Extension Foundation Life Extension Mix	US	5.0	
NSI (Neutraceutical Sciences Institute) Synergy Men's Version 2	US	5.0	
Rejuvenation Science Maximum Vitality	US	5.0	
Source Naturals Élan Vital Multiple	US	5.0	
Source Naturals Life Force Multiple	US	5.0	
Swanson Lee Swanson Signature Line Longevital	US	5.0	
Vitamin Research Products Optimum 18	US	5.0	
Country Life Superior	US	4.5	
HealthyWize Vital Greens	US	4.5	
New Roots Herbal Multi-Max Immune	CA	4.5	
NSI (Neutraceutical Sciences Institute) Synergy Version 9	US	4.5	
NSI (Neutraceutical Sciences Institute) Synergy Women's Version 4	US	4.5	
Ortho Molecular Products Alpha Base Capsules without Iron	US	4.5	
Ortho Molecular Products Alpha Base Capsules without Iron or Copper	US	4.5	
Ortho Molecular Products Alpha Base Tablets	US	4.5	
Selekta Selekta-Clear	CA	4.5	
Vitamin Research Products Extend Plus	US	4.5	
Vitamin Shoppe Life Essentials Multi	US	4.5	
Allergy Research Group Steady On	US	4.0	
amni Added Protection III (iron free with copper)	US	4.0	
amni Basic Preventive 5 Plus Extra Vitamin D	US	4.0	
Biogenesis Nutraceuticals UltraGenesis without iron	US	4.0	
CanPrev Immuno-Pro Formula	CA	4.0	
DaVinci Laboratories Spectra Multi Age	US	4.0	
Doctor's Nutrition UltraNutrient	US	4.0	
Douglas Laboratories Added Protection III Iron Free	US	4.0	
Douglas Laboratories Basic Preventive 5 Plus Extra Vitamin D	US	4.0	
Douglas Laboratories Ultra Balance III (tablets)	CA	4.0	
Douglas Laboratories Ultra Preventive D with Copper	US	4.0	
Douglas Laboratories Ultra Preventive III (tablets)	US	4.0	
Douglas Laboratories Ultra Preventive III with Copper (tablets)	US	4.0	
Douglas Laboratories Ultra-AM & Ultra-PM	US	4.0	
Dr. Cranton's PrimeNutrients	US	4.0	
Enzymatic Therapy Doctor's Choice for 50-Plus Men	US	4.0	
FoodScience of Vermont Superior Multi Age	US	4.0	
Gary Null's Super AM Formula & Super PM Formula	US	4.0	
Jean Carper's Stop Aging Now!	US	4.0	
Jean Carper's Stop Aging Now! PLUS	US	4.0	
Mountain Naturals of Vermont Superior Multi Age Powder	US	4.0	
Nutriex Sport	US	4.0	
Ortho Molecular Products Alpha Base Capsules	US	4.0	
PhytoPharmica Clinical Nutrients for 45-Plus Women	US	4.0	
PhytoPharmica Clinical Nutrients for 50-Plus Men	US	4.0	
ProThera MultiThera 1	US	4.0	
Pure Encapsulations UltraNutrient	US	4.0	
Pure Essence Labs Life Essence Powder	US	4.0	
Pure Essence Labs Life Essence Tablets	US	4.0	
Rainbow Light RejuvenAge 40+	US	4.0	
Schwarzbein Institute Ultra Preventive III (tablets)	US	4.0	
Source Naturals Wellness Multiple	US	4.0	
SuperNutrition Men's Blend	US	4.0	
Vitamin Research Products Optimum 6	US	4.0	
Advanced Physician's Products Maximum MultiVitamin/Mineral without Iron	US	3.5	
All One Multiple for Active Seniors	US	3.5	
amni Added Protection III (copper and iron free)	US	3.5	
amni Added Protection III (copper free with iron)	US	3.5	
amni Added Protection III (with copper & iron)	US	3.5	
amni Basic Preventive 1	US	3.5	
amni Basic Preventive 2	US	3.5	
amni Basic Preventive 3	US	3.5	
amni Basic Preventive 4	US	3.5	
amni Basic Preventive 5	US	3.5	
AOR Ortho-Core	US	3.5	
Biogenesis Nutraceuticals UltraGenesis	US	3.5	dosage derived
Bluebonnet Super Vita-CoQ10 Formula	US	3.5	

Body Wise Right Choice A.M. + P.M. Formulas	CA/US	3.5	
Bronson Laboratories Vegi Source	US	3.5	
DaVinci Laboratories GENEssentials Spectra SNP	US	3.5	
DaVinci Laboratories Spectra	US	3.5	
DaVinci Laboratories Spectra Man	US	3.5	
DaVinci Laboratories Spectra Senior	US	3.5	
DaVinci Laboratories Spectra without Copper & Iron	US	3.5	
DaVinci Laboratories Spectra Woman	US	3.5	
Doctor's Nutrition Mega Vites Man	US	3.5	
Doctor's Nutrition Mega Vites without Copper & Iron	US	3.5	
Doctor's Nutrition Mega Vites Woman	US	3.5	
Don Lemmon's All Natural Balanced Multi-Nutrient	US	3.5	
Douglas Laboratories Added Protection III	US	3.5	
Douglas Laboratories Added Protection III Copper & Iron Free	US	3.5	
Douglas Laboratories Added Protection III Copper Free	US	3.5	
Douglas Laboratories Basic Preventive 1	US	3.5	
Douglas Laboratories Basic Preventive 2	US	3.5	
Douglas Laboratories Basic Preventive 3	US	3.5	
Douglas Laboratories Basic Preventive 4	US	3.5	
Douglas Laboratories Basic Preventive 5	US	3.5	
Douglas Laboratories Ultra Balance III with Iron (tablets)	CA	3.5	
Douglas Laboratories Ultra Preventive Beta	US	3.5	
Douglas Laboratories Ultra Preventive Beta with Copper	US	3.5	
Douglas Laboratories Ultra Preventive Beta with Copper & Iron	US	3.5	
Douglas Laboratories Ultra Preventive D	US	3.5	
Douglas Laboratories Ultra Preventive D with Copper & Iron	US	3.5	
Douglas Laboratories Ultra Preventive III with Copper & Iron (tablets)	US	3.5	
Douglas Laboratories Vitaworx	US	3.5	
Eclectic Institute Opti Gyn Formula	CA/US	3.5	
Enzymatic Therapy Doctor's Choice for 45-Plus Women	US	3.5	
Enzymatic Therapy Doctor's Choice for Men	CA	3.5	
Enzymatic Therapy Doctor's Choice for Men	US	3.5	
Enzymatic Therapy Doctor's Choice for Women	US	3.5	
FoodScience of Vermont Men's Superior	US	3.5	
FoodScience of Vermont Senior's Superior	US	3.5	
FoodScience of Vermont Superior Care without Copper and Iron	US	3.5	
FoodScience of Vermont Women's Superior	US	3.5	
Genuine Health greens+ multi+ powder	CA	3.5	
Great Earth TNT Extra Strength Timed Release	US	3.5	dosage derived
Jarrow Formulas Longevity Multi	US	3.5	
Karuna Maxxum 4	US	3.5	
Metagenics Multigenics Intensive Care	US	3.5	
Metagenics Multigenics Intensive Care (without iron)	US	3.5	
Metagenics Multigenics without iron	US	3.5	
MMS Pro Preventamins Iron Free	US	3.5	
Mountain Naturals of Vermont Men's Superior	US	3.5	
Mountain Naturals of Vermont Senior Superior	US	3.5	
Mountain Naturals of Vermont Women's Superior	US	3.5	
Natural Factors Multi Flow Oral Chelation Formula	CA	3.5	
Natural Factors MultiStart Women's	CA	3.5	
Natural Factors MultiStart Women's 45+	CA	3.5	
Natural Factors Women's MultiStart	US	3.5	
Nature's Way Multi Vitamin Iron-Free	US	3.5	
Nutriex Health	US	3.5	
Nutrition Dynamics Day Start & Day End Essentials	US	3.5	
Oregon Health Multi-GuarD with CoQ10	US	3.5	
PhytoPharmica Clinical Nutrients for Men	US	3.5	
PhytoPharmica Clinical Nutrients for Women	US	3.5	
ProThera MultiThera 2	US	3.5	
Pure Encapsulations Nutrient 950 without copper, iron & iodine	US	3.5	
Pure Encapsulations Nutrient 950 without iron	US	3.5	
Purity Products The Perfect Multi	US	3.5	
Purity Products The Perfect Multi Super Greens	US	3.5	
QCI Nutritionals Daily Preventive #1	US	3.5	
QCI Nutritionals Ultra Vitality #3	US	3.5	
QCI Nutritionals Ultra Vitality Elite	US	3.5	
Rainbow Light Advanced Nutritional System Iron-Free	US	3.5	additional nutrient amounts not specified
Solgar Male Multiple	US	3.5	dosage derived
Solgar Omnium Iron-Free	US	3.5	
SuperNutrition Perfect Blend	US	3.5	
Thorne Research Al's Formula	US	3.5	
Thorne Research Extra Nutrients	US	3.5	
Thorne Research Meta-Fem	US	3.5	
Ultimate Nutrition Super Complete	US	3.5	
Vital Nutrients Multi-Nutrients No Iron or Iodine	US	3.5	
Vitamin Research Products Optimum D	US	3.5	
4Life RiteStart Men	US	3.0	additional nutrient amounts not specified
4Life RiteStart Women	US	3.0	additional nutrient amounts not specified
Advanced Nutritional Innovations (ANI) CORALadvantage Bone & Joint Multi	US	3.0	
All One Multiple Green Phyto Base	US	3.0	
All One Multiple Original Formula	US	3.0	

Product	Region	Rating	Notes
All One Multiple Rice Base	US	3.0	
amni Essential Basics	US	3.0	
AOR Essential Mix	CA/US	3.0	additional nutrient amounts not specified
AOR Ortho-Core	CA	3.0	
Bluebonnet Super Earth Iron-Free	US	3.0	
CNC (Creative Nutrition Canada) Vitamost Plus Formula	CA/US	3.0	dosage derived
Colgan Institute First Defense Multi	US	3.0	
Country Life Beyond Food	US	3.0	
Country Life Max for Men	US	3.0	
Country Life Maxine for Women Iron-Free	US	3.0	
Designs for Health DFH Complete Multi	US	3.0	
Designs for Health DFH Complete Multi without copper & iron	US	3.0	
Doctor's Nutrition Mega Vites Senior	US	3.0	
Douglas Laboratories Essential Basics	US	3.0	
Douglas Laboratories Ultra Fem	US	3.0	
Douglas Laboratories Ultra Preventive III (capsules)	US	3.0	
Douglas Laboratories Ultra Preventive III with Iron (tablets)	US	3.0	
Douglas Laboratories Ultra Preventive III with Zinc Picolinate (tablets)	US	3.0	
Eclectic Institute Vital Force	US	3.0	
FoodScience of Vermont Superior Care	US	3.0	
Genesis Today 4 Total Nutrition	US	3.0	
Genuine Health greens+ multi+	CA	3.0	dosage derived
Genuine Health multi+ complete	CA	3.0	dosage derived
GNC Multi Liquid Ultra Mega	US	3.0	
Highland Laboratories Energy with Whole Food Concentrates	US	3.0	
Intensive Nutrition Multi-VM	US	3.0	
Julian Whitaker, M.D. Forward Multi-Nutrient	US	3.0	dosage derived
Kal Enhanced Energy	US	3.0	
Kal Multi-Active	US	3.0	
Karuna HIM	US	3.0	
Karuna Maxxum 1	US	3.0	
Karuna Maxxum 2	US	3.0	
Karuna Maxxum 3	US	3.0	
Longevity Science Revitalize	US	3.0	
Majestic Earth Ultimate Classic	US	3.0	dosage derived
MaxiVision Whole Body Formula	US	3.0	
MD's Choice Complete Formula for Mature Women	US	3.0	dosage derived
MD's Choice Complete Formula for Men	US	3.0	dosage derived
MD's Choice Complete Formula for Young Women	US	3.0	dosage derived
MegaFood Maximum Life	US	3.0	
Metagenics Multigenics	US	3.0	
More than a Multiple for Men	US	3.0	
More than a Multiple Iron Free/Vegetarian	US	3.0	
Mountain Peak Nutritionals Ultra High	US	3.0	
Natural Factors Men's MultiStart	US	3.0	
Natural Factors MultiStart Men's 50+	CA	3.0	
Natural Factors WellBetX	CA	3.0	
Natural Factors Women's Plus MultiStart	US	3.0	
Nature's Life Full Spectrum Antioxidant Soft Multi	US	3.0	dosage derived
Nature's Plus ReGeneration Soft Gels	US	3.0	
Nature's Way Alive! Drink Mix Powder	US	3.0	dosage derived
Nature's Way Alive! Vcaps/Tablets, no Iron added	US	3.0	
Nature's Way Daily Two Multi Iron Free	US	3.0	
Nature's Way Multi Vitamin with Iron	US	3.0	
New Roots Herbal Multi-Max	CA	3.0	
Now Eco-Green Multi	US	3.0	
NSI (Neutraceutical Sciences Institute) Synergy Basic Version 2	US	3.0	additional nutrient amounts not specified
NutriCare NutriDaily	US	3.0	
Nutrition Dynamics Balanced Vita-Plus-Min	US	3.0	
Nutrition Dynamics Ultra Fem	US	3.0	
NuTriVene-D Full Spectrum Formula	US	3.0	
Ola Loa Super Multi (Tropical)	US	3.0	
Ola Loa Super Multi (Orange)	US	3.0	
Optimox Androvite for Men	US	3.0	
Oregon Health Women's Multiple	US	3.0	
Pharmacist's Ultimate Health Man's Ultimate Formula	US	3.0	
Pharmacist's Ultimate Health Woman's Ultimate Formula	US	3.0	
Pioneer Vegetarian 1+ Vitamin Mineral	US	3.0	
Platinum Active EasyMulti Plus for Men	CA	3.0	
Platinum Active EasyMulti Plus for Women	CA	3.0	
Platinum Super EasyMulti Plus for Men 45+	CA	3.0	
Platinum Super EasyMulti Plus for Women 45+	CA	3.0	
Prairie Naturals Multi-Force	CA	3.0	
Pro Health Super Multiple without Iron	US	3.0	
Pro-Caps Laboratories Cholox	US	3.0	
Progressive for Active Men	CA	3.0	
Progressive for Active Women	CA	3.0	
Progressive for Men Over 50	CA	3.0	
Progressive for Women Over 50	CA	3.0	
Pure Encapsulations Nutrient 950	US	3.0	
Pure Encapsulations Nutrient 950 with NAC	US	3.0	

Pure Encapsulations Nutrient 950 without copper & iron	US	3.0	
Puritan's Pride Ultra Man 75	US	3.0	
QCI Nutritionals Ultra Vitality #2	US	3.0	
Rainbow Light Advanced Nutritional System	US	3.0	additional nutrient amounts not specified
Rx Vitamins Revitalize	US	3.0	
Rx Vitamins Revitalize without Iron	US	3.0	
Schwarzbein Institute Ultra Preventive III (capsules)	US	3.0	
Solaray Spectro 3	US	3.0	
Solaray Spectro 3 Iron Free	US	3.0	
Solaray Spectro Multi-Vita-Min	US	3.0	
Solaray Spectro Smoothie Once Daily	US	3.0	
Solaray Three Daily Super Energy Iron Free	US	3.0	
Solaray Vegetarian Spectro Multi-Vita-Min	US	3.0	
Solgar Female Multiple	US	3.0	dosage derived
Solgar Omnium	US	3.0	dosage derived
Source Naturals Life Defense	US	3.0	additional nutrient amounts not specified
SupraLife Ultra Body Toddy with Cell Shield	US	3.0	dosage based on 150 lb. body weight; additional nutrient amounts not specified
Swanson All-Day Complete for Seniors without Iron	US	3.0	
Swiss Swiss Total One Men	CA	3.0	
Swiss Total One	CA	3.0	
The Green Turtle Bay Vitamin Co. Diabetiks & PowerVites	US	3.0	
Thorne Research Basic Nutrients I	US	3.0	
Thorne Research Basic Nutrients II	US	3.0	
Thorne Research Basic Nutrients III	US	3.0	
Thorne Research Basic Nutrients III without Copper & Iron	US	3.0	
Thorne Research Basic Nutrients IV	US	3.0	
Thorne Research Basic Nutrients V	US	3.0	
Thorne Research Nutri-Fem	US	3.0	
Trophic Complete	CA	3.0	
VegLife Iron Free MultiVeg Energy	US	3.0	
Vital Nutrients Multi-Nutrients II	US	3.0	
Vital Nutrients Multi-Nutrients III	US	3.0	
Vital Nutrients Multi-Nutrients Veg Caps No Iron or Iodine	US	3.0	
Vital Nutrients Multi-Nutrients with Iron and Iodine	US	3.0	
Vitamin Research Products Extend Core	US	3.0	
Vitamin Research Products Optimum Silver	US	3.0	
Vitamin Research Products Women's Essentials	US	3.0	
Vitamin Shoppe Daily 3 Complete	US	3.0	
Vitazan Multi-Power	CA	3.0	dosage derived
WellBetX Complete Diabetic	CA	3.0	
Xtend-Life Total Balance Women's Plus	NZ/US	3.0	
Xymogen ActivNutrients	US	3.0	
Young Again Nutrients UltraHigh	US	3.0	
Advanced Physician's Products Complete MultiVitamin/Mineral without iron	US	2.5	
Avena Originals Vitamin Supreme	CA	2.5	additional nutrient amounts not specified
BioX Ultimate Once A Day	CA	2.5	dosage derived
Bluebonnet Maxi Two	US	2.5	
Bluebonnet Multi-Vita Softgels	US	2.5	
Bluebonnet Super Earth mini-caplets	US	2.5	
Bluebonnet Super Earth with Iron	US	2.5	
Carlson Multi-Gel	US	2.5	
Carlson Super 2 Daily	US	2.5	
CNC (Creative Nutrition Canada) Vitamost Prime Formula	CA	2.5	dosage derived
CNC (Creative Nutrition Canada) Vitamost RTRE Formula	CA/US	2.5	
Cooper Complete Iron Free	US	2.5	
Cooper Complete with Iron	US	2.5	
Country Life Esssential Life	US	2.5	
Country Life Maxine for Women	US	2.5	
Country Life Maxine for Women Vegetarian Caps	US	2.5	
Cyto Charge Life Assurance	US	2.5	
Douglas Laboratories Nutri-Smart Formula	US	2.5	
Douglas Laboratories Ultra Balance III (capsules)	CA	2.5	
Douglas Laboratories Ultra Preventive III with Copper (capsules)	US	2.5	
Douglas Laboratories Vita-Chel-Plus	US	2.5	
Dr. Donsbach's Ora-Flo	US	2.5	
Drucker Labs intraMAX	US	2.5	additional nutrient amounts not specified
Enerex Sona Rx	CA	2.5	
Freeda Ultra Freeda, Iron-Free	US	2.5	
Freeda Ultra Freeda, with Iron	US	2.5	
Genuine Health greens+ multi+ tablets	CA	2.5	
GNC Mega Men	US	2.5	
GNC Multi Ultra Mega Gold	US	2.5	
GNC Multi Ultra Mega Gold without Iron	US	2.5	
Great American Products Master Green Multi	US	2.5	
Great Earth Super Hy-Vites Ultra Strength	US	2.5	dosage derived
Highland Laboratories Men's 30 Plus Multi	US	2.5	
Highland Laboratories OMNI	US	2.5	
Highland Laboratories Women's 30 Plus Multi	US	2.5	
Innate Response Formulas Food Multi IV	US	2.5	
Innate Response Formulas Men Over 40	US	2.5	
Intensive Nutrition Mega-VM	US	2.5	

Jarrow Formulas Multi 1-to-3	US	2.5	
Jarrow Formulas Multi Easy Powder	CA/US	2.5	
Kal Multi-Four+	US	2.5	
Kal Multiple Energy	US	2.5	
Life Plus Daily BioBasics	US	2.5	
Life Solutions Super Multi Vitamins and Minerals	US	2.5	
Life-Line Theravits 100	US	2.5	
LifeSource Nutrition Multi Vitamin & Minerals	US	2.5	
Mannatech Glycentials	US	2.5	
MegaFood Essentials FoodBased Mini's	US	2.5	
MegaFood Essentials for Menopause	US	2.5	
Metabolic Maintenance Men's Maintenance	US	2.5	
Metabolic Maintenance Women's Maintenance without Iron	US	2.5	
MHP Activite Sport	US	2.5	additional nutrient amounts not specified
Michael's Active Senior Tabs	US	2.5	dosage derived; additional nutrient amounts not specified
Michael's For Men	US	2.5	dosage derived
Michael's For Women	US	2.5	dosage derived
More than a Multiple	US	2.5	
More than a Multiple for Women	US	2.5	
Mountain Peak Nutritionals Energy Formula	US	2.5	dosage derived
MultiSure for Women 50+	CA	2.5	
Natrol My Favorite Multiple (original)	US	2.5	
Natural Nutrition Active Men's	US	2.5	
Natural Nutrition Active Woman's	US	2.5	
Natural Nutrition Life Essentials	US	2.5	
Natural Nutrition Ultra VMT	US	2.5	
Natural Nutrition Vi-Min	US	2.5	
Natural Nutrition Vita-Min 75	US	2.5	
Natural Nutrition Vita-Min 75 No Iron	US	2.5	
Naturally Preferred Men's Multi	US	2.5	
Nature's Plus Source of Life Men Liquid	US	2.5	
Nature's Plus Source of Life Women	US	2.5	
Nature's Plus Source of Life Women Liquid	US	2.5	
Nature's Plus Ultra Source of Life	US	2.5	additional nutrient amounts not specified
Nature's Plus Ultra Source of Life No Iron	US	2.5	additional nutrient amounts not specified
Nature's Way Alive! Tablets with Iron	US	2.5	
NF Formulas, Inc. Women's Formula	US	2.5	
NF Formulas, Inc. Women's Formula without iron	US	2.5	
Now Adam	US	2.5	
Now Eve	US	2.5	
Now Vit-Min 100	US	2.5	
Now Vit-Min Caps	US	2.5	
Nu-Life The Legend	CA	2.5	
Nu-Life The Legend High Stress/Activity for Men	CA	2.5	additional nutrient amounts not specified
Nu-Life The Legend Max Stress/Activity for Men	CA	2.5	additional nutrient amounts not specified
Nu-Life The Legend Max Stress/Activity for Women	CA	2.5	additional nutrient amounts not specified
Nu-Life Ultimate One for Men Active	CA	2.5	additional nutrient amounts not specified
Nu-Life Ultimate One Right Weight	CA	2.5	additional nutrient amounts not specified
Nutri-Betics Nutra Balance For Men	CA	2.5	additional nutrient amounts not specified
Nutrina Champion Formula	US	2.5	dosage derived
Nutrina Marathon Formula	US	2.5	
Nutrition Dynamics Iodine Free "Vegi" Formula	US	2.5	
Nutrition House Men's Multi Extra	CA	2.5	
Nutrition House Women's Multi Extra	CA	2.5	
Nutrition Now Multi Earth Force	US	2.5	
NuTriVene-D Advanced Formula Daily Supplement	US	2.5	
Nutri-West Core Level Health Reserve	US	2.5	
Olympian Labs Vita Vitamin	US	2.5	dosage derived
Olympian Labs Vita-One	US	2.5	dosage derived
Optimox Optivite PMT for Women	US	2.5	
Pioneer Chewable	US	2.5	
Prevention Dieter's Complete	CA	2.5	
Prevention for Men	CA/US	2.5	
Prevention for Men 50 Plus	CA	2.5	
Prevention for Men 50 Plus	US	2.5	
Prevention for Women	US	2.5	
Prevention for Women	CA	2.5	
Prevention for Women 50 Plus	US	2.5	
Prevention for Women 50 Plus	CA	2.5	
Pro Health Multiple One	US	2.5	
Professional Health Products Multi-Pro	CA	2.5	
Progressive for Adult Men	CA	2.5	
Progressive for Adult Women	CA	2.5	
ProThera LDA Multi-Vitamin & LDA Trace Mineral Complex	US	2.5	
ProThera VItaPrime	US	2.5	
Puritan's Pride Daily 3 Caps	US	2.5	
Puritan's Pride Green Source Iron Free	US	2.5	
Quest Maximum Once A Day	CA	2.5	
Radiance Green Source Iron Free	US	2.5	
Rainbow Light Complete Nutritional System	US	2.5	
Rainbow Light Women's Nutritional System	US	2.5	

Ripple Creek Mega-100	US	2.5	
Sangster's Men's Choice	US	2.5	dosage derived
Seroyal Super Orti Vite	CA	2.5	2003 data
SISU Vegi Mins	CA	2.5	
Solaray Multi-Vita Mega Mineral Multi-Vita-Min	US	2.5	
Solaray Provide Iron Free	US	2.5	
Solaray Spectro Multi-Vita-Min Iron Free	US	2.5	
Solaray Spectro Multi-Vita-Min Iron Free	CA	2.5	
Solaray Three Daily Super Energy	US	2.5	
Solaray Twice Daily Iron Free	US	2.5	
Solaray Twice Daily Multi Energy Iron Free	US	2.5	
Solaray VitaPrime for Men	US	2.5	
Solaray VitaPrime for Women	US	2.5	
Solaray Women's Golden Multi-Vita-Min	US	2.5	
SomaLife SomaVit Plus	CA/US	2.5	
SupraLife Formula Plus	US	2.5	
SupraLife Maxum Essentials	US	2.5	
Swanson All-Day Complete	US	2.5	
Swanson High Potency Soft Multiple Iron Free	US	2.5	
Swanson Ultra Whole Food	US	2.5	
Swiss Swiss Total One Women	CA	2.5	
The Synergy Company Vita Synergy for Men	US	2.5	dosage derived
The Synergy Company Vita Synergy for Women	US	2.5	dosage derived
Trace Minerals Complete Foods Multi	US	2.5	
TRC Nutritional Laboratories Liquid Life	US	2.5	
Twinlab Men's Ultra Daily	US	2.5	
Twinlab Women's Ultra Daily	US	2.5	
VegLife Spectro Veg High Energy	US	2.5	
VirtuVites Iron-Free Vita-Min 75	US	2.5	
Vital Nutrients Multi Nutrients V	US	2.5	
Vital Nutrients Multi-Nutrients IV	US	2.5	
Vitamin Research Products Extend Liquid	US	2.5	
Vitamin Shoppe From the Earth (without Iron)	US	2.5	
Vitamin World Daily 3 Caps	US	2.5	
Vitamin World Green Source	US	2.5	
VIVA Life Science LiquiGuard	US	2.5	additional nutrient amounts not specified
Wellness International Network Phyto-Vite	US	2.5	
Wellness Resources Daily Energy	US	2.5	
Women's International Pharmacy Nutri-Woman	US	2.5	
Women's International Pharmacy OsteoEmphasis	US	2.5	
Xtend-Life Total Balance Men's Plus	NZ/US	2.5	
Xtend-Life Total Balance Unisex	NZ/US	2.5	
Young Again Nutrients UltraMan	US	2.5	
21st Century Mega Multi for Women	US	2.0	
4Life Start Plus	US	2.0	dosage derived
Action Labs Action Man Multi Once Daily	US	2.0	
Advocare CorePlex	US	2.0	
Albi Imports Rocky Mountain Multiple	CA	2.0	DPD data; 2003 data
Alive Vitamins Super One Plus	CA	2.0	DPD data; 2003 data
Allergy Research Group Multi-Vi-Min without Copper & Iron	US	2.0	
American Health Nutri Mega	US	2.0	
American Nutrition Ultra VM-T	US	2.0	
Anabolic Laboratories Aved-Digest Multi	US	2.0	
Anabolic Laboratories Aved-Multi Iron Free	US	2.0	
Anabolic Laboratories Multigel Caps	US	2.0	
Atkins Basic 3	CA	2.0	
AuMed Coremed	US	2.0	dosage derived; additional nutrient amounts not specified
Bluebonnet Iron Free Multi One	US	2.0	
Bluebonnet Maxi One	US	2.0	
Body Guard Antioxidant Formula	CA/US	2.0	
Botanic Choice Complete Assurance for Men	US	2.0	
Botanic Choice Complete Assurance for Women	US	2.0	
Bronson Laboratories Mega Multi Softcaps	US	2.0	
Bronson Laboratories Men's Complete Formula with 7-Keto	US	2.0	
Bronson Laboratories Performance Edge for Men	US	2.0	
Bronson Laboratories Performance Edge for Women	US	2.0	
Bronson Laboratories Vitamin & Mineral Insurance Formula	US	2.0	
Canadian Sun One Plus	CA	2.0	
Carlson Super-75	US	2.0	
Country Life Multi-100	US	2.0	
Country Life Vegetarian Support	US	2.0	
Curves Multivitamin	CA	2.0	
CVS Pharmacy Mega Multi	US	2.0	
DaVinci Laboratories Daily Best	US	2.0	
Dr. Rath's Women's Health Program	US	2.0	
EcoNugenics Women's Longevity Rhythms	US	2.0	
EcoNugenics Women's Longevity Rhythms Gold	US	2.0	
Enerex Sona	CA	2.0	
epic4health Physician's Multi Vitamin Formula	US	2.0	
Essence-of-Life Liquid Nutrition Plus/Essence	US	2.0	dosage derived
Exact Multi Max 1	CA	2.0	

Product	Region	Rating	Notes
Flora Multi Vitamins	CA	2.0	
FoodScience of Vermont Daily Best	US	2.0	
ForMor International AnOx	US	2.0	dosage derived
Freeda Ultra Freeda, A-Free	US	2.0	
FutureBiotics Hi Energy Multi for Men	US	2.0	
FutureBiotics Vegetarian Super Multi	US	2.0	
Garden of Life Living Multi	US	2.0	
Garden of Life Living Multi Iron Free	CA	2.0	
Garden of Life Living Multi Men's Formula	CA/US	2.0	
Gary Null's Super AM Formula	US	2.0	
Genuine Health multi+ daily trim	CA	2.0	
Global Health Trax (GHT) Daily Vita Plus & Mega Minerals Plus	US	2.0	dosage derived
GNC Mega Men 50 Plus	US	2.0	
GNC Multi Ultra Mega Green	US	2.0	
GNC Multi Ultra Mega Softgels	CA	2.0	
GNC Women's Ultra Mega	CA	2.0	
GNC Women's Ultra Mega without iron	CA	2.0	
GNC Women's Women's Ultra Mega	US	2.0	
GNC Women's Women's Ultra Mega Bone Density	US	2.0	
Goldshield Total Multivitamin & Mineral Formula	US	2.0	
Great Earth Super Hy-Vites Extra Strength	US	2.0	dosage derived
Health First Iron Free Multi-First	CA	2.0	
Henry's Farmer's Market 75 Complete	US	2.0	
Henry's Farmer's Market Iron Free Multi Caps	US	2.0	
Henry's Farmer's Market Iron Free Ultimate One	US	2.0	
Henry's Farmer's Market Life Multi Complete	US	2.0	
Henry's Farmer's Market Softgel Multi	US	2.0	
Henry's Farmer's Market Ultimate One	US	2.0	
Henry's Farmer's Market Ultimate Two	US	2.0	
Henry's Farmer's Market Ultimate Vegetarian Multi	US	2.0	
Highland Laboratories Mega II Daily	US	2.0	
Highland Laboratories Mega II Daily Iron-free	US	2.0	
Hillestad Pharmaceuticals Sterling	US	2.0	dosage derived
Hillestad Pharmaceuticals Summit Gold Special Formula	US	2.0	dosage derived
Innate Response Formulas Women Over 40	US	2.0	
Intelligent Nutrients NutriBase	US	2.0	dosage derived; additional nutrient amounts not specified
Isotonix Champion Blend	US	2.0	
Jarrow Formulas Women's Multi	CA/US	2.0	
Kal Enhanced-75	US	2.0	
Kal High Potency Soft Multiple Iron Free	US	2.0	
Kal Mega Vita-Min	US	2.0	
Kal Multi-Max 1	US	2.0	
Kal Vitality for Women	US	2.0	
Levity+Plus Multivitamin for Women	US	2.0	
Life-Line Maximum Daily Greens	US	2.0	
LifeTime Life's Basics	US	2.0	
LifeTime Multi-Vitamin & Mineral Soft Gels	US	2.0	
London Naturals Iron-Free	CA	2.0	
London Naturals Premier	CA	2.0	
Longs Men's Multivitamin/Mineral Supplement with Herbs	US	2.0	
Mannatech Glycentials	CA	2.0	additional nutrient amounts not specified
Matol MegaVitamins	CA	2.0	
Matol MegaVitamins	US	2.0	
MegaFood LifeStyle DailyFoods	US	2.0	
MegaFood Maximum Man	US	2.0	
MegaFood Maximum Woman	US	2.0	
MegaFood Men Over 40 DailyFoods	US	2.0	
MegaFood Women Over 40 DailyFoods	US	2.0	
Melaleuca Vitality Gold for Men	US	2.0	dosage derived; additional nutrient amounts not specified
Melaleuca Vitality Gold for Women	US	2.0	dosage derived; additional nutrient amounts not specified
Metabolic Maintenance Basic Maintenance without Iron	US	2.0	
Metabolic Maintenance The Big One without Iron	US	2.0	
Metabolic Maintenance Women's Maintenance with Iron	US	2.0	
Michael's Just One	US	2.0	dosage derived; additional nutrient amounts not specified
Miracle 2000 Total Body Nutrition	US	2.0	dosage derived
MultiSure for Men	CA	2.0	
MultiSure for Men 50+	CA	2.0	
MultiSure for Women	CA	2.0	
Natural Factors Hi Potency Multi	CA	2.0	
Natural Factors Ultra Multi Plus	CA	2.0	
Naturally Preferred 75 Complete	US	2.0	
Naturally Preferred Life Multi Complete	US	2.0	
Naturally Preferred Nutri-Max	US	2.0	
Naturally Preferred Vita Max	US	2.0	
Naturally Preferred Women's Multi	US	2.0	
Nature's Answer Liquid Multiple Vitamins & Liquid Multiple Minerals	US	2.0	
Nature's Best TR Mega 100	US	2.0	dosage derived
Nature's Bounty Ultra Man	US	2.0	dosage derived
Nature's Bounty Ultra Woman	US	2.0	dosage derived
Nature's Harmony High Potency One Per Day	CA	2.0	
Nature's Life Green Multi	US	2.0	

Nature's Life Soft Gelatin Multiple	US	2.0	dosage derived
Nature's Life Ultra Mega Vite	US	2.0	
Nature's Life Vegetarian Green Multi	US	2.0	dosage derived
Nature's Plus Nutri-Genic	US	2.0	
Nature's Plus ReGeneration Liquid Sunshine	US	2.0	dosage derived
Nature's Plus Source of Life Liquid	US	2.0	dosage derived
Nature's Plus Source of Life Tablets/Capsules	US	2.0	
Nature's Plus Ultra I	US	2.0	
Nature's Plus Ultra II	US	2.0	
Nature's Sunshine Super Supplemental without Iron	US	2.0	
Nature's Sunshine VitaWave	US	2.0	additional nutrient amounts not specified
Nature's Valley Women's Formula	US	2.0	dosage derived
Nature's Way Completia Ultra Energy (Iron-Free)	US	2.0	
Nature's Way Completia Ultra Energy Multivitamin	US	2.0	
Nature's Way Once Daily Multi	US	2.0	
Nikken Kenzen	US	2.0	
North American Pharmacal Polyvite A & Phytocal A	US	2.0	dosage derived
North American Pharmacal Polyvite AB & Phytocal AB	US	2.0	dosage derived
Now Special Two	CA/US	2.0	
Now Vit-Min 75+ Iron Free	US	2.0	
Nu-Life The Legend High Stress/Activity for Women	CA	2.0	additional nutrient amounts not specified
Nu-Life Ultimate One for Men 50 Plus	CA	2.0	additional nutrient amounts not specified
Nu-Life Ultimate One for Men Adult	CA	2.0	additional nutrient amounts not specified
Nu-Life Ultimate One for Women 50 Plus	CA	2.0	additional nutrient amounts not specified
Nu-Life Ultimate One for Women Active	CA	2.0	additional nutrient amounts not specified
Nu-Life Ultimate One Women Adult	CA	2.0	additional nutrient amounts not specified
Nutra Therapeutics All-In-One	CA/US	2.0	
NutriCology Multi-Vi-Min without Copper & Iron	US	2.0	
Nutrina Athlete Formula	US	2.0	dosage derived
Nutrina Mega Greens	US	2.0	
Nutrina Vitamax Powder	US	2.0	dosage derived
Nutrition House Multi-Vitamin Extra Iron Free	CA	2.0	
OneSource Men's	US	2.0	
OneSource Women's	US	2.0	
Optimox Gynovite Plus	US	2.0	
Original Medicine NutraSyn	US	2.0	
Peter Gillham's Natural Vitality Liquid Organic life Vitamins	US	2.0	
Physician Formulas MultiVit-Rx	US	2.0	
Prairie Naturals Multi-Force Powder	CA	2.0	
Prevention Diabetic Support	US	2.0	
Prevention Dieter's Complete	US	2.0	
Pro Health Super Multiple II	US	2.0	
Pure Advantage Womens Multiple	US	2.0	
Pure Essence Labs One'n'Only	US	2.0	additional nutrient amounts not specified
Puritan's Pride Formula 100	US	2.0	
Puritan's Pride Green Source	US	2.0	additional nutrient amounts not specified
Puritan's Pride Mega Vita Gel	US	2.0	
Puritan's Pride Mega Vita Min	US	2.0	
Puritan's Pride Mega Vita Min for Seniors	US	2.0	
Puritan's Pride Mega Vita Min for Women	US	2.0	
Puritan's Pride Mega Vita Min for Women Iron Free	US	2.0	
Puritan's Pride Mega Vita Min Iron Free	US	2.0	
Puritan's Pride Ultra Vita Man	US	2.0	
Radiance Mega Vita Gel	US	2.0	
Radiance Mega Vita-Min Iron Free	US	2.0	dosage derived
Rainbow Light Just Once Active Senior	US	2.0	
Ripple Creek Mega-Caps 2	US	2.0	
Safeway Select Super Women's Multivitamin	US	2.0	
Sangster's Senior's Choice	US	2.0	dosage derived
Sangster's Vege Choice	US	2.0	dosage derived
Sangster's Women's Choice	US	2.0	dosage derived
Schiff Single Day	US	2.0	
Selekta Multi II's with Copper & Iron	CA	2.0	
Selekta Multi's without Copper & Iron	CA	2.0	
SISU Multi Active	CA	2.0	
SISU Multi Active Woman	CA	2.0	
Solaray Men's Golden Multi-Vita-Min	US	2.0	
Solaray Provide	US	2.0	
Solaray Spectro Multi-Vita-Min	CA	2.0	
Solaray Twice Daily Multi Energy	US	2.0	
Solgar Earth Source Multi-Nutrient	US	2.0	
Solgar Formula VM-2000	US	2.0	dosage derived
Solgar Formula VM-75	US	2.0	
Solgar Formula VM-75 Iron-Free	US	2.0	
Solgar Formula VM-Prime	US	2.0	
Source Naturals Ultra Multiple	US	2.0	additional nutrient amounts not specified
SuperNutrition Longevity	US	2.0	
SuperNutrition Multi Vitamin & Mineral	CA	2.0	
SuperNutrition Simply One	US	2.0	
SuperNutrition Simply One Men	US	2.0	additional nutrient amounts not specified
SuperNutrition Simply One Women	US	2.0	additional nutrient amounts not specified

Product	Country	Rating	Notes
SupraLife Total Toddy	US	2.0	dosage based on 150 lb. body weight
Swanson Active One without Iron	US	2.0	
Swanson High Potency Soft Multiple	US	2.0	
Swiss Adult Multi One Formula	CA	2.0	
Swiss Hi Potency Swiss One "80"	CA	2.0	
Swiss Slim Essentials	CA	2.0	
Swiss Vege Multivitamin and Mineral	CA	2.0	
The Greatest Vitamin in the World	US	2.0	
Thompson Adult-Plex	US	2.0	
Thompson Coach's Formula	US	2.0	
Thompson Mega 80	US	2.0	
Trace Minerals Liquid Multi Vita-Mineral	US	2.0	
TriVita VitaDaily AM/PM	US	2.0	
Trophic Select	CA	2.0	
Twinlab Dualtabs	US	2.0	dosage derived
Unicity CoreHealth for Men	US	2.0	
Unicity CoreHealth for Women	US	2.0	
Universal Nutrition Genesis	CA	2.0	
Universal Nutrition Mega Edge	CA	2.0	
Växa Daily Essentials	US	2.0	dosage derived
VegLife Vegan One Multiple	CA/US	2.0	
Vision for Life Body Force	US	2.0	additional nutrient amounts not specified
Vital Nutrients Minimal and Essential	US	2.0	
Vitality New Generation	US	2.0	
Vitality Products Multi-Vitamins and Minerals	US	2.0	
Vitamin Power Power Source 100	US	2.0	dosage derived
Vitamin Power Ultra Multi 90 Plus	US	2.0	
Vitamin Research Products Extend One	US	2.0	
Vitamin Shoppe Mega-Vites 75	US	2.0	
Vitamin Shoppe Ultimate Man	US	2.0	
Vitamin Shoppe Ultimate Woman	US	2.0	
Vitamin Shoppe Ultimate Woman No Iron	US	2.0	
Vitamin World Mega Vita Gel	US	2.0	
Vitamin World Mega Vita Min for Seniors	US	2.0	
Vitamin World Mega Vita Min for Women	US	2.0	
Vitamin World Mega Vita Min for Women with Iron	US	2.0	
Vitamin World Mega Vita-Min	US	2.0	
Vitamin World Mega Vita-Min Iron Free	US	2.0	
Vitamin World Nutri-100 Gold	US	2.0	
Vitamin World Ultra Vita Man	US	2.0	
Vitaplex Total One Daily	CA	2.0	
Vitasmart Select Men's Multi	US	2.0	
VIVA Life Science DailyGuard	US	2.0	
Weil Daily Multivitamin for Optimum Health	US	2.0	
Weil Daily Multivitamin Formula	CA	2.0	
Wild Oats Iron Free Multi Caps	US	2.0	dosage derived
Wild Oats Iron Free Ultimate One	US	2.0	
Wild Oats Life Multi Complete	US	2.0	dosage derived
Wild Oats Ultimate One	US	2.0	
Wild Oats Ultimate Two	US	2.0	
Wild Oats Ultimate Vegetarian Multi	US	2.0	
Xymogen ActivNutrients Women (with Iron)	US	2.0	
Xymogen ActivNutrients Women (without iron)	US	2.0	
Xymogen InsuLean Soy	US	2.0	
Young Again Nutrients Complete One	US	2.0	
Young Again Nutrients UltraWoman	US	2.0	
Zand Herbal Formulas Zanergy	US	2.0	dosage derived
21st Century Mega Multi for Men	US	1.5	
4Life MultiPlex	CA/US	1.5	dosage derived
agel Min	US	1.5	
agel Min	CA	1.5	
Alacer Super-Gram III	US	1.5	
Albi Imports Super One a Day	CA	1.5	DPD data; 2003 data
Allergy Research Group Multi-Vi-Min	US	1.5	
Anabolic Laboratories Aved-Multi	US	1.5	
Arbonne Complete Essentials for Men	US	1.5	
Atkins Basic 3	US	1.5	
Awareness Life Daily Complete	US	1.5	additional nutrient amounts not specified
Biogenesis Nutraceuticals BioFocus	US	1.5	
Bio-lumin Essence Daily Essence	US	1.5	dosage derived
Biotics Research Corporation Bio-Multi Plus Iron & Copper Free	US	1.5	
Biotics Research Corporation Bio-Multi Plus Iron-Free	US	1.5	
Bluebonnet Multi One	US	1.5	
Body Rewards Daily Multiple	US	1.5	
Botanic Choice Senior Multi-Vitamin	US	1.5	
Botanic Choice Whole Foods Power Multi	US	1.5	
Bronson Laboratories Fortified Vitamin & Mineral Insurance Formula	US	1.5	
Bronson Laboratories Multi Formula with Lutein	US	1.5	
Canadian Sun Formula Flow	CA	1.5	
Carlson Super 1 Daily	US	1.5	
Clinician's Formula Vitality Multivite	US	1.5	additional nutrient amounts not specified

Colorado Nutrition Ultimate Men's Formula	US	1.5	
Colorado Nutrition Ultimate Women's Formula	US	1.5	
Comprehensive Formula Men's	US	1.5	2003 data
Country Life Daily Total One	US	1.5	
Country Life Enhanced QM-1	US	1.5	
Country Life Green Edge II	US	1.5	dosage derived
Country Life Seniority	US	1.5	
Curves Complete	US	1.5	new data unavailable, 2004 data
Curves Complete Biomultiple	US	1.5	
CVS Pharmacy Today's Life Women's	US	1.5	
DaVinci Laboratories Omni	US	1.5	
dc (Dee Cee Laboratories) Formula 75	US	1.5	
dc (Dee Cee Laboratories) Ultra VM	US	1.5	
EcoNugenics Men's Longevity Essentials Plus	US	1.5	
Eniva Essential Phytamins & Cell-Ready Minerals (Cranberry-Grapefruit Blend)	US	1.5	
Eniva Essential Phytamins and Cell-Ready Minerals (original formula)	US	1.5	additional nutrient amounts not specified
Eniva Vibe	US	1.5	additional nutrient amounts not specified
Enzyme Labs Nutraceuticals Multi-Life	US	1.5	additional nutrient amounts not specified
FoodScience of Vermont Total Care	US	1.5	
Freeda Quintabs-M Iron-Free	US	1.5	
Future Formulations Advance (Iron Free)	CA	1.5	
FutureBiotics MultiVitamin Energy Plus for Women	US	1.5	
Garden of Life Living Multi	CA	1.5	
Garden of Life Living Multi Optimal Women's Formula	CA	1.5	
Garden of Life Living Multi Optimal Women's Formula	US	1.5	
Gary Null's Super PM Formula	US	1.5	
GNC Mega Men	CA	1.5	
GNC Multi Solotron without iron	US	1.5	
GNC Multi Ultra Mega	CA	1.5	
GNC Multi Ultra Mega	US	1.5	
GNC Multi-Gel	US	1.5	dosage derived
GNC Preventive Nutrition Men's Multiple	US	1.5	
GNC Preventive Nutrition Premium One without Iron	US	1.5	
GNC Preventive Nutrition Women's Multiple	US	1.5	
GNLD International Formula IV Plus	US	1.5	
Great Earth Super Hy-Vites Regular Strength	US	1.5	dosage derived
greens+ greens+ powder	US	1.5	
Health First Multi-First	CA	1.5	
Henry's Farmer's Market Ultimate Capsule	US	1.5	
Henry's Marketplace Ultimate Senior Multi	US	1.5	
HerbaSway Laboratories MultiVitamin Magic & MultiMineral Magic	US	1.5	
Highland Laboratories Mega I Daily	US	1.5	
Highland Laboratories Mega I Daily Iron-free	US	1.5	
Hillestad Pharmaceuticals Summit Gold	US	1.5	dosage derived
Holista Advanz	US	1.5	
Holista Advanz Iron Free	US	1.5	
Innate Response Formulas Men's Multi Without Iron	US	1.5	
Inno-Vite Formula H.H.	CA	1.5	
Inno-Vite Total NRG Lift	CA	1.5	2003 data; additional nutrient amounts not specified
Isagenix Essentials for Men	CA	1.5	dosage derived
Isagenix Essentials for Men	US	1.5	dosage derived; additional nutrient amounts not specified
Isagenix Essentials for Women	US	1.5	dosage derived; additional nutrient amounts not specified
Isagenix Women's Essentials	CA	1.5	dosage derived
Jamieson Power Vitamins for Men	CA	1.5	
Jamieson Super Vita-Vim	CA	1.5	
Jamieson Vita Slim	CA	1.5	
Juvio Rejuvionate Green Perfection	CA/US	1.5	dosage derived; additional nutrient amounts not specified
Kal SoftOne Multi with Lutein	US	1.5	
Kirkman EveryDay & NuThera EveryDay Companion Capsules	US	1.5	
Kroger Men	US	1.5	
Life Spectrum with Beta Carotene	CA	1.5	
LifeSource Nutrition Liquid Multi Vitamin & Immune Booster	US	1.5	additional nutrient amounts not specified
Majestic Earth Ultimate Daily	US	1.5	
Maxion Formula F-L-W	CA	1.5	
Maxion Nutrition Artr-E-Clnz	US	1.5	
MegaFood Alpha DailyFoods	US	1.5	
MegaFood Essentials Iron Free One Daily	US	1.5	
MegaFood Essentials One Daily	US	1.5	
MegaFood Optimum Foods	US	1.5	
Metabolic Maintenance Basic Maintenance with Iron	US	1.5	
Metabolic Maintenance Multi-Vitamin Powder	US	1.5	
Metabolic Maintenance The Big One with Iron	US	1.5	
Molecular Biologics Allervimin	US	1.5	
Molecular Biologics Derma-Vites	US	1.5	dosage derived
N.V. Perricone, M.D. Physician's Super Antioxidant	US	1.5	
Natura Select Food Based Men's Multi	CA/US	1.5	
Natura Select Food Based Women's Multi	CA/US	1.5	dosage derived
Natural Factors MultiStart	CA	1.5	
Natural Factors Super Multi Iron Free	CA	1.5	
Natural Factors Super Multi Plus Iron	CA	1.5	
Natural Nutrition Vita Super	US	1.5	

Nature's Best TR Mega 50	US	1.5	dosage derived
Nature's Life One Daily Multiple	US	1.5	
Nature's Life Vegetarian Mega-Vita-Min	US	1.5	
Nature's Life Vegetarian Super Mega Vite	US	1.5	dosage derived
Nature's Plus Source of Life Adult's Chewable Wafers	US	1.5	dosage derived
Nature's Way Completia Energy	CA	1.5	
New Roots Herbal Phytomax	CA	1.5	
Neways ProZinger	US	1.5	
NewChapter Every Man	CA	1.5	
NewChapter Organics Every Man	US	1.5	
NewChapter Organics Every Man II	US	1.5	
NewChapter Organics Every Man II	CA	1.5	
North American Pharmacal Polyvite B & Phytocal B	US	1.5	dosage derived
North American Pharmacal Polyvite O & Phytocal O	US	1.5	dosage derived
Now Special One	US	1.5	
Nu-Life Gourmet Chewables Multiple	CA	1.5	
Nutra Perfect VitaPerfect	US	1.5	
NutriCology Multi-Vi-Min	US	1.5	
Nutrina Vitamax Tablets	US	1.5	dosage derived
Nutrition Dynamics Ultra Vitaplex	US	1.5	
Nutrition House Multi-Vitamin Extra	CA	1.5	
Nutri-West Multibalance for Men	US	1.5	
Nutri-West Multibalance for Women	US	1.5	
Omnitrition Shield Antioxidant	US	1.5	
Organika One Daily	CA	1.5	
Pataki USA 2001 Formula	US	1.5	dosage derived; additional nutrient amounts not specified
PharmAssure Men's Biomultiple	US	1.5	
PharmAssure Women's Biomultiple	US	1.5	
Professional Health Products Multidyn	CA	1.5	
Pure Encapsulations Nutrient 280	US	1.5	
Puritan's Pride Potent 75 Super VM	US	1.5	
Puritan's Pride Women's Exclusive Formula	US	1.5	
Quest Premium Multi-One	CA	1.5	
Quest Super Once A Day	CA	1.5	
Rainbow Light Just Once Men's Energy	US	1.5	
Rainbow Light Just Once Men's One	US	1.5	
Rainbow Light Just Once Women's One	US	1.5	
Rainbow Light Master Nutrient System Plus	US	1.5	
RBC Life Sciences 24Seven Life Essentials	CA/US	1.5	additional nutrient amounts not specified
Resource Optisource	US	1.5	
Resurgex	US	1.5	
Resurgex Plus	US	1.5	
R-Garden Vitamin Mineral Formula	US	1.5	
Ripple Creek Mega-One 75	US	1.5	
Rite Aid Whole Source Complete Formula for Women	US	1.5	
Safeway Select Super Men's Multivitamin	US	1.5	
Sangster's Multi Vitamin	US	1.5	
Sangster's Multi Vitamin	CA	1.5	
Shaklee Vita-Lea Gold with Vitamin K	US	1.5	
Shaklee Vita-Lea Gold without Vitamin K	US	1.5	
SISU Mini Vits	CA	1.5	
SISU Only One	CA	1.5	
SISU Only One Iron Free	CA	1.5	
Solaray Once Daily High Energy	US	1.5	
Solaray Once Daily High Energy Iron Free	US	1.5	
Solaray Once Daily High Energy Softgel	CA	1.5	
Solgar Naturvite	US	1.5	dosage derived
Solgar Vegetarian Multiple	US	1.5	
Sonergy Mega Plan	US	1.5	
Swanson Active One	US	1.5	
Swiss Super Adult	CA	1.5	
Swiss Super Swiss One "50"	CA	1.5	
The Green Turtle Bay Co. PowerVites	US	1.5	
Thompson Super Maxicaps	US	1.5	
Trace Minerals Electro-Vita-Min	US	1.5	
Trace Minerals Electro-Vita-Min (New & Improved)	US	1.5	
TRC Nutritional Laboratories Male Basic Multiple	US	1.5	
TRC Nutritional Laboratories Vast Vitality	US	1.5	
TriVita Daily Men	US	1.5	additional nutrient amounts not specified
TriVita Daily Women	US	1.5	additional nutrient amounts not specified
Tropical Oasis Tropical Plus	US	1.5	dosage derived
Twinlab Daily One Caps with Iron	US	1.5	
Twinlab Daily One Caps without Iron	US	1.5	
ViSalus Nutri-One	US	1.5	
Vitality Products Two-A-Day	US	1.5	
Vitamin Power SuperFem Multiple	US	1.5	
Vitamin Shoppe One Daily	US	1.5	
Vitasmart Men's Premium Multivitamin	US	1.5	
Vitasmart Select Women's Multi	US	1.5	
Watkins Super Multi	CA	1.5	
Watkins Superfood Multiple	US	1.5	

Wild Oats Food Origins Men's Prime Plus Multi-Vitamin	US	1.5	dosage derived
Wild Oats Food Origins Women's Prime Plus Multi-Vitamin	US	1.5	dosage derived
Ziquin Mind & Body Tonic	US	1.5	additional nutrient amounts not specified
21st Century One Daily Adults 50+	US	1.0	
21st Century One Daily CarbHealth	US	1.0	
Action Labs Action-Tabs Made for Men	US	1.0	
Adrien Gagnon Feminex Multi	CA	1.0	
Adrien Gagnon Sélect Multi	CA	1.0	
Advanced Nutritional Innovations (ANI) CORALadvantage	US	1.0	
alpha betic Once-A-Day Multi-Vitamin	US	1.0	
Apex Fitness FIT 50 Plus	US	1.0	
Apex Fitness FIT Performance	US	1.0	
Arbonne Complete Essentials for Women I	US	1.0	
Arbonne Complete Essentials for Women II	US	1.0	
Biotics Research Corporation Bio-Multi Plus	US	1.0	
Bronson Laboratories The Bronson Formula	US	1.0	
Bronson Laboratories Therapeutic Vitamin & Mineral Formula - without iron	US	1.0	
Canadian Sun Seniors Only	CA	1.0	
Centrum Advantage	CA	1.0	
Colorado Nutrition Ultimate One	US	1.0	
Comprehensive Formula Women's	US	1.0	2003 data
Cooper Complete Basic One Iron Free	US	1.0	
Cooper Complete Basic One with Iron	US	1.0	
Country Life Adult Multi	US	1.0	
CVS Pharmacy Today's Life Men's	US	1.0	
CVS Pharmacy Weight Sharp	US	1.0	
dc (Dee Cee Laboratories) Formula 249 Iron Free	US	1.0	
Douglas Laboratories Geri-Vite 25	US	1.0	
Douglas Laboratories Ultra Vite 75 II	US	1.0	
Dr. Fuhrman's Gentle Care Formula	US	1.0	dosage derived
Dr. Rath's Vitacor Plus	US	1.0	
Equaline One Daily Dieter's Support Formula	US	1.0	
Essence-of-Life Only One Cell-Ready Nutrition	US	1.0	additional nutrient amounts not specified
First Organics Daily Multiple	US	1.0	
Freeda Quintabs-M	US	1.0	
GNC Multi Preventron	US	1.0	
GNC Multi Solotron	US	1.0	
GNC Multi Solotron	CA	1.0	
GNC Multi Solotron Platinum	US	1.0	
GNC Platinum Years	CA	1.0	
GNLD International Formula IV	US	1.0	
GNLD International Vegetarian Multi	US	1.0	
Heaven Sent Naturals Balanced Essentials	US	1.0	
Herbalife ShapeWorks Garden 7	US	1.0	
Herbalife Shapeworks Multivitamin Complex (Formula 2)	US	1.0	additional nutrient amounts not specified
Highland Laboratories Nature's Daily	US	1.0	
Hillestad Pharmaceuticals Vitamin/Mineral Complex Unit A	US	1.0	dosage derived
Innate Response Formulas Food Multi II	US	1.0	
Innate Response Formulas Men's Multi	US	1.0	
Innate Response Formulas Women's Multi	US	1.0	
Isotonix MultiTech	US	1.0	dosage derived
Jamieson Regular Vita-Vim	CA	1.0	
Jamieson Vita-Vim Adult 50+	CA	1.0	
Kirkman Nu-Thera without Vitamins A & D	US	1.0	
Kirkman Super Nu-Thera	US	1.0	
LA Weight Loss Centers Vita-Max	CA	1.0	dosage derived
Life Daily-One Weight Sense	CA	1.0	
LifeScript Daily Essentials, plus Calcium Complete	US	1.0	
Lifestyles Lifecycles for Mature Men	CA/US	1.0	2003 data
Lifestyles Lifecycles for Mature Women	CA/US	1.0	2003 data
Lifestyles Lifecycles for Men	CA/US	1.0	2003 data
Lifestyles Lifecycles for Women	CA/US	1.0	2003 data
LifeTime Adult Vit-Mins	US	1.0	
LifeTime Nutrilife Soft Gels	CA	1.0	
LiquiMax Complete Nutrition	US	1.0	additional nutrient amounts not specified
London Drugs Multi Premium	CA	1.0	
London Drugs Multi Silver	CA	1.0	
London Drugs One Adults 50+	CA	1.0	
Longs One Daily Dieter's Support Formula	US	1.0	
Longs Women's Multivitamin/Multimineral/Herbs	US	1.0	
Mason Super Multiple	US	1.0	
Maxion Nutrition Max Multi Liquid Vitamin	CA/US	1.0	
MD Healthline Ad-ditions	US	1.0	
MegaFood Maximum Man One Daily	US	1.0	
MegaFood Maximum Woman One Daily	US	1.0	
MegaFood Women's DailyFoods	US	1.0	
Melaleuca Vitality for Men	US	1.0	dosage derived; additional nutrient amounts not specified
Melaleuca Vitality for Women	US	1.0	dosage derived; additional nutrient amounts not specified
Melaleuca Vitality Pack for Men	US	1.0	dosage derived; additional nutrient amounts not specified
Melaleuca Vitality Pack for Women	US	1.0	dosage derived; additional nutrient amounts not specified
Moducare Multi-mune	US	1.0	

Molecular Biologics Bio-Naturalvite	US	1.0	dosage derived
Molecular Biologics Fruit Colloidal Mineral & Vitamin Elixir	US	1.0	
Natrol My Favorite Multiple Energizer	US	1.0	
Natura Select Adult Food-Based Multivitamin	CA/US	1.0	dosage derived
Nature Made Essential Mega	US	1.0	
Nature Made Multi Max	US	1.0	
Nature's Blend Mega Multivitamin with Minerals	US	1.0	
Nature's Harmony Adult Chewable	CA	1.0	
Nature's Harmony Superior One Per Day Iron Free	CA	1.0	
Nature's Life E-Z Vite Multiple	US	1.0	dosage derived; additional nutrient amounts not specified
Nature's Plus Adult's Chewable	US	1.0	
Nature's Plus Ultra Juice	US	1.0	
Nature's Way Completia Energy Plus Iron	CA	1.0	
New Vision JuicePower Fruit/Vegetable Caps	US	1.0	
NewChapter Everyone's Multiple	CA	1.0	dosage derived
NewChapter Only One	CA	1.0	
NewChapter Organics Every Man's One Daily	CA	1.0	
NewChapter Organics Every Woman	US	1.0	
NewChapter Organics Every Woman II	US	1.0	
NewChapter Organics Every Woman's One Daily	US	1.0	
NewChapter Organics Every Woman's One Daily	CA	1.0	
NewChapter Organics Only One	US	1.0	
Now Daily Vits	US	1.0	
nutraMetrix MultiVitamins & MultiMinerals with Iron	US	1.0	
nutraMetrix MultiVitamins & MultiMinerals without Iron	US	1.0	
Nutri-West Multi Complex	US	1.0	
One A Day Weight Smart	US	1.0	
One A Day Weight Smart	CA	1.0	
Pataki USA 2101 Formula	US	1.0	dosage derived; additional nutrient amounts not specified
Pharmanex Life Essentials	US	1.0	
Pharmanex Life Essentials	CA	1.0	
Platinum EasyMulti	CA	1.0	
Puritan's Pride Puritron	US	1.0	
Puritan's Pride Ultra Vita-Min	US	1.0	
Puritan's Pride Ultra Vita-Min Iron Free	US	1.0	
Purity Products Fizz-5 Formula	US	1.0	
Quest Adults	CA	1.0	
Quest Extra Once a Day	CA	1.0	
Quest Premium Multi-Cap	CA	1.0	
Rainbow Light Just Once	US	1.0	
Rainbow Light Just Once Iron-Free	US	1.0	
Reliv Classic	US	1.0	
Reliv Classic	CA	1.0	
Reliv Now	US	1.0	
Reliv Now	CA	1.0	additional nutrient amounts not specified
Resurgex Select	US	1.0	dosage derived
Revival Firm Foundation	US	1.0	
Rexall One Weigh	CA	1.0	
Rite Aid Whole Source Mature Adult	US	1.0	
Rite Aid Whole Source Men	US	1.0	
Rite Aid Whole Source Women	US	1.0	
Safeway Select One Tablet Daily Dieter's Support Formula	US	1.0	
Safeway Select Weight-Conscious	CA	1.0	
Sangster's Daily Choice	CA/US	1.0	
Schiff Prime Years	US	1.0	
Shaklee Advanced Formula Vita-Lea	CA	1.0	
Shaklee Vita-Lea with Iron	US	1.0	
Shaklee Vita-Lea without Iron	US	1.0	
SISU Multi-Vi-Min	CA	1.0	
Solaray Once Daily Iron Free	US	1.0	
Solgar Solovite Iron Free	US	1.0	
Sundown Complete Ultra	US	1.0	
Swanson Century Formula without Iron	US	1.0	
Swiss Mega Swiss One "25"	CA	1.0	
Symmetry Ultra Vitality	US	1.0	additional nutrient amounts not specified
Target Weight Sense	US	1.0	
The Green Turtle Bay Vitamin Co. Maple Melts	US	1.0	
Trace Minerals Maxi Multi	US	1.0	
TRC Nutritional Laboratories Female Basic Multiple	US	1.0	
Trophic Multiple Vitamins & Minerals	CA	1.0	
Truly Weight One	CA	1.0	
Twinlab Food-Based Ultra Daily	US	1.0	additional nutrient amounts not specified
Ultima For Men	US	1.0	
Unicity LifeHealth on the go	US	1.0	dosage derived
Vitamin Power Mega Multiple 85	US	1.0	dosage derived
Vitamin Power Super-Vite	US	1.0	
Vitamin Power Vita-Max	US	1.0	dosage derived
Vitamin World Ultra Vita-Min Iron Free	US	1.0	
Vitaminerals Combadult	US	1.0	
Vitaminerals Combadult M	US	1.0	
Vitasmart Daily Diet Support	US	1.0	

Vitosophy	US	1.0	additional nutrient amounts not specified
VIVA Life Science VIVA for Life	US	1.0	
Walgreens UltraChoice Mature	US	1.0	dosage derived
Western Family Daily Diet Support	US	1.0	
Western Family Multra 50+	CA	1.0	
Wheaties Multivitamin	US	1.0	dosage derived
Xymogen InsuLean Rice	US	1.0	dosage derived
21st Century One Daily Active	US	0.5	
Apex Fitness FIT Vegan/High Carb	US	0.5	
Bio-Actif Phytobec	CA	0.5	
Botanic Choice High Potency Vitamin & Mineral	US	0.5	
Bronson Laboratories Therapeutic Vitamin & Mineral Formula	US	0.5	
Burns Drugs Multi-Max	US	0.5	
Centrum Carb Assist	US	0.5	
Centrum Performance	US	0.5	
Centrum Protegra	CA	0.5	
Centrum Select	CA	0.5	
Centrum Silver	US	0.5	
Centrum Silver Chewables	US	0.5	
Club Vitamin Best	CA	0.5	dosage derived
CVS Pharmacy Daily Multiple 50 Plus	US	0.5	
CVS Pharmacy Daily Multiple for Men	US	0.5	
CVS Pharmacy Spectravite Performance	US	0.5	
CVS Pharmacy Spectravite Senior	US	0.5	
CVS Pharmacy Spectravite Senior Chewables	US	0.5	
CVS Pharmacy Thera Plus	US	0.5	
CVS Pharmacy Today's Life 50+	US	0.5	
CVS Pharmacy Today's Life Active+	US	0.5	
dc (Dee Cee Laboratories) 6BG+	US	0.5	
dc (Dee Cee Laboratories) Formula 19	US	0.5	
dc (Dee Cee Laboratories) Formula 360	US	0.5	
dc (Dee Cee Laboratories) Formula 814	US	0.5	
dc (Dee Cee Laboratories) Vidoplex-ML	US	0.5	
Drinkables Multi Vitamins for Seniors	US	0.5	
Endurance Products Endur-VM	US	0.5	
Endurance Products Endur-VM without Iron	US	0.5	
Equaline Central-Vite Carb Dieter Formula	US	0.5	
Equaline Central-Vite Performance	US	0.5	
Equaline Central-Vite Select	US	0.5	
Equaline One Daily 50 Plus	US	0.5	
Equaline One Daily Active	US	0.5	
Equaline One Daily Men's Health Formula	US	0.5	
Equate Century Premium	CA	0.5	
Equate Century Silver	CA	0.5	
Equate Century Silver Chewable	CA	0.5	
Equate Complete Mature	US	0.5	
Equate One Daily Men's	CA	0.5	
Equate One Daily Men's	US	0.5	
Equate One Tablet Daily	CA	0.5	
Equate One Tablet Daily Adults 50+	CA	0.5	
Exact Essentra Elite	CA	0.5	
Exact Essentra Platinum	CA	0.5	
Exact Vital One Men's Formula	CA	0.5	
Freeda MonoCaps	US	0.5	dosage derived
GNC Chewable Solotron	US	0.5	
Goldshield Centural Silver	US	0.5	
Good Neighbor Pharmacy Century Advantage	US	0.5	
Good Neighbor Pharmacy Century Senior	US	0.5	
Good Neighbor Pharmacy Maximum One Daily	US	0.5	
Good Neighbor Pharmacy One Daily Carb-Vantage	US	0.5	
Good Neighbor Pharmacy Therapeutic-M Complete	US	0.5	
H-E-B Complete Advantage	US	0.5	
H-E-B Complete Senior	US	0.5	
H-E-B Multiple Vitamins Men's	US	0.5	
H-E-B Multiple Vitamins 50 Plus	US	0.5	
H-E-B Therapeutic-M	US	0.5	
Henry's Farmer's Market Basic Multi	US	0.5	
Henry's Farmer's Market Iron Free Basic Multi	US	0.5	
Immunotec Research Vitamin/Mineral Supplement	CA	0.5	dosage derived
Immuvit Original Swiss Formula	US	0.5	
Innate Response Formulas BioMax Food Multi III	US	0.5	
Innate Response Formulas Men's One Daily	US	0.5	
Innate Response Formulas One Daily I	US	0.5	
Innate Response Formulas One Daily II	US	0.5	
Innate Response Formulas Women's One Daily	US	0.5	
Isotonix MultiTech with Iron	US	0.5	dosage derived
Jamieson Stamina	CA	0.5	
Jamieson Vita-Vim Adult Chewable	CA	0.5	
Kirkland Daily Multi	US	0.5	
Kirkland Premium Performance Multivitamin	US	0.5	
Kirkman EveryDay	US	0.5	

Product	Region	Rating	Notes
Klamath Blue Green Algae	US	0.5	
Klamath Power 3	US	0.5	
Kroger Fortify	US	0.5	
Kroger One Daily Men's Health Formula	US	0.5	
Kroger Thera Plus	US	0.5	
Leader Century Senior	US	0.5	
Leader Men's One Daily	US	0.5	
Life Chewable Tablets	CA	0.5	
Life Daily-One 50+	CA	0.5	
Life Daily-One Carb Sense	CA	0.5	
Life Daily-One Men's Formula	CA	0.5	
Life Optimum	CA	0.5	
Life Optimum 50+	CA	0.5	
Life Spectrum Gold	CA	0.5	
Life Spectrum Performa	CA	0.5	
Life-Line Daily Plus 50	US	0.5	
Liquid Health Daily Multiple	US	0.5	
London Drugs Multi Plus	CA	0.5	
London Drugs Multi Vitamin & Minerals	CA	0.5	
London Drugs One Tablet Daily Adults	CA	0.5	
Longs Central Vite Carb Dieter Formula	US	0.5	
Longs Central Vite Performance	US	0.5	
Longs Central Vite Select	US	0.5	
Longs One Daily Men's Health Formula	US	0.5	
Mason VitaTrum Endurance	US	0.5	
Mason Vitrum Senior	US	0.5	
MegaFood Iron Free One Daily	US	0.5	
MegaFood Medi-Safe DailyFoods	US	0.5	
MegaFood Men's DailyFoods	US	0.5	
MegaFood One Daily DailyFoods	US	0.5	
Member's Mark Mature Multi	US	0.5	
Molecular Biologics Liqui-Vimin	US	0.5	
Natura Select Basic Adult Multi	CA/US	0.5	dosage derived
Naturally Preferred One Daily Multi	US	0.5	
Nature Made Adult Multivitamin Chewable	US	0.5	
Nature Made Essential 50+	US	0.5	
Nature Made Essential Man	US	0.5	
Nature Made Essential Woman	US	0.5	
Nature Made Multi 50+	US	0.5	
Nature Made Multi For Her 50+	US	0.5	
Nature Made Multi For Him	US	0.5	
Nature Made Multi For Him 50+	US	0.5	
Nature's Bounty Weight Trim	US	0.5	
NewChapter Organics Tiny Tabs Multi	US	0.5	
NewChapter Tiny Tabs Multiple	CA	0.5	
NHK Laboratories Multi-Vitamin and Mineral	US	0.5	dosage derived
NHK Laboratories Multi-Vitamin and Mineral with Lutein	US	0.5	dosage derived
NHK Laboratories Senior Multi-Vitamin and Mineral	US	0.5	dosage derived
NutriCare Prime Greens	US	0.5	additional nutrient amounts not specified
NutriCare Prime Greens Capsules	US	0.5	additional nutrient amounts not specified
Nutrilite Daily	US	0.5	
Nutri-West Total Male	US	0.5	
Olay Complete 50+ Multivitamin	US	0.5	
Olay Complete Multivitamin	US	0.5	
Olay Complete Woman's Multivitamin	US	0.5	
Olay Complete Woman's Multivitamin 50+	US	0.5	
Omnilife Magnus	US	0.5	
Omnitrition Omni IV	US	0.5	additional nutrient amounts not specified
One A Day 50 Plus	US	0.5	
One A Day Active	US	0.5	
One A Day Adults 50+	CA	0.5	
One A Day CarbSmart	US	0.5	
One A Day Cholesterol Plus	US	0.5	
One A Day Men's	CA	0.5	
One A Day Men's Health Formula	US	0.5	
OneSource 50 Plus	US	0.5	
OneSource Advanced Formula	US	0.5	
OneSource Micro	US	0.5	
OneSource Pure Performance	US	0.5	
Performance Labs Vitalert	US	0.5	
Personnelle Natura Senior	CA	0.5	
Personnelle Senior	CA	0.5	
Personnelle Superia	CA	0.5	
Pharmaton Ginsana Gold Formula	US	0.5	
Phytobec	CA	0.5	
Plante Gummi 50+	CA/US	0.5	
Platinum MegaVita Minerals with Hempseed Oil	CA	0.5	
Rexall Complete for Adults 50+	CA	0.5	
Rexall One Tablet Daily Adults 50+	CA	0.5	
Rite Aid Central-Vite Select	US	0.5	
Rite Aid One Daily Low Carb Support	US	0.5	

Rite Aid One Daily Men's Multi	US	0.5	
Rite Aid Trim Support	US	0.5	
Rite Aid Whole Source	US	0.5	
Safeway Select Central-Vite Performance	US	0.5	
Safeway Select Central-Vite Senior Formula	US	0.5	
Safeway Select Formula Forte Senior	CA	0.5	
Safeway Select Formule pour 50+	CA	0.5	
Safeway Select Formule pour hommes	CA	0.5	
Safeway Select One Tablet Daily Men's Health	US	0.5	
Sangster's Choice Apex	CA	0.5	
Sangster's Choice Apex	US	0.5	dosage derived
Schiff Vegetarian Multiple	US	0.5	
Spring Valley Naturally Complete Multivitamin	US	0.5	
Spring Valley Sentury-Vite	US	0.5	
Standard Process Immunoplex	US	0.5	
Sundown Complete 50+	US	0.5	
Sundown Complete Daily	US	0.5	
Sundown Complete Multi 50+	US	0.5	
Sundown Complete Women's	US	0.5	
Sunmark Complete Senior	US	0.5	
Sunmark Therapeutic-M	US	0.5	
Swiss Swiss One	CA	0.5	
Synergy Multiple Vitamin/Mineral	US	0.5	
Target Men's Daily Multivitamin	US	0.5	
Target Multivitamin/Multimineral for Adults 50+	US	0.5	
Theragran-M Advanced Formula	US	0.5	
Theragran-M Premier	US	0.5	
Theragran-M Premier 50 Plus	US	0.5	
Thompson Multi Formula for Women	US	0.5	
Thompson Multi-Vitamins	US	0.5	
Thompson Nuplex	US	0.5	
Top Care Complete Advantage	US	0.5	dosage derived
Top Care Complete Senior	US	0.5	
Top Care One Daily 50+	US	0.5	
Top Care One Daily Men's	US	0.5	
Total Multivitamin	US	0.5	
TotalOne SuperMulti	US	0.5	
Trace Minerals ImmunoMax	US	0.5	
Tropical Oasis Multiple Vitamin/Mineral	US	0.5	
Truly Century Premium	CA	0.5	
Truly Century Silver	CA	0.5	
Ultima For Women	US	0.5	
Vita-Complete AA (Anti-Aging)	CA/US	0.5	
Vitalert	US	0.5	
Vitamin World Ultra Vita-Min	US	0.5	
Vitaplen Complete	US	0.5	additional nutrient amounts not specified
Vitasmart Carb-Vantage	US	0.5	
Vitasmart Century Advantage	US	0.5	
Vitasmart Complete Senior	US	0.5	
Vitasmart Men's Health Formula	US	0.5	
Vitasmart Select Super Multi 50+	US	0.5	
Walgreens A thru Z Advantage	US	0.5	
Walgreens A thru Z Select	US	0.5	
Walgreens One Daily 50 Plus	US	0.5	
Walgreens One Daily Men's	US	0.5	
Walgreens One Daily Women's 50 Plus	US	0.5	
Walgreens Super Aytinal for Adults 50 Plus	US	0.5	
Walgreens Therapeutic M	US	0.5	
Walgreens UltraChoice Adult	US	0.5	
Wampole Adult Chewable	CA	0.5	
Wampole HSN Formula Women's	CA	0.5	
Westcoast Naturals Multi-Plus	CA	0.5	
Western Family Active Women 50+	US	0.5	
Western Family Complete Premium	US	0.5	
Western Family Complete Senior Formula	US	0.5	
Western Family Multi Vitamins with Minerals	CA	0.5	
Western Family Multra	CA	0.5	
Western Family Multra with Iron	CA	0.5	additional nutrient amounts not specified
Western Family Therapeutic M	US	0.5	
Wild Oats Basic Multi	US	0.5	
Wild Oats Food Origins Multi-Vitamin One	US	0.5	
Win Fuel Men's formula	US	0.5	
21st Century One Daily Women's	US	-	
Burns Drugs Super-T	US	-	
Cell Tech International Alpha Sun	US	-	
Cell Tech International Omega Sun	US	-	
Centrum	US	-	
Centrum	CA	-	
Centrum Forte	CA	-	
Centrum Chewables	US	-	
Centrum Liquid	US	-	

Centrum Performance	CA	-	
Curves Protein Drink	US	-	new data unavailable, 2004 data
CVS Pharmacy Daily Multiple for Women	US	-	
CVS Pharmacy Multivitamin & Minerals	US	-	
CVS Pharmacy Spectravite	US	-	
dc (Dee Cee Laboratories) Formula 784	US	-	
Douglas Laboratories Multivite	US	-	
Equaline Central-Vite	US	-	
Equaline One Daily Maximum	US	-	
Equaline One Daily Women's	US	-	
Equate Century Complete	CA	-	
Equate Century Perform	CA	-	
Equate Century Plus	CA	-	
Equate Complete	US	-	
Equate One Daily Women's	US	-	
Equate One Tablet Daily Adults	CA	-	
Equate One Tablet Daily Women's	CA	-	
Exact Essentra Balance	CA	-	
Exact Essentra Forte	CA	-	
Exact for Adults over 50	CA	-	
Exact Vital-Fem 1	CA	-	
Geritol Complete	US	-	
Good Neighbor Pharmacy Century	US	-	
Good Neighbor Pharmacy Women's One Daily	US	-	
H-E-B Complete	US	-	
H-E-B Multiple Vitamins Maximum	US	-	
Kirkland Formula Forte	CA	-	
Kroger Complete	US	-	dosage derived
Kroger One Daily Maximum	US	-	
Kroger One Daily Women's Health	US	-	
Leader Century	US	-	
Leader Women's One Daily	US	-	
Life Adult	CA	-	
Life Daily-One Adult	CA	-	
Life Daily-One for Women	CA	-	
Life For People over 50	CA	-	
Life Spectrum	CA	-	
London Drugs Multi Complete	CA	-	
London Drugs Women's Formula	CA	-	
Longs Advanced Formula Central Vite	US	-	
Longs One Daily Women's	US	-	
Longs Thera Plus	US	-	
Longs Wellness High Potency Multi Vitamin & Mineral	US	-	
Mason Daily Multiple Vitamins with Minerals	US	-	
Mason VitaTrum Complete	US	-	
MD Healthline Advanced Green Multi Formula	US	-	additional nutrient amounts not specified
MegaFood Men's One Daily DailyFoods	US	-	
MegaFood Women's One Daily DailyFoods	US	-	
Member's Mark Complete Multi	US	-	
Myadec Professional Formula	US	-	
Nature Made Essential Balance	US	-	
Nature Made Essential Daily	US	-	
Nature Made Multi Complete	US	-	
Nature Made Multi Daily	US	-	
Nature Made Multi For Her	US	-	
Nature's Blend Multi-Vitamin with Minerals	US	-	
Nature's Blend Theratrum Complete	US	-	
Nature's Bounty Multi-Day Womens	US	-	
Neways Maximol Solutions	US	-	
Nutrition Dynamics Multi-vitasorb	US	-	
Nutrition Now Adult Formula	US	-	
Nutri-West Total Female	US	-	
One A Day Adults	CA	-	
One A Day Maximum	US	-	
One A Day Women's	US	-	
One A Day Women's	CA	-	
Origin Complete Multi-Vitamin & Mineral	US	-	
Personnelle Complete	CA	-	
Personnelle Forte	CA	-	
Pro Image Pro Vitamin Complete	US	-	dosage derived; additional ingredient amounts not specified
Puritan's Pride Multi-Day Plus Minerals	US	-	
Puritan's Pride Theravim-M	US	-	
Rexall Complete	CA	-	
Rexall Complete Forte	CA	-	
Rexall Multiple Vitamins & Minerals	CA	-	
Rexall Multivitamin + Multimineral Forte	CA	-	additional nutrient amounts not specified
Rexall One Tablet Daily Adult	CA	-	
Rexall One Tablet Daily Women's	CA	-	
Rite Aid Central-Vite	US	-	
Rite Aid High Potency Multi	US	-	
Rite Aid One Daily	US	-	

Rite Aid One Daily Women's	US	-	
Rite Aid Therapeutic M	US	-	
Safeway Select Central-Vite	US	-	
Safeway Select Formula Forte	CA	-	
Safeway Select Formule Régulière	CA	-	
Safeway Select Maximum One Tablet Daily	US	-	
Safeway Select Multivitamin & Mineral	US	-	
Safeway Select One Tablet Daily Women's	US	-	
Safeway Select Women's Formula	CA	-	
Sav-on Osco One Daily Maximum	US	-	
Sonergy One Daily Multiple with Iron	US	-	
Standard Process Catalyn	US	-	
Sundown SunVite	US	-	
Sunmark Complete Advanced	US	-	
SunMark Multiple Vitamins Women's	US	-	
Target Adult Multivitamin/Multimineral	US	-	
Target Multivitamin/Multimineral	US	-	
Target Women's Daily Multivitamin	US	-	
Top Care Complete	US	-	
Top Care Multi for Women	US	-	
Top Care One Daily Dieter's Support Formula	US	-	
Top Care One Daily Maximum	US	-	
Top Care One Daily Women's	US	-	
Truly Century Plus	CA	-	
Unicap M Dietary Supplement	US	-	
Unicap Sr. Dietary Supplement	US	-	
Unicity Bios Life 2 Original	US	-	
Viactiv Multi-Vitamin	US	-	dosage derived
Vicon-C High Potency Multivitamin/Mineral	US	-	
Vita-Complete Vita-Complete 29	CA/US	-	dosage derived
Vitamin World ABC Plus	US	-	
Vitamin World Theravim-M	US	-	
Vitasmart Advanced Formula Complete	US	-	
Vitasmart Hi Potency Complete	US	-	
Vitasmart Maximum	US	-	
Vitasmart Women's	US	-	
Walgreens A thru Z	US	-	
Walgreens One Daily Women's	US	-	
Walgreens Super Aytinal for Active Adults	US	-	
Western Family Complete Advanced	US	-	
Western Family One Daily Maximum	US	-	
Western Family One Daily Women's	US	-	
Wild Oats Multi-Vitamin One	US	-	
Win Fuel Women's formula	US	-	

Appendix C: Combination Products Alphabetically

Manufacturer & Product Name	Country	# of Stars	Dosages and Considerations
AmeriSciences Men's Master Multi	US	2.5	additional nutrient amounts not specified
AmeriSciences Women's Master Multi	US	2.5	additional nutrient amounts not specified
Arbonne International Daily Power Packs for Men	US	2.5	additional nutrient amounts not specified
Arbonne International Daily Power Packs for Women	US	2.5	additional nutrient amounts not specified
BioX Multi Vitamin Pack	CA	4.0	dosage derived
Bronson Laboratories Daily Nutrional Packets	US	1.5	
Bronson Laboratories Nutritional Packets for Active Men	US	1.5	
Bronson Laboratories Nutritional Packets for Active Women	US	1.5	
Club Vitamin Mega Vitamin Kit	CA	1.5	dosage derived
Colgan Institute Basic Body Armor	US	2.5	
Colgan Institute Men's Active Pak	US	4.5	
Colgan Institute Men's First Defense Pak	US	3.0	
Colgan Institute Men's Pak	US	5.0	
Colgan Institute Men's+ 50 Pak	US	5.0	
Colgan Institute Sports Pak	US	5.0	
Colgan Institute Women's 50+ Pak	US	5.0	
Colgan Institute Women's Active Pak	US	5.0	
Colgan Institute Women's First Defense	US	3.0	
Colgan Institute Women's Pak	US	5.0	
CVC 4 Health Unit Pac Original	US	1.5	dosage derived
CVC 4 Health Unit Pac Royal	US	2.0	dosage derived
CVC 4 Health Unit Pac Supreme	US	2.0	dosage derived
CVC 4 Health Unit Pac Ultimate	US	3.0	dosage derived
dc (Dee Cee Laboratories) Mega Vita-Min	US	3.0	
Douglas Laboratories Basic Antiox	US	4.0	
Douglas Laboratories Dad's Pack	US	4.5	
Douglas Laboratories Daily Core Essentials	CA	5.0	**NutriSearch GOLD Medal of Achievement Recipient**
Douglas Laboratories Essential-4 Nutrition Pack	US	4.0	
Douglas Laboratories Longevity Support Pack	US	5.0	**NutriSearch GOLD Medal of Achievement Recipient**
Douglas Laboratories Met-A-Syn X-Pack	US	2.5	
Douglas Laboratories Nutri-Pak for Men	US	4.0	
Douglas Laboratories Nutri-Pak for Women	US	4.0	
Douglas Laboratories OC Pack	US	4.0	
Douglas Laboratories Ultra Preventive V plus Chel-Supplement Pack	US	3.0	
Dr. Lark Daily Answer MultiNutrient for Women	US	3.5	dosage derived
Dr. Lark Daily Balance Women's Multinutrient	US	3.5	dosage derived
Enerex Optimal Health Pack	CA	2.0	
Enzymatic Therapy Energy Revitalization System (Citrus Delight)	US	3.5	
epic4health Physician's Rx Complete Formula	US	3.0	
Equaline Daily Vitamin Packets	US	2.0	
ForMor International Core Nutrition	US	3.5	
FreeLife Basic Mindell Plus	US	3.0	additional nutrient amounts not specified
Global Health Trax Basic Five	US	2.0	additional nutrient amounts not specified
GNC Maximum Nutrition VitaPak	US	2.0	
GNC Mega Men Performance and Vitality Program	US	2.0	dosage derived; additional nutrients amounts not specified
GNC Women's Ultra Mega Wellness Program	US	2.0	dosage derived; additional nutrients amounts not specified
GNLD International Daily Vitality Pack Active 40+	US	2.5	
GNLD International Daily Vitality Pack Sports 30	US	2.5	
GNLD International Daily Vitality Pack Stress 30	US	2.5	
Great American Products Master Health Pack	US	3.5	
Great Earth Nutritional Starter Pack (Extra Strength)	US	3.0	additional nutrient amounts not specified
Great Earth Nutritional Starter Pack (Regular Strength)	US	2.0	additional nutrient amounts not specified
Great Earth Nutritional Starter Pack (Ultra Strength)	US	3.5	additional nutrient amounts not specified
Guthy-Renker Nutrition GRN Vitapower	US	1.0	
Hannen Health Daily Essentials	US	1.5	
HerbaSway Laboratories Daily Maintenance Group	US	1.5	
Highland Laboratories Men's Sports Pak	US	3.5	
Highland Laboratories Super Athlete Packs	US	3.0	
Highland Laboratories Women's Sports Pak	US	3.5	
InVite Multi-Vitamin	US	3.0	
Jarrow Formulas All Capsule Health Pak	US	4.0	
Jarrow Formulas Jarrow Pak Plus	US	3.5	
Jean Carper's Stop Aging Now! Anti-Aging Power-Pak	US	4.5	
Julian Whitaker, M.D. Forward Plus Daily Regimen	CA	4.0	additional nutrient amounts not specified
Julian Whitaker, M.D. Forward Plus Daily Regimen	US	4.5	dosage derived; additional nutrients amounts not specified
Kirkland Daily Multivitamin Pack	US	1.5	
Life-Line Men's Life-Pack	US	1.5	dosage derived
Life-Line Total Health Formula	US	3.5	
Life-Line Women's Life-Pack	US	1.0	
Lorna Vanderhaeghe FemmEssentials	CA/US	4.0	
Melaleuca Daily for Life Total Nutrition for Men	US	2.0	additional nutrient amounts not specified
Melaleuca Daily for Life Total Nutrition for Women	US	2.0	additional nutrient amounts not specified
Melaleuca Vitality Pack with Cellwise and ProVexCV for Men	US	2.0	additional nutrient amounts not specified
Melaleuca Vitality Pack with Cellwise and ProVexCV for Women	US	1.5	additional nutrient amounts not specified
Member's Mark Daily Vitamin Pack	US	1.5	
Metagenics Wellness Essentials	US	4.0	

Product	Region	Rating	Notes
Metagenics Wellness Essentials for Women	US	3.5	
Mountain Home Daily Advantage	US	4.5	
Nature Made Diabetes Health Pack	US	1.5	
Nature Made Maximin Pack	US	2.0	
Nature Made Men's Pack	US	1.0	
Nature Made Stress Pack	US	1.5	dosage derived
Nature Made Women's Pack	US	1.0	
Nature's Best Perfect Fitness Pak	US	1.5	
Nature's Best Perfect Hardcore Pak	US	2.5	
Nature's Best Perfect Super Multi Power Pak	US	2.5	
Nature's Bounty Prescriptive Formulas Men's	US	1.0	
Nature's Bounty Prescriptive Formulas Women's	US	1.5	
Nature's Code Men's Over 50	US	2.0	dosage derived
Nature's Code Men's Under 50	US	1.5	dosage derived
Nature's Code Women's Over 50	US	1.5	dosage derived
Nature's Code Women's Under 50	US	1.5	dosage derived
Nature's Life Mega Pak	US	3.0	
Nature's Peak Fresh Start	CA	2.0	
Nature's Peak Great Start	CA	1.5	
New Vision Men's Essentials Pack	US	1.5	additional nutrient amounts not specified
New Vision Prime Pack	US	1.5	additional nutrient amounts not specified
New Vision Women's Essentials Pack (Coral Calcium)	US	1.5	additional nutrient amounts not specified
New Vision Women's Essentials Pack (Essential Calcium)	US	2.0	additional nutrient amounts not specified
Nikken Kenzen Dansei/Men	US/CA	2.5	additional nutrient amounts not specified
Nikken Kenzen Josei/Women	US/CA	2.5	additional nutrient amounts not specified
NSI (Neutraceutical Sciences Institute) Synergy Advanced	US	4.5	additional nutrient amounts not specified
NSI (Neutraceutical Sciences Institute) Synergy Max	US	5.0	additional nutrient amounts not specified
NSI (Neutraceutical Sciences Institute) Synergy Ultra	US	5.0	
Nutricology Super Immuno Complex	US	3.0	
Nutrilite Double X	CA/US	2.5	
Nutrilite Perfect Health Pack	US	4.0	
Nutristart Nutri-Pods	CA	3.0	
Nutrition Dynamics Busy Dad Pack	US	2.5	
Nutrition Dynamics Busy Mom Pack	US	1.0	
Nutrition Dynamics Cholestavita Forte Pack	US	3.0	
Nutrition Dynamics Just For Dad	US	4.5	
NuTriVene-D Complete Program	US	2.5	dosage derived
Olay Vitamins Daily Energy Pack for Women	US	1.0	
Olay Vitamins Total Effects Beautiful Skin & Wellness	US	2.0	
Olay Vitamins Total Effects Beautiful Skin & Wellness 7x	US	1.5	
Ortho Molecular Products Alpha Base Foundation Pak	US	4.5	
Ortho Molecular Products Alpha Base Ultimate Pak	US	5.0	
Pharmanex LifePak	CA	3.5	
Pharmanex LifePak	US	3.0	
Pharmanex lifepak nano	CA/US	4.0	
Pharmanex LifePak Prime	US	3.5	
Pharmanex LifePak Women	CA	3.0	
Pharmanex LifePak Women	US	3.0	
Pharmax Four Pillar Pack	US	2.5	
Prescriptive Formulas Men's Optimal Vitamin Packs	US	1.5	
Prescriptive Formulas Women's Optimal Vitamin Packs	US	1.5	
Pro-Caps Laboratories Complete for Men	US	3.0	
Pro-Caps Laboratories Complete for Women	US	3.5	
Pro-Caps Laboratories Men's Complete Life Rx	US	3.5	
Pro-Caps Laboratories Men's Maximum Complete	US	3.5	
Pro-Caps Laboratories Ultimate Complete for Men	US	4.0	
Pro-Caps Laboratories Ultimate Complete for Women	US	4.5	
Propax with NT Factor	US	4.0	
R Garden Essential Nutrition Pack	US	3.0	
R-Garden Essential Nutrition Plus	US	3.0	
Safeway Select Maximum Daily Pack	US	2.0	
Safeway Select Men's Daily Pack	US	1.0	
Safeway Select Women's Daily Pack	US	1.0	additional nutrient amounts not specified
Schiff Multi-Nutrient Pack	US	2.5	
Shaklee Basics Iron Formula	US	2.5	additional nutrient amounts not specified
Shaklee Basics With Iron	CA	2.0	additional nutrient amounts not specified
Shaklee Basics Without Iron	CA	2.5	additional nutrient amounts not specified
Shaklee Basics Without Iron	US	2.5	additional nutrient amounts not specified
SomaLife SomaLifePak	US	2.5	additional nutrient amounts not specified
SomaLife SomaLifePak C	CA	2.5	additional nutrient amounts not specified
Sundown Vitamins To Go Maximum	US	1.5	
Sundown Vitamins To Go Men	US	1.0	additional nutrient amounts not specified
Sundown Vitamins To Go Women	US	1.0	additional nutrient amounts not specified
Symmetry Ultra Vitality NutraPack	US	1.5	additional nutrient amounts not specified
Total High Potency Daily Vitamin Pack	US	1.0	
TriVita Healthy Aging Pack with B-12	US	2.5	
TriVita Healthy Aging Pack with HCY Guard	US	2.5	additional nutrient amounts not specified
TrueStar Health TrueBASICS Plus for Men	CA	5.0	**NutriSearch GOLD Medal of Achievement Recipient**
TrueStar Health TrueBASICS Plus for Women	CA	5.0	**NutriSearch GOLD Medal of Achievement Recipient**
Universal Nutrition Animal Pak	US	2.0	
Universal Nutrition Spa Pak	US	2.0	

USANA Health Sciences HealthPak 100	CA	5.0	**NutriSearch GOLD Medal of Achievement Recipient**
USANA Health Sciences HealthPak 100	US	5.0	**NutriSearch GOLD Medal of Achievement Recipient**
ViSalus Vi-PAK	US	4.5	
Vision for Life Body Force Travel Packs	US	2.0	additional nutrient amounts not specified
Vitamin Shoppe Health & Fitness	US	2.5	
Vitamin Shoppe Mature Female	US	2.0	
Vitamin Shoppe Mature Male Pack	US	2.0	
Vitamin Shoppe Multi-Vitamin Pack	US	3.0	
Weil Complete Daily Pack	CA	3.0	
Weil Complete Daily Pack	US	3.0	
Wheaties Daily Performance Vitamin Pack	US	0.5	
Xymogen Activ Essentials	US	2.0	
Xymogen Activ Essentials Women	US	2.0	
YourLife Daily Pak Maximum	US	1.5	
YourLife Daily Pak Men's 50+	US	1.5	
YourLife Daily Pak Women's 50+	US	1.0	

Appendix D: Combination Products Alphabetically by Star Rating

Manufacturer & Product Name	Country	# of Stars	Dosages and Considerations
Douglas Laboratories Daily Core Essentials	CA	5.0	NutriSearch GOLD Medal of Achievement Recipient
Douglas Laboratories Longevity Support Pack	US	5.0	NutriSearch GOLD Medal of Achievement Recipient
TrueStar Health TrueBASICS Plus for Men	CA	5.0	NutriSearch GOLD Medal of Achievement Recipient
TrueStar Health TrueBASICS Plus for Women	CA	5.0	NutriSearch GOLD Medal of Achievement Recipient
USANA Health Sciences HealthPak 100	CA	5.0	NutriSearch GOLD Medal of Achievement Recipient
USANA Health Sciences HealthPak 100	US	5.0	NutriSearch GOLD Medal of Achievement Recipient
Colgan Institute Men's Pak	US	5.0	
Colgan Institute Men's+ 50 Pak	US	5.0	
Colgan Institute Sports Pak	US	5.0	
Colgan Institute Women's 50+ Pak	US	5.0	
Colgan Institute Women's Active Pak	US	5.0	
Colgan Institute Women's Pak	US	5.0	
NSI (Neutraceutical Sciences Institute) Synergy Max	US	5.0	additional nutrient amounts not specified
NSI (Neutraceutical Sciences Institute) Synergy Ultra	US	5.0	
Ortho Molecular Products Alpha Base Ultimate Pak	US	5.0	
Colgan Institute Men's Active Pak	US	4.5	
Douglas Laboratories Dad's Pack	US	4.5	
Jean Carper's Stop Aging Now! Anti-Aging Power-Pak	US	4.5	
Julian Whitaker, M.D. Forward Plus Daily Regimen	US	4.5	dosage derived; additional nutrient amounts not specified
Mountain Home Daily Advantage	US	4.5	
NSI (Neutraceutical Sciences Institute) Synergy Advanced	US	4.5	additional nutrient amounts not specified
Nutrition Dynamics Just For Dad	US	4.5	
Ortho Molecular Products Alpha Base Foundation Pak	US	4.5	
Pro-Caps Laboratories Ultimate Complete for Women	US	4.5	
ViSalus Vi-PAK	US	4.5	
BioX Multi Vitamin Pack	CA	4.0	dosage derived
Douglas Laboratories Basic Antiox	US	4.0	
Douglas Laboratories Essential-4 Nutrition Pack	US	4.0	
Douglas Laboratories Nutri-Pak for Men	US	4.0	
Douglas Laboratories Nutri-Pak for Women	US	4.0	
Douglas Laboratories OC Pack	US	4.0	
Jarrow Formulas All Capsule Health Pak	US	4.0	
Julian Whitaker, M.D. Forward Plus Daily Regimen	CA	4.0	additional nutrient amounts not specified
Lorna Vanderhaeghe FemmEssentials	CA/US	4.0	
Metagenics Wellness Essentials	US	4.0	
Nutrilite Perfect Health Pack	US	4.0	
Pharmanex lifepak nano	CA/US	4.0	
Pro-Caps Laboratories Ultimate Complete for Men	US	4.0	
Propax with NT Factor	US	4.0	
Dr. Lark Daily Answer MultiNutrient for Women	US	3.5	dosage derived
Dr. Lark Daily Balance Women's Multinutrient	US	3.5	dosage derived
Enzymatic Therapy Energy Revitalization System (Citrus Delight)	US	3.5	
ForMor International Core Nutrition	US	3.5	
Great American Products Master Health Pack	US	3.5	
Great Earth Nutritional Starter Pack (Ultra Strength)	US	3.5	additional nutrient amounts not specified
Highland Laboratories Men's Sports Pak	US	3.5	
Highland Laboratories Women's Sports Pak	US	3.5	
Jarrow Formulas Jarrow Pak Plus	US	3.5	
Life-Line Total Health Formula	US	3.5	
Metagenics Wellness Essentials for Women	US	3.5	
Pharmanex LifePak	CA	3.5	
Pharmanex LifePak Prime	US	3.5	
Pro-Caps Laboratories Complete for Women	US	3.5	
Pro-Caps Laboratories Men's Complete Life Rx	US	3.5	
Pro-Caps Laboratories Men's Maximum Complete	US	3.5	
Colgan Institute Men's First Defense Pak	US	3.0	
Colgan Institute Women's First Defense	US	3.0	
CVC 4 Health Unit Pac Ultimate	US	3.0	dosage derived
dc (Dee Cee Laboratories) Mega Vita-Min	US	3.0	
Douglas Laboratories Ultra Preventive V plus Chel-Supplement Pack	US	3.0	
epic4health Physician's Rx Complete Formula	US	3.0	
FreeLife Basic Mindell Plus	US	3.0	additional nutrient amounts not specified
Great Earth Nutritional Starter Pack (Extra Strength)	US	3.0	additional nutrient amounts not specified
Highland Laboratories Super Athlete Packs	US	3.0	
InVite Multi-Vitamin	US	3.0	
Nature's Life Mega Pak	US	3.0	
Nutricology Super Immuno Complex	US	3.0	
Nutristart Nutri-Pods	CA	3.0	
Nutrition Dynamics Cholestavita Forte Pack	US	3.0	
Pharmanex LifePak	US	3.0	
Pharmanex LifePak Women	CA	3.0	
Pharmanex LifePak Women	US	3.0	
Pro-Caps Laboratories Complete for Men	US	3.0	
R Garden Essential Nutrition Pack	US	3.0	
R-Garden Essential Nutrition Plus	US	3.0	
Vitamin Shoppe Multi-Vitamin Pack	US	3.0	

Weil Complete Daily Pack	CA	3.0	
Weil Complete Daily Pack	US	3.0	
AmeriSciences Men's Master Multi	US	2.5	additional nutrient amounts not specified
AmeriSciences Women's Master Multi	US	2.5	additional nutrient amounts not specified
Arbonne International Daily Power Packs for Men	US	2.5	additional nutrient amounts not specified
Arbonne International Daily Power Packs for Women	US	2.5	additional nutrient amounts not specified
Colgan Institute Basic Body Armor	US	2.5	
Douglas Laboratories Met-A-Syn X-Pack	US	2.5	
GNLD International Daily Vitality Pack Active 40+	US	2.5	
GNLD International Daily Vitality Pack Sports 30	US	2.5	
GNLD International Daily Vitality Pack Stress 30	US	2.5	
Nature's Best Perfect Hardcore Pak	US	2.5	
Nature's Best Perfect Super Multi Power Pak	US	2.5	
Nikken Kenzen Dansei/Men	US/CA	2.5	additional nutrient amounts not specified
Nikken Kenzen Josei/Women	US/CA	2.5	additional nutrient amounts not specified
Nutrilite Double X	CA/US	2.5	
Nutrition Dynamics Busy Dad Pack	US	2.5	
NuTriVene-D Complete Program	US	2.5	dosage derived
Pharmax Four Pillar Pack	US	2.5	
Schiff Multi-Nutrient Pack	US	2.5	
Shaklee Basics Iron Formula	US	2.5	additional nutrient amounts not specified
Shaklee Basics Without Iron	CA	2.5	additional nutrient amounts not specified
Shaklee Basics Without Iron	US	2.5	additional nutrient amounts not specified
SomaLife SomaLifePak	US	2.5	additional nutrient amounts not specified
SomaLife SomaLifePak C	CA	2.5	additional nutrient amounts not specified
TriVita Healthy Aging Pack with B-12	US	2.5	
TriVita Healthy Aging Pack with HCY Guard	US	2.5	additional nutrient amounts not specified
Vitamin Shoppe Health & Fitness	US	2.5	
CVC 4 Health Unit Pac Royal	US	2.0	dosage derived
CVC 4 Health Unit Pac Supreme	US	2.0	dosage derived
Enerex Optimal Health Pack	CA	2.0	
Equaline Daily Vitamin Packets	US	2.0	
Global Health Trax Basic Five	US	2.0	additional nutrient amounts not specified
GNC Maximum Nutrition VitaPak	US	2.0	
GNC Mega Men Performance and Vitality Program	US	2.0	dosage derived; additional nutrient amounts not specified
GNC Women's Ultra Mega Wellness Program	US	2.0	dosage derived; additional nutrient amounts not specified
Great Earth Nutritional Starter Pack (Regular Strength)	US	2.0	additional nutrient amounts not specified
Melaleuca Daily for Life Total Nutrition for Men	US	2.0	additional nutrient amounts not specified
Melaleuca Daily for Life Total Nutrition for Women	US	2.0	additional nutrient amounts not specified
Melaleuca Vitality Pack with Cellwise and ProVexCV for Men	US	2.0	additional nutrient amounts not specified
Nature Made Maximin Pack	US	2.0	
Nature's Code Men's Over 50	US	2.0	dosage derived
Nature's Peak Fresh Start	CA	2.0	
New Vision Women's Essentials Pack (Essential Calcium)	US	2.0	additional nutrient amounts not specified
Olay Vitamins Total Effects Beautiful Skin & Wellness	US	2.0	
Safeway Select Maximum Daily Pack	US	2.0	
Shaklee Basics With Iron	CA	2.0	additional nutrient amounts not specified
Universal Nutrition Animal Pak	US	2.0	
Universal Nutrition Spa Pak	US	2.0	
Vision for Life Body Force Travel Packs	US	2.0	additional nutrient amounts not specified
Vitamin Shoppe Mature Female	US	2.0	
Vitamin Shoppe Mature Male Pack	US	2.0	
Xymogen Activ Essentials	US	2.0	
Xymogen Activ Essentials Women	US	2.0	
Bronson Laboratories Daily Nutrional Packets	US	1.5	
Bronson Laboratories Nutritional Packets for Active Men	US	1.5	
Bronson Laboratories Nutritional Packets for Active Women	US	1.5	
Club Vitamin Mega Vitamin Kit	CA	1.5	dosage derived
CVC 4 Health Unit Pac Original	US	1.5	dosage derived
Hannen Health Daily Essentials	US	1.5	
HerbaSway Laboratories Daily Maintenance Group	US	1.5	
Kirkland Daily Multivitamin Pack	US	1.5	
Life-Line Men's Life-Pack	US	1.5	dosage derived
Melaleuca Vitality Pack with Cellwise and ProVexCV for Women	US	1.5	additional nutrient amounts not specified
Member's Mark Daily Vitamin Pack	US	1.5	
Nature Made Diabetes Health Pack	US	1.5	
Nature Made Stress Pack	US	1.5	dosage derived
Nature's Best Perfect Fitness Pak	US	1.5	
Nature's Bounty Prescriptive Formulas Women's	US	1.5	
Nature's Code Men's Under 50	US	1.5	dosage derived
Nature's Code Women's Over 50	US	1.5	dosage derived
Nature's Code Women's Under 50	US	1.5	dosage derived
Nature's Peak Great Start	CA	1.5	
New Vision Men's Essentials Pack	US	1.5	additional nutrient amounts not specified
New Vision Prime Pack	US	1.5	additional nutrient amounts not specified
New Vision Women's Essentials Pack (Coral Calcium)	US	1.5	additional nutrient amounts not specified
Olay Vitamins Total Effects Beautiful Skin & Wellness 7x	US	1.5	
Prescriptive Formulas Men's Optimal Vitamin Packs	US	1.5	
Prescriptive Formulas Women's Optimal Vitamin Packs	US	1.5	
Sundown Vitamins To Go Maximum	US	1.5	
Symmetry Ultra Vitality NutraPack	US	1.5	additional nutrient amounts not specified

YourLife Daily Pak Maximum	US	1.5	
YourLife Daily Pak Men's 50+	US	1.5	
Guthy-Renker Nutrition GRN Vitapower	US	1.0	
Life-Line Women's Life-Pack	US	1.0	
Nature Made Men's Pack	US	1.0	
Nature Made Women's Pack	US	1.0	
Nature's Bounty Prescriptive Formulas Men's	US	1.0	
Nutrition Dynamics Busy Mom Pack	US	1.0	
Olay Vitamins Daily Energy Pack for Women	US	1.0	
Safeway Select Men's Daily Pack	US	1.0	
Safeway Select Women's Daily Pack	US	1.0	additional nutrient amounts not specified
Sundown Vitamins To Go Men	US	1.0	additional nutrient amounts not specified
Sundown Vitamins To Go Women	US	1.0	additional nutrient amounts not specified
Total High Potency Daily Vitamin Pack	US	1.0	
YourLife Daily Pak Women's 50+	US	1.0	
Wheaties Daily Performance Vitamin Pack	US	0.5	

Appendix E: Products Exceeding Upper Limits

Manufacturer & Product Name	Country	Status	Dosages & Considerations
BioMax Vitamins & Minerals Plus	US	disqualified	three or more nutrients exceeding Upper Limits
Colgan Institute Athlete's Pak	US	disqualified	three or more nutrients exceeding Upper Limits
Douglas Laboratories Ultra Preventive III Forte-Chel	US	disqualified	three or more nutrients exceeding Upper Limits
Douglas Laboratories Ultra Preventive III Forte-Chel with Copper	US	disqualified	three or more nutrients exceeding Upper Limits
Douglas Laboratories Ultra Preventive III Forte-Chel with Iron	US	disqualified	three or more nutrients exceeding Upper Limits
Douglas Laboratories Ultra Preventive III Forte-Chel with Zinc Picolinate	US	disqualified	three or more nutrients exceeding Upper Limits
Gary Null Beginner's Health Startup Kit	US	disqualified	three or more nutrients exceeding Upper Limits
Gary Null's Supreme Health Formula	US	disqualified	three or more nutrients exceeding Upper Limits
Nature's Best Perfect Multi Pak	US	disqualified	three or more nutrients exceeding Upper Limits
NSI (Neutraceutical Sciences Institute) Synergy Supreme	US	disqualified	three or more nutrients exceeding Upper Limits
Nutrition Dynamics Optimum Health Essentials	US	disqualified	three or more nutrients exceeding Upper Limits
O'Brien Pharmacy Optimal Daily Allowance	US	disqualified	three or more nutrients exceeding Upper Limits
Pro Health Mega Multiple III	US	disqualified	three or more nutrients exceeding Upper Limits
Super Nutrition Iron Free Opti-Pack	US	disqualified	three or more nutrients exceeding Upper Limits
Super Nutrition Opti-Pack	US	disqualified	three or more nutrients exceeding Upper Limits
SuperNutrition Super Blend	US	disqualified	three or more nutrients exceeding Upper Limits
SuperNutrition Women's Blend	US	disqualified	three or more nutrients exceeding Upper Limits
TRC Nutritional Laboratories Liquid Life Complete	US	disqualified	three or more nutrients exceeding Upper Limits
Vitality Lifetime	US	disqualified	three or more nutrients exceeding Upper Limits
Vitamin Research Products Extend Ultra	US	disqualified	three or more nutrients exceeding Upper Limits
Wellness Resources Daily Super Pack	US	disqualified	three or more nutrients exceeding Upper Limits

Bibliography: References by Chapter

Chapter One

(1) Fairfield KM, Fletcher RH. Vitamins for chronic disease prevention in adults: scientific review. *JAMA* 2002 June 19;287(23):3116-26.

(2) Fletcher RH, Fairfield KM. Vitamins for chronic disease prevention in adults: clinical applications. *JAMA* 2002 June 19;287(23):3127-9.

(3) Cavadini C, Siega-Riz AM, Popkin BM. US adolescent food intake trends from 1965 to 1996. *West J Med* 2000 December;173(6):378-83.

(4) Brady LM, Lindquist CH, Herd SL, Goran MI. Comparison of children's dietary intake patterns with US dietary guidelines. *Br J Nutr* 2000 September;84(3):361-7.

(5) Krebs-Smith SM, Cook A, Subar AF, Cleveland L, Friday J, Kahle LL. Fruit and vegetable intakes of children and adolescents in the United States. *Arch Pediatr Adolesc Med* 1996 January;150(1):81-6.

(6) McClelland JW, mark-Wahnefried W, Mustian RD, Cowan AT, Campbell MK. Fruit and vegetable consumption of rural African Americans: baseline survey results of the Black Churches United for Better Health 5 A Day Project. *Nutr Cancer* 1998;30(2):148-57.

(7) Charlet B, Henneberry SR. A profile of food consumption trends and changing market institutions.In: OSU Extension Facts Report #F-511. Oklahoma Cooperative Extension Service, Oklahoma State University; 2002.

(8) Tucker KL, Hallfrisch J, Qiao N, Muller D, Andres R, Fleg JL. The combination of high fruit and vegetable and low saturated fat intakes is more protective against mortality in aging men than is either alone: the Baltimore Longitudinal Study of Aging. *J Nutr* 2005 March;135(3):556-61.

(9) Li R, Serdula M, Bland S, Mokdad A, Bowman B, Nelson D. Trends in fruit and vegetable consumption among adults in 16 US states: Behavioral Risk Factor Surveillance System, 1990-1996. *Am J Public Health* 2000 May;90(5):777-81.

(10) Colgan M. We Have Fouled Our Land. *The New Nutrition: Medicine for the Millennium.*Vancouver, BC: Apple Publishing; 1995. p. 10-1.

(11) Berenson GS, Srinivasan SR, Bao W, Newman WP, III, Tracy RE, Wattigney WA. Association between multiple cardiovascular risk factors and atherosclerosis in children and young adults. The Bogalusa Heart Study. *N Engl J Med* 1998 June 4;338(23):1650-6.

(12) Bazzano LA, He J, Ogden LG et al. Fruit and vegetable intake and risk of cardiovascular disease in US adults: the first National Health and Nutrition Examination Survey Epidemiologic Follow-up Study. *Am J Clin Nutr* 2002 July;76(1):93-9.

(13) WHO Study Group. Diet, nutrition and the prevention of chronic diseases. World Health Organization; 1990.

(14) American Heart Association. An eating plan for healthy Americans. Dallas: American Heart Association; 2000.

(15) Hung HC, Joshipura KJ, Jiang R et al. Fruit and vegetable intake and risk of major chronic disease. *J Natl Cancer Inst* 2004 November 3;96(21):1577-84.

(16) Flood A, Schatzkin A. Colorectal cancer: does it matter if you eat your fruits and vegetables? *J Natl Cancer Inst* 2000 November 1;92(21):1706-7.

(17) Lichtenstein P, Holm NV, Verkasalo PK et al. Environmental and heritable factors in the causation of cancer--analyses of cohorts of twins from Sweden, Denmark, and Finland. *N Engl J Med* 2000 July 13;343(2):78-85.

(18) Potter JD, Chavez A, Chen J. Food, Nutrition and the Prevention of Cancer: A Global Perspective. American Institute for Cancer Research and the World Cancer Fund; 1997 Sep.

(19) Block G, Patterson B, Subar A. Fruit, vegetables, and cancer prevention: a review of the epidemiological evidence. *Nutr Cancer* 1992;18(1):1-29.

(20) Davis DL, Dinse GE, Hoel DG. Decreasing cardiovascular disease and increasing cancer among whites in the United States from 1973 through 1987. Good news and bad news. *JAMA* 1994 February 9;271(6):431-7.

(21) Ahn J, Gammon MD, Santella RM et al. Associations between breast cancer risk and the catalase genotype, fruit and vegetable consumption, and supplement use. *Am J Epidemiol* 2005 November 15;162(10):943-52.

(22) Campos FG, Logullo Waitzberg AG, Kiss DR, Waitzberg DL, Habr-Gama A, Gama-Rodrigues J. Diet and colorectal cancer: current evidence for etiology and prevention. *Nutr Hosp* 2005 January;20(1):18-25.

(23) Chan JM, Wang F, Holly EA. Vegetable and fruit intake and pancreatic cancer in a population-based case-control study in the San Francisco bay area. *Cancer Epidemiol Biomarkers Prev* 2005 September;14(9):2093-7.

(24) De SE, Boffetta P, eo-Pellegrini H, Ronco AL, Correa P, Mendilaharsu M. The role of vegetable and fruit consumption in the aetiology of squamous cell carcinoma of the oesophagus: a case-control study in Uruguay. *Int J Cancer* 2005 August 10;116(1):130-5.

(25) Gonzalez CA, Pera G, Agudo A et al. Fruit and vegetable intake and the risk of stomach and oesophagus adenocarcinoma in the European Prospective Investigation into Cancer and Nutrition (EPIC-EURGAST). *Int J Cancer* 2006 May 15;118(10):2559-66.

(26) Hayes DP. The protective role of fruits and vegetables against radiation-induced cancer. *Nutr Rev* 2005 September;63(9):303-11.

(27) Kellen E, Zeegers M, Paulussen A, Van DM, Buntinx F. Fruit consumption reduces the effect of smoking on bladder cancer risk. The Belgian case control study on bladder cancer. *Int J Cancer* 2006 May 15;118(10):2572-8.

(28) Lunet N, Lacerda-Vieira A, Barros H. Fruit and vegetables consumption and gastric cancer: a systematic review and meta-analysis of cohort studies. *Nutr Cancer* 2005;53(1):1-10.

(29) Meyskens FL, Jr., Szabo E. Diet and cancer: the disconnect between epidemiology and randomized clinical trials. *Cancer Epidemiol Biomarkers Prev* 2005 June;14(6):1366-9.

(30) Rylander R, Axelsson G. Lung cancer risks in relation to vegetable and fruit consumption and smoking. *Int J Cancer* 2006 February 1;118(3):739-43.

(31) Steinmetz KA, Potter JD. Vegetables, fruit, and cancer prevention: a review. *J Am Diet Assoc* 1996 October;96(10):1027-39.

(32) Goodwin JS, Brodwick M. Diet, aging, and cancer. *Clin Geriatr Med* 1995 November;11(4):577-89.

(33) Bonita R, Stewart A, Beaglehole R. International trends in stroke mortality: 1970-1985. *Stroke* 1990 July;21(7):989-92.

(34) Gillum RF, Sempos CT. The end of the long-term decline in stroke mortality in the United States? *Stroke* 1997 August;28(8):1527-9.

(35) Thom TJ. Stroke mortality trends. An international perspective. *Ann Epidemiol* 1993 September;3(5):509-18.

(36) Uemura K, Pisa Z. Trends in cardiovascular disease mortality in industrialized countries since 1950. *World Health Stat Q* 1988;41(3-4):155-78.

(37) Yang Q, Botto LD, Erickson JD et al. Improvement in stroke mortality in Canada and the United States, 1990 to 2002. *Circulation* 2006 March 14;113(10):1335-43.

(38) Broderick J, Brott T, Kothari R et al. The Greater Cincinnati/Northern Kentucky Stroke Study: preliminary first-ever and total incidence rates of stroke among blacks. *Stroke* 1998 February;29(2):415-21.

(39) Lock K, Pomerleau J, Causer L, Altmann DR, McKee M. The global burden of disease attributable to low consumption of fruits and vegetables: implications for the global strategy on diet. *Bull World Health Organ* 2005 February;83(2):100-8.

(40) Dauchet L, Amouyel P, Dallongeville J. Fruit and vegetable consumption and risk of stroke: a meta-analysis of cohort studies. *Neurology* 2005 October 25;65(8):1193-7.

(41) He FJ, Nowson CA, MacGregor GA. Fruit and vegetable consumption and stroke: meta-analysis of cohort studies. *Lancet* 2006 January 28;367(9507):320-6.

(42) Feldman EB. Fruits and vegetables and the risk of stroke. *Nutr Rev* 2001 January;59(1 Pt 1):24-7.

(43) Eskin NAM, Henderson HN, Townsend RJ. *The Biochemistry of Foods.* New York, NY: Academic Press; 1971.

(44) Mertz W. *Trace Elements in Human and Animal Nutrition.* 5th ed. New York, NY: Academic Press; 1986.

Chapter Two

(1) Wan H, Sengupta M, Velkoff VA, DeBarros KA. 65+ in the United States 2005. *U S Census Bureau* 2006;Available at: URL: www.census.gov. AccessedApril 14, 2006.

(2) Ahlburg DA, Vaupel JW. Alternative projections of the U.S. population. *Demography* 1990 November;27(4):639-52.

(3) Manton KG, Stallard E. Cross-sectional estimates of active life expectancy for the U.S. elderly and oldest-old populations. *J Gerontol* 1991 May;46(3):S170-S182.

(4) Kurzweil R, Grossman T. You can Live Long Enough to Live Forever. *Fantastic Voyage.* Holtzbrinck Publishers; 2004. p. 1-13.

(5) Anderson RN, Smith BL. Deaths: Leading Causes for 2002. National Vital Statistics Reports: U.S. Department of Health and Human Services; 2005 Mar 7. Report No.: 53(17).

(6) Extracts of The Surgeon General's Report on Nutrition and Health. Washington, DC: U.S. Department of Health and Human Services; 1988.

(7) Potter JD, Chavez A, Chen J et al. Food, Nutrition and the Prevention of Cancer: A Global Perspective. American Institute for Cancer Research and the World Cancer Research Fund; 1997 Sep.

(8)   Reid IR. Therapy of osteoporosis: calcium, vitamin D, and exercise. *Am J Med Sci* 1996 December;312(6):278-86.

(9)   Extracts of The Surgeon General's Report on Nutrition and Health. Washington, DC: U.S. Department of Health and Human Services; 1988.

(10) WISQARS Internet program. WISQARS Leading Causes of Death Reports, 1999 - 2004. Atlanta, GA: Office of Statistics and Programming, National Center for Injury Prevention and Control, Centers for Disease Control and Prevention; 2004.

(11) Greenwell I. The Role of Inflammation in Chronic Disease. Life Extension Magazine Feb. 2001. Life Extension Media. Ref Type: Magazine Article

Chapter Three

(1)   Calden EF. *Fast Reactions in Solution*. New York, NY: John Wiley & Sons; 1964.

(2)   Roughton FJW, Chance B. *Techniques of Organic Chemistry*. 2nd ed. Interscience; 1963.

(3)   Forman HJ, Boveris A. Superoxide radical and hydrogen peroxide in mitochondria. In: Pryor WA, editor. *Free Radicals in Biology*. New York, NY: Academic Press; 1982. p. 65-89.

(4)   Patel RP, McAndrew J, Sellak H et al. Biological aspects of reactive nitrogen species. *Biochim Biophys Acta* 1999 May 5;1411(2-3):385-400.

(5)   West ES, Todd W, Mason HS, van Bruggen JT. Biological Oxidation-Reduction. *Textbook of Biochemistry*. 4 ed. The Macmillan Company; 1970. p. 897-969.

(6)   Davies K. Oxidative Stress: the Paradox of Aerobic Life. *Biochemical Society Symposia* 1995;61:1-31.

(7)   Strand R. *Bionutrition: Winning the War Within*. Rapid City, SD: Comprehensive Wellness Publishing; 1998.

(8)   Harman D. Free radical theory of aging: effect of free radical reaction inhibitors on the mortality rate of male LAF mice. *J Gerontol* 1968 October;23(4):476-82.

(9)   MacWilliam LD. Radiation-Induced Changes in the Profiles of Certain Key Enzymes in Rat Myocardium and Serum: Effects of Exercise and Dietary Supplementation with Vitamin E [Kinesiology]. Burnaby, BC: Simon Fraser University; 1974.

(10) MacWilliam LD, Bhakthan NMG. Radiation-induced efflux from rat heart: sedentary animals. In: Roy PE, Dhalla NS, editors. *Recent Advances in Studies on Cardiac Structure and Metabolism: The Sarcolema*. 9 ed. Baltimore: University Park Press; 1976. p. 447-60.

(11) Passwater RA. The Basics of Antioxidants. *All About Antioxidants*. New York, NY: Avery Publishing; 1998. p. 9-30.

Chapter Four

(1)   Studer M, Briel M, Leimenstoll B, Glass TR, Bucher HC. Effect of different antilipidemic agents and diets on mortality: a systematic review. *Arch Intern Med* 2005 April 11;165(7):725-30.

(2)   Ross R. Atherosclerosis is an inflammatory disease. *Am Heart J* 1999 November;138(5 Pt 2):S419-S420.

(3)   Albert CM, Ma J, Rifai N, Stampfer MJ, Ridker PM. Prospective study of C-reactive protein, homocysteine, and plasma lipid levels as predictors of sudden cardiac death. *Circulation* 2002 June 4;105(22):2595-9.

(4)   Bermudez EA, Ridker PM. C-reactive protein, statins, and the primary prevention of atherosclerotic cardiovascular disease. *Prev Cardiol* 2002;5(1):42-6.

(5)   Rifai N, Ridker PM. Inflammatory markers and coronary heart disease. *Curr Opin Lipidol* 2002 August;13(4):383-9.

(6)   Gorman C, Park A. The Fires Within. Time February 23. 2004. Time Publishers. Ref Type: Magazine Article

(7)   Jager A, van H, V, Kostense PJ et al. von Willebrand factor, C-reactive protein, and 5-year mortality in diabetic and nondiabetic subjects: the Hoorn Study. *Arterioscler Thromb Vasc Biol* 1999 December;19(12):3071-8.

(8)   Ridker PM, Cushman M, Stampfer MJ, Tracy RP, Hennekens CH. Inflammation, aspirin, and the risk of cardiovascular disease in apparently healthy men. *N Engl J Med* 1997 April 3;336(14):973-9.

(9)   Ridker PM, Buring JE, Shih J, Matias M, Hennekens CH. Prospective study of C-reactive protein and the risk of future cardiovascular events among apparently healthy women. *Circulation* 1998 August 25;98(8):731-3.

(10) Libby P, Ridker PM, Maseri A. Inflammation and atherosclerosis. *Circulation* 2002 March 5;105(9):1135-43.

(11) Packard CJ, O'Reilly DS, Caslake MJ et al. Lipoprotein-associated phospholipase A2 as an independent predictor of coronary heart disease. West of Scotland Coronary Prevention Study Group. *N Engl J Med* 2000 October 19;343(16):1148-55.

(12) Ridker PM, Rifai N, Stampfer MJ, Hennekens CH. Plasma concentration of interleukin-6 and the risk of future myocardial infarction among apparently healthy men. *Circulation* 2000 April 18;101(15):1767-72.

(13) Jialal I, Devaraj S. Inflammation and atherosclerosis: the value of the high-sensitivity C-reactive protein assay as a risk marker. *Am J Clin Pathol* 2001 December;116 Suppl:S108-S115.

(14) Zairis MN, Papadaki OA, Manousakis SJ et al. C-reactive protein and multiple complex coronary artery plaques in patients with primary unstable angina. *Atherosclerosis* 2002 October;164(2):355-9.

(15) Sears B. *The Anti-Inflammation Zone*. New York, NY: HaperCollins Publishers Inc.; 2005.

(16) Pompl PN, Ho L, Bianchi M, McManus T, Qin W, Pasinetti GM. A therapeutic role for cyclooxygenase-2 inhibitors in a transgenic mouse model of amyotrophic lateral sclerosis. *FASEB J* 2003 April;17(6):725-7.

(17) Schmidt R, Schmidt H, Curb JD, Masaki K, White LR, Launer LJ. Early inflammation and dementia: a 25-year follow-up of the Honolulu-Asia Aging Study. *Ann Neurol* 2002 August;52(2):168-74.

(18) Pradhan AD, Ridker PM. Do atherosclerosis and type 2 diabetes share a common inflammatory basis? *Eur Heart J* 2002 June;23(11):831-4.

(19) Kurzweil R, Grossman T. *Fantastic Voyage: Live Long Enough to Live Forever*. New York, NY: Rodale; 2004.

(20) Floyd RA. Neuroinflammatory processes are important in neurodegenerative diseases: an hypothesis to explain the increased formation of reactive oxygen and nitrogen species as major factors involved in neurodegenerative disease development. *Free Radic Biol Med* 1999 May;26(9-10):1346-55.

(21) Arden NK, Cooper C. Osteoporosis in patients with inflammatory bowel disease. *Gut* 2002 January;50(1):9-10.

(22) Van Staa TP, Brusse LS, Javid MK. Inflammatory bowel disease and the risk of fracture. 2002.

(23) Valentine JF, Sninsky CA. Prevention and treatment of osteoporosis in patients with inflammatory bowel disease. *Am J Gastroenterol* 1999 April;94(4):878-83.

(24) Chung YC, Chang YF. Serum interleukin-6 levels reflect the disease status of colorectal cancer. *J Surg Oncol* 2003 August;83(4):222-6.

(25) Erlinger TP, Platz EA, Rifai N, Helzlsouer KJ. C-reactive protein and the risk of incident colorectal cancer. *JAMA* 2004 February 4;291(5):585-90.

(26) Burskins CJ, Ristimaki A, Offerhaus GJ ea. Role of Cyclooxygenase-2 in the development and treatment of oesophageal adenocarcinoma. *Scand J Gastroenterol* 2003;239:87-93.

(27) Reddy BS, Tokumo K, Kulkarni N, Aligia C, Kelloff G. Inhibition of colon carcinogenesis by prostaglandin synthesis inhibitors and related compounds. *Carcinogenesis* 1992 June;13(6):1019-23.

(28) Akhmedkhanov A, Toniolo P, Zeleniuch-Jacquotte A, Koenig KL, Shore RE. Aspirin and lung cancer in women. *Br J Cancer* 2002 July 1;87(1):49-53.

(29) Duenwald M. Body's Defender Goes on the Attack. The New York Times 2002 Jan 22.

(30) Sears B. The Cause and the Cure for Silent Inflammation. *The Anti-Inflammation Zone*. New York, NY: HaperCollins Publishers Inc.; 2005. p. 21-30.

(31) Cunningham DS. Quenching the Flames of Inflammation. Life Extension , 27-34. 2004. Ref Type: Magazine Article

(32) Griffiths RJ, Pettipher ER, Koch K et al. Leukotriene B4 plays a critical role in the progression of collagen-induced arthritis. *Proc Natl Acad Sci U S A* 1995 January 17;92(2):517-21.

(33) Turner CR, Breslow R, Conklyn MJ et al. In vitro and in vivo effects of leukotriene B4 antagonism in a primate model of asthma. *J Clin Invest* 1996 January 15;97(2):381-7.

(34) Weringer EJ, Perry BD, Sawyer PS, Gilman SC, Showell HJ. Antagonizing leukotriene B4 receptors delays cardiac allograft rejection in mice. *Transplantation* 1999 March 27;67(6):808-15.

(35) Jiang Q, Elson-Schwab I, Courtemanche C, Ames BN. gamma-tocopherol and its major metabolite, in contrast to alpha-tocopherol, inhibit cyclooxygenase activity in macrophages and epithelial cells. *Proc Natl Acad Sci U S A* 2000 October 10;97(21):11494-9.

(36) Jiang Q, Christen S, Shigenaga MK, Ames BN. gamma-tocopherol, the major form of vitamin E in the US diet, deserves more attention. *Am J Clin Nutr* 2001 December;74(6):714-22.

(37) Bengmark S. Curcumin, an atoxic antioxidant and natural NFkappaB, cyclooxygenase-2, lipooxygenase, and inducible nitric oxide synthase inhibitor: a shield against acute and chronic diseases. *JPEN J Parenter Enteral Nutr* 2006 January;30(1):45-51.

(38) Kurzweil R, Grossman T. Inflammation-the Latest "Smoking Gun". *Fantastic Voyage: Live Long Enough to Live Forever*.New York, NY: Rodale; 2004. p. 160-71.

(39) Jenkins DJ, Kendall CW, Marchie A et al. Direct comparison of dietary portfolio vs statin on C-reactive protein. *Eur J Clin Nutr* 2005 July;59(7):851-60.

(40) Schmidt MA. *Smart Fats: How Dietary Fats and Oils affect Mental, Physical, and Emotional Intelligence*. Berkely, CA: Frog Ltd.; 1997.

(41) Kelley VE, Ferretti A, Izui S, Strom TB. A fish oil diet rich in eicosapentaenoic acid reduces cyclooxygenase metabolites, and suppresses lupus in MRL-lpr mice. *J Immunol* 1985 March;134(3):1914-9.

(42) Watanabe S, Katagiri K, Onozaki K et al. Dietary docosahexaenoic acid but not eicosapentaenoic acid suppresses lipopolysaccharide-induced interleukin-1 beta mRNA induction in mouse spleen leukocytes. *Prostaglandins Leukot Essent Fatty Acids* 2000 March;62(3):147-52.

(43) Murray MT. Essential Fatty Acid Supplementation. *Encyclopedia of Nutritional Supplements.*Rocklin, CA: Prima Health; 1996. p. 249-78.

(44) Conner EM, Grisham MB. Inflammation, free radicals, and antioxidants. *Nutrition* 1996 April;12(4):274-7.

(45) Djordjevic VB. Free radicals in cell biology. *Int Rev Cytol* 2004;237:57-89.

(46) Rahman I. Oxidative stress, chromatin remodeling and gene transcription in inflammation and chronic lung diseases. *J Biochem Mol Biol* 2003 January 31;36(1):95-109.

(47) Winrow VR, Winyard PG, Morris CJ, Blake DR. Free radicals in inflammation: second messengers and mediators of tissue destruction. *Br Med Bull* 1993 July;49(3):506-22.

(48) Perricone N. The Inflammation-Aging-Disease-Obesity Connection. *The Perricone Weight-Loss Diet*. New York, NY: Ballantine Books; 2005. p. 9-16.

(49) Goepp JG. What is Nuclear Factor kappa Beta? Life Extension July, 31-40. 2006. Ref Type: Magazine Article

(50) Ahn KS, Aggarwal BB. Transcription Factor NF-kB: A Sensor for Smoke and Stress Signals. *Ann NY Acad Sci* 2005;1056:218-33.

(51) Aggarwal BB, Shishodia S. Suppression of Nuclear Factor-kB Acivation Pathway by Spice-Derived Phytochemicals: Reasoning for Seasoning. *Ann NY Acad Sci* 2004;1030:434.

(52) Greenwell I. The Role of Inflammation in Chronic Disease. Life Extension Magazine Feb. 2001. Life Extension Media. Ref Type: Magazine Article

(53) Egan RW, Gale PH, Beveridge GC, Phillips GB, Marnett LJ. Radical scavenging as the mechanism for stimulation of prostaglandin cyclooxygenase and depression of inflammation by lipoic acid and sodium iodide. *Prostaglandins* 1978 December;16(6):861-9.

(54) Lee HA, Hughes DA. Alpha-lipoic acid modulates NF-kappaB activity in human monocytic cells by direct interaction with DNA. *Exp Gerontol* 2002 January;37(2-3):401-10.

(55) Ha H, Lee JH, Kim HN et al. alpha-Lipoic acid inhibits inflammatory bone resorption by suppressing prostaglandin E2 synthesis. *J Immunol* 2006 January 1;176(1):111-7.

(56) Burkart V, Koike T, Brenner HH, Imai Y, Kolb H. Dihydrolipoic acid protects pancreatic islet cells from inflammatory attack. *Agents Actions* 1993 January;38(1-2):60-5.

(57) Cho YS, Lee J, Lee TH et al. alpha-Lipoic acid inhibits airway inflammation and hyperresponsiveness in a mouse model of asthma. *J Allergy Clin Immunol* 2004 August;114(2):429-35.

(58) Grimble RF. Effect of antioxidative vitamins on immune function with clinical applications. *Int J Vitam Nutr Res* 1997;67(5):312-20.

(59) Majewicz J, Rimbach G, Proteggente AR, Lodge JK, Kraemer K, Minihane AM. Dietary vitamin C down-regulates inflammatory gene expression in apoE4 smokers. *Biochem Biophys Res Commun* 2005 December 16;338(2):951-5.

(60) Tahir M, Foley B, Pate G et al. Impact of vitamin E and C supplementation on serum adhesion molecules in chronic degenerative aortic stenosis: a randomized controlled trial. *Am Heart J* 2005 August;150(2):302-6.

(61) Majano PL, Garcia-Monzon C, Garcia-Trevijano ER et al. S-Adenosylmethionine modulates inducible nitric oxide synthase gene expression in rat liver and isolated hepatocytes. *J Hepatol* 2001 December;35(6):692-9.

Chapter Five

(1) Waly M, Olteanu H, Banerjee R et al. Activation of methionine synthase by insulin-like growth factor-1 and dopamine: a target for neurodevelopmental toxins and thimerosal. *Mol Psychiatry* 2004 April;9(4):358-70.

(2) Watson WA, Litovitz TL, Rodgers GC, Jr. et al. 2004 Annual report of the American Association of Poison Control Centers Toxic Exposure Surveillance System. *Am J Emerg Med* 2005 September;23(5):589-666.

(3) Lazarou J, Pomeranz BH, Corey PN. Incidence of adverse drug reactions in hospitalized patients: a meta-analysis of prospective studies. *JAMA* 1998 April 15;279(15):1200-5.

(4) Starfield B. Deficiencies in US medical care. *JAMA* 2000 November 1;284(17):2184-5.

(5) Saul AW. How Safe are Vitamins? *Orthomolecular News Service* 2006;Available at: URL: www.orthomolecular.org.

(6) *To Err is Human: Building a Safer Health System*. Washington, DC: National Academy Press; 1999.

(7) Schuster M. How good is the quality of health care in the United States? *Milbank Q* 1998;76:517-63.

(8) Leape LL. Unnecessary surgery. *Annu Rev Public Health* 1992;13:363-83.

(9) Phillips DP, Christenfeld N, Glynn LM. Increase in US medication-error deaths between 1983 and 1993. *Lancet* 1998 February 28;351(9103):643-4.

(10) Hatoff DE, Gertler SL, Miyai K, Parker BA, Weiss JB. Hypervitaminosis A unmasked by acute viral hepatitis. *Gastroenterology* 1982 January;82(1):124-8.

(11) Murray MT. Vitamin A and Carotenes. *Encyclopedia of Nutritional Supplements*. Rockland, CA: Prima Publishing; 1996. p. 19-38.

(12) Rothman KJ, Moore LL, Singer MR, Nguyen US, Mannino S, Milunsky A. Teratogenicity of high vitamin A intake. *N Engl J Med* 1995 November 23;333(21):1369-73.

(13) Gordeuk VR, Bacon BR, Brittenham GM. Iron overload: causes and consequences. *Annu Rev Nutr* 1987;7:485-508.

(14) Salonen JT, Nyyssonen K, Korpela H, Tuomilehto J, Seppanen R, Salonen R. High stored iron levels are associated with excess risk of myocardial infarction in eastern Finnish men. *Circulation* 1992 September;86(3):803-11.

(15) Uhland V, Lewis K, Spehar C. American Top 25: Supplements Climbing the Charts. Natural Foods Merchandiser . 2004. Ref Type: Magazine Article

(16) Murray MT, Pizzorno J. Osteoporosis. *Encyclopedia of Natural Medicine*. Revised 2nd ed. Prima Publishing; 1998. p. 717-8.

(17) Bourgoin BP, Evans DR, Cornett JR, Lingard SM, Quattrone AJ. Lead content in 70 brands of dietary calcium supplements. *Am J Public Health* 1993 August;83(8):1155-60.

(18) Murray MT. Herbal Preparations. *The Healing Power of Herbs*. 2nd ed. Rockland, CA: Prima Publishing; 1995. p. 15-26.

(19) Murray MT. Panax ginseng. *The Healing Power of Herbs*. 2nd ed. Rockland, CA: Prima Publishing; 1995. p. 265-79.

(20) Transition Team OoNHP. A Fresh Start: Final Report of the ONHP Transition Team. Government of Canada; 2000 Mar 31.

(21) Slifman NR, Obermeyer WR, Aloi BK et al. Contamination of botanical dietary supplements by Digitalis lanata. *N Engl J Med* 1998 September 17;339(12):806-11.

(22) Melethil S. Proposed rule: current good manufacturing practice in manufacturing, packing, or holding dietary ingredients and dietary supplements. *Life Sci* 2006 March 27;78(18):2049-53.

(23) Saper RB, Kales SN, Paquin J et al. Heavy metal content of ayurvedic herbal medicine products. *JAMA* 2004 December 15;292(23):2868-73.

(24) FDA News. FDA Proposes Labeling and Manufacturing Standards For All Dietary Supplements. Press Release 2003 Mar 7.

(25) Food and Drug Adminstration. Current Good Manufacturing Practice in Manufacturing, Packing, or Holding Dietary Ingredients and Dietary Supplements; Proposed Rule. National Archives and Records Administration: Federal Register; 2003 Mar 13.

(26) Center for Food Safety and Applied Nutrition. Overview of Dietary Supplements. *Center for Food Safety and Applied Nutrition* 2001;Available at: URL: www.cfsan.fda.gov.

(27) ConsumerLab.com. Product Review: Multivuitamin/Multimineral Supplements. ConsumerLab com 2007;Available at: URL: www.consumerlab.com.

(28) Lobenberg R, Steinke W. Investigation of vitamin and mineral tablets and capsules on the Canadian market. *J Pharm Pharm Sci* 2006;9(1):40-9.

Chapter Six

(1) South J. Vitamin Safety, RDAs and the Assault on Vitamin Freedom. *Vitamin Research Products website* 2006;Available at: URL: www.vrp.com.

(2) Commission on Life Sciences. Recommended Dietary Allowances: 10th Edition (1989). Washington, DC: National Academies Press; 1989.

(3) Hathcock JN. Vitamin and Mineral Safety, 2nd Edition. *Council for Responsible Nutrition* 2004;Available at: URL: crnusa.org. Accessed July 2, 2006.

(4) BRIN M. Erythrocyte as a biopsy tissue for functional evaluation of thiamine adequacy. *JAMA* 1964 March 7;187:762-6.

(5) Stephens NG, Parsons A, Schofield PM, Kelly F, Cheeseman K, Mitchinson MJ. Randomised controlled trial of vitamin E in patients with coronary disease: Cambridge Heart Antioxidant Study (CHAOS). *Lancet* 1996 March 23;347(9004):781-6.

(6) Rimm EB, Stampfer MJ, Ascherio A, Giovannucci E, Colditz GA, Willett WC. Vitamin E consumption and the risk of coronary heart disease in men. *N Engl J Med* 1993 May 20;328(20):1450-6.

(7) Stampfer MJ, Hennekens CH, Manson JE, Colditz GA, Rosner B, Willett WC. Vitamin E consumption and the risk of coronary disease in women. *N Engl J Med* 1993 May 20;328(20):1444-9.

(8) Losonczy KG, Harris TB, Havlik RJ. Vitamin E and vitamin C supplement use and risk of all-cause and coronary heart disease mortality in older persons: the Established Populations for Epidemiologic Studies of the Elderly. *Am J Clin Nutr* 1996 August;64(2):190-6.

(9) Meyer F, Bairati I, Dagenais GR. Lower ischemic heart disease incidence and mortality among vitamin supplement users. *Can J Cardiol* 1996 October;12(10):930-4.

(10) Clark LC, Combs GF, Jr., Turnbull BW et al. Effects of selenium supplementation for cancer prevention in patients with carcinoma of the skin. A randomized controlled trial. Nutritional Prevention of Cancer Study Group. *JAMA* 1996 December 25;276(24):1957-63.

(11) Flicker L, Vasikaran SD, Thomas J et al. Efficacy of B vitamins in lowering homocysteine in older men: maximal effects for those with B12 deficiency and hyperhomocysteinemia. *Stroke* 2006 February;37(2):547-9.

(12) Jacques PF, Taylor A, Hankinson SE et al. Long-term vitamin C supplement use and prevalence of early age-related lens opacities. *Am J Clin Nutr* 1997 October;66(4):911-6.

(13) Dawson-Hughes B, Harris SS, Krall EA, Dallal GE. Effect of calcium and vitamin D supplementation on bone density in men and women 65 years of age or older. *N Engl J Med* 1997 September 4;337(10):670-6.

(14) Reid IR, Ames RW, Evans MC, Gamble GD, Sharpe SJ. Long-term effects of calcium supplementation on bone loss and fractures in postmenopausal women: a randomized controlled trial. *Am J Med* 1995 April;98(4):331-5.

(15) NIH Consensus conference. Optimal calcium intake. NIH Consensus Development Panel on Optimal Calcium Intake. *JAMA* 1994 December 28;272(24):1942-8.

(16) Klatz R, Goldman R. Vitamins, Co-vitamins and Cofactors. *Anti-Aging Revolution.* third ed. North Bergen, NJ: Basic Health Publications Inc.; 2003. p. 169-204.

(17) Ames BN, Elson-Schwab I, Silver EA. High-dose vitamin therapy stimulates variant enzymes with decreased coenzyme binding affinity (increased K(m)): relevance to genetic disease and polymorphisms. *Am J Clin Nutr* 2002 April;75(4):616-58.

(18) Higdon J. Folic Acid. *An Evidence-based Approach to Vitamins and Minerals.* New York, NY: Thieme Medical Publishers Inc.; 2003. p. 6-14.

(19) Choi SW, Mason JB. Folate and carcinogenesis: an integrated scheme. *J Nutr* 2000 February;130(2):129-32.

(20) Ames BN, Elson-Schwab I, Silver EA. High-dose vitamin therapy stimulates variant enzymes with decreased coenzyme binding affinity (increased K(m)): relevance to genetic disease and polymorphisms. *Am J Clin Nutr* 2002 April;75(4):616-58.

(21) Megavitamins may be useful treatment for many genetic diseases, or just good insurance to tune up body's metabolism. *University of California, Berkeley* 2002 April 4. AccessedJune 29, 2006.

(22) Stampfer MJ, Malinow MR, Willett WC et al. A prospective study of plasma homocyst(e)ine and risk of myocardial infarction in US physicians. *JAMA* 1992 August 19;268(7):877-81.

(23) Glueck CJ, Shaw P, Lang JE, Tracy T, Sieve-Smith L, Wang Y. Evidence that homocysteine is an independent risk factor for atherosclerosis in hyperlipidemic patients. *Am J Cardiol* 1995 January 15;75(2):132-6.

(24) Loehrer FM, Angst CP, Haefeli WE, Jordan PP, Ritz R, Fowler B. Low whole-blood S-adenosylmethionine and correlation between 5-methyltetrahydrofolate and homocysteine in coronary artery disease. *Arterioscler Thromb Vasc Biol* 1996 June;16(6):727-33.

(25) Franken DG, Boers GH, Blom HJ, Trijbels FJ, Kloppenborg PW. Treatment of mild hyperhomocysteinemia in vascular disease patients. *Arterioscler Thromb* 1994 March;14(3):465-70.

(26) Firshein R. *The Nutraceutical Revolution.* New York, NY: Riverhead Books; 21998. p. 144-60.

(27) Selhub J, Jacques PF, Bostom AG et al. Association between plasma homocysteine concentrations and extracranial carotid-artery stenosis. *N Engl J Med* 1995 February 2;332(5):286-91.

(28) Arnesen E, Refsum H, Bonaa KH, Ueland PM, Forde OH, Nordrehaug JE. Serum total homocysteine and coronary heart disease. *Int J Epidemiol* 1995 August;24(4):704-9.

(29) Boushey CJ, Beresford SA, Omenn GS, Motulsky AG. A quantitative assessment of plasma homocysteine as a risk factor for vascular disease. Probable benefits of increasing folic acid intakes. *JAMA* 1995 October 4;274(13):1049-57.

(30) Firshein R. *The Nutraceutical Revolution.* New York, NY: Riverhead Books; 21998. p. 144-60.

(31) Munshi MN, Stone A, Fink L, Fonseca V. Hyperhomocysteinemia following a methionine load in patients with non-insulin-dependent diabetes mellitus and macrovascular disease. *Metabolism* 1996 January;45(1):133-5.

(32) Bottiglieri T. Folate, vitamin B12, and neuropsychiatric disorders. *Nutr Rev* 1996 December;54(12):382-90.

(33) Bailey LB, Gregory JF, III. Polymorphisms of methylenetetrahydrofolate reductase and other enzymes: metabolic significance, risks and impact on folate requirement. *J Nutr* 1999 May;129(5):919-22.

(34) Kauwell GP, Wilsky CE, Cerda JJ et al. Methylenetetrahydrofolate reductase mutation (677C-->T) negatively influences plasma homocysteine response to marginal folate intake in elderly women. *Metabolism* 2000 November;49(11):1440-3.

(35) Shpichinetsky V, Raz I, Friedlander Y et al. The association between two common mutations C677T and A1298C in human methylenetetrahydrofolate reductase gene and the risk for diabetic nephropathy in type II diabetic patients. *J Nutr* 2000 October;130(10):2493-7.

(36) Ames BN, Elson-Schwab I, Silver EA. High-dose vitamin therapy stimulates variant enzymes with decreased coenzyme binding affinity (increased K(m)): relevance to genetic disease and polymorphisms. *Am J Clin Nutr* 2002 April;75(4):616-58.

(37) Yoo JH, Choi GD, Kang SS. Pathogenicity of thermolabile methylenetetrahydrofolate reductase for vascular dementia. *Arterioscler Thromb Vasc Biol* 2000 August;20(8):1921-5.

(38) Bates CJ, Fuller NJ. The effect of riboflavin deficiency on methylenetetrahydrofolate reductase (NADPH) (EC 1.5.1.20) and folate metabolism in the rat. *Br J Nutr* 1986 March;55(2):455-64.

(39) Ames BN, Elson-Schwab I, Silver EA. High-dose vitamin therapy stimulates variant enzymes with decreased coenzyme binding affinity (increased K(m)): relevance to genetic disease and polymorphisms. *Am J Clin Nutr* 2002 April;75(4):616-58.

Chapter Seven

(1) Wartenberg D, Ramsey D, Warner J. A Guide to Statistics and Data Analyses. *FacsNet Reporting Tools* 2006;Available at: URL: www.facsnet.org/tools/ref_tutor/epidem/data.php3. AccessedMarch 15, 2006.

(2) Ioannidis JP. Why most published research findings are false. *PLoS Med* 2005 August;2(8):e124.

(3) Ullom-Minnich P. Prevention of osteoporosis and fractures. *Am Fam Physician* 1999 July;60(1):194-202.

(4) Prince RL, Devine A, Dhaliwal SS, Dick IM. Effects of calcium supplementation on clinical fracture and bone structure: results of a 5-year, double-blind, placebo-controlled trial in elderly women. *Arch Intern Med* 2006 April 24;166(8):869-75.

(5) Hooper L, Thompson RL, Harrison RA et al. Risks and benefits of omega 3 fats for mortality, cardiovascular disease, and cancer: systematic review. *BMJ* 2006 March 24.

(6) Clegg DO, Reda DJ, Harris CL et al. Glucosamine, chondroitin sulfate, and the two in combination for painful knee osteoarthritis. *N Engl J Med* 2006 February 23;354(8):795-808.

(7) Hochberg MC. Nutritional supplements for knee osteoarthritis--still no resolution. *N Engl J Med* 2006 February 23;354(8):858-60.

(8) Jackson RD, LaCroix AZ, Gass M et al. Calcium plus vitamin D supplementation and the risk of fractures. *N Engl J Med* 2006 February 16;354(7):669-83.

(9) Dreosti IE. Magnesium status and health. *Nutr Rev* 1995 September;53(9 Pt 2):S23-S27.

(10) Gallai V, Sarchielli P, Morucci P, Abbritti G. Magnesium content of mononuclear blood cells in migraine patients. *Headache* 1994 March;34(3):160-5.

(11) Cohen L, Kitzes R. Infrared spectroscopy and magnesium content of bone mineral in osteoporotic women. *Isr J Med Sci* 1981 December;17(12):1123-5.

(12) Murray M. Calcium. *Encyclopedia of Nutritional Supplements.* Rocklin, CA: Prima Health; 2006. p. 149-58.

(13) Lips P, Graafmans WC, Ooms ME, Bezemer PD, Bouter LM. Vitamin D supplementation and fracture incidence in elderly persons. A randomized, placebo-controlled clinical trial. *Ann Intern Med* 1996 February 15;124(4):400-6.

(14) Meyer HE, Smedshaug GB, Kvaavik E, Falch JA, Tverdal A, Pedersen JI. Can vitamin D supplementation reduce the risk of fracture in the elderly? A randomized controlled trial. *J Bone Miner Res* 2002 April;17(4):709-15.

(15) Bischoff-Ferrari HA, Zhang Y, Kiel DP, Felson DT. Positive association between serum 25-hydroxyvitamin D level and bone density in osteoarthritis. *Arthritis Rheum* 2005 December 15;53(6):821-6.

(16) Chapuy MC, Arlot ME, Duboeuf F et al. Vitamin D3 and calcium to prevent hip fractures in the elderly women. *N Engl J Med* 1992 December 3;327(23):1637-42.

(17) Chapuy MC, Pamphile R, Paris E et al. Combined calcium and vitamin D3 supplementation in elderly women: confirmation of reversal of secondary hyperparathyroidism and hip fracture risk: the Decalyos II study. *Osteoporos Int* 2002 March;13(3):257-64.

(18) Trivedi DP, Doll R, Khaw KT. Effect of four monthly oral vitamin D3 (cholecalciferol) supplementation on fractures and mortality in men and women living in the community: randomised double blind controlled trial. *BMJ* 2003 March 1;326(7387):469.

(19) Vieth R. Why the optimal requirement for Vitamin D3 is probably much higher than what is officially recommended for adults. *J Steroid Biochem Mol Biol* 2004 May;89-90(1-5):575-9.

(20) Grossman MI, Kirsner JB, Gillespie IE. Basal and histalog-stimulated gastric secretion in control subjects and in patients with peptic ulcer or gastric cancer. *Gastroenterology* 1963 July;45:14-26.

(21) Recker RR. Calcium absorption and achlorhydria. *N Engl J Med* 1985 July 11;313(2):70-3.

(22) Howard BV, Van HL, Hsia J et al. Low-fat dietary pattern and risk of cardiovascular disease: the Women's Health Initiative Randomized Controlled Dietary Modification Trial. *JAMA* 2006 February 8;295(6):655-66.

(23) Prentice RL, Caan B, Chlebowski RT et al. Low-fat dietary pattern and risk of invasive breast cancer: the Women's Health Initiative Randomized Controlled Dietary Modification Trial. *JAMA* 2006 February 8;295(6):629-42.

(24) Beresford SA, Johnson KC, Ritenbaugh C et al. Low-fat dietary pattern and risk of colorectal cancer: the Women's Health Initiative Randomized Controlled Dietary Modification Trial. *JAMA* 2006 February 8;295(6):643-54.

(25) Howard BV, Van HL, Hsia J et al. Low-fat dietary pattern and risk of cardiovascular disease: the Women's Health Initiative Randomized Controlled Dietary Modification Trial. *JAMA* 2006 February 8;295(6):655-66.

(26) Prentice RL, Caan B, Chlebowski RT et al. Low-fat dietary pattern and risk of invasive breast cancer: the Women's Health Initiative Randomized Controlled Dietary Modification Trial. *JAMA* 2006 February 8;295(6):629-42.

(27) Howell A, Cuzick J, Baum M et al. Results of the ATAC (Arimidex, Tamoxifen, Alone or in Combination) trial after completion of 5 years' adjuvant treatment for breast cancer. *Lancet* 2005 January 1;365(9453):60-2.

(28) Beresford SA, Johnson KC, Ritenbaugh C et al. Low-fat dietary pattern and risk of colorectal cancer: the Women's Health Initiative Randomized Controlled Dietary Modification Trial. *JAMA* 2006 February 8;295(6):643-54.

(29) MacWilliam LD. What Makes Gamma Tocopherol Superior to Alpha Tocopherol. Life Extension Magazine [April], 25-31. 2006. Life Extension Publications Inc. Ref Type: Magazine Article

(30) Brookes L, Gruberg L. Medscape Conference Coverage, based on selected sessions at the European Society of Cardiology Congress. *WebMD* 2006;Available at: URL: www.medscape.com. AccessedFebruary 20, 2006.

(31) Campbell S, Stone W, Whaley S, Krishnan K. Development of gamma (gamma)-tocopherol as a colorectal cancer chemopreventive agent. *Crit Rev Oncol Hematol* 2003 September;47(3):249-59.

(32) Campbell SE, Stone WL, Whaley SG, Qui M, Krishnan K. Gamma (gamma) tocopherol upregulates peroxisome proliferator activated receptor (PPAR) gamma (gamma) expression in SW 480 human colon cancer cell lines. *BMC Cancer* 2003 October 1;3:25.

(33) Christen S HTSMAB. Chronic Inflammation, Mutation and Cancer. In: Parsonnet J, editor. *Microbes and Malignancy: Infection as a Cause of Human Cancers.*New York: Oxford University Press; 1999. p. 35-88.

(34) Stone WL, Papas AM. Tocopherols and the etiology of colon cancer. *J Natl Cancer Inst* 1997 July 16;89(14):1006-14.

(35) Traub M. Is Homocysteine Dead? *Holistic Primary Care* 2006;Available at: URL: www.holisticprimarycare.net. AccessedMarch 1, 2006.

(36) Bonaa KH, Njolstad I, Ueland PM et al. Homocysteine lowering and cardiovascular events after acute myocardial infarction. *N Engl J Med* 2006 April 13;354(15):1578-88.

(37) Homocysteine and risk of ischemic heart disease and stroke: a meta-analysis. *JAMA* 2002 October 23;288(16):2015-22.

(38) Arnesen E, Refsum H, Bonaa KH, Ueland PM, Forde OH, Nordrehaug JE. Serum total homocysteine and coronary heart disease. *Int J Epidemiol* 1995 August;24(4):704-9.

(39) Miller ER, III, Pastor-Barriuso R, Dalal D, Riemersma RA, Appel LJ, Guallar E. Meta-analysis: high-dosage vitamin E supplementation may increase all-cause mortality. *Ann Intern Med* 2005 January 4;142(1):37-46.

(40) Wood T. The Case for Nutritional Supplements. article submitted for publication. 2006. Ref Type: Unpublished Work

(41) Blumberg J, Block G. The Alpha-Tocopherol, Beta-Carotene Cancer Prevention Study in Finland. *Nutr Rev* 1994 July;52(7):242-5.

(42) Wright ME, Mayne ST, Stolzenberg-Solomon RZ et al. Development of a comprehensive dietary antioxidant index and application to lung cancer risk in a cohort of male smokers. *Am J Epidemiol* 2004 July 1;160(1):68-76.

Chapter Eight

(1) MacWilliam LD. What Makes Gamma Tocopherol Superior to Alpha Tocopherol? Life Extension Magazine [April 2006], 25-31. 2006. Ft. Lauderdale, FL, Life Extension Publications. Ref Type: Magazine Article

(2) Visioli F, Vinceri FF, Galli C. 'Waste waters' from olive oil production are rich in natural antioxidants. *Experientia* 1995 January 15;51(1):32-4.

(3) Canavese C, Bergamo D, Ciccone G et al. Low-dose continuous iron therapy leads to a positive iron balance and decreased serum transferrin levels in chronic haemodialysis patients. *Nephrol Dial Transplant* 2004 June;19(6):1564-70.

(4) Colgan M. Vitamins: Nuts and Bolts of Life. *The New Nutrition: Medicine for the Millennium.*Vancouver: Apple Publishing; 1995. p. 76-115.

(5) Atkins R. Vitamins. *Dr. Atkin's Vita-Nutrient Solution.*New York: Simon and Schuster; 1998. p. 87-9.

(6) Murray MT. Some Practical Recommendations. *Encyclopedia of Nutritional Supplements.*Rocklin CA: Prima Health; 1996. p. 10-3.

(7) Passwater RA. The New Supernutrition Plan. *The New Supernutrition* .New York, NY: Simon & Schuster Inc.; 1991. p. 295-306.

(8) Strand RD. Putting It All Together. *Bionutrition 1998.*Rapid City, SD: Comprehensive Wellness Publishing; 1998. p. 128-36.

(9) Strand RD. Cellular Nutrition: Putting It All Together. *What Your Doctor Doesn't Know About Nutritional Medicine May Be Killing You.*Nashville, TE: Thomas Nelson Inc.; 2002. p. 192-204.

(10) Mindell E. My Basic Adult Vitamin-Mineral Program. *Dr. Earl Mindell's What You Should Know About Creating Your Own Health Plan* .New Canaan, KT: Keats Publishing Inc; 1996. p. 52-3.

(11) Whitaker J. The Whitaker Wellness Program. *Dr. Whitaker's Guide to Natural Healing* .Roseville, CA: Prima Publishing; 1996. p. 26-58.

(12) Balch PA. Nutrition, Diet and Wellness. *Prescription for Natural Healing: The A-to-Z Guide to Supplements* . 2nd ed. New York, NY: Pengiun Putnam Inc; 2002. p. 1-23.

(13) Balch PA and Balch JF. Nutrition, Diet and Wellness. *Prescription for Natural Healing: A Practical A-to-Z Reference to Drug-Free Remedies Using Vitamins, Herbs & Food Supplements.* 3rd ed. New York, NY: Pengiun Putnam Inc. 2000. p. 3-12.

(14) Kurzweil R GT. Aggressive Supplementation. *Fantastic Voyage: Live Long Enough to Live Forever.* Holtzbrinck Publishers; 2004. p. 312-36.

(15) Colgan M. Hormonal Nutrition. *Hormonal Health.* 1st ed. Vancouver, BC: Apple Publishing; 1996. p. 218-41.

(16) Perricone N. 12 Nutritional Supplements That Faciltate Weight Loss While Maintaining Muscle Mass. *The Perricone Weight-Loss Diet.*New York, NY: Ballantine Books; 2005. p. 94-115.

(17) Atkins RC. Applying the Program. *Dr. Atkins' Vita-Nutrient Solution.*New York, NY: Fireside; 1998. p. 315-26.

(18) Miller PE, Reinagel M. Individualizing Your Antiaging Program. *The Life Extension Revolution.*New York, NY : Bantam Dell ; 2005. p. 262-70.

(19) Higdon J. *An Evidence-Based Approach to Vitamins and Minerals*. New York, NY: Thieme; 2003.

Chapter Nine

(1) Canavese C, Bergamo D, Ciccone G et al. Low-dose continuous iron therapy leads to a positive iron balance and decreased serum transferrin levels in chronic haemodialysis patients. *Nephrol Dial Transplant* 2004 June;19(6):1564-70.

(2) Balch PA. Minerals. *Prescription for Nutritional Healing*. 2 ed. New York, NY: Avery; 2002. p. 53-76.

(3) Albion Laboratories. A Healthy Start. *Alblion Research Notes Newsletter* 1997 July;6(2):1-5.

(4) Knudsen E et al. Zinc, copper and magnesium absorption from a fiber-rich diet. *J Trace Elem Med Biol* 1996;2(10):68-76.

(5) Schardt FZ. Effects of doses of certain cereal foods and zinc on different blood parameters in performing althletes. *Ernahrungswuiss* 1994;3(33):207-16.

(6) Greger JL, Krashoc CL. Effects of a variety of calcium sources on mineral metabolism in anemic rats. *Drug Nutr Interact* 1988;5(4):387-94.

(7) Murray MT. Magnesium. *Encyclopedia of Nutritional Supplements.*Rocklin, CA: Prima Health; 1996. p. 159-75.

(8) Reavley N. Vitamins, minerals and diet: the basics. *New Encyclopedia of Vitamins, Minerals and Herbs.*New York, NY: M. Evans and Company; 1998. p. 4-30.

(9) Heaney RP, Dowell MS, Bierman J, Hale CA, Bendich A. Absorbability and cost effectiveness in calcium supplementation. *J Am Coll Nutr* 2001 June;20(3):239-46.

(10) Rojas LX, McDowell LR, Martin FG, Wilkinson NS, Johnson AB, Njeru CA. Relative bioavailability of zinc methionine and two inorganic zinc sources fed to cattle. *J Trace Elem Med Biol* 1996 December;10(4):205-9.

(11) Wapnir RA. Copper absorption and bioavailability. *Am J Clin Nutr* 1998 May;67(5 Suppl):1054S-60S.

(12) Johnson MA, Smith MM, Edmonds JT. Copper, iron, zinc, and manganese in dietary supplements, infant formulas, and ready-to-eat breakfast cereals. *Am J Clin Nutr* 1998 May;67(5 Suppl):1035S-40S.

(13) Kincaid RL, Chew BP, Cronrath JD. Zinc oxide and amino acids as sources of dietary zinc for calves: effects on uptake and immunity. *J Dairy Sci* 1997 July;80(7):1381-8.

(14) Fairweather-Tait SJ, Fox TE, Wharf SG, Ghani NA. A preliminary study of the bioavailability of iron- and zinc-glycine chelates. *Food Addit Contam* 1992 January;9(1):97-101.

(15) Smith AM, Picciano MF. Relative bioavailability of seleno-compounds in the lactating rat. *J Nutr* 1987 April;117(4):725-31.

(16) Nicar MJ, Pak CY. Calcium bioavailability from calcium carbonate and calcium citrate. *J Clin Endocrinol Metab* 1985 August;61(2):391-3.

(17) Strand RD. Putting it All Together. *Bionutrition: Winning the War Within.* Rapid City, SD: Comprehensive Wellness Publishing; 1998. p. 128-36.

(18) Colgan M. Minerals Are Your Framework. *The New Nutrition: Medicine for the Millennium.* Vancouver, BC: Apple Publishing; 1995. p. 89-99.

(19) Murray MT, Pizzorno J. *Encyclopedia of Natural Medicine.* 2nd ed. Rocklin, CA: Prima Publishing; 1998. p. 718.

(20) Murray MT. *Encyclopedia of Nutritional Supplements.* Rocklin, CA: Prima Health; 1996. p. 162.

(21) Traber MG. The Biological Activity of Vitamin E. Linus Pauling Institute, Oregon State University; 1998.

(22) National Academies Press. Dietary Reference Intakes for Vitamin C, Vitamin E, Selenium, and Carotenoids. Washington, DC: Food and Nutrition Board, Institute of Medicine; 2000.

(23) Kushi LH, Folsom AR, Prineas RJ, Mink PJ, Wu Y, Bostick RM. Dietary antioxidant vitamins and death from coronary heart disease in postmenopausal women. *N Engl J Med* 1996 May 2;334(18):1156-62.

(24) Yochum LA, Folsom AR, Kushi LH. Intake of antioxidant vitamins and risk of death from stroke in postmenopausal women. *Am J Clin Nutr* 2000 August;72(2):476-83.

(25) Stampfer MJ, Hennekens CH, Manson JE, Colditz GA, Rosner B, Willett WC. Vitamin E consumption and the risk of coronary disease in women. *N Engl J Med* 1993 May 20;328(20):1444-9.

(26) Keaney JF, Jr., Simon DI, Freedman JE. Vitamin E and vascular homeostasis: implications for atherosclerosis. *FASEB J* 1999 June;13(9):965-75.

(27) Greenwell I. Newly Discovered Benefits of Gamma Tocopherol. Life Extension Magazine [Collector's edition], 61-64. 2003. Ft. Lauderdale, FL, LE Publications Inc. Ref Type: Magazine Article

(28) Olmedilla B, Granado F, Southon S et al. Serum concentrations of carotenoids and vitamins A, E, and C in control subjects from five European countries. *Br J Nutr* 2001 February;85(2):227-38.

(29) Friedrich MJ. To "E" or not to "E," vitamin E's role in health and disease is the question. *JAMA* 2004 August 11;292(6):671-3.

(30) Dietary supplementation with n-3 polyunsaturated fatty acids and vitamin E after myocardial infarction: results of the GISSI-Prevenzione trial. Gruppo Italiano per lo Studio della Sopravvivenza nell'Infarto miocardico. *Lancet* 1999 August 7;354(9177):447-55.

(31) Yusuf S, Dagenais G, Pogue J, Bosch J, Sleight P. Vitamin E supplementation and cardiovascular events in high-risk patients. The Heart Outcomes Prevention Evaluation Study Investigators. *N Engl J Med* 2000 January 20;342(3):154-60.

(32) Kushi LH, Folsom AR, Prineas RJ, Mink PJ, Wu Y, Bostick RM. Dietary antioxidant vitamins and death from coronary heart disease in postmenopausal women. *N Engl J Med* 1996 May 2;334(18):1156-62.

(33) Jha P, Flather M, Lonn E, Farkouh M, Yusuf S. The antioxidant vitamins and cardiovascular disease. A critical review of epidemiologic and clinical trial data. *Ann Intern Med* 1995 December 1;123(11):860-72.

(34) The effect of vitamin E and beta carotene on the incidence of lung cancer and other cancers in male smokers. The Alpha-Tocopherol, Beta Carotene Cancer Prevention Study Group. *N Engl J Med* 1994 April 14;330(15):1029-35.

(35) Campbell SE, Stone WL, Whaley SG, Qui M, Krishnan K. Gamma (gamma) tocopherol upregulates peroxisome proliferator activated receptor (PPAR) gamma (gamma) expression in SW 480 human colon cancer cell lines. *BMC Cancer* 2003 October 1;3:25.

(36) Huang HY, Appel LJ. Supplementation of diets with alpha-tocopherol reduces serum concentrations of gamma- and delta-tocopherol in humans. *J Nutr* 2003 October;133(10):3137-40.

(37) Saldeen T, Li D, Mehta JL. Differential effects of alpha- and gamma-tocopherol on low-density lipoprotein oxidation, superoxide activity, platelet aggregation and arterial thrombogenesis. *J Am Coll Cardiol* 1999 October;34(4):1208-15.

(38) Tomasch R, Wagner KH, Elmadfa I. Antioxidative power of plant oils in humans: the influence of alpha- and gamma-tocopherol. *Ann Nutr Metab* 2001;45(3):110-5.

(39) Li D, Saldeen T, Romeo F, Mehta JL. Relative Effects of alpha- and gamma-Tocopherol on Low-Density Lipoprotein Oxidation and Superoxide Dismutase and Nitric Oxide Synthase Activity and Protein Expression in Rats. *J Cardiovasc Pharmacol Ther* 1999 October;4(4):219-26.

(40) Jiang Q, Elson-Schwab I, Courtemanche C, Ames BN. gamma-tocopherol and its major metabolite, in contrast to alpha-tocopherol, inhibit cyclooxygenase activity in macrophages and epithelial cells. *Proc Natl Acad Sci U S A* 2000 October 10;97(21):11494-9.

(41) Stone WL, Krishnan K, Campbell SE, Qui M, Whaley SG, Yang H. Tocopherols and the treatment of colon cancer. *Ann N Y Acad Sci* 2004 December;1031:223-33.

(42) Azzi A, Gysin R, Kempna P et al. The role of alpha-tocopherol in preventing disease: from epidemiology to molecular events. *Mol Aspects Med* 2003 December;24(6):325-36.

(43) Williamson KS, Gabbita SP, Mou S et al. The nitration product 5-nitro-gamma-tocopherol is increased in the Alzheimer brain. *Nitric Oxide* 2002 March;6(2):221-7.

(44) Sanders R. UC Berkeley and Australian researchers call into question current formulation of Vitamin E supplements. 4-1-1997. 2-12-2005. Ref Type: Internet Communication

(45) Crary EJ, McCarty MF. Potential clinical applications for high-dose nutritional antioxidants. *Med Hypotheses* 1984 January;13(1):77-98.

(46) Saldeen T, Li D, Mehta JL. Differential effects of alpha- and gamma-tocopherol on low-density lipoprotein oxidation, superoxide activity, platelet aggregation and arterial thrombogenesis. *J Am Coll Cardiol* 1999 October;34(4):1208-15.

(47) Handelman GJ. Carotenoids as scavengers of active oxygen species. In: Cadenas E, Parker L, editors. *Handbook of Antioxidants.* New York, NY: Marcel Dekker Inc.; 1996. p. 259-314.

(48) Balch PA, Balch JF. Antioxidants. *Prescription for Nutritional Healing.* New York, NY: Avery; 2000. p. 53-62.

(49) Murray MT, Pizzorno J. Osteoporosis. *Encyclopedia of Natural Medicine.* 2nd ed. Rocklin, CA: Prima Publishing; 1998. p. 706-21.

(50) Reavley N. Osteoporosis. *New Encyclopedia of Vitamins, Minerals and Herbs.* New York, NY: M. Evans and Company; 1998. p. 653-60.

(51) Murray MT. Zinc. *Encyclopedia of Nutritional Supplements.* Rocklin, CA: Prima Health; 1996. p. 181-9.

(52) Mancini M, Parfitt VJ, Rubba P. Antioxidants in the Mediterranean diet. *Can J Cardiol* 1995 October;11 Suppl G:105G-9G.

(53) Steinberg D. Antioxidants in the prevention of human atherosclerosis. Summary of the proceedings of a National Heart, Lung, and Blood Institute Workshop: September 5-6, 1991, Bethesda, Maryland. *Circulation* 1992 June;85(6):2337-44.

(54) Gottlieb SS, Baruch L, Kukin ML, Bernstein JL, Fisher ML, Packer M. Prognostic importance of the serum magnesium concentration in patients with congestive heart failure. *J Am Coll Cardiol* 1990 October;16(4):827-31.

(55) Bellizzi MC, Franklin MF, Duthie GG, James WP. Vitamin E and coronary heart disease: the European paradox. *Eur J Clin Nutr* 1994 November;48(11):822-31.

(56) Rimm EB, Stampfer MJ, Ascherio A, Giovannucci E, Colditz GA, Willett WC. Vitamin E consumption and the risk of coronary heart disease in men. *N Engl J Med* 1993 May 20;328(20):1450-6.

(57) Cappuccio FP, Elliott P, Allender PS, Pryer J, Follman DA, Cutler JA. Epidemiologic association between dietary calcium intake and blood pressure: a meta-analysis of published data. *Am J Epidemiol* 1995 November 1;142(9):935-45.

(58) Murray MT. Calcium. *Encyclopedia of Nutritional Supplements.* Rocklin, CA: Prima Health; 1996. p. 149-58.

(59) Karppanen H, Karppanen P, Mervaala E. Why and how to implement sodium, potassium, calcium, and magnesium changes in food items and diets? *J Hum Hypertens* 2005 December;19 Suppl 3:S10-S19.

(60) Zemel MB. Calcium modulation of hypertension and obesity: mechanisms and implications. *J Am Coll Nutr* 2001 October;20(5 Suppl):428S-35S.

(61) Altura BM. Ischemic heart disease and magnesium. *Magnesium* 1988;7(2):57-67.

(62) Altura BM. Basic biochemistry and physiology of magnesium: a brief review. *Magnes Trace Elem* 1991;10(2-4):167-71.

(63) McLean RM. Magnesium and its therapeutic uses: a review. *Am J Med* 1994 January;96(1):63-76.

(64) Purvis JR, Movahed A. Magnesium disorders and cardiovascular diseases. *Clin Cardiol* 1992 August;15(8):556-68.

(65) Galland LD, Baker SM, McLellan RK. Magnesium deficiency in the pathogenesis of mitral valve prolapse. *Magnesium* 1986;5(3-4):165-74.

(66) Simoes FJ, Pereira T, Carvalho J et al. Therapeutic effect of a magnesium salt in patients suffering from mitral valvular prolapse and latent tetany. *Magnesium* 1985;4(5-6):283-90.

(67) Brodsky MA, Orlov MV, Capparelli EV et al. Magnesium therapy in new-onset atrial fibrillation. *Am J Cardiol* 1994 June 15;73(16):1227-9.

(68) Langsjoen PH, Vadhanavikit S, Folkers K. Response of patients in classes III and IV of cardiomyopathy to therapy in a blind and crossover trial with coenzyme Q10. *Proc Natl Acad Sci U S A* 1985 June;82(12):4240-4.

(69) Digiesi V, Cantini F, Oradei A et al. Coenzyme Q10 in essential hypertension. *Mol Aspects Med* 1994;15 Suppl:s257-s263.

(70) Langsjoen P, Langsjoen P, Willis R, Folkers K. Treatment of essential hypertension with coenzyme Q10. *Mol Aspects Med* 1994;15 Suppl:S265-S272.

(71) Langsjoen PH, Langsjoen PH, Folkers K. Isolated diastolic dysfunction of the myocardium and its response to CoQ10 treatment. *Clin Investig* 1993;71(8 Suppl):S140-S144.

(72) Duke RC, Ojcius DM, Young JD. Cell suicide in health and disease. *Sci Am* 1996 December;275(6):80-7.

(73) Slater AF, Stefan C, Nobel I, van den Dobbelsteen DJ, Orrenius S. Signalling mechanisms and oxidative stress in apoptosis. *Toxicol Lett* 1995 December;82-83:149-53.

(74) Kidd PM. Glutathione: Systemic Protectant aginst Oxidative and Free Radical Damage. *www thorne com/altmedrev* 2002. AccessedMarch 3, 2002.

(75) Forman HJ, Boveris A. Superoxide radical and hydrogen peroxide in mitochondria. In: Pryor WA, editor.New York, NY: Academy Press; 1982. p. 65-90.

(76) Kidd PM. Natural Antioxidants' First Line of Defense. *Living with the AIDS Virus: A Strategy for Long-term Survival.*Albany, CA: PMK Biomedical-Nutritional Consulting; 1991. p. 115-42.

(77) Cross CE, Halliwell B, Borish ET et al. Oxygen radicals and human disease. *Ann Intern Med* 1987 October;107(4):526-45.

(78) Meister A. Glutathione-ascorbic acid antioxidant system in animals. *J Biol Chem* 1994 April 1;269(13):9397-400.

(79) Anderson ME. Glutathione and glutathione delivery compounds. *Adv Pharmacol* 1997;38:65-78.

(80) Meister A. Mitochondrial changes associated with glutathione deficiency. *Biochim Biophys Acta* 1995 May 24;1271(1):35-42.

(81) Hunjan MK, Evered DF. Absorption of glutathione from the gastro-intestinal tract. *Biochim Biophys Acta* 1985 May 14;815(2):184-8.

(82) Witschi A, Reddy S, Stofer B, Lauterburg BH. The systemic availability of oral glutathione. *Eur J Clin Pharmacol* 1992;43(6):667-9.

(83) Campbell PJ, Carlson MG. Impact of obesity on insulin action in NIDDM. *Diabetes* 1993 March;42(3):405-10.

(84) Hughes TA, Gwynne JT, Switzer BR, Herbst C, White G. Effects of caloric restriction and weight loss on glycemic control, insulin release and resistance, and atherosclerotic risk in obese patients with type II diabetes mellitus. *Am J Med* 1984 July;77(1):7-17.

(85) Murray MT. Vitamin A and Carotenoids. *Encyclopedia of Nutritional Supplements.*Rocklin, CA: Prima Health; 1996. p. 19-38.

(86) Pitchon E, Sahli O, Borruat FX. Night blindness, yellow vision, and yellow skin: symptoms and signs of malabsorption. *Klin Monatsbl Augenheilkd* 2006 May;223(5):443-6.

(87) Chichili GR, Nohr D, Schaffer M, von LJ, Biesalski HK. beta-Carotene conversion into vitamin A in human retinal pigment epithelial cells. *Invest Ophthalmol Vis Sci* 2005 October;46(10):3562-9.

(88) Hammond BR, Jr., Wooten BR, Snodderly DM. Density of the human crystalline lens is related to the macular pigment carotenoids, lutein and zeaxanthin. *Optom Vis Sci* 1997 July;74(7):499-504.

(89) Knekt P, Heliovaara M, Rissanen A, Aromaa A, Aaran RK. Serum antioxidant vitamins and risk of cataract. *BMJ* 1992 December 5;305(6866):1392-4.

(90) Jacques PF, Chylack LT, Jr., McGandy RB, Hartz SC. Antioxidant status in persons with and without senile cataract. *Arch Ophthalmol* 1988 March;106(3):337-40.

(91) Robertson JM, Donner AP, Trevithick JR. Vitamin E intake and risk of cataracts in humans. *Ann N Y Acad Sci* 1989;570:372-82.

(92) Burton GW, Ingold KU. beta-Carotene: an unusual type of lipid antioxidant. *Science* 1984 May 11;224(4649):569-73.

(93) Palozza P, Krinsky NI. beta-Carotene and alpha-tocopherol are synergistic antioxidants. *Arch Biochem Biophys* 1992 August 15;297(1):184-7.

(94) Glueck CJ, Shaw P, Lang JE, Tracy T, Sieve-Smith L, Wang Y. Evidence that homocysteine is an independent risk factor for atherosclerosis in hyperlipidemic patients. *Am J Cardiol* 1995 January 15;75(2):132-6.

(95) Landgren F, Israelsson B, Lindgren A, Hultberg B, Andersson A, Brattstrom L. Plasma homocysteine in acute myocardial infarction: homocysteine-lowering effect of folic acid. *J Intern Med* 1995 April;237(4):381-8.

(96) Bates CJ, Fuller NJ. The effect of riboflavin deficiency on methylenetetrahydrofolate reductase (NADPH) (EC 1.5.1.20) and folate metabolism in the rat. *Br J Nutr* 1986 March;55(2):455-64.

(97) Ames BN, Elson-Schwab I, Silver EA. High-dose vitamin therapy stimulates variant enzymes with decreased coenzyme binding affinity (increased K(m)): relevance to genetic disease and polymorphisms. *Am J Clin Nutr* 2002 April;75(4):616-58.

(98) Wilcken DE, Dudman NP, Tyrrell PA. Homocystinuria due to cystathionine beta-synthase deficiency--the effects of betaine treatment in pyridoxine-responsive patients. *Metabolism* 1985 December;34(12):1115-21.

(99) Dudman NP, Guo XW, Gordon RB, Dawson PA, Wilcken DE. Human homocysteine catabolism: three major pathways and their relevance to development of arterial occlusive disease. *J Nutr* 1996 April;126(4 Suppl):1295S-300S.

(100) Flora SJ, Singh S, Tandon SK. Prevention of lead intoxication by vitamin-B complex. *Z Gesamte Hyg* 1984 July;30(7):409-11.

(101) Shakman RA. Nutritional influences on the toxicity of environmental pollutants: a review. *Arch Environ Health* 1974 February;28(2):105-13.

(102) Schmidt MA. *Smart Fats: How Dietary Fats and Oils affect Mental, Physical, and Emotional Intelligence.* Berkely, CA: Frog Ltd.; 1997.

(103) Kelley VE, Ferretti A, Izui S, Strom TB. A fish oil diet rich in eicosapentaenoic acid reduces cyclooxygenase metabolites, and suppresses lupus in MRL-lpr mice. *J Immunol* 1985 March;134(3):1914-9.

(104) Watanabe S, Katagiri K, Onozaki K et al. Dietary docosahexaenoic acid but not eicosapentaenoic acid suppresses lipopolysaccharide-induced interleukin-1 beta mRNA induction in mouse spleen leukocytes. *Prostaglandins Leukot Essent Fatty Acids* 2000 March;62(3):147-52.

(105) Murray MT. Essential Fatty Acid Supplementation. *Encyclopedia of Nutritional Supplements.*Rocklin, CA: Prima Health; 1996. p. 249-78.

(106) Christen S, Jiang Q, Shigenaga MK, Ames BN. Analysis of plasma tocopherols alpha, gamma, and 5-nitro-gamma in rats with inflammation by HPLC coulometric detection. *J Lipid Res* 2002 November;43(11):1978-85.

(107) Christen S, Woodall AA, Shigenaga MK, Southwell-Keely PT, Duncan MW, Ames BN. gamma-tocopherol traps mutagenic electrophiles such as NO(X) and complements alpha-tocopherol: physiological implications. *Proc Natl Acad Sci U S A* 1997 April 1;94(7):3217-22.

(108) Jiang Q, Ames BN. Gamma-tocopherol, but not alpha-tocopherol, decreases proinflammatory eicosanoids and inflammation damage in rats. *FASEB J* 2003 May;17(8):816-22.

(109) Moini H, Packer L, Saris NE. Antioxidant and prooxidant activities of alpha-lipoic acid and dihydrolipoic acid. *Toxicol Appl Pharmacol* 2002 July 1;182(1):84-90.

(110) Greenwell I. The Role of Inflammation in Chronic Disease. Life Extension Magazine Feb. 2001. Life Extension Media. Ref Type: Magazine Article

(111) Ha H, Lee JH, Kim HN et al. alpha-Lipoic acid inhibits inflammatory bone resorption by suppressing prostaglandin E2 synthesis. *J Immunol* 2006 January 1;176(1):111-7.

(112) Majewicz J, Rimbach G, Proteggente AR, Lodge JK, Kraemer K, Minihane AM. Dietary vitamin C down-regulates inflammatory gene expression in apoE4 smokers. *Biochem Biophys Res Commun* 2005 December 16;338(2):951-5.

(113) Tahir M, Foley B, Pate G et al. Impact of vitamin E and C supplementation on serum adhesion molecules in chronic degenerative aortic stenosis: a randomized controlled trial. *Am Heart J* 2005 August;150(2):302-6.

(114) Korantzopoulos P, Kolettis TM, Kountouris E et al. Oral vitamin C administration reduces early recurrence rates after electrical cardioversion of persistent atrial fibrillation and attenuates associated inflammation. *Int J Cardiol* 2005 July 10;102(2):321-6.

(115) Carcamo JM, Pedraza A, Borquez-Ojeda O, Golde DW. Vitamin C suppresses TNF alpha-induced NF kappa B activation by inhibiting I kappa B alpha phosphorylation. *Biochemistry* 2002 October 29;41(43):12995-3002.

(116) Pleiner J, Mittermayer F, Schaller G, Macallister RJ, Wolzt M. High doses of vitamin C reverse Escherichia coli endotoxin-induced hyporeactivity to acetylcholine in the human forearm. *Circulation* 2002 September 17;106(12):1460-4.

(117) Rossig L, Hoffmann J, Hugel B et al. Vitamin C inhibits endothelial cell apoptosis in congestive heart failure. *Circulation* 2001 October 30;104(18):2182-7.

(118) Aggarwal BB, Shishodia S. Suppression of Nuclear Factor-kB Activation Pathway by Spice-Derived Phytochemicals: Reasoning for Seasoning. *Ann N Y Acad Sci* 2004;1030:-434.

(119) Chen CC, Chow MP, Huang WC, Lin YC, Chang YJ. Flavonoids inhibit tumor necrosis factor-alpha-induced up-regulation of intercellular adhesion molecule-1 (ICAM-1) in respiratory epithelial cells through activator protein-1 and nuclear factor-kappaB: structure-activity relationships. *Mol Pharmacol* 2004 September;66(3):683-93.

(120) Lim H, Son KH, Chang HW, Kang SS, Kim HP. Inhibition of chronic skin inflammation by topical anti-inflammatory flavonoid preparation, Ato Formula. *Arch Pharm Res* 2006 June;29(6):503-7.

(121) Lotito SB, Frei B. Dietary flavonoids attenuate TNFalpha -induced adhesion molecule expression in human aortic endothelial cells: Structure-function relationships and activity after first-pass metabolism. *J Biol Chem* 2006 September 20.

(122) O'Leary KA, de Pascual-Tereasa S, Needs PW, Bao YP, O'Brien NM, Williamson G. Effect of flavonoids and vitamin E on cyclooxygenase-2 (COX-2) transcription. *Mutat Res* 2004 July 13;551(1-2):245-54.

(123) Gutierrez-Venegas G, Kawasaki-Cardenas P, rroyo-Cruz SR, Maldonado-Frias S. Luteolin inhibits lipopolysaccharide actions on human gingival fibroblasts. *Eur J Pharmacol* 2006 July 10;541(1-2):95-105.

(124) Birrell MA, McCluskie K, Wong S, Donnelly LE, Barnes PJ, Belvisi MG. Resveratrol, an extract of red wine, inhibits lipopolysaccharide induced airway neutrophilia and inflammatory mediators through an NF-kappaB-independent mechanism. *FASEB J* 2005 May;19(7):840-1.

(125) Manna SK, Mukhopadhyay A, Aggarwal BB. Resveratrol suppresses TNF-induced activation of nuclear transcription factors NF-kappa B, activator protein-1, and apoptosis: potential role of reactive oxygen intermediates and lipid peroxidation. *J Immunol* 2000 June 15;164(12):6509-19.

(126) Martin AR, Villegas I, La CC, de la Lastra CA. Resveratrol, a polyphenol found in grapes, suppresses oxidative damage and stimulates apoptosis during early colonic inflammation in rats. *Biochem Pharmacol* 2004 April 1;67(7):1399-410.

(127) Mandel S, Youdim MB. Catechin polyphenols: neurodegeneration and neuroprotection in neurodegenerative diseases. *Free Radic Biol Med* 2004 August 1;37(3):304-17.

(128) Weinreb O, Mandel S, Amit T, Youdim MB. Neurological mechanisms of green tea polyphenols in Alzheimer's and Parkinson's diseases. *J Nutr Biochem* 2004 September;15(9):506-16.

(129) Bengmark S. Curcumin, an atoxic antioxidant and natural NFkappaB, cyclooxygenase-2, lipooxygenase, and inducible nitric oxide synthase inhibitor: a shield against acute and chronic diseases. *JPEN J Parenter Enteral Nutr* 2006 January;30(1):45-51.

(130) Bitler CM, Viale TM, Damaj B, Crea R. Hydrolyzed olive vegetation water in mice has anti-inflammatory activity. *J Nutr* 2005 June;135(6):1475-9.

(131) El Seweidy MM, El-Swefy SE, Abdallah FR, Hashem RM. Dietary fatty acid unsaturation levels, lipoprotein oxidation and circulating chemokine in experimentally induced atherosclerotic rats. *J Pharm Pharmacol* 2005 November;57(11):1467-74.

(132) Perez-Jimenez F, varez de CG, Badimon L et al. International conference on the healthy effect of virgin olive oil. *Eur J Clin Invest* 2005 July;35(7):421-4.

(133) Camuesco D, Galvez J, Nieto A et al. Dietary olive oil supplemented with fish oil, rich in EPA and DHA (n-3) polyunsaturated fatty acids, attenuates colonic inflammation in rats with DSS-induced colitis. *J Nutr* 2005 April;135(4):687-94.

(134) Baynes JW. The Maillard hypothesis on aging: time to focus on DNA. *Ann N Y Acad Sci* 2002 April;959:360-7.

(135) le-Donne I, Giustarini D, Colombo R, Rossi R, Milzani A. Protein carbonylation in human diseases. *Trends Mol Med* 2003 April;9(4):169-76.

(136) Berlett BS, Stadtman ER. Protein oxidation in aging, disease, and oxidative stress. *J Biol Chem* 1997 August 15;272(33):20313-6.

(137) Baynes JW. The role of AGEs in aging: causation or correlation. *Exp Gerontol* 2001 September;36(9):1527-37.

(138) Stadtman ER, Levine RL. Protein oxidation. *Ann N Y Acad Sci* 2000;899:191-208.

(139) DeGroot J. The AGE of the matrix: chemistry, consequence and cure. *Curr Opin Pharmacol* 2004 June;4(3):301-5.

(140) Harding JJ. Viewing molecular mechanisms of ageing through a lens. *Ageing Res Rev* 2002 June;1(3):465-79.

(141) Onorato JM, Jenkins AJ, Thorpe SR, Baynes JW. Pyridoxamine, an inhibitor of advanced glycation reactions, also inhibits advanced lipoxidation reactions. Mechanism of action of pyridoxamine. *J Biol Chem* 2000 July 14;275(28):21177-84.

(142) Vlassara H. Advanced glycation in health and disease: role of the modern environment. *Ann N Y Acad Sci* 2005 June;1043:452-60.

(143) Jordan KG. Carnosine - Nature's pluripotent life extension agent. Life Extension Magazine [January]. 2001. Ft. Lauderdale, FL, Life Extension Media. Ref Type: Magazine Article

(144) Gallant S, Semyonova M, Yuneva M. Carnosine as a potential anti-senescence drug. *Biochemistry (Mosc)* 2000 July;65(7):866-8.

(145) Guiotto A, Calderan A, Ruzza P, Borin G. Carnosine and carnosine-related antioxidants: a review. *Curr Med Chem* 2005;12(20):2293-315.

(146) Hipkiss AR. Carnosine, a protective, anti-ageing peptide? *Int J Biochem Cell Biol* 1998 August;30(8):863-8.

(147) Rosick ER. How Carnosine Protects Against Age-Related Disease. Life Extension Magazine [January]. 2006. Ft. Lauderdale, FL, Life Extension Media. Ref Type: Magazine Article

(148) Brownson C, Hipkiss AR. Carnosine reacts with a glycated protein. *Free Radic Biol Med* 2000 May 15;28(10):1564-70.

(149) Miller PL, Reinagel M. Preventing Glycation: Age-Proofing Your Organs. *Life Extension Revolution.* New York, NY: Bantam Dell; 2005. p. 220-31.

(150) Hipkiss AR, Michaelis J, Syrris P. Non-enzymatic glycosylation of the dipeptide L-carnosine, a potential anti-protein-cross-linking agent. *FEBS Lett* 1995 August 28;371(1):81-5.

(151) Balch PA, Balch JF. Diabetes. *Prescription for Nutritional Healing.* 3rd ed. New York, NY: Avery; 2000. p. 321-6.

(152) Murray MT, Pizzorno J. Diabetes Mellitis. *Encyclopedia of Natural Medicine.* 2nd ed. Rocklin, CA: Prima Publishing; 1998. p. 401-30.

(153) Rutter K, Sell DR, Fraser N et al. Green tea extract suppresses the age-related increase in collagen crosslinking and fluorescent products in C57BL/6 mice. *Int J Vitam Nutr Res* 2003 November;73(6):453-60.

(154) Qian P, Cheng S, Guo J, Niu Y. [Effects of vitamin E and vitamin C on nonenzymatic glycation and peroxidation in experimental diabetic rats]. *Wei Sheng Yan Jiu* 2000 July;29(4):226-8.

(155) Boeing H, Weisgerber UM, Jeckel A, Rose HJ, Kroke A. Association between glycated hemoglobin and diet and other lifestyle factors in a nondiabetic population: cross-sectional evaluation of data from the Potsdam cohort of the European Prospective Investigation into Cancer and Nutrition Study. *Am J Clin Nutr* 2000 May;71(5):1115-22.

(156) Midaoui AE, Elimadi A, Wu L, Haddad PS, de CJ. Lipoic acid prevents hypertension, hyperglycemia, and the increase in heart mitochondrial superoxide production. *Am J Hypertens* 2003 March;16(3):173-9.

(157) Suzuki YJ, Tsuchiya M, Packer L. Lipoate prevents glucose-induced protein modifications. *Free Radic Res Commun* 1992;17(3):211-7.

(158) Munch G, Kuhla B, Luth HJ, Arendt T, Robinson SR. Anti-AGEing defences against Alzheimer's disease. *Biochem Soc Trans* 2003 December;31(Pt 6):1397-9.

(159) Thirunavukkarasu V, nitha Nandhini AT, Anuradha CV. Lipoic acid improves glucose utilisation and prevents protein glycation and AGE formation. *Pharmazie* 2005 October;60(10):772-5.

(160) Visioli F, Galli C. Natural antioxidants and prevention of coronary heart disease: the potential role of olive oil and its minor constituents. *Nutr Metab Cardiovasc Dis* 1995;5:306-14.

(161) Visioli F, Bellomo G, Montedoro G, Galli C. Low density lipoprotein oxidation is inhibited in vitro by olive oil constituents. *Atherosclerosis* 1995 September;117(1):25-32.

(162) Block G. The data support a role for antioxidants in reducing cancer risk. *Nutr Rev* 1992 July;50(7):207-13.

(163) Hertog MGL, et al. Content of potentially anticarcinogenic flavonoids of 28 vegetables and 9 fruits commonly consumed in the Netherlands. *J Agric Food Chem* 1992;40:2379-83.

(164) Havsteen B. Flavonoids, a class of natural products of high pharmacological potency. *Biochem Pharmacol* 1983 April 1;32(7):1141-8.

(165) Muosi I, Pragai BM. Inhibition of virus multiplication and alteration of cyclic AMP level in cell cultures by flavonoids. *Experimentia* 1985;41:930-1.

(166) Bagchi D, Bagchi M, Stohs SJ et al. Free radicals and grape seed proanthocyanidin extract: importance in human health and disease prevention. *Toxicology* 2000 August 7;148(2-3):187-97.

(167) Masquelier J. Procyanidolic Oligomers. *J Parfums Cosm Arom* 1990;95:89-97.

(168) Schwitters B, Masquelier J. OPC in Practice: Bioflavonoids and their Application. *Alpha Omega* 1993.

(169) Hertog MG, Feskens EJ, Hollman PC, Katan MB, Kromhout D. Dietary antioxidant flavonoids and risk of coronary heart disease: the Zutphen Elderly Study. *Lancet* 1993 October 23;342(8878):1007-11.

(170) Hertog MG, Kromhout D, Aravanis C et al. Flavonoid intake and long-term risk of coronary heart disease and cancer in the seven countries study. *Arch Intern Med* 1995 February 27;155(4):381-6.

(171) Cavallini L, Bindoli A, Siliprandi N. Comparative evaluation of antiperoxidative action of silymarin and other flavonoids. *Pharmacol Res Commun* 1978 February;10(2):133-6.

(172) Duarte J, Perez VF, Utrilla P, Jimenez J, Tamargo J, Zarzuelo A. Vasodilatory effects of flavonoids in rat aortic smooth muscle. Structure-activity relationships. *Gen Pharmacol* 1993 July;24(4):857-62.

(173) Hanasaki Y, Ogawa S, Fukui S. The correlation between active oxygens scavenging and antioxidative effects of flavonoids. *Free Radic Biol Med* 1994 June;16(6):845-50.

(174) Hope WC, Welton AF, Fiedler-Nagy C, Batula-Bernardo C, Coffey JW. In vitro inhibition of the biosynthesis of slow reacting substance of anaphylaxis (SRS-A) and lipoxygenase activity by quercetin. *Biochem Pharmacol* 1983 January 15;32(2):367-71.

(175) Ratty AK, Das NP. Effects of flavonoids on nonenzymatic lipid peroxidation: structure-activity relationship. *Biochem Med Metab Biol* 1988 February;39(1):69-79.

(176) Hasegawa R, Chujo T, Sai-Kato K, Umemura T, Tanimura A, Kurokawa Y. Preventive effects of green tea against liver oxidative DNA damage and hepatotoxicity in rats treated with 2-nitropropane. *Food Chem Toxicol* 1995 November;33(11):961-70.

(177) Visioli F, Vinceri FF, Galli C. 'Waste waters' from olive oil production are rich in natural antioxidants. *Experientia* 1995 January 15;51(1):32-4.

(178) Reavley N. Vitamin A and Carotenes. *New Encyclopedia of Vitamins, Minerals and Herbs.*New York, NY: M. Evans and Company; 1998. p. 33-57.

(179) Cooper K. Nutrimedicine from A to Z: Vitamin A and its Relatives. *Advanced Nutritional Therapies.*Nashville, TN: Thomas Nelson Publishers; 1996. p. 65-72.

(180) Murray MT. Vitamin A and Carotenes. *Encyclopedia of Nutritional Supplements.*Rocklin, CA: Prima Health; 1996. p. 19-38.

(181) Rothman KJ, Moore LL, Singer MR, Nguyen US, Mannino S, Milunsky A. Teratogenicity of high vitamin A intake. *N Engl J Med* 1995 November 23;333(21):1369-73.

(182) Cooper K. Nutrimedicine from A to Z: Iron. *Advanced Nutritional Therapies.*Nashville, TN: Thomas Nelson Publishers; 1996. p. 263-7.

(183) Kiechl S, Willeit J, Egger G, Poewe W, Oberhollenzer F. Body iron stores and the risk of carotid atherosclerosis: prospective results from the Bruneck study. *Circulation* 1997 November 18;96(10):3300-7.

(184) Tuomainen TP, Punnonen K, Nyyssonen K, Salonen JT. Association between body iron stores and the risk of acute myocardial infarction in men. *Circulation* 1998 April 21;97(15):1461-6.

(185) Gordeuk VR, Bacon BR, Brittenham GM. Iron overload: causes and consequences. *Annu Rev Nutr* 1987;7:485-508.

(186) Reavley N. Iron. *New Encyclopedia of Vitamins, Minerals and Herbs.*New York, NY: M. Evans and Company; 1998. p. 249-62.

(187) Stevens RG, Graubard BI, Micozzi MS, Neriishi K, Blumberg BS. Moderate elevation of body iron level and increased risk of cancer occurrence and death. *Int J Cancer* 1994 February 1;56(3):364-9.

Index of Terms

2002 World Health Report 4

A

absorption 45, 50, 51, 55
acetaminophen 57
acetyl l-carnitine 45
acetyl-l-carnitine 54
AGE 44, 50, 56, 57, 59, 60, 63
aging 3, 7, 8, 10, 12, 13, 14, 17, 18
alcohol 3
aldehydes 60
Allen, Woody 6
alpha-linolenic acid 45, 47, 58
Alzheimer's 6, 7, 13, 14, 15, 18, 59, 60
AMA 2
    American Medical Association 2, 3
American Academy of Dermatology 44
American Board of Anti-Aging Medicine 44
American Board of Dermatology 44
American Chemical Society 43
American College for Advancement in Medicine 43
American College of Surgeons 42
American Institute for Cancer Research 4, 7
American Institute of Chemistry 43
American Preventive Medicine Association 43
Ames, Bruce 31
amino acid 31, 32
amino acids 46, 50, 54, 59, 60
    beta-alanine 60
    l-histidine 60
amino-acid chelates 51
amyloid 14
amyotrophic lateral sclerosis 13
ANSI 68
    American National Standards Institute 68
anti-aging 42, 43, 44, 60
antibiotics 6
antioxidant 9, 10, 11, 12, 18, 43, 48, 49, 51, 52, 53, 54, 55, 56, 58, 59, 60, 61, 62, 63
Antioxidant Support 48, 49, 52, 53
antioxidants 4, 5, 7, 8, 10, 11, 12, 18
apoptosis 54, 58
arachidonic acid 15
arsenic 10
arteries 3, 4, 14, 15, 57, 61
arthritis 6, 7, 13, 14, 15, 17, 63
    rheumatoid arthritis 13
atherosclerosis 3, 11, 15
Atkins Center for Complementary Medicine 43
Atkins, Robert 43
ATP 9, 10
    adenosine triphosphate 9

B

Balch, James 42
Balch, Phyllis 42
Bastyr University 42
B-complex 5
Bernadean University 43
beta-amyloid 14

beta-carotene 46, 52, 53, 54, 56, 57, 61, 63
Bioactivity of Vitamin E 51
bioavailability 50, 51
Bioflavonoid Profile 61
bioflavonoids 4, 11, 18
biotin 21, 31, 55
birth defects 5
black current seed oil 15
Blended Standard 41, 42, 44, 45, 46, 47, 48, 49, 50, 52, 53, 54, 55, 56, 57, 58, 59, 60, 61, 62, 63, 64
blood flow 4
blood pressure 3, 4, 15, 16, 54, 61
    diastolic 54
    systolic 54
blood sugar 14
body fat 13
body-mass index 3
bone 53, 58
Bone Health 53
borage oil 15
boron 5, 53
Boston Museum of Science 44
botulism 25
brain 4, 14, 15, 18
British Institute of Homeopathy 42

C

calcium 2, 3, 5, 7, 21, 22, 25, 29, 35, 36, 39, 46, 47, 53, 54
    bone meal 22
    dolomite 22
California Orthomolecular Medical Society 43
Canada 2, 3, 4, 5
Canadian Heart and Stroke Foundation 4
cancer 2, 3, 4, 5, 6, 7, 8, 11, 14, 15, 17, 18, 21, 29, 32, 34, 36, 37, 38, 39, 43, 44, 45, 60, 61, 62, 63
    breast 2, 7, 36, 37
    colon 4, 7, 29, 36, 37
    colorectal 36, 37
    endometrium 4
    lung 2, 4, 18
    oesophagus 4
    oral cavity 4
    pancreas 4, 14
    pharynx 4
    prostate 2, 7
    stomach 4
capillaries 61
Capital University of Integrative Medicine 43
carbohydrates 7, 8
    complex 5, 7, 9, 10, 18
    fibre 7
arbonylation 59, 60
carcinogens 10
cardiac 53, 54
cardiomyopathy 53, 54
cardiovascular 45, 53, 54, 55, 57, 59, 61, 62, 63
    arrhythmias 53, 54
cardiovascular disease 2, 3, 4, 13, 18, 31, 34, 36, 38, 39
cardiovascular risk factors 3
Carnegie Mellon University 44

carnosine 45, 60

carotenoids 2, 11, 45, 55, 56, 61

catabolic 8

catalase 11, 12

cataracts 7, 56, 60

catechins 62

CH3 30, 31

    methyl group 29, 30

CHD 3, 36, 37

    coronary heart disease 3, 36

chemotherapy 8

cholesterol 3, 7, 13

choline 57, 58

chondroitin 24, 34, 35, 39

    chondroitin sulphate 34, 35

chromium 5, 43, 55

chronic 2, 4, 5, 6, 7, 8, 10, 12, 13, 14, 15, 16, 17, 18

chronic disease 2, 4, 7, 8

CNS 13, 18

    central nervous system 13, 18

cobalt 5

coenzyme Q10 53, 54, 55

    CoQ10 53, 54

Colgan, Michael 42

Completeness 47, 48, 49, 50, 64

congestive heart failure 53, 54

contaminants 22, 24, 25

copper 5, 11, 21, 26

COX-2 52, 58, 59

C-reactive protein 58

Crohn's disease 13

curcumin 46, 59, 62

curry 62

CVD 37

cysteine 54, 55

cytokines 8, 14, 15, 17, 18, 58, 59

cytotoxic 60

D

Dartmouth College 43

DASH 54

    Dietary Approaches to Stop Hypertension 54

degenerative disease 1, 5, 6, 7, 8, 10, 13, 14, 15, 16, 17, 18

dementia 4, 13

DHA 47, 58

    docosahexaenoic acid 45, 58, 59

diabetes 6, 7, 11, 13, 14, 15, 18, 43, 55, 60, 61, 63

    type 2 55

DIN 65, 66, 68

    Drug Identification Number 65, 66, 68

disintegration 25, 26

DNA 8, 10, 17, 53, 54, 59, 62, 63

    nucleic acids 8, 10

DRI 48

    Dietary Reference Intake 48

DRIs 50

    recommended dietary intakes 50

drugs 19, 20, 21, 23, 25, 28, 32, 34, 35, 39

    pharmaceutical drugs 19, 20

DSHEA 24

    Dietary Supplementation and Health Education Act 24

E

egg 15

eicosanoids 14, 15, 16, 17

Einstein, Albert 9

Emory University Medical School 43

endothelial 58, 59

environment 3, 8, 9, 17

enzymes 50, 54, 59, 63

EPA 47, 58

    eicosapentaenoic acid 45, 58, 59

essential fatty acids 14, 15, 17

evening primrose oil 15

exercise 3, 7, 10

extracts 46, 59, 61, 62

    berry 46, 61, 62

    grape seed 46, 61, 62

    pine bark 46, 61, 62

F

FAD 57

    flavin adenine dinucleotide 57

FADH2 9

Fairfield, Kathleen 2

fatty acids 44, 46, 47, 48, 50, 58, 59, 64

FDA 20, 22, 23, 24, 25, 66, 67

    Food and Drug Administration 20

    Food and Drug Authority 66

fertilizers 5

    NPK 5

fiber 7

fish 5, 13, 15, 17

fish oil 58

Five-Star Rating 46, 48, 64

flavonoids 46, 58, 59, 61, 62

Fletcher, Robert 2, 5

flour 7

folate 31, 32

folic acid 2, 3, 4, 5, 21, 24, 25, 27, 29, 30, 31, 32, 38, 45, 53, 57

Ford Medical Center 44

Ford, Henry 65

free radical 8, 9, 10, 11, 12, 17, 18

free radicals 8, 9, 10, 11, 12, 13, 14, 17

fruit 3, 4, 5

fruits 2, 3, 4, 5, 7, 11, 18, 50, 61

    black currents 61

    cherries 61

    grapefruit 61

    grapes 59, 61

    kiwi 61

    lemons 61

    limes 61

    olive 45, 46, 59, 62

    oranges 61

G

genetic 3, 8, 10, 12, 17

ginseng 20, 23

    Panax quinquefolius 23

glucosamine 24, 34, 35, 39

glutamic acid 54

glutathione 11, 12, 49, 54, 55, 57

glutathione peroxidase 11, 12

glycation 49, 59, 60
Glycation Control 49, 59, 60
glycine 54
glycosides 62
glycosylation 59
GMP 65, 66, 67, 68, 69, 72
    Good Manufacturing Practice 65, 68, 69
Grady Memorial Hospital 43
grain 4
grains 4, 5, 17, 33, 36
green tea 46, 58, 59, 62
Grey, Aubrey de 7
Grossman, Terry 43, 44

H
H2O2 10, 54
    hydrogen peroxide 10, 12, 54
Harman, Denham 8, 11
Harvard School of Public Health 54
Health Professionals' Follow-up Study 3
Health Support Profile 48, 49
Health Support Profiles 47
heart 21, 24, 27, 28, 29, 31, 32, 33, 34, 36, 37, 38, 39, 40
    heart attacks 29, 36
heart disease 2, 3, 5, 6, 7, 11, 13, 15, 18, 43, 44, 51, 52, 54, 55, 57
Heart Health 48, 49, 53, 54
heavy metal 24, 25
    lead 22, 23, 24, 25, 31, 34, 38, 39
herbal products 22, 23
    berberine 22
    digitalis 22, 24
    ephedra 20, 22
    foxglove 22
    kava 22
    lobelia 22
    Ma huang 20, 22
    mistletoe 22
herbs 61
    bilberry 46, 61, 62
    ginkgo 43, 61
    hawthorn 61
    milk thistle 61
    yarrow 61
hesperidin 46, 61, 62
Higdon, Jane 44
Hippocrates 49
homocysteine 2, 4, 13, 29, 30, 31, 32, 37, 38, 49, 53, 57
Huntington's 13, 14
hydrocarbon 62
hydroxytyrosol 62
hygiene 6
hypertension 54, 60

I
Illinois College of Physicians and Surgeons 42
infectious 7, 8
inflammation 1, 8, 10, 13, 14, 15, 16, 17, 18, 45, 47, 48, 49, 58, 59, 64
Inflammation Control 47, 48, 49, 58, 59, 64
inflammatory 6, 8, 10, 12, 13, 14, 15, 16, 17, 18
inflammatory bowel disorder 6, 14
inositol 57, 58
insulin 6, 14, 15, 16, 17

insulin resistance 55
Insulin Resistance Syndrome 55
iodine 5
iron 3, 5, 9, 20, 21, 25, 26, 45, 46, 47, 48, 49, 62, 63, 64
ISO 65, 69
    International Standards Organization 69
    ISO 17025 65, 69
    ISO 9000 69
    ISO/IEC-17025 69

J
JAMA 2, 5

K
kidney 7, 14, 15
Koop, Everett 7
Krebs cycle 51
Kurzweil, Ray 43, 44

L
LA 58
    lipoic acid 53, 58, 59, 60, 61
l-carnitine 45, 54
lead 7, 8, 10, 14
lecithin 57, 58
    phosphatidylcholine 57, 58
life expectancy 6, 7
Life Extension Foundation 17, 44
lifespan 6, 7, 9, 10
lifestyle 3, 4, 7, 8, 18
linoleic acid 15
Linus Pauling Institute 44, 51
lipid 9, 11, 17, 18
lipid peroxides 59
lipoproteins 60
lipotropic factors 57, 58
liver 7, 13, 48, 49, 50, 51, 54, 55, 57, 63
Liver Health 48, 49, 54, 55
longevity 7, 14, 18
lupus 13, 14
lutein 45, 56
lycopene 2, 53, 54

M
macular degeneration 7
magnesium 5, 21, 22, 35, 46, 53, 54, 55
manganese 11, 55
median 44, 45, 48, 57, 62, 63
mercury 10
Metabolic Health 49, 55
Michigan State University 44
Michigan State University's College of Human Medicine 44
milk 2
Miller, Phillip Lee 44
Mindell, Earl 42
Mineral Forms 50, 51
mitochondria 52, 54
mixed carotenoids 45
molybdenum 5, 21
mortality 3, 4, 6, 13
MTHFR 30, 31, 32, 57
    methylene tetrahydrofolate reductase 30, 32, 57

multiple sclerosis 13
Murray, Michael 42

N

n-acetyl-cysteine 11, 55
NADH 9
National Inventor Hall of Fame 44
New York Academy of Sciences 42, 44
NFkB 8, 17, 18
    Nuclear factor kappa Beta 8, 17
NHANES 63
    National Health and Nutrition Examination Survey 63
NHPD 65, 66, 68
    Canadian Natural Health Products Directorate 65
nitrogen 5, 10
NO iv, vi, 3, 5, 6, 7, 10, 12, 13
    nitric oxide 10, 17
NPA 65, 66, 67, 68
NPN 65, 66, 68
    Natural Product Number 65, 66, 68
NSF 65, 66, 67, 68, 69
nucleotide 31, 32
Nurses' Health Study 3
nutritional deficiencies 5

O

O2 10
    oxygen 9, 10, 12, 18
obesity 3, 7, 13, 16, 43, 54, 55
Ocular Health 49, 55, 56
OH 58
    hydroxyl 58
OH· 10
    hydroxyl radical 10
oleuropeine 62
olive oil 45, 59, 62
omega-3 58
omega-6 58
Oregon State University 44
organic-acid complexes 51
osteoporosis 2, 5, 6, 7, 14, 27, 29, 35, 39, 53, 63
oxidation 8, 9, 10, 11, 17, 51, 52, 54, 59, 61, 63
oxidative damage 8, 10, 12, 13, 17
oxidative Stress 1, 8, 9, 10, 12, 16, 17, 18
oxygen 52, 53, 54, 55, 58
    reactive oxygen species 54

P

PABA 45
pantothenic acid 21, 29
Paracelsus 2
Parkinson's 6, 13, 14
Parkinson's Disease 59, 60
Passwater, Richard 43
Pauling, Linus 8, 21, 27, 42, 43, 44, 51
PCOs 18, 46, 54, 61, 62
    grape seed extract 46, 61
    pine bark extract 46
    proanthocyanidins 61
    procyanidolic oligomers 46, 54, 59, 61
    red wine 18
    resveratrol 18, 46, 59, 61, 62

pellagra 2
Perricone, Nicholas 44
PG-E2 58
    prostaglandin E-2 58
pH 50
phenolic compounds 45, 46, 50, 54, 59, 61, 62
    Polyphenol 45, 59, 61
Phenolic Compounds Profile 62
phosphorus 5, 53
plaque 3
polymorphism 31, 32
polyphenol 18
polyphenols 4, 18
    catechins 18
    epicatechin 18
    gallic acid 18
    green tea 18
    pine bark 11, 18
    turmeric 15, 18
potassium 4, 5
potency 22, 23, 25, 26, 28, 46, 47, 48, 49, 50, 51, 52, 62, 64
Potential Toxicities 45, 49, 62, 64
prevention 3, 4, 7
Pritikin Longevity Center 43
proinflammatory 8, 14, 15, 16, 17
pro-inflammatory 58, 59
protein 13, 14, 17, 18
proteins 8, 9, 10, 14, 15, 17, 46, 51, 54, 55, 56, 59, 60
    glycosylated proteins 60
purity 22, 23, 25, 26

Q

quercetin 46, 61, 62
quercitrin 46, 61, 62

R

radiation 8, 11
red meats 15, 17
repiratory 7
respiration 9, 10, 11, 12
retina 55, 56
RNS 10
    reactive nitrogen species 10
Rockefeller University 42
ROS 10, 12, 18
    reactive oxygen species 10, 18

S

salmonella 25
SAMe 24, 26, 34, 35, 39, 40, 57
    s-adenosyl methionine 24, 57
saturated fat 7
saturated fats 3, 17
scurvy 2
selenium 5, 11, 43, 53, 55
shellfish 15
silicon 53
smoking 3, 4, 16
Society of Investigative Dermatology 44
SOD 11
    superoxide dismutase 11, 12
sodium 7, 54